Why Do You Need This New Edition?

If you're wondering why you should buy this new edition of *Essentials of Argument*, here are six good reasons!

1 This edition features **new argument** readings by professional writers on issues of both current and enduring concern: racial profiling and racism, and government bureaucratic doublespeak.

2 **Fifteen new photographs with discussion** and writing assignments expand the exploration of important, contemporary issues, including border security, immigration, and war.

3 **A new organization helps you to write** a more powerful research paper by learning about visual argument and arguing for common ground

before beginning the argument research paper assignment.

4 **The descriptions and criteria** for detecting the ethical and unethical qualities of arguments have been enhanced to provide deeper insight into arguing fairly and avoiding being misled by others.

5 **A new section on bias** in Chapter 9 helps you detect potential agendas that may compromise objectivity. Also in this chapter is a new "worksheet" to help you formulate effective arguments that incorporate images.

6 **MLA and APA documentation** sections conform to the specifications in the 2009 MLA and 2010 APA style manuals so that you may cite sources accurately in your assignments.

PEARSON

ESSENTIALS OF ARGUMENT

Third Edition

Nancy V. Wood

University of Texas at Arlington

Prentice Hall
Boston   Columbus   Indianapolis   New York   San Francisco   Upper Saddle River
Amsterdam   Cape Town   Dubai   London   Madrid   Milan   Munich   Paris   Montreal   Toronto
Delhi   Mexico   City   São Paulo   Sydney   Hong Kong   Seoul   Singapore   Taipei   Tokyo

Senior Acquisitions Editor: Brad Potthoff
Assistant Editor: Nancy C. Lee
Director of Marketing: Megan Galvin-Fak
Senior Marketing Manager: Sandra McGuire
Senior Supplements Editor: Donna Campion
Production Manager: Raegan Keida Heerema
Associate Managing Editor: Bayani Mendoza de Leon
Managing Editor: Linda Mihatov Behrens
Project Coordination, Text Design, and Electronic Page Makeup: Electronic Publishing Services Inc.
Cover Design Manager: Miguel Ortiz
Cover Designer: Nancy Sacks
Cover Illustration/Photo: Front cover: Apomares/iStockphoto, Blend Images/Superstock, Blend Images/Superstock
Back cover: Photoshot
Image Permission Coordinator: Lee Scher
Photo Researcher: Kate Cebik
Senior Manufacturing Buyer: Mary Anne Gloriande
Printer and Binder: Edwards Brothers Malloy
Cover Printer: Lehigh-Phoenix Color/Hagerstown

For permission to use copyrighted material, grateful acknowledgment is made to the copyright holders on p. 313, which are hereby made part of this copyright page.

Library of Congress Cataloging-in-Publication Data

Wood, Nancy V.
   Essentials of argument / Nancy V. Wood. — 3rd ed.
     p. cm.
   Includes bibliographical references and index.
   ISBN 978-0-205-82702-2
1. Persuasion (Rhetoric)   2. Debates and debating.   I. Title.
   PN207.W66 2011
   808.53—dc22

               2010035567

3 4 5 6 7 8 9 10—EBM—13 12

Prentice Hall
is an imprint of

www.pearsonhighered.com

ISBN-13: 978-0-205-82702-2
ISBN-10:   0-205-82702-0

Contents

The author examines the issue of racial profiling, using facts and personal narrative.
This student issue proposal examines the controversy associated with Barbie dolls.

This is a student-written annotated bibliography about human cloning.

This author considers different perspectives on how to pay children for doing the chores.

PART II   Using Argument Theory for Reading and Writing   93

5   The Toulmin Model of Argument: Understanding the Parts   95

6   The Types of Claims: Establishing Purpose and Organization   122

7   The Types of Proof: Supporting the Claim   140

Preface

PURPOSE

Essentials of Argument, third edition, presents instruction in critical reading, critical thinking, research, and writing about argument in a brief and clear format. This book's basic assumption is that students need to learn to participate productively in all forms of argument, including those they encounter in school, at home, on the job, and in the national and international spheres. Such participation is critical not only in a democratic society but also in a global society, in which issues become more complex each year. Students who use this book will learn to identify topics of personal and social consequence, to read and form reactions and opinions of their own, to analyze a potential audience, and to write argument papers that express their individual views and perspectives so they will appeal to an audience. They will also learn to present their arguments in visual as well as written form.

A central idea of this text is that modern argument is not always polarized as right versus wrong, but instead often invites a variety of perspectives on an issue. Another important idea is that not all argument results in the declaration of a winner. The development of common ground and forms of consensus and/or compromise is as acceptable sometimes as declaring winners in argument. Students will learn to take a variety of approaches to argument, including taking a position and defending it, seeking common ground when it is called for, withholding opinion at other times, negotiating when necessary, and even changing their original beliefs when they can no longer make a case for them. The perspectives and abilities taught here are those that an educated populace in a world community within which the need to coexist cooperatively and to avoid needless destructive conflict is becoming essential.

The assignments in *Essentials of Argument* encourage students to write early and often. At the outset, students are taught to select topics, analyze audiences, and conduct library and online research that leads to the development of a variety of argument projects, including written papers, oral reports, and visual arguments. This book will be useful in classes that teach both research and writing. It will also be useful in classes for which the instructor has selected a reader or has compiled a packet of readings and needs an accompanying textbook focused on instruction and assignments for argumentative writing. Finally, this book is suitable for classes where the instructor wants students to spend relatively little time reading about argument and more time discussing and writing about issues.

SPECIAL FEATURES

- **Reading, Critical Thinking, and Writing** are taught as integrated and interdependent processes. Instruction on the reading and writing processes shows how they can be adapted to argument.
- **The Rhetorical Situation,** with its focus on the **audience**, the **exigence** for the argument, the **constraints**, the **author**, and the **text**, is explained in Chapter 2 so that students can use this information to analyze the arguments they read and to plan the arguments they write.
- **Research Methods Are Introduced Early**. In Chapter 3, students are taught to locate, read, evaluate, and take notes on both print and online sources.
- **Several Types of Argument Paper Assignments** provide students with a variety of strategies to draw on as they respond to different rhetorical situations.
    Exploratory Argument Paper Students examine an issue from several perspectives.
    Argument Analysis Paper Students analyze the methods and strategies well-known authors use to create effective arguments.
    Rogerian Argument Paper Students search for points of agreement through the establishment of common ground and seek to resolve conflict by reaching consensus.
    Researched Position Paper Students provide evidence for a point of view on a controversial issue and attempt to persuade an audience to agree with it.
- **The Toulmin Model of Argument, the Types of Claims (based on classical stasis theory), and the Classical Proofs (*logos*, *ethos*, and *pathos*)** are explained as useful to both the reader and writer of argument. Heuristics based on these ideas help students develop material for their papers.
- **All six parts of the Toulmin model, with special attention to backing**, show how different parts of the model are used, as needed, to make an argument more convincing to a particular audience.
- **Chapter 9 on Visual Argument** teaches students to analyze the argument they see every day and also to create visual arguments of their own. **A Color Portfolio of 17 Visual Arguments** (follows page 224), accompanied by **Questions for Discussion and Questions for Writing**, provides students with opportunities to practice analyzing visual argument.
- **Nine Worksheets Help Students Plan Strategies for Invention and Organization.** These can be used by individuals or by groups of students

in class to help them plan and execute assignments. **Boxes** also highlight particularly useful material that students will refer to repeatedly.

- **An Optional On-going Writing Assignment Sequence** presents an incremental set of assignments, each part of which is labeled with a diamond ◆ in the margin in the Class Activities and Writing Assignments section at the end of each chapter. This sequence of assignments is optional. Instructors may assign all of it, parts of it, or none of it. Each assignment can stand alone.

- **Methods for Avoiding Plagiarism** are taught throughout the book. The Council of Writing Program Administrators' definition of plagiarism is presented, followed by clear examples of actual plagiarism that show students exactly what to avoid and what to do instead.

- **Essays for Analysis Written by Professional Writers** appear at the ends of the chapters. They provide examples of argumentation strategies. Instructors who want to use longer and more complex essays for analysis in their classes may want to bring in their own packets of essays, use a Reader, or consider *Perspectives on Argument*, a longer version of this textbook that includes a Reader.

- **The Apparatus for Analysis in Chapter 8** can be applied to any long, complex argument that an instructor decides to assign.

- **Nine Essays Written by Students** serve as models and as master examples of the papers students are assigned to write.

- **How to Document Sources Using MLA and APA Style** is described in Appendix 1. A sample MLA student paper and the first page and the References page from an APA paper provide models to teach students to use both types of style.

- **Summary Charts** in Appendix 2 present the main points of argument, including the rhetorical situation, the Toulmin model, the types of claims, and the types of proofs. The charts also integrate the reading and writing processes by placing reading and writing strategies for analyzing and using these points of argument side by side to show the interconnections.

- **WHERE IS IT? A Quick Reference to Major Writing Assignments and Sample Papers by Students** appears on the inside front cover of the book to help students quickly locate frequently visited pages.

- **WRITING A RESEARCH PAPER THAT MAKES AN ARGUMENT: Suggestions and Ideas** appears on the inside back cover of the book so that students can locate pertinent sections quickly.

NEW TO THIS EDITION

- **Chapters have been condensed and reduced in length for easier reading.** The third edition is 24 pages shorter than the second edition.

- **Chapter 9, "Visual Argument," now precedes Chapter 10, "Writing the Rogerian Argument Paper" and Chapter 11, "Writing the Researched Position Paper"** to create a more effective sequence of assignments. This new order allows students to use both Rogerian strategies and visual arguments in their research papers.

- **A new section on bias in visual argument** has been added to Chapter 9.

- **A new set of images in the color portfolio** teaches students to explore issues through visual images.
- **Two new readings, one new student paper, and 15 new images** have been added for analysis.
- **All charts and graphs** have been updated with new data. **Examples and student papers** have also been updated.
- **A new Visual Argument Development Worksheet** has been added to Chapter 9.
- **Descriptions and criteria for judging the ethical and unethical qualities of argument, including Rogerian argument,** have been added or expanded.
- **An expanded assignment on how to conduct a class symposium of student research** has been added to Chapter 11.
- **MLA and APA sections have been updated** to conform to the specifications in the 2009 MLA and 2010 APA style manuals.

ORGANIZATION

Essentials of Argument, third edition, is organized into three parts and, as much as possible, the eleven chapters have been written so that each stands alone. Thus instructors can assign them either in the book's sequence or in an order they prefer to best supplement their own course organizations.

PART I: Understanding Argument and Conducting Research. Chapter 1 teaches the special characteristics of argument, explains individual argument styles, and invites students to identify issues for future papers; Chapter 2 explains the rhetorical situation, with special emphasis on audience analysis; Chapter 3 teaches research, reading, and evaluation strategies, note taking strategies, and how to avoid plagiarism; and Chapter 4 characterizes the writing process and suggests that students learn to examine an issue from several different perspectives. Writing assignments include the argument style paper, the issue proposal, the annotated bibliography, summary-response papers, and the exploratory paper.

PART II: Using Argument Theory for Reading and Writing. Chapter 5 identifies and explains the parts of an argument according to Stephen Toulmin's model of argument; Chapter 6 explains the types of claims and purposes for argument; and Chapter 7 presents the types of proofs, organized under the headings of *logos, ethos,* and *pathos,* along with the language, warrants, and fallacies associated with each of them. Chapter 8 teaches students to apply what they have learned in Chapters 1–7 to analyze a famous classical argument. Writing assignments include the Toulmin analysis; papers that develop particular types of claims, including fact, definition, cause, value, and policy; and the argument analysis paper.

PART III: Writing and Presenting Arguments. Chapter 9 teaches students to analyze and create visual arguments; Chapter 10 demonstrates how to write a Rogerian argument paper; and Chapter 11 teaches students to organize, write, revise, and prepare the final manuscript for a researched position paper. Assignments include creating a visual argument, the Rogerian argument paper, the researched position paper and adapting it for oral presentation in a class symposium.

APPENDICES: MLA and APA Documentation and Summary Charts.

THE INSTRUCTOR'S MANUAL

The *Instructor's Manual* that accompanies *Essentials of Argument*, third edition, provides a glossary of argument terms, answers to chapter review questions, suggestions for working with the class activities and writing assignments that appear at the end of each chapter, and syllabi for argument classes that use *Essentials of Argument* as the textbook. A set of class handouts is also provided. Copies of this manual may be obtained from your Prentice Hall representative or accessed electronically at www.prenhall.com on this text's catalog page.

MYCOMPLAB

MyCompLab empowers student writers and facilitates writing instruction by uniquely integrating a composing space and assessment tools with market-leading instruction, multimedia tutorials, and exercises for writing, grammar and research.

Students can use MyCompLab on their own, benefiting from self-paced diagnostics and a personal study plan that recommends the instruction and practice each student needs to improve her writing skills. The composing space and its integrated resources, tools, and services (such as online tutoring) are also available to each student as he writes.

MyCompLab is an eminently flexible application that instructors can use in ways that best complement their course and teaching style. They can recommend it to students for self-study, set up courses to track student progress, or leverage the power of administrative features to be more effective and save time. The assignment builder and commenting tools, developed specifically for writing instruction, bring instructors closer to their student writers, make managing assignments and evaluating papers more efficient, and put powerful assessment within reach. Students receive feedback within the context of their own writing, which encourages critical thinking and revision and helps them to develop skills based on their individual needs.

ACKNOWLEDGMENTS

It is difficult to imagine writing a book like this without the students who try it out, offer their suggestions for improvement, and contribute argument papers that serve as examples of successfully completed assignments. I am grateful to all of the students who participated in these ways. I particularly want to thank Prisna Virasin, Angela Boatwright, Mohamed T. Diaby Jr., Eric Hartman, Elizabeth Nabhan, Darrell Greer, and Karen Hernandez, all of whom gave their permission to publish their papers as models for other student writers. These papers were written in argument classes, and they appear in several chapters throughout this book. Also, even though this is a different book, it nonetheless owes a debt to the 6th edition of my longer book *Perspectives on Argument.*

At Prentice Hall, I owe a great debt to the individuals who have supported and encouraged me with this project. Brad Potthoff, Senior Acquisitions Editor, has provided valuable recommendations and encouragement to help me complete it successfully. Thanks also to Brandy Dawson, Executive Marketing Manager, who has always encouraged me with her good cheer and positive outlook. Carrie Fox, Production Editor, has done a swift and competent job of seeing this book through all the phases of production. Diane Nesin has checked and proofread this book, and I am grateful for her careful and accurate work. Kate Cebik, Lee Scher and Julie Brown secured permission to use the various printed and visual arguments reproduced in the book. It has been a privilege to work with such conscientious and capable professionals. I thank them for all the care they took.

Colleagues around the country who have provided additional ideas and recommended changes include Emily Golson, University of Northern Colorado; Julie Townsend, University of North Carolina at Charlotte; Julie Foust, Utah State; Lara B. Whelan, Berry College; Shelley N. Harper, Rowan Cabarrus Community College; Kyle Taylor, University of West Georgia; David Alan Sapp, Fairfield University; Jeannine M. Jordan, Rowan Cabarrus CC/Winthrop University; Peggy Lindsey, Wright State College; Robert Arnold III, University of North Carolina at Charlotte; Cynthia Bowers, Kennesaw State University; Stuart Brown, New Mexico State University; James Cornish, McLennan Community College; JoAnn Dadisman, West Virginia University; Dan Ferguson, Amarillo College; Daniel Gross, University of Iowa; Paul Hagood, Linn-Benton Community College; Ella Hairston, Guildford Technical Community College; Alisa Klinger, Cuesta College; Jody Malcolm, University of West Florida; Carol Marion, Guilford Technical Community College; Mary Trachsel, University of Iowa; David Bockoven, Linn-Benton Community College; Sydney Brown, Grossmont College; Ruth A. Gerik, University of Texas at Arlington; Rebecca B. Hewett, California State University, Bakersfield; Matt Hollrah, University of Central Oklahoma; Matthew S.S. Johnson, Southern Illinois University Edwardsville; Jeff Pruchnic, Wayne State University; and Patrick Shaw, University of Southern Indiana. I am grateful to all of these individuals for the time and care they took reviewing the manuscript. I hope they will be pleased when they see how many of their suggestions have helped shape this book.

Finally, I owe a profound debt to my husband, James A. Wood, who has also taught and written about argument. As a speech professor and former debate coach, he has his own unique perspectives on argument, and he has helped me, through many long discussions, develop my own. Most writers, I am convinced, profit from talking through their ideas with someone else. I have been lucky to work with someone so knowledgeable and generous with his time and insights.

This book has been a genuinely collaborative effort. I hope students will profit from the example and learn to draw on the expertise of their instructors and classmates to help them write their papers. I continue to believe that writing is more fun and more successful when it is, at least partly, a social process.

N. V. W.

UNDERSTANDING ARGUMENT AND CONDUCTING RESEARCH

The strategy in Part One is, in Chapter 1, to introduce you to the special characteristics of argument, your personal argument style, and some issues you may want to write about; in Chapter 2, to teach you to analyze the context and motivation for an argument, with special emphasis on analyzing your audience; in Chapter 3, to teach you to conduct research, read for ideas, and evaluate the sources of information you use in your papers; and in Chapter 4, to teach you to explore a variety of positions on your issue to help you establish your own. The focus in these chapters is on you and how you will engage with argument both as a reader and as a writer. When you finish reading Part One:

- You will understand what argument is and why it is important in a democratic society.

- You will have analyzed your present style of argument and considered ways to adapt it for special contexts.

- You will have found some issues (topics) to read and write about yourself.

- You will know how to analyze the rhetorical situation, including the audience, for arguments you read and write.

- You will know how to organize and conduct library and online research and incorporate it into your writing to support the ideas in your papers.

- You will have new strategies and ideas to help you read argument critically, think critically, and write argument papers.

- You will have experience with writing an issue proposal, an annotated bibliography, and an exploratory argument paper.

Recognizing Argument and Finding Issues

What do you think about when you see the word *argument*? It is best to begin the study of any new subject by thinking about what you already know. You can then use what you know to learn more, which is the way all of us acquire new knowledge. See the short list of five actual student responses describing some of their initial views about argument provided here. Check the responses that match your own, and add others if you like.

✓ **1.** Argument attempts to resolve issues between two or more parties.
✓ **2.** Argument is rational disagreement, but it can get emotional.
✓ **3.** Argument can result in agreement or compromise.
✓ **4.** Argument is angry people yelling at each other.
✓ **5.** Argument is standing up for your ideas, defending them, and minimizing the opposition by being persuasive.

The responses in the list, with the exception of response 4, "angry people yelling at each other," are consistent with the approach to argument that appears in this book. We omit response 4 because no argument is effective if people stop listening, stop thinking, and engage in vocal fighting. "Yes, it is!"—"No, it isn't!" accompanied by a fist pounding on the table gets people nowhere.

Now answer this question: What would happen if a society were to outlaw all forms of argument? In effect, under the law all individuals are to share the same views, and there is to be no disagreement. Here are some student responses to the question. With which descriptions do you agree?

_____ **1.** Everyone would think the same thing.
✓ **2.** There would not be any progress.
✓ **3.** There would be no new knowledge.
✓ **4.** Life would be boring.

A key idea in this book is that argument is literally to be found everywhere[1] and that without it, we would have the stagnant society suggested in these student responses. You will become more aware of argument as it impacts your life if you consider the notion that argument can be found in virtually any context in which human beings interact and hold divergent views about topics that are at issue. Further, argument can appear in a variety of forms: it can be written, spoken, sung, or chanted, and it can be read, heard, or observed in pictures that are either still or moving. Argument can be explicit, with a clear purpose and position, as in an advertisement for a soft drink or a brand of blue jeans; or it can be implicit, communicating a more subtle position on an issue that the audience has to think about and figure out, as in some of the photographs taken in war zones. Most issues invite a spectrum of perspectives and views for individuals to hold. Few issues are black and white, nor can most issues be viewed in pro and con terms anymore. Keep these complexities in mind as we now attempt to define argument and describe why it is important to study it and learn to argue well.

A DEFINITION OF ARGUMENT

Since the classical era, argument theorists have defined and described argument in different ways. Some definitions focus on providing convincing evidence for a point of view on a controversial issue and persuading an audience to agree with it. In this argument situation, a judge or a vote sometimes declares a winner. Examples of this type of argument can be found in courts of law where lawyers argue about whether the defendant is guilty or not guilty or in legislative assemblies where legislators argue in favor of or against new legislation. Another group of definitions of argument emphasize the importance of multiple views and perspectives, learning about them and making comparisons, and reasoning and gaining insights toward reaching an agreement or consensus on a position or point of view that is acceptable to everyone, at least for the present time. Examples of this type of argument can be found in policy meetings in which participants must agree on courses of action and in classrooms where students and professors reason together to establish viable solutions to puzzling questions and problems.

The definition of argument we shall use in this book is a broad one that includes both of these types of argument: *The goal of argument is to bring about a change in an audience's initial position on a controversial issue. Depending on the situation and audience, at times this goal is achieved by an arguer who presents a claim along with reasons and evidence to convince an audience to agree with the position taken; at other times, arguers create the possibility of agreement by acknowledging different points of view and working to identify one view or a combination of views that are acceptable to most or all audience members.* Both kinds of argument are taught in this book.

---

[1]I am indebted to Wayne Brockriede for this observation and for some of the other ideas in this chapter. See his article "Where Is Argument?" *Journal of the American Forensic Association* 11 (1975): 179–82.

The basic method that argument of both kinds employs can be described as (**making a claim** expressing a point of view on an issue that is communicated by the arguer) and (**supporting it with reasons and evidence** to convince an audience to change the way they think about the issue. All forms of productive argument include these components.

WHY STUDY ARGUMENT?

Argument classes are taught in college because they improve students' ability to read and think critically and write or speak about significant problems and issues that have social consequences. These abilities are routinely identified by college faculty and the general public as crucial competencies for college graduates. The positions individuals take on many issues and ultimately the decisions and actions they take in regard *to* them can affect their lives in significant ways. In college you will be expected to participate in argument to contribute to the development of new knowledge. As a member of society you will be expected to engage in effective argument and contribute to the gradual development and improvement of the society. You will also be expected to make moral judgments and to evaluate the decisions and ideas that emerge from engaging in argument at all levels of human interaction.

The concept of all people knowing how to argue effectively to resolve differences in personal, national, and international relationships is potentially a very powerful idea. Think of a country and a world where major problems are resolved through profitable argument instead of through confrontation, shouting, fighting, or war. You will often fervently disagree with other people; in fact, life would be boring if you never disagreed. Yet even when you disagree, even when you decide to enter an ongoing argument, you can learn to use a style that is comfortable and natural for you and also ethical and effective. This is preferable to the alternatives: either remaining silent or becoming involved in destructive arguments that solve nothing and may even cause harm.

The purpose of this book is, first, to teach you to read, observe, listen to, and evaluate other people's arguments, and, second, to think critically and write or present visual or oral arguments of your own that succeed with particular audiences. This chapter will help you recognize argument in a variety of different forms and will also present some issues that will interest both you and a potential audience. Chapter 2 will explain the context and motivation for arguments, whether written, oral, or visual, with special emphasis on analyzing an audience. You will also learn to write an issue proposal. You will then learn to reason and think about your issue, conduct research, and evaluate this information in Chapter 3. You will learn to write an exploratory paper in Chapter 4 in which you will identify several different perspectives on your issue and begin to plan your future argument papers. Chapters 5 through 7 will help you understand the nature of argument as you learn about its essential parts and how to make your arguments convincing. In Chapter 8 you will practice applying what you have learned in the first seven chapters of this book as you read a classical argument essay and write an argument analysis paper about it. In Chapter 9, you will extend what you have learned in previous chapters as you apply it to analyze and create effective visual arguments. In Chapter 10, you will learn to write a Rogerian argument paper in which you work for consensus on an issue. You will write a researched position paper in Chapter 11 in which you state your position on an issue and prove it. Also, in Chapter 11, you will learn how to present your final paper as an oral argument.

Appendix 1 at the end of the book presents a handy reference to the basics of MLA and APA documentation style. Appendix 2 presents summary charts of major ideas about argument that are explained in this book for quick reference. All chapters and appendices present information that will also be useful to you in your other college classes.

RECOGNIZING TRADITIONAL AND CONSENSUAL ARGUMENT

The definition of argument presented in this chapter allows for two basic approaches to argument, the traditional and the consensual. The traditional approach to argument has been dominant in Western culture. That approach is founded in Greek classical philosophy and rhetoric. Aristotle made it clear in the *Rhetoric*, written sometime between 360 and 334 B.C., that a person making an argument should find all of the available means of persuasion in order to convince an audience to change positions and agree with the arguer. You are familiar with this model of argument. You observe it every day when you watch news programs and political talk shows on television or when you read editorials and letters to the editor in magazines and newspapers. When you engage in argument, either orally or in writing, you probably quite naturally turn to the traditional approach.

Examples of traditional argument. One example of traditional argument is the *public debate* among candidates for public office or among other individuals who want to convince their audiences to side with them and accept their points of view. Public debates are often televised, allowing candidates to state and explain their views on many subjects; people also write about their views, explaining how their analyses or views are better than opposing positions or views. The judge, or decider, is the viewing public or a reader, who may or may not pick a winner. *Courtroom argument,* with lawyers pleading a case (opposed sets of alleged facts) before a judge and jury, is another example of traditional argument. As in debate, lawyers take opposing sides and argue to convince a judge and jury of the guilt or innocence of a defendant. One of them wins.

Another example of traditional argument, known as *single-perspective argument,* occurs when one person develops a perspective on an issue and argues to convince a mass audience to agree with this single view. You encounter this type of argument frequently on television and in newspapers, journals, books, and public speeches. The issue and the arguer's position are usually clear. Opposing views, if referred to at all, are refuted or otherwise dismissed. An example might be a politician who wants to convince the public that marriage should exist only between a man and a woman. This arguer provides reasons and evidence and refutes the views of another politician who favors gay marriage. It may not be clear whether anyone "wins" such an argument. Polls, letters to the editor, or a change in policy may present indications about how some members of the audience have reacted.

One-on-one, everyday argument, also a type of traditional argument, can be very different from convincing a judge or a large unspecified audience. In the one-on-one situation, the person arguing needs to focus on and identify with the other person, think about what that person wants and values, and be conciliatory, if necessary. Each participant either wins, loses, or succeeds in part. Examples might be a salesperson who wants to sell a customer a car or a student who writes a letter to convince a professor to accept a late paper.

Examples of consensual argument. In contrast to traditional argument with its emphasis on winning, consensual argument emphasizes agreement. You will probably encounter both traditional and consensual argument in your college classes. In *dialectic,* one type of consensual argument, two or more people participate as equals in a dialogue to try to discover what seems to be the best position on an issue. A questioning strategy is often used to test the validity of differing views. The ancient philosopher Plato used this form of argument in his *Dialogues* to examine such questions as *What is truth?* and *What is the ideal type of government?* You may have seen this kind of exchange referred to as "the Socratic method" because Plato's teacher, the philosopher Socrates, asks many of the questions in these dialogues.

Professors sometimes use dialectic to help students think about and finally arrive at positions that can be generally accepted by most of the class. In a philosophy class, for example, the professor may ask the question, *How can one establish a personal hierarchy of values?* and then describe a situation in which an individual is faced with a conflict of values. For example, can one remain loyal to a friend if one must break a law in the process? The professor first asks class members to describe the values that are in conflict in this situation, then to compare the relative strength and importance of these values, and finally to prioritize them in a way that is agreed to by the class. The objective is to discover, through questions and answers, a common bedrock of ideas that most or all of the class can accept in common. There are no winners. There is instead a consensual discovery of a new way to look at a difficult issue. Students then may be asked to write papers in which they describe their understanding of this new consensual view.

Another type of consensual argument is *academic inquiry.* The purpose of academic inquiry is to discover, through reading, discussion, and writing, new views, new knowledge, and new truths about complex issues. For example, English majors engage in academic inquiry when they read, discuss, and write about their insights into the motivation of a character in a novel. Political science majors take part in academic inquiry when they find themselves contributing to a new understanding of the benefits of strong state governments. The participants in such inquiry find that there are few clear-cut *pro* and *con* positions; there is no judge; the emphasis is not on winning. Anyone can participate; there are potentially as many views as there are participants. The result of academic inquiry, ideally, is to reach well-founded consensus on academic and social issues. Consensus may take some time to emerge, and it may also be challenged later when someone proposes a whole new way of looking at a particular issue.

Negotiation and *mediation* are conducted in arenas in which people employ argument to reach consensus on plans of action that solve problems. Both the Palestinians and the Israelis, for example, cannot claim ownership of the same land, so other solutions continue to be negotiated. *Negotiation* can take place between two people, one-on-one, or in a group meeting. A special characteristic of negotiation is that the negotiators usually represent an entire business, organization, or government, and, as a result, many people not present at the negotiating table must ultimately be as satisfied with the final agreements as the negotiators themselves. Often, negotiation involves both competition (for example, both parties claim rights to fish in the same waters) and cooperation (they have to figure out how to make that possible). For negotiation to be successful, all those involved must state their positions, including the views or claims of the groups or governments they represent, and support them with reasons and evidence both in writing and orally. Everyone must be willing to consider alternative views and reasons and modify their original views in order to reach consensus and resolve the problem.

Mediation is becoming a frequent alternative to a court trial. A judge assigns trained mediators to help parties who are in conflict resolve a problem that would otherwise have to be solved by a judge and possibly a jury. The mediators act as go-betweens and help the individuals involved see their problems in new ways so that they can figure out how to solve them outside of the courtroom. You may be taught methods for negotiation or mediation in your business or other classes, in which case you will be able to draw on what you know about argument to help you understand and use these practices.

A final type of consensual argument you may use frequently is known as *internal argument.* Most of us argue with ourselves when we experience internal conflict because we need to increase personal motivation, make a decision, or solve a problem. New Year's resolutions, to-do lists, and time management charts are examples of internal argument and decision making. As in other forms of consensual argument, different possibilities are identified, reasons for and against are considered, and a satisfactory resolution is finally reached.

EVALUATING TRADITIONAL AND CONSENSUAL ARGUMENT

Since traditional argument is so prevalent in American society, you need to be able to recognize it, evaluate it, and use it yourself when the audience and occasion call for it. In some situations, however, you may find traditional argument limiting and even ineffective with a particular audience and consensual argument more promising. Some modern authors now suggest that the traditional approach may not always be the best approach in all situations. In *The Argument Culture: Moving from Debate to Dialogue,* sociologist Deborah Tannen states that all topics, all audiences, and all occasions do not call for the same approach to argument.[2] She claims that in our culture we often take an extreme approach to traditional argument. We present it as a fight between two opposing sides.

---

[2]Deborah Tannen, *The Argument Culture: Moving from Debate to Dialogue* (New York: Random House, 1998).

We use war metaphors when we engage with issues: the war on drugs, the war on cancer, or the battle for health care. We live in an argument culture, Tannen claims, in which war metaphors pervade our talk and shape our thinking. As a result, we look at many issues in an adversarial frame of mind since our assumption is that opposition is the best way to solve problems or to get anything done.

The three groups in our society who are most likely to engage with issues as conflicts are politicians, lawyers, and journalists. When an issue comes to public attention, journalists, for example, often set up a debate between politicians and then jump in themselves to keep the debate going. Journalists look for politicians who are willing to express the most extreme, polarized views on an issue, with the ostensible objective of presenting both sides.

Our culture also likes to settle issues with litigation that pits one party against the other. We have frequent opportunities to watch trial argument on television and to read about it in the newspaper. The objective is always to declare a winner. The argument culture as exhibited in the media, in the courts, and in the political arena sometimes carries over to the classroom, according to Tannen. Often students learn to start essays with opposition, and some students are quick to criticize and attack most of what they read. These approaches are necessary at times, as in courtroom argument, in public and collegiate debate, or when an author seems clearly to be wrong according to a reader's standards or values. Sometimes rebuttals and a declaration of winners is required. However, if this is regarded as the only approach to controversial issues, we can create more problems than we solve.

Tannen claims that as a society we have to find constructive and creative ways of resolving disputes and differences. She notes the value of studying argument in other cultures because some cultures work for agreement more than others. Her subtitle, *Moving from Debate to Dialogue*, suggests an alternative to the win–lose model of argument. She points out that other ways exist for dealing with issues, ways that focus on resolving issues, finding agreement, and achieving consensus in order to get things done.

Part of evaluating argument requires that you read, listen, look, and analyze objectively, without making negative prejudgments. This can be difficult when you encounter opinions and values different from your own. To help you maintain your objectivity, think of yourself as a fair, unbiased person who needs to gain information and understand it before you respond. When you do respond, think of yourself as a capable and ethical arguer who is willing to evaluate and participate in argument because it is important to you and to the society in which you live.

DISTINGUISH BETWEEN ETHICAL AND UNETHICAL ARGUMENT

Throughout this book you will be given information to help you distinguish between *ethical argument*, which approaches issues in insightful, useful, and beneficial ways, and *unethical argument*, which manipulates an audience and may even harm it. An example of an ethical argument might be a plan for an effective and economical way to rebuild an area that has been destroyed by hurricanes and floods. An example of unethical argument might be an invitation to acquire a new credit card that tempts the user to incur a huge debt with high interest that will be difficult or impossible to pay back. To help you distinguish ethical from unethical argument, consider the arguer's general approach (traditional or consensual), the specific purpose (to restore a community or to make money at others' expense), general competency and reliability, and the quantity and quality of information presented. Learn to detect misleading and biased information as well as information that is untrue. Chapter 7 will help you do this, but you can use your common sense and moral values now to help you make such judgments.

WHAT IS YOUR PERSONAL STYLE OF ARGUMENT?

Most argument classes contain a mix of students who favor either the adversarial or the consensual style of argument. Some students exhibit a combination of these styles. The adversarial approach to argument is usually associated with the traditional approach. Adversarial arguers have strong opinions and are often intent on changing other people's minds. They also enjoy refutation and work to make their ideas prevail. Consensual arguers try to find elements of the opponent's position that they can agree with and are sometimes even willing to change their own views in order to reach a compromise agreeable to both parties. Completing the checklist on page 23 will give you an idea which style you favor.

Adversarial arguers usually welcome the idea of taking an argument class and view it as a forum where they can present their positions on issues. Consensual arguers are sometimes less enthusiastic about argument class, at least at first. These students may resist the idea of finding issues and participating in argument because they think they will be required to take an opposing view, to debate, or to be contentious or aggressive in class, and they feel they do not do these things well. With some conscious effort on the part of students and the instructor, everyone in an argument class can and should find ways to participate even though not everyone may participate in the same way.

When students are asked to describe their styles of argument—that is, what they do when they have to be convincing—the individual differences in style and strategy they describe seem to be related to various possible causes. Home training and role models are frequently mentioned. Other influences may be related to gender or to the background and experience provided by different cultures or nationalities. Modern research indicates that men and women describe different approaches to argument often enough to suggest that gender may partly account for differences in argument style. African American, Asian American, Hispanic American, and Native American cultures may also produce recognizably distinct styles and approaches; students from non-Western cultures sometimes describe approaches to argument that strike Americans as distinctive and even unique.

Here is an example of what one young man in an argument class wrote about his argument style, which he claims is influenced by his gender. He also considers what he might do to make his style more effective.

> I strongly believe my adversarial style is determined almost entirely by my gender. Men tend to be more competitive than women. Women are generally more compassionate towards each other, whereas men are constantly flaming each other. It takes a real tragedy to get a man to turn to another and actually show some compassion. I am very confrontational, so I think being a little more open-minded wouldn't hurt me. I have noticed that my friends and I tend to build a wall when we argue, and we just entrench ourselves on the opposite sides of the argument and never make an inch of headway. If I were more open-minded, this would be less of a problem.[3]

This second example was written by a young woman in an argument class who thinks her style has been influenced by her mother, her culture, and her gender. She also writes about how she could profitably modify her style.

> My style of argument is mostly influenced by my mother. Whenever my mother argues with someone, I know what the results will be. I am sure that she will not stand up for her opinions long if the other person is insistent. I think the Vietnamese culture and her gender have influenced her. In our culture, women are taught not to argue, especially with elders and their husbands. It is considered bad behavior for a woman. Plus, my mom always thinks that a woman should keep the peace so that other people will respect her. She prefers listening to others rather than trying to achieve her point of view on an issue. I have always looked at my mom as a perfect role model. I just did not realize how much my argument style has become similar to hers. To be honest, I would like to be a more aggressive arguer because that would help me become more involved in arguments with others. I would love to be more direct and open instead of keeping quiet and peaceful like now.[4]

Expressed differences in styles among various demographic groups of students are usually neither consistent nor strong enough for typecasting. In fact, in some studies, a sizable minority of men indicate they prefer the styles that some researchers have identified as predominantly female,[5] and certainly not all Asian men and women remain reluctant to argue even if they were not encouraged in this practice at home or in schools in their own countries.

The final purpose for considering individual styles in argument is to encourage you and your classmates to become aware at the outset of how each of you argues best. Such preferences will often influence how you plan and write argument papers. One style may seem more natural to you, while you may need to exert more effort to write in another style. Thus you will learn to recognize, rely on, and perhaps even improve your existing style of writing argument. You will also learn how to modify or change to another style in certain situations when your preferred style may not be effective with a particular audience. This process will help you learn flexibility as you write in response to various argumentation situations.

---

[3]From a student paper by Allen Duck; used with permission.
[4]From a student paper by Oanh Pham; used with permission.
[5]Carol S. Pearson, "Women as Learners: Diversity and Educational Quality," *Journal of Developmental Education* 16 (1992): 10.

The examples of types of argument and differing styles of individual argument demonstrate that the effectiveness of an argument is based on situational elements and conditions. Let's take a look at some of the specific conditions that can help you improve your argument skills. You can strive to create these conditions when you participate in argument.

UNDER WHAT CONDITIONS DOES ARGUMENT WORK BEST?

To work best, a productive and potentially successful argument, whether presented in writing, in speech, or in images, requires the following elements.

■ *An issue.* An argument needs to have as its central focus an issue that has not yet been settled. Furthermore, there must be the potential for at least two or more views on that issue. For example, the handgun issue has more than the two extreme views that people should either be allowed or not allowed to own them. Between these extremes, people take a variety of positions, including the view that owning and using handguns may be acceptable for certain purposes, such as hunting, or that handguns themselves can be modified to limit their use.

■ *An arguer.* Ideally, every argument requires a person who is motivated to initiate the argument, to take a position on the issue, to obtain and consider information, and to communicate a position to others. This person needs to develop expertise on an issue and be willing to take a risk to express his or her own ideas about it. Furthermore, the arguer should seek to go beyond the "current wisdom" about an issue and find fresh perspectives and approaches that will suggest original insights to the audience. For example, an individual arguing for tougher handgun laws needs to present fresh reasons and evidence to get people's attention and agreement. Michael Moore did this in his persuasive Oscar-winning film documentary about handguns, *Bowling for Columbine* (2002).

■ *An audience.* An audience for an argument, whether friendly or hostile, should ideally be willing to listen to or read and consider new views or perspectives. The audience should also be capable of understanding, thinking, questioning, discussing, and answering. The arguer may be familiar with the audience's background and values or, in the case of a totally unknown audience, the arguer may have to imagine their backgrounds, motives, and values. The arguer should respect the audience and want to communicate with them. It is a compliment to draw someone into discussion on an issue, so the arguer should try to show that he or she cares about the audience, the members' interests, and their state of mind. This approach will ensure an open audience, one who reads, views, or listens and does not shut the arguer out or otherwise try to escape. Receptive audiences are potentially willing to change their minds, a desirable outcome of argument.[6]

■ *Common ground.* Effective argument requires the establishment of some common ground between the audience and the arguer that is relevant to the issue.

---

[6]Some of the observations in this chapter about the special conditions for argument, especially for the audience, are derived from Chaim Perelman and Lucie Olbrechts-Tyteca, *The New Rhetoric: A Treatise on Argumentation* (Notre Dame, IN: University of Notre Dame Press, 1969), pt. 1.

If two parties are too far apart and share no common ground, they usually do not understand one another well enough to engage in dialogue. For example, people who disagree on the abortion issue often find themselves at a standoff, they fight rather than argue, and their disagreement sometimes results in violence. At the other extreme, if two parties are already in complete agreement, there is usually no need to argue. For example, two parents who agree that their child should go to college do not argue about that part of the child's future. Common ground may be established between an arguer and the audience through the discovery of common interests—common ideas, experiences, motives, or values—or even through recognizing common friends or enemies. As soon as two parties realize they have something in common, they can more easily achieve identification, even if it is minimal, and engage in constructive argument. Figure 1.1 (on this page) diagrams a possible situation.

THE ISSUE: SHOULD LIMITS BE PLACED ON HANDGUN OWNERSHIP?

Possibility 1: *Complete agreement and no argument.* Two individuals believe that all private citizens should be allowed to own one or more handguns to protect themselves from random shooters. They agree totally and share the same common ground. They have nothing to argue about with this statement of the issue.

Possibility 2: *Total disagreement, no common ground, and no argument.* One individual believes private citizens should have the right to own handguns to protect themselves from random shooters, and another believes that no private citizen should own handguns for any purpose. They disagree totally, and there is no common ground. Productive argument is nearly impossible.

Possibility 3: *Two parties discover something in common, and there is a possibility of argument.* The two parties discover they each hold their positions because of their fear of random shooters. One wants to own a handgun to kill a random shooter in self-defense. The other wants to banish handguns so that random shooters will have trouble obtaining them. They have an important point in common: they both want to stop random shootings. They share common ground on that point, even though they may disagree on other points. The common ground creates the possibility for productive argument about what can be done to stop random shooting, the ultimate goal.

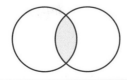

FIGURE 1.1 Establishing Common Ground.

■ *A forum.* People need forums for argument so they can feel creative and know they will be heard. Such widely available forums include public places for argument, such as a courtroom or legislative assembly. They also include various media, such as magazines, newspapers, and other print sources, television and radio, motion pictures, the arts, and photographs and other graphic materials. College is a forum for argument. Professors and students argue in class, at meals, and in dorms and apartments. Outside speakers present argument. The argument class, with its discussions, papers, and other assignments, can be an excellent forum for practicing argument, particularly if both the students and the instructor work to create an environment in which all students participate and respect one another.

■ *Audience outcomes.* Successful arguments should produce changes in the audience. At times, the arguer convinces the audience and the members of the audience to change their minds. Or a successful negotiation is achieved, people find themselves in consensus, a decision is reached, and a plan of action is started. Other arguments may not have such clear-cut results. A hostile audience may be brought to a neutral point of view. A neutral audience may decide to take a stand. Sometimes it is a significant accomplishment to get the audience's attention and to raise consciousness of your issue. This success can lay the groundwork for a possible future change of mind.

UNDER WHAT CONDITIONS DOES ARGUMENT FAIL?

We have just examined the optimal conditions for argument. Now let's look at the conditions that can cause it to flounder or fail.

■ *No disagreement or reason to argue.* We have already seen that no argument can take place when there is no real disagreement, no uncertainty, or no possibility for two or more views. Also, neutral people who do not have enough interest in an issue to form an opinion do not argue. For example, people who do not use computers may be neutral about the issues surrounding unlimited access to certain Internet sites. Argument also cannot take place unless people perceive an issue as a subject for argument. Orientation leaders who try to persuade students to consider one major over another will not succeed with students who have already decided on their majors.

■ *Risky or trivial issues.* Big or risky problems that may call for radical change are difficult to argue about for some people. Finding a new career or dissolving a long-time relationship may fit into this category, and many people, wisely or not, tend to leave such difficult issues alone rather than argue about them. Religious issues or issues that threaten global disaster are also sometimes too big, too emotional, or too scary to argue about for many people. At the other extreme, some issues may be perceived as low risk, trivial, boring, or even ridiculous. Some family arguments fall into this category, like what to eat for dinner or who should take out the trash. One person may care, but the rest do not.

■ *Difficulty in establishing common ground.* We have pointed out that arguments that lack common ground among participants are not effective. You may encounter difficulties when trying to establish common ground with those who have made up their minds on certain issues and who do not desire to listen or change. Those individuals who hold fast to prejudiced beliefs about various groups of people, for example, may dismiss information that defies their favorite stereotypes. It is also difficult to argue with some religious people who take certain issues on faith and do not perceive them as subjects for argument. Finally, argument cannot take place when one party is not motivated to argue. "Don't bring that up again" or "I don't want to discuss that" puts an end to most argument.

■ *Standoffs or fights which result in negative outcomes.* When argument is not working, as in some of the situations just described, the outcomes are negative also. A standoff occurs, parties agree to keep their original views, and they refuse to cross the line. Or emotions may be strong, verbal fighting breaks out, and extreme views are expressed. No one agrees with anyone else. People shake their heads and walk away, or they become hurt and upset. Some individuals may become strident, wanting to debate everyone to demonstrate they are right. When classroom argument results in such negative outcomes, some students drop the class, others fall silent and refuse to participate, and everyone becomes anxious.

One important aim of this book is to provide you with the insight and skill to manage these negative situations so that more constructive argument can take place. Students are in an excellent position to overcome some of the fear, resistance, and aversion associated with difficult issues and, by using evidence and good sense, get to work and face some of them. Understanding audience members, especially their attitudes, needs, and values, is an important first step. Another useful idea to keep in mind is that most arguers have more success with some audiences than with others, depending on the amount of common ground.

Arguing effectively in difficult situations requires a conscious effort to avoid both stereotypical reactions and the entrenched behavioral patterns that you have relied on in the past when you have argued. You can learn to replace past habits, such as never varying your argument style or formulating a response before you fully understand the other point of view, with new strategies that work better. It is sometimes difficult to make such changes because habits can be strong, but it is possible to do so. The stakes are often high, especially when the choice is constructive argument or verbal fighting and standoffs. You may also find that you prefer written to spoken argument in some situations because you have more time to consider your audience, formulate your ideas, and plan your argumentation strategies.

Now it is time to think about issues that you might want to write about as you practice changing past habits and experiment with new strategies to help you argue more effectively.

ENGAGING WITH ISSUES

What will help you find your arguable issues? Your issues may emerge from the parts of your life that demand your greatest attention and energy. For example, people who are compellingly engaged with their professions think about work issues, new parents think about child-rearing issues, dedicated students think about the issues raised in class, and many teenagers think about peer-group issues. Examine the areas of your life that take up much of your time or attention. Think about what you enjoy or about what aggravates you. It may also help you to think about some of the special characteristics of issues in general. Here are a few of them.

Issues Are Compelling. People get excited about issues, and they usually identify with a few in particular. Most people can quickly name one or more issues that are so important and so interesting to them that they think about them often, sometimes daily. If you live in the Northwest, the preservation of old-growth forests may be an issue for you. If you are preparing for a career in education, creating equal access to quality education may be an issue you care about. Can you think of some issues that are particularly compelling to you?

Issues Often Originate in Dramatic Life Situations. Things happen all around us—people find they can access news on the Internet for free, which threatens the existence of print newspapers, the government proposes security measures that interfere with individual privacy, the number of illegal immigrants entering the United States increases. As the issues around us change, we inevitably respond with questions: Should individuals pay to read the news on the Internet? Should individuals be willing to forgo privacy in order to improve national security, or is privacy an important personal freedom in America that should be protected at all costs? Should U.S. borders be fenced off and patrolled, should immigrants be offered work permits, or should all be granted amnesty? Pay attention to the stories that are newsworthy this week, and identify the issues associated with them. Select the ones that interest you the most.

Current Issues Can Be Linked to Enduring Issues That Have Engaged People for Ages. For example, the controversy about stem cell research is related to age-old issues associated with the preservation of life as it has evolved on this planet: Will stem cell research help cure human disease? Or will it be profoundly destructive to existing life-forms? Affirmative action issues are linked to the enduring issue of whether or not all people are created equal: Will affirmative action contribute to racial profiling? Or will it actually decrease discrimination? Look at Box 1.1 (pages 17–19) for additional examples of contemporary public issues that have been linked with enduring issues to demonstrate the timeless quality of most of them. See if you can add examples as you read through those in the "current" column.

BOX 1.1	Examples of Current and Enduring Public Issues.

What Are Some Public Issues?

CURRENT ISSUES	ENDURING ISSUES
Ways and Means Issues	
Should everyone pay taxes? In what proportion to their incomes?	From what sources should a government obtain money, and how should it spend it?
Should free trade be limited?	
How much business profit can be sacrificed to keep the environment clean and safe?	
How can we reduce our dependence on foreign oil?	
Should scholarships and fellowships be taxed?	
Is the national debt too high, and if so, what should be done about it?	
How should we finance health care?	
Quality of Life Issues	
Should more resources be directed to protecting the environment?	What is a minimum quality of life, and how do we achieve it?
Are inner cities or rural areas better places to live?	
How can we improve the quality of life for children and senior citizens?	
What effect will global climate change have on our lives?	
Personal Rights versus Social Rights Issues	
Should individuals, the government, private business, or charitable organizations be responsible for the unemployed? Health care? Day care? The homeless? Senior citizens? Drug addicts? People with AIDS? Race problems? Minority problems? Dealing with criminals? Worker safety? Deciding who should buy guns?	Can individuals be responsible for their own destinies, or should social institutions be responsible? Can individuals be trusted to do what is best for society?

(continued)

BOX 1.1	*(continued)*

CURRENT ISSUES	ENDURING ISSUES

War and Peace Issues

How much should the government spend on the military?	Is war ever justified, and should countries stay prepared for war?
Should the United States remain prepared for a major world war?	
Should you, your friends, or your family be required to register for the draft?	
To what extent should a government pursue negotiation as an alternative to war?	

Self-Development Issues

What opportunities for education and training should be available to everyone?	What opportunities for self-development should societies make available to individuals?
How well are job-training programs helping people get off welfare and find employment?	
Should undocumented workers be allowed the same opportunities to participate in society as citizens?	

Human Life Issues

Should abortions be permitted?	Should human life be protected under any conditions?
Should capital punishment be permitted?	What or who will define the limits of a person's control of his or her own life? And what or who limits a government's interest or control?
Is mercy killing ever justifiable?	
Should stem cell research be allowed?	

Foreign Affairs Issues

Which is wiser, to support an American economy or a global economy?	In world politics, how do we balance the rights of smaller countries and different ethnic groups against the needs of larger countries and international organizations?
How much foreign aid should we provide, and to which countries?	
Should college graduates be encouraged to participate in some type of foreign service like the Peace Corps?	
Should the United States defend foreign countries from aggressors?	

(continued)

BOX 1.1	*(continued)*

CURRENT ISSUES   **ENDURING ISSUES**

Law and Order Issues

Is the judicial system effective?	What is an appropriate balance between the welfare and protection of society as a whole and the rights of the individul?
Does the punishment always fit the crime?	
How serious a problem is racial profiling?	
How can global terrorism be eradicated?	
To what degree have we sacrificed our privacy for national security?	

Issues Go Underground and Then Resurface. Public concern with particular issues is not constant. Experts may think about their issues continuously, but the public usually thinks about an issue only when something happens that brings it to public attention. Issues associated with global warming, war and peace, and human rights, for example, resurface when new information about them is released. What are some of the issues that used to concern you that you have neither thought about nor read about for a long time?

Issues Are Everywhere. Listen for issues in lectures and look for them in your textbooks. Ask your professors to identify the major issues in their fields. Box 1.2 (page 20) illustrates some of the issues you are likely to encounter in your other classes in college. These are examples of issues that your professors argue about, the subjects for academic inquiry. You may be expected to take positions and develop arguments yourself on these or similar issues if you take classes in some of these subjects.

As you read, try to add examples from your own classes. Read newspapers and newsmagazines, listen to public radio, and watch television programs in or on which issues are discussed. Browse through some of the newly acquired books in the library and look for issues. Listen for issues in conversations and discussions with friends and families. Identify campus issues. If you attend a house of worship or belong to organizations, listen to the issues that surface there.

As you watch for and think about the issues that might engage you, start making a list of those you particularly want to learn more about. Make a corresponding list of some of the other groups or individuals who may also be interested in these topics, and jot down the views they may hold. Such lists will be useful to you when it is time to select topics for your argument papers and begin analyses of your potential audiences.

BOX 1.2	Examples of Academic Issues Across the Disciplines.

What Are Some Academic Issues?

In **Physics**—Is there a unifying force in the universe? Is there enough matter in the universe to cause it eventually to stop expanding and then to collapse? What is the nature of this matter?

In **Astronomy**—What elements can be found in interstellar gas? What is the nature of the asteroids? What criteria should be used to identify a new planet?

In **Biology**—How can stem cell research best be managed?

In **Chemistry**—How can toxic wastes best be managed?

In **Sociology**—Is the cause of crime social or individual? Does television have a significant negative effect on society? What effects do computers have on their users?

In **Psychology**—Which is the better approach for understanding human behavior, nature or nurture? Can artificial intelligence ever duplicate human thought?

In **Anthropology**—Which is more reliable in dating evolutionary stages, DNA or fossils?

In **Business**—Can small, privately owned businesses still compete with giant conglomerate companies? Are chief executive officers paid too much?

In **Mathematics**—Are boys naturally better than girls at math? Should the use of calculators be encouraged? How might calculators be used in testing situations?

In **Engineering**—How important should environmental concerns be in determining engineering processes? To what extent, if any, are engineers responsible for the social use of what they produce? How aggressive should we be in seeking and implementing alternative sources of energy? Should the government fund the development of consumer-oriented technologies to the same extent that it funds military-oriented technologies?

In **History**—Have historians been too restrictive in their perspectives? Does history need to be retold, and if so, how? Is the course of history influenced more by unusual individuals or by socioeconomic forces?

In **Political Science**—Where should ultimate authority to govern reside: with the individual, the church, the state, or social institutions? Is power properly divided among the three branches of government in the United States?

In **Communication**—How can the best balance be struck between the needs of society and freedom of expression in the mass media? How much impact, if any, do the mass media have on the fears, beliefs, values, and behavior of individuals in society?

In **English**—Is the concept of traditional literature too narrowly focused in English departments? If yes, what else might be considered topics for study in literature classes?

REVIEW QUESTIONS

1. What did you think of when you encountered the word *argument* as you began reading this chapter? What do you think now?
2. Provide three examples of your own to illustrate the statement "Argument is everywhere."
3. Describe traditional and consensual argument. Give two examples of each.
4. What are some of the conditions necessary for argument to work best?
5. What are some of the conditions that may cause argument to fail?

CLASS ACTIVITIES AND WRITING ASSIGNMENTS

1. **Understand Common Ground**

   a. *Build common ground with your classmates.* Create pairs of students, appoint one in each pair as the scribe, and have each pair take five minutes to discuss and record characteristics and interests they have in common. Now create groups of four students by teaming two pairs, appoint a scribe for each group, and have the groups take five minutes to discuss and record what all four members have in common. The scribes then give one-minute reports about what each group has in common. As you listen to these reports, get a sense of what the whole class has in common.

   b. *Discover common ground about argument.* Return to your groups of four for five minutes and have the scribes write answers to these questions: (1) What do you think of when you hear the word *argument*? (2) What effect might finding common ground have on your ideas about argument? Finally, have the scribes take two minutes to report to the class the findings of their groups.

   c. *Write about common ground.* Write for five minutes about the common ground you think already exists in your classroom. What do you and your classmates have in common? How do you differ? How are your ideas about argument and common ground similar to or different from those of your classmates? What effect will common ground in your class have on the argument that takes place there? Discuss what you have written with the class.

2. **Demonstrate That "Argument Is Everywhere"**

   a. Test the idea that argument can be found everywhere. Each member of the class should bring in an example of an argument and explain why it can be defined as argument. Each example should focus on an issue that people are still arguing about and on which there is no general agreement. Look for examples in a variety of contexts: newspapers, magazines, the Internet, television, motion pictures, music, sermons, other college classes, conversations, and printed material you find at work, at school, and at home.

Bring in actual examples of articles, letters to the editor, bumper stickers, advertisements, or other easily transportable argument formats, or provide clear and complete descriptions and explanations of argument sources you cannot bring to class, such as lectures, television shows, or billboards. Students should give two- to three-minute oral reports on the example of argument they have selected, including a description of the issue and some of the reasons and evidence offered. This is most easily achieved by completing the statement "This arguer wants us to believe . . . because . . . ." The class should decide whether all examples described in this activity are indeed examples of argument.

b. State whether you think the argument you have provided is ethical or unethical, and say why.[7]

3. **Discover Your Predominant Argument Style**

a. *Is your personal argument style consensual or adversarial?* Do you visualize yourself as a lawyer writing briefs and arguing in the courtroom, a politician writing on public issues and arguing for votes, or a journalist writing an argument in favor of a controversial new policy? Alternatively, is it easier to imagine yourself as a professor conducting a class discussion to help students reach consensus and write what they have discovered or as a negotiator writing out plans to resolve a conflict? Box 1.3 (on page 23) provides a summary of some of the characteristics of consensual and adversarial styles of argument. Check the items that are most typical of you. Does one list describe your style of argument better than the other? Or can your style best be described by items derived from both lists? From this analysis, how would you say you prefer to argue?

b. *Write an argument-style paper.* Think about the last time you had to argue convincingly, either in writing or orally, for a certain point of view. Write a 300- to 500-word paper in which you describe your predominant argument style. Include the following information:

1. Identify when you argued, the issue, the audience, what you were trying to achieve, and what you did to achieve it.
2. Is what you have described typical of your usual style of argument? If yes, explain why; if no, explain why not and describe your usual style.
3. What has influenced your style of argument? Consider home training, role models, gender, culture, nationality, national heritage, or any other life experiences that have influenced you.
4. What do you like best about your current style of argument? What would you like to change? How can you become more flexible in your style?

c. *Create a classroom environment for argument and understand your class as an audience.*

1. Read aloud the argument-style papers written by class members. Discuss the different styles described in these papers and some of the influences that have helped create them.

---

[7] I am indebted to Cedrick May for the basic idea for this project.

BOX 1.3 | **Two Styles of Argument.**

Which Style Best Describes You?

Check all statements that apply in both columns. Does one style tend to predominate, or do you have a mixed style?

CONSENSUAL STYLE

___✓___ I prefer to be indirect.

___✓___ I like to give reasons.

___✓___ I prefer cooperation.

___✓___ I favor group consensus.

_____ I like affiliation.

___✓___ I hate to fight.

_____ I prefer to avoid confrontation.

_____ I dislike contentious argument.

_____ I am nonaggressive.

_____ I solicit many views on an issue.

_____ I am both logical and emotional.

_____ I try to make connections.

_____ I prefer negotiating.

_____ I favor the personal example, story, or anecdote.

_____ I want to keep the community strong.

ADVERSARIAL STYLE

_____ I am direct and open.

_____ I like to reach conclusions.

_____ I prefer competition.

___✓___ I favor individual opinions.

_____ I like conflict.

___✓___ I like to fight.

___✓___ I like confrontation.

_____ I like contentious argument.

_____ I am aggressive.

_____ I tend to see issues as two-sided, pro and con, right or wrong.

_____ I am primarily logical.

_____ I tend to be adversarial.

_____ I prefer winning.

_____ I favor abstract ideas.

_____ I want to keep the individual strong.

---

2. Characterize your class as an audience after reading all their argument-style papers. Write for five minutes about the characteristics your class holds in common and also about the types of diversity that are evident in your class. What generalizations can you finally make about your class as an audience? How can you maintain a classroom environment where people do not feel threatened and where they feel they are being heard?

◆ **4. Identify and Test Issues for Future Argument Papers**

This is the first in an optional sequence of writing assignments. Additional assignments in this sequence are marked with an icon (◆) in the Class Activities and Writing Assignments sections in subsequent chapters.

a. *Make an issue list.* You will need one or more topics for the argument papers you will write. Argument papers taught in this book include the issue proposal on page 43, the exploratory paper on page 92, the Rogerian argument paper on page 230, and the researched position paper on pages 253–254.

Find "your" issues. Most students have issues that they really care about. What are yours? Think about what has affected you in the past. Think about your pet peeves. Think about recent news items on television or in the newspaper that have raised issues for you. Make a class list of the issues that concern you and those of the other students in your class.

b. *Apply the twelve tests of an arguable issue.* Before you write about an issue, apply the twelve tests that appear below in Box 1.4 to make certain that it is arguable. If all of your answers are yes, you will be able to work with your issue productively. If any of your answers are no, you may want to modify your issue or switch to another one.

| **BOX 1.4** | **Twelve Tests of an Arguable Issue.** |

Do You Have an Arguable Issue?

If you cannot answer yes to all of these questions, change or modify your issue.

Your issue (phrased as a question as in the lists on pages 17–19): _____

Yes _____ No _____ 1. Is this an issue that has not been resolved or settled?

Yes _____ No _____ 2. Does this issue potentially inspire two or more views?

Yes _____ No _____ 3. Are you willing to consider a position different from your own and, perhaps, even modify your views on this issue?

Yes _____ No _____ 4. Are you sufficiently interested and engaged with this issue to inspire your audience also to become interested?

Yes _____ No _____ 5. Do other people perceive this as an issue?

Yes _____ No _____ 6. Is this issue significant enough to be worth your time?

Yes _____ No _____ 7. Is this a safe issue for you? Not too risky? Scary? Will you be willing to express your ideas?

Yes _____ No _____ 8. Can you establish common ground with your audience on this issue—common terms, common background, and related values?

Yes _____ No _____ 9. Will you be able to get information and come up with convincing insights on this issue?

Yes _____ No _____ 10. Can you eventually get a clear and limited focus on this issue, even if it is a complicated one?

Yes _____ No _____ 11. Is it an enduring issue, or can you build perspective by linking it to an enduring issue?

Yes _____ No _____ 12. Can you predict one or more audience outcomes? (Think of your classmates as the audience. Will they be convinced? Hostile? Neutral? Attentive? Remember that any outcomes at all can be regarded as significant in argument.)

5. **Read and Write about Campus Issues**

a. *Read the student editorial below about grading policies.* It first appeared in a college newspaper. Answer the questions for discussion.

> **BEFORE YOU READ:** What are your opinions about the grading policies in your classes?

Essay 1

"A" IS FOR "ABSENT"*

Chris Piper

Chris Piper was a broadcast journalism major at the University of Texas at Arlington when he wrote this essay for the student newspaper, for which he also worked as a proofreader.

1   Last semester, I enrolled in one of the most dreaded courses in any communication degree plan. Most save it until the very end of their college career, but I took it as a sophomore.

2   Remarkably, I did very well on all of the tests. Also, the professor gave me high marks on almost every project. But when final grades came out, I ended up with a "C." My absences dropped my average more than 10 points. Admittedly, I earned the grade given to me. The syllabus clearly stated what would occur if I missed more than my allotted "freebies."

3   But my refusal to attend class does not excuse policies that subvert the value of learning and education, emphasizing attendance instead.

4   Professors who implement attendance policies often argue, "If this were a job, and you failed to show up, you would be fired." There is, however, one big difference between going to work versus going to class.

5   A job pays for my service, but I pay my professors for their services. I spend plenty of money on my education, and my choice to fully take advantage of the expense is exactly that—my choice.

6   When evaluating superior standardized test scores, such as what one might make on the SAT and ACT, admissions officers don't ask whether students attended prep courses before the exam. Obviously, a high score denotes that a test taker knows the material.

7   I truly believe most professors want their students to score well, which is why they implement attendance policies. I am touched by the sentiment. But if missing class leads to poor results by traditional grading methods—tests, quizzes, projects, etc.—then so be it. The student body could use some winnowing out.

8   I imagine a few instructors adopt attendance policies to stroke their own egos—to ensure a crowd is present when they enlighten the eager masses. But I'm

---

*Chris Piper, "'A' is for 'Absent,'" *Shorthorn*, October 21, 2003, p. 3.

arguing the validity of such rules regardless of any questionable motives. If a student can earn good grades on required work without attending class, then instructors should grade that student accordingly.

9   I encourage professors to give pop quizzes in place of attendance policies. At the very least, a quiz measures comprehension of pertinent material. Of course, such a change would mean more work for professors.

10   But that's what students are paying for.

FOR DISCUSSION:

What is the issue? What is the author's position on the issue? What reasons and evidence are given to support the author's position? What are the strengths and weaknesses in this argument? What is your position on this issue? How much common ground do you share with your instructor on this issue?

---

b. *Write a short essay on a campus issue.* Select the campus issue that interests or aggravates you the most, apply the twelve tests in Box 1.4 (page 24), and write a 250- to 300-word argument about it. Write a title that identifies your issue. Then make a statement (a claim) that explains your position on the issue, followed by reasons and supportive evidence to convince a college official to accept your views and perhaps take action to improve the situation.

Chapter 2

The Rhetorical Situation: Understanding Audience and Context

You are probably beginning to realize by now that argument does not take place in a vacuum. Instead, a situation occurs that raises questions in people's minds and motivates them to discuss and argue in an attempt to resolve the issues and problems that emerge. For example, the price per barrel of crude oil goes up, and issues emerge: How can the United States become less dependent on foreign oil? What are viable alternate energy sources? Or, how effective are hybrid cars? Professor Lloyd Bitzer calls a situation that motivates issues and argument a *rhetorical situation* because it stimulates discussion and encourages change. Rhetorical situations existed for the Declaration of Independence in 1776 when the issue was independence and its authors declared that the North American colonies should be independent from Great Britain, and for Abraham Lincoln's Gettysburg Address, delivered in 1863 on the site of a deadly Civil War battle. The issue was national unity. The time, place, and existing circumstances of these rhetorical situations provided the motivation for the authors of these documents to write them.[1] Five elements, according to Bitzer, are present in every rhetorical situation, and they can be analyzed.

In this chapter we focus on the rhetorical situation as readers and writers employ it. Analyzing the rhetorical situation is an important critical reading strategy: it can be used as a tool for analysis throughout the reading process; and it is a potent critical thinking strategy that can help the writer plan and write a better argument. It can also be employed to help you understand visual argument, which is the subject of Chapter 9.

---

[1]Lloyd Bitzer, "The Rhetorical Situation," *Philosophy and Rhetoric* 1 (January 1968): 1–14.

ANALYZE THE RHETORICAL SITUATION WHEN YOU READ AN ARGUMENT

According to Bitzer, a rhetorical situation has five elements. We rearrange the elements in order to form the acronym TRACE, from the initial letters of these five elements, to help you remember them: the *Text*, the *Reader* or audience, the *Author*, the *Constraints*, and the *Exigence* or cause. Now look at each of them to see how they can help you read, understand, and evaluate arguments.

1. The **text** is the written argument, which has characteristics you can analyze. These include the type of text (essay, letter, book, etc.), the content of the text, and the format, organization, argumentation strategies, language, and style that are employed by the author.

2. The potential **reader** or audience for the text ideally must care enough to read and pay attention, might change personal perceptions as a result, and perhaps will mediate change or act in a new way. A rhetorical situation invites such audience responses and outcomes. Most authors have a targeted or intended reading audience in mind. You may identify with the targeted audience, or you may not, particularly if you belong to a different culture or live in a different time. As you read, compare your reactions to the text with the reactions you imagine the targeted or intended reading audience might have had.

3. The **author** writes an argument to convince a particular audience. You can analyze the author's position, motives, values, and degree of expertise. If you do not have direct information about the author, you will need to infer or guess at much of this information as you read the text.

4. **Constraints** include the people, events, circumstances, and traditions that are part of the situation and that constrain or limit a targeted audience and cause them to analyze and react to the situation in a particular way. Constraints also include the beliefs, attitudes, prejudices, interests, and habits that influence the audience's perceptions of the situation. The author brings another set of constraints to the situation. These include the author's character, background, available resources, and style. The limits inherent in the type of text being produced, whether written, spoken, or visual, can also provide constraints. Constraints may draw the author and audience together, or they may drive them apart. They influence the amount of common ground that will be established between an author and an audience.

Here are some examples of constraints: (1) An audience feels constrained to mistrust the media because often people think reporters exaggerate or lie. This constraint may cause this audience to be cynical and suspicious of an essay written by an editor who praises reporters for always writing the truth. (2) Another essay, by a famous biologist, presents the global environmental and overpopulation crisis in such catastrophic and frightening terms that a particular audience is constrained, through fear, to shut out the argument and refuse to consider it. (3) Some voters have lost their faith in political leaders. When they are mailed brochures that argue in favor of particular candidates and that ask them to support these candidates with donations, their constraints cause these potential voters to throw these materials away without looking at them.

Here are two more examples of constraints that may be closer to you: (1) You parked your car in a no-parking zone because you were late to class, and the police feel constrained by law to give you a ticket. You have different constraints, and you write to the hearings board that more and closer parking should be available to students to help them get to class on time. The hearings board has its own constraints and will probably turn down your plea. (2) You believe everyone should share the household chores equally, and the person you live with disagrees. Both of you are constrained by your past experiences in living with other people, possibly by traditions that influence your ideas about gender roles in this type of division of labor, and also by perceptions about who has the most time to spend on the chores. Both parties may have to work hard to create the common ground necessary to resolve this issue. Notice how the constraints present on both sides in these examples influence the way the audience and the arguer react to the rhetorical situation and to the issues it generates.

5. Exigence is the part of the situation that signals that something controversial has occurred or is present and that a problem needs to be resolved by some response from an audience. Here are some examples of exigence for argument: the glaciers in the Himalaya mountains and other parts of the world are melting at a rapid rate; a higher than usual unemployment rate in the United States has just been announced; the government provides bailout money for banks and automotive industries during a recession; many people in the United States cannot afford health insurance and cannot pay medical bills; a general calls for more troops to escalate an existing war. In all cases, something is wrong, imperfect, defective, or in conflict. Exigence invites analysis and discussion, and sometimes also a written response to encourage both individual public awareness and discourse about problematic situations.

Study the following set of questions. They will help you analyze the rhetorical situation and gain insight into its component parts when you are the reader.

1. *Text.* What kind of text is it? What are its special qualities and features? What is it about?
2. ***Reader or audience.*** Who is the *targeted (intended) audience*? What is the nature of this group? Can they be convinced? What are the anticipated outcomes? If you are reading a historical document—for example, the Declaration of Independence—you might ask further, How did the readers at the time the text was written differ from other readers of the time or from modern readers? Were they convinced? Did they act on their convictions?

   Now consider how *you as a reader* compare with the targeted audience and ask, Am I typical of one of the readers the writer anticipated? Or, am I better described as an *unintended audience*? How does my answer influence my answers to the next questions? What is my initial position? What are my constraints? Do I share common ground with the author and other audience members? Am I open to change? Does this argument convince me? Am I motivated to change my mind or modify the situation? How?

3. *Author.* Who is the author? Consider background, experience, education, affiliations, and values. What is motivating the author to write?
4. *Constraints.* What special constraining circumstances will influence the reader's and the author's responses to the subject? Think about the people, events, circumstances, and traditions that are already in place along with the beliefs, attitudes, prejudices, interests, habits, and motives held by both the author and the reader that may limit or constrain their perceptions. Do the constraints create common ground, or do they drive the reader and author apart?
5. *Exigence.* What happened to cause this argument? Why is it perceived as a defect or problem? Is it new or recurring?

Here is an analysis of the rhetorical situation for "'A' Is for 'Absent'" (pages 25–26).

Example of an Analysis of a Rhetorical Situation from the Reader's Point of View

1. *Text.* This is an argumentive editorial in the student newspaper that provides reasons and personal experience to prove that professors should not have attendance policies that lower students' grades for excessive absences.
2. *Reader or audience.* The targeted readers are other students who have had or could have similar experiences. The author expects the students to identify with him and agree that such policies should be abolished. Other readers might include professors and administrators who would probably be less likely to agree with the somewhat combative position taken by the author.
3. *Author.* The author is a sophomore majoring in communications who had good grades on tests and projects but who lost ten points and ended up with a C for missing more classes than the syllabus allowed. The author also is a proofreader for the college newspaper.
4. *Constraints.* The author is constrained by the belief that students are customers who pay professors for their services and should be able to take advantage of those services on their own terms. He is also constrained by the idea that students can learn enough material to merit good grades without going to class. He expects his readers to hold the same beliefs.
5. *Exigence.* The student received a C in a course in which he thought he should have had a higher grade.

Understanding the rhetorical situation of written argument also helps you as a writer.

USE THE RHETORICAL SITUATION WHEN YOU WRITE AN ARGUMENT

As a writer, you can also use the rhetorical situation to help you think critically and make decisions about your own writing. All five elements of the rhetorical situation are important considerations for writers. Three elements are in place

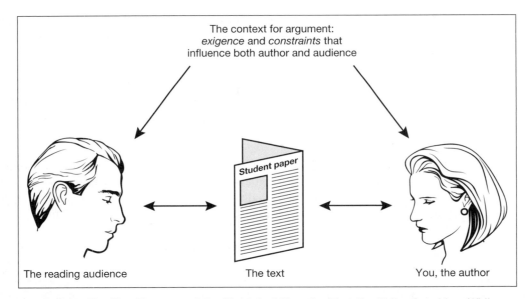

The context for argument:
exigence and *constraints* that
influence both author and audience

Student paper

The reading audience   The text   You, the author

FIGURE 2.1 The Five Elements of the Rhetorical Situation That the Writer Considers While Planning and Writing Argument.

before you begin to write. They are the *exigence*, the *reader or audience*, and the *constraints*. When you begin to write, the other two elements are added: you, the *author*, and the *text* that you create. Figure 2.1 above provides a diagram of these five elements to suggest some of the relationships among them.

Now consider each of the five elements from the writer's point of view. Use TRACE to help you remember the elements. As a writer, however, you will think about them not in the order presented in the mnemonic but in the order just suggested in the previous paragraph.

What Is the Exigence? The exigence of a situation will provide an author with the motivation to write about an issue. Issues often emerge from real-life events that signal something is wrong. One student found a topic when a relative who had spent time in jail could not get employment after he was released. Another student from a country outside of the United States became interested in intercultural differences and decided to write about the relative value of retaining her own culture or assimilating with a new one. Yet another student discovered an exigence when she read a negative article about Barbie dolls and remembered her positive experiences with them when she was younger.

Such occurrences can cause the writer to ask the questions associated with exigence: *What issues, including problems or defects, are revealed? Are these new issues or recurring issues? How severe is the problem or defect?*

Who Is the Reader or Audience? According to the definition of argument established in Chapter 1, productive argument must create common ground and achieve some definable audience outcomes. To do this, a writer needs to analyze the audience's present opinions, values, and motives, and show as often as possible that the author shares them. Both audience and author must cooperate to a certain degree for argument to achieve any outcomes at all. To help you analyze the values and motives you hold in common with your audience, refer to Box 2.1 below for a list of the needs and values that motivate most audiences.

To help you understand your audience, ask: *Who are my readers? Where do they stand on my issue? How can I establish common ground with them? If they disagree with me, will they be willing to change or modify their views, or not?*

What Are Some of the Constraints? Remember that constraints influence the ways in which both you and your audience think about the issues. What background, events, experiences, traditions, values, or associations are influencing both you and them? If your audience has no experience with criminals and you decide to write to convince them to hire people with criminal records, what are their constraints likely to be? How hard will it be for them to adopt your views?

BOX 2.1	Needs and Values That Motivate Most Audiences.

What Motivates an Audience?[2]

1. *Survival needs:* food, warmth, and shelter; physical safety

2. *Health:* physical well-being, strength, endurance, energy; mental stability, optimism

3. *Financial well-being:* accumulation of wealth; increased earning capacity; lower costs and expenses; financial security

4. *Affection and friendship:* identification in a group; being accepted, liked, loved; being attractive to others; having others as friends or objects of affection

5. *Respect and esteem of others:* having the approval of others; having status in a group; being admired; having fame

6. *Self-esteem:* meeting one's own standards in such virtues as courage, fairness, honesty, generosity, good judgment, and compassion; meeting self-accepted obligations of one's role as employee, child or parent, citizen, member of an organization

7. *New experience:* travel; change in employment or location; new hobbies or leisure activities; new food or consumer products; variety in friends and acquaintances

8. *Self-actualization:* developing one's potential in skills and abilities; achieving ambitions; being creative; gaining the power to influence events and other people

9. *Convenience:* conserving time or energy; satisfying the other motives with considerable ease

---

[2]The list in Box 2.1 is based on Abraham Maslow's hierarchy of needs and motives from his book *Motion and Personality*, expanded by James A. Wood in *Speaking Effectively* (New York: Random House, 1988), pp. 203–204. Used with permission.

Or if you are an international student who is comparing your culture with the American culture to decide how much to change and adapt to American ways, and your audience is only familiar with its own culture, what will you do to help them see this problem as you see it? If you are writing for an audience that is mostly male and has no experience with or memories of Barbie dolls, what constraints would you run into if you tried to convince them that Barbie dolls are an important part of children's experience?

To help you understand the constraints held by both you and your audience, ask: *How are our training, background, affiliations, and values either in harmony or in conflict? Will constraints drive us apart or help us build common ground? If they drive us apart, what additional information can I provide to build common ground and bring us closer together? Where will my argument appear? Will it be a paper for an instructor, a letter to a supervisor, a letter to an editor, or a posting in an online chat room?* Each medium has its own requirements.

You are in a position now to think about the remaining two elements of the rhetorical situation: you, the *author*, and the *text* you will write.

Who Is the Author? You will now need to think of yourself as an author of argument. You may have selected one or more issues to write about at this point. Before beginning your research, reflect on what you already know about your issue and what you still need to learn. Draw on your own experience, if you have some that applies. For instance, one student might think about her relative's experiences in prison and imagine a better life for him, another might feel out of place in America and wonder how much he should change, and yet another student may still have her Barbie dolls and looks back with pleasure on the many hours she spent playing with them. Make brief notes on this experience to use later in your paper. If you have no direct experience to draw on, research, reading, and critical thinking will provide the material for the paper.

To better consider your role as the author, ask these questions: *Why am I interested in this issue? Why do I perceive it as a defect or problem? Is it a new or old issue for me? What is my personal background or experience with this issue? What makes me qualified to write about it? Which of my personal values are involved? How can I get more information? What is my purpose and perspective? How can I make my paper convincing?*

How Should the Text Be Developed to Fit the Situation? Your text (paper) may be written in response to an assignment in your argument class, in which case it should meticulously follow the assignment requirements. You might also, however, write a paper for another class, a proposal at work, or a letter to the editor of a newspaper, to name a few possibilities.

Questions such as the following will help you decide what your completed argument text might look like: *What is the assignment? What final form should this paper take? Should I use an adversarial or a consensual style? How can I build common ground? Should I state the issue and my position on it right away, or should I lead up to it? How can I make my position original and interesting? What types of support should I use? How will I conclude my argument?*

Example of an Analysis of a Rhetorical Situation When You Are the Writer

1. *Exigence: What is motivating you to write on this issue?* You neglected to turn in two early assignments in a course, and you suddenly realize that the zeroes you received then will lower your final grade from a B to a C. If you get a C, you will lose your scholarship. You decide to write to your instructor to find a way to raise your grade.

2. *Reader or Audience: Who is going to read this?* Your instructor (the audience) has already announced a policy of no late work. Nothing has been said about extra-credit work, however. You will try to establish common ground with the instructor by proposing an extra-credit project that will benefit not just you, but the entire class. You will describe in detail a successful experience you had with online research on your paper topic. The class is struggling with online research, the teacher wants the students to learn it, she does not have much time to teach it, and you can help fill the gap.

3. *Constraints: Will your values and attitudes drive you and your instructor apart, or will they help you develop common ground?* The instructor will have time constraints in class and may be unwilling to give you class time for your project. To address that constraint, you decide to ask for only five minutes, and you offer to prepare handouts that describe your online research in a way that will benefit your classmates.

The instructor may also have constraints about replacing missed assignments with extra-credit work. If one student is allowed to do this, she reasons, will all the others want to also? You point out that the project you are proposing is more difficult than the early assignments you missed and probably few, if any, students will want to follow your example.

You create common ground with your instructor by showing you are serious about the course and its standards. You decide to admit to your bad judgment when you failed to complete assignments, to point out that you have done well since then, and to commit to completing the remaining assignments carefully and on time. You also explain the importance of the extra-credit work to your future as a student. Without your scholarship, you will have to drop out of school. You know that you and your teacher share a desire to keep students in school. You and your instructor have common ground on that matter as well.

4. *Author: What do you know? What do you need to learn?* You are the author. You have read the class policies in the syllabus and know you have to work with them. You know you have computer expertise that many others in the class lack. You need to learn how to present what you know both orally and in written handouts to help the rest of the class.

5. *Text: What should your argument look like?* You will write a one-page proposal to your instructor in which you describe in detail what you would like to present to the class about online research. You ask that this assignment be used to raise the zero grades you received earlier in the course. You attach a second page that shows a sample of the handouts you will prepare for the class.

The class activities and writing assignments at the end of this chapter will help you use the information about the rhetorical situation that you have learned in this chapter. For example, one of the activities instructs you to analyze the rhetorical situation for each issue you select to write about in future papers and another asks you to conduct an audience analysis of your class members who will read the various drafts of your papers. Finally, you will be given instructions for writing an issue proposal in which you will organize and develop your initial thoughts on an issue you intend to develop in later papers. This short paper will pave the way for conducting research, which you will learn more about in Chapter 3. Before you turn to the activities and writing assignments, however, you will need additional information to help you think about and analyze an audience for an argument paper.

CONDUCTING AN AUDIENCE ANALYSIS

The purpose of argument is to bring about some change in an audience. Here are several additional considerations to help you understand your audience and plan your argument strategies to bring about change.

Determine the Audience's Initial Position and Consider How It Might Change

As part of your planning, project what you would regard as acceptable audience outcomes for your argument. Think particularly about the degree of common ground you initially share with your audience because it is then easier to plan for audience change. There are several possibilities of initial audience positions and possible changes or outcomes.

- *A friendly audience.* You may be writing for a friendly audience, one that is in *near or total agreement with you* from the outset. The planned outcome is to *confirm this audience's beliefs and strengthen their commitment.* You can be straightforward with such an audience, addressing them directly and openly with your claim at the beginning, supported with evidence that they can accept. Political rallies, religious sermons, and public demonstrations by special-interest groups, such as civil rights or environmental groups, all serve to make members more strongly committed to their original beliefs. When you write for a friendly audience, you will achieve the same effect.
- *An undecided audience.* An undecided audience *may possess no clear reasons for their tendencies or beliefs.* Possible outcomes in this case usually include (1) *final agreement* with you, (2) *a new interest* in the issue and a commitment to work out a position on it, or (3) *a tentative decision* to accept what seems to be true for now. To establish common ground with this kind of audience, get to the point quickly, and use support that will establish connections. Types of support that establish connections with an audience are described in Chapter 7.
- *A neutral audience.* Other audiences may be *neutral on your issue, uncommitted and uninterested in how it is resolved.* Your aim will be to *change the*

level of indifference and encourage readers to take a position. You may only be able to get their attention or raise their level of consciousness. As with other audiences, you will establish common ground with a neutral audience by analyzing audience needs and by appealing to those needs.

- **A hostile, resistant audience.** A hostile audience consciously *disagrees with you and may be closed to the idea of change*, at least at first. Anticipated outcomes for such audiences might include *avoiding more hostility* and *getting people to listen and consider possible alternative views.* You will learn strategies in Chapter 10 to help you appeal to such audiences. It is always possible that members of a hostile audience might *change their minds* or at least *compromise.* If all else fails, sometimes you can get a hostile audience to *agree to disagree,* which is much better than increasing its hostility.
- **An unfamiliar audience.** When you do not know your audience's position, it is best to *imagine it as neutral to mildly opposed* to your views and direct your argument with that in mind. Imagining an unfamiliar audience as either hostile or friendly can lead to extreme positions that may cause the argument to fail. Imagining the audience as neutral or mildly opposed ensures *an even tone* to the argument that *promotes audience interest and receptivity.*

Think of your relationship with your audience as if it were plotted on a sliding scale. At one end are the people who agree with you and at the other end are those who disagree. In the middle is the neutral audience and the unknown audience. Other mildly hostile or mildly favorable audiences are positioned at various points in between. Your knowledge of human nature and argument theory will help you plan strategies of argument that will address all these audience types and perhaps cause them to change their initial position on the sliding scale.

Analyze the Audience's Discourse Community

Besides analyzing your audience's initial position and how it might change, it is also useful to identify the audience's *discourse community.* An audience's affiliations can help define the nature of the audience itself. Specialized groups who share subject matter, background, experience, values, and a common language (including specialized and technical vocabulary, jargon, or slang) are known as discourse communities.

Consider discourse communities composed of all scientists, all engineers, or all mathematicians. Their common background, training, language, and knowledge make it easier for them to connect, achieve common ground, and work toward conclusions. The discourse community itself creates some of the common ground necessary for successful academic inquiry or for other types of argument.

You are a member of the university or college discourse community where you attend classes. This community is characterized by reasonable and educated people who share common backgrounds and interests that enable them to inquire into matters that are still at issue. You are also a member of the discourse community in your argument class, which has a common vocabulary and common tasks and assignments. Outsiders visiting your class would not be members of this community in the same way that you and your classmates are. To what other discourse communities do you belong?

Compare argument in your class with argument at home, at work, online, or chatting or texting with your friends. The strategies for connecting with others, building common ground, and arguing within the context of each of your discourse communities can vary considerably. With some reflection, you will be able to think of examples of the ways you have analyzed and adapted to each of them already. You can improve your natural ability to work with audiences by learning some conscious strategies for analyzing and adapting to both familiar and unfamiliar audiences.

Analyze and Adapt to a Familiar Audience

In working with a familiar audience, ask questions like the following to learn more about them:

- Who are the members of your audience, and what do you have in common with them?
- What are some of the demographic characteristics of this audience? Consider number, age, organizational affiliations, interests, and college majors.
- What is the present position of audience members on your issue, and what audience outcomes can you anticipate?
- What experience do audience members have with your issue? Ask about their knowledge and background, including both positive and negative experiences and obstacles.
- What beliefs, values, motives, goals, or aims about your issue do you share?

Construct an Unfamiliar Audience

Sometimes you will not be able to gather direct information about your audience because they are unfamiliar to you and unavailable for study. In this case, you will need to draw on your past experience for audience analysis. To do so, imagine a particular kind of audience, a *universal audience*, to write for when you cannot get direct audience information.

Chaim Perelman, who has written extensively about the difficulty of identifying the qualities of audiences with certainty, developed the concept of the universal audience.[3] He suggests planning an argument for a *composite audience*, one with distinct individual differences but also important common qualities. This universal audience is educated, reasonable, normal, adult, and willing to listen. Every arguer constructs the universal audience from his or her own past experiences, and consequently the concept of the universal audience varies somewhat from individual to individual and culture to culture.

The construct of the universal audience can be useful when you write papers for your other college classes. It is especially useful when the audience is largely unknown and you cannot obtain much information about its members. Imagine writing for a universal audience on those occasions. Your professors and classmates as a group possess the general qualities of this audience.

---

[3]See Perelman and Olbrechts-Tyteca, *The New Rhetoric*, for additional details on the universal audience.

When you complete the analysis of your audience, go back through the information you have gathered and consciously decide which audience characteristics to appeal to in your paper. Then you will be in a position to gather materials for your paper that will be convincing to this particular audience. You will develop reasoning and support that audience members can link to their personal values, motives, beliefs, knowledge, and experience. Similarity you need to show the same care in adapting to the needs of a universal audience. Since this audience is reasonable, educated, and adult, reasoning and support must be on its level and should also have broad applicability and acceptance. The universal audience inspires a high level of argumentation. *Careful research, intelligent reasoning, and clear writing style are requirements for this audience.*

Use your understanding of the rhetorical situation to help you read and also to help you get ideas and plan your own argument writing. It can be useful at every stage when you are reading, thinking, and writing about issues. The Summary Chart of the Rhetorical Situation (page 303) provides a brief version of the elements of the rhetorical situation as it applies to both reading and writing. Use it as a quick reference as you read or plan and write argument.

REVIEW QUESTIONS

1. What are the five elements in the rhetorical situation? Use TRACE to help you remember.
2. How can a reader use the rhetorical situation to analyze an argument essay? How can a writer use the rhetorical situation during the planning phase of writing a paper?
3. Why is the audience important in argument? What types of positions might an audience initially hold? What possible outcomes are associated with arguments directed to each of these audiences?
4. What is a discourse community? To what discourse communities do you belong? How does a discourse community help establish common ground for its members?
5. What is the universal audience? What are the special qualities of this audience? Why is it a useful idea?

CLASS ACTIVITIES AND WRITING ASSIGNMENTS

1. **Understand the Rhetorical Situation**
   a. *Analyze the rhetorical situation in a written argument.* Read the essay on page 39 by Charles M. Blow. Then answer the questions for discussion that follow the essay.

BEFORE YOU READ: Do you have knowledge about, or have you personally experienced, racial profiling? Describe your knowledge or experience.

Essay 1

WELCOME TO THE CLUB*

Charles M. Blow

The author is the *New York Times* visual op-ed columnist. His columns appear on Saturdays and are usually accompanied with visual graphics or images.

1   This week, the fog of racial profiling hung heavy over Harvard Square:

2   The arrest of Professor Henry Louis Gates Jr.,[1] the eminent Harvard scholar, at his own home thrust the police's treatment of minorities, particularly black men, back into the spotlight.

3   Whether one thinks race was a factor in this arrest may depend largely on the prism through which the conflicting accounts are viewed. For many black men, it's through a prism stained by the fact that a negative, sometimes racially charged, encounter with a policeman is a far-too-common rite of passage.

4   A New York Times/CBS News poll conducted last July asked: "Have you ever felt you were stopped by the police just because of your race or ethnic background? Sixty-six percent of black men said yes. Only 9 percent of white men said the same.

5   These views are not without merit. A series of racial-profiling studies across the country have found that blacks and Hispanics are more likely to be stopped and searched than whites.

6   In fact, last year the Center for Constitutional Rights, a New York law firm specializing in human rights, released a damning study of the racial-profiling practices of the New York Police Department. It found that more than 80 percent of those stopped and frisked were black or Hispanic. The report also said that when stopped, 45 percent of blacks and Hispanics were frisked, compared with 29 percent of whites, even though white suspects were 70 percent more likely than black suspects to have a weapon.

7   It's such a sensitive issue for black men that even the Black Man in Chief dove into the fray on Wednesday, reiterating that the issue of racial profiling "still haunts us." So passionate was his empathy that it caused him to err. His comment that the police behaved "stupidly" was not very smart. On Friday, he acknowledged as much.

8   Mr. Gates may be able to take some solace in the fact that his rite of passage came later in his life—a life that he told me on Thursday has been insulated "by a cocoon of racial tolerance, enlightenment and reason." Still, as one commenter on my Facebook page put it: "Tell Doc, welcome to the 'club.'"

9   My own induction into the "club" came when I was an 18-year-old college freshman. I was in a car with my friend Andre. We were young black men in a mostly white section of the mostly white town in Louisiana, about three miles from the college town where we lived.

New York Times, July 25, 2009, p. A15.
[1]Professor Gates was attempting to enter his home when local police arrested him.

10   As we drove, a police car began to trail us. Before we reached the city limits, its lights came on.

11   We stopped, and a white police officer approached. Andre got his license and motioned to me to get the registration from the glove box. When I opened it, a switch blade comb fell out. It was like the one the Fonz had on "Happy Days." They were popular prizes at local fairs and carnivals at the time.

12   The officer drew his gun. I froze. Then, realizing that it was just a comb, I told him so and pushed the button to make the comb pop up. I thought it was kind of funny. I was the only one. The officer grew irritated. He commanded me to "drop the weapon" and told Andre to exit the car.

13   Andre insisted on knowing why we had been stopped. The officer gave a reason. It wasn't true. Then he said something I will never forget: that if he wanted to, he could make us lie down in the middle of the road and shoot us in the back of the head and no one would say anything about it. Then he walked to his car and drove away.

14   He had raised the specter of executing us. He wanted to impress upon us his power and our worth, or lack thereof. We were shocked, afraid, humiliated and furious. We were the good guys—dean's list students with academic scholarships. I was the freshman class president. This wasn't supposed to happen to us.

15   As a child, I had been taught, in subtle ways, to be leery of the police. It wasn't that they were all bad, but you never wanted to have to find out which ones were. As my mother would say, they were to be "fed with a long-handled spoon." This was the first day that I fully understood what that meant.

16   We drove back to our college town and stopped at the house of Andre's father. Andre asked him what we should do. Happy that we were alive, he just told us to drop it. I have spent 20 years trying to drop it.

17   Even so, I committed myself to breaking this cycle when I had my own kids. That became impossible the day after Thanksgiving a couple of years ago. A white police officer stopped me when I was in the car with my children. He said that I was using my cellphone while driving. In fact, I had answered a call at a stoplight. When the light turned green, I put the phone away. I thought this was a case that could be debated, so I debated it. That didn't sit well with the officer. He went back to his car to write up a ticket. When he returned, he had two tickets. The second one, he told me, was for not wearing a seat belt, that he believed I had only put it on as I was being pulled over. That was not true. My kids were flabbergasted. They knew the officer was wrong, so they began to protest. I quieted them. When the officer drove off, I had a frank talk with them.

18   I told them that although most officers are brave and honorable men and women doing their best to protect and serve, there were, unfortunately, some bad seeds. Although I could not be sure that race had any bearing on what the officer had done, I felt the need to tell my boys that as black men, we may sometimes take more of the brunt of those bad officers' actions. As I spoke, my heart sank. Despite my best efforts to prevent it, the cycle of suspicion and mutual mistrust was tumbling forward into yet another generation. My children were one step closer to joining the "club."

FOR DISCUSSION:

Use TRACE to analyze this essay. How would you describe the text itself? How would you characterize the reader or audience that the author may have had in mind when writing this essay? What do you learn about the author? What are some of the possible constraints that might have influenced the author? What constraints influenced you as you read this essay? What is the exigence for this essay? How much common ground do you share with this author? Do you find this argument convincing or not? Why?

◆   b. *Apply the rhetorical situation to your issue by completing the rhetorical situation worksheet.* The worksheet below will help you understand the rhetorical situation for any issue you have selected to write about and have also tested to see if it is arguable (page 24). Complete the worksheet by yourself. You are working with limited information, so you may need to guess at some of the answers.

2. **Understand the Audience**

   a. *Write a letter to a specific audience.* Read the rhetorical situation on the next page and write a letter in response to one of the four individuals in the prompts that appear immediately after it. Do not confer with other members of the class. Make sure at least some students write in response to each of the four prompts.

Worksheet 1: Rhetorical Situation

1. *Exigence*

   What is motivating you to write on this issue? What happened? Why is it compelling to you?

2. *Reader or Audience*

   Who is going to read this? Where do you think they might stand on your issue right now? What are the chances of establishing common ground? What is the best approach to change their minds?

3. *Constraints*

   How do you think your training, background, affiliations, values, and attitudes about your issue are either in harmony or in conflict with those of your audience? What constraints can you use to build common ground?

4. *Author*

   What is your position or perspective on your issue? What do you already know? What do you need to learn? How can you be convincing?

5. *Text*

   What are you writing? What should it look like? What specifications do you need to follow? Review your assignment for your paper.

The Rhetorical Situation

You are enrolled in a first-year English class and your teacher allows you to be absent five times before she gives you an F for the course. If you are tardy to class three times, it counts as an absence. You have been absent five times and tardy to class twice. Your parents are angry at you for missing class so much, and they say that if you fail English you will have to get a job and start paying rent to live at home. Your teacher has explained that if you are tardy or absent from class one more time, she is going to fail you. You really want to do better; you are determined to change your ways.

On the way to class you have a blowout on the freeway. You pull over to change the tire and when you get the spare from the trunk, it is flat. This is not your fault, as you have just had your car serviced and the tires checked. A fellow motorist pulls over and helps you, but by the time you get a good tire on your car and drive to class, you are forty-five minutes late. You enter the classroom as quietly as you can. Your best friend raises her eyebrows. Your teacher gives you a stern look. You feel terrible.

The Writing Prompts

1. You are too embarrassed to talk to your teacher. Write her a letter to explain what happened and ask her for another chance.
2. Your parents are too angry to talk to you. Write them a letter to explain what happened and to ask their forgiveness.
3. You are very upset with the tire company. Write them a letter to explain what happened and ask for a reimbursement.
4. You don't have time to talk to your best friend after class. Write her a note to explain what happened and tell her what you intend to do about it.[4]

You and your classmates should now read some of these letters aloud. When you read them, do not divulge who the intended audience is. Ask the other students to guess who the intended reader of the letter is. Continue doing this until you have a sampling of all four letters and the class has guessed to whom each has been written.

Discuss the Results

What clues helped you guess the audience for each letter? How are the letters different from each other? In your discussion, consider how each audience influenced the purpose for writing each letter, the tone of each letter, and the type and level of vocabulary used in each letter.

◆   b. *Analyze your class as an audience.* The following worksheet will provide you with more specific information about the audience of your peers who will read your paper. This audience may consist of a small group of four or five individuals in your class who will serve as readers and critics of drafts of

---

[4]I am indebted to Samantha Masterton for this assignment.

Worksheet 2: Audience Analysis _____

1. Describe your issue. What is your audience's present position on this issue? Describe some other perspectives on your issue, and ask for reactions to those ideas. State your claim and ask if there is anyone who cannot accept it as stated. If there is, ask why.

2. How significant is your issue to the audience? If it is not considered significant, describe why it is significant to you. Talk about ways you can make it more significant to the audience.

3. How involved are audience members in the ongoing conversation about the issue? What do they already know about it?

4. How will you build common ground? What beliefs and values do you and your audience share about your issue? What motivates audience members in regard to your issue? What do they _want, think,_ and _believe_ in relation to your issue?

5. What argument style will work best with them? A direct adversarial style? Or a consensual style? Why?

6. Write what you have learned from this analysis to help you plan your appeal to this audience. Include values and motives in your discussion. (See Box 2.1 on page 32).

---

your paper from now until you hand it in. Your aim is to get an idea of how your audience regards your issue now before you begin your research and writing. You will then continue to consider your audience's thoughts during all phases of the writing process. This will help your audience members become interested in reading your paper and will perhaps ultimately change some of their views on your issue. Conduct the audience analysis as a group project, with each group member in turn interviewing the others and jotting down answers to the questions in Worksheet 2.

◆ **3. Write a One-Page Issue Proposal**

If you have not yet selected an issue to write future papers about, do so now. Refer to pages 16–20 to help you select an issue, write it as a question, and use the twelve tests of an arguable issue (see Box 1.4 on page 24) to make certain it is arguable.

Now write an issue proposal to help you organize and develop your thoughts and direct your future research for longer argument papers such as those assigned in Chapters 4 and 11. Your proposal should be 250 to 300 words long, and it should respond to the following four items:

a. Introduce the issue, and then present it in question form.
b. Explain why it is compelling to you.
c. Describe what you already know about it.
d. Explain what more you need to learn.

The example on the next page is an issue proposal written by a student.

Prisna Virasin
Issue Proposal
Professor Wood
English 1302
2 February 2010

The Barbie Controversy*

Introduce the issue.

1   It is interesting that a small, blond, blue-eyed, plastic doll could cause an uproar. Barbie has succeeded (intentionally or not) in inciting heated opinion on whether she is fit to be the image of the perfect woman for millions of impressionable young girls. Some people have stated that Barbie's proportions are humanly impossible, with her exaggerated bustline and minuscule waist. They claim that these impossible proportions could lead girls to develop a poor body image. Barbie doll defenders state that Barbie is a part of most girls' lives while they are growing up. Is Barbie bad? Does she have the power to affect girls psychologically all over the country or perhaps the world? When Barbie turned 50 in 2009, the media evaluated her once again, and, as usual, the results were mixed.

Present it in question form.

Explain why it is compelling to you.

2   I am interested in the Barbie controversy because, like many girls growing up in America, I was obsessed with Barbie when I was a child. Now, as a college student, I am very interested in female icons and their role in self-image development. I also have to fight the voices in my head telling me that I am too short and too fat, and I am not sure exactly where these voices have come from.

Describe what you already know about it.

3   I know that the Barbie doll product is pervasive in American society. I have never met a woman or girl who hasn't played with at least one Barbie. Barbie's image has appeared in McDonald's Happy Meals, in computer programs, on her own clothing line, on school supplies, and in every major American store with a toy section.

Explain what more you need to learn.

4   I need to do more research on the validity of the claim that Barbie affects girls' self-images either detrimentally or positively. I would like to explore the pervasiveness of Barbie internationally and compare the domestic sales figures to the international sales figures. Also, if Barbie proves to be a detriment to girls' self-images, I would like to seek out some proposed solutions and discuss their feasibility.

*The format shown in this paper and similar student papers throughout this book is reflective of MLA documentation style but has been modified to accommodate space limitations. All MLA-style student papers are double-spaced throughout. For actual MLA guidelines and a sample student paper showing the correct MLA format, see Appendix 1.

Learning More about Issues: Conducting Research

In Chapters 1 and 2 you learned to find issues for argument papers and to understand the contexts in which they occur. This chapter provides ways to learn more about your issue. It presents research and note-taking strategies to help you write papers that are uniquely yours. You will learn to use what you already know as you read and evaluate the opinions of others. As a result, your voice will become the major voice in your papers, and your ideas will dominate those of others. Information and ideas from other sources will be brought in to back up what you ultimately have to say.

Research takes time. Begin it early, and set up a system derived from the ideas in this chapter to preserve and organize what you may want to use in future papers. You can read this chapter now to get started on your thinking and research, and read it again when you are working to complete a particular assignment. The research materials and ideas you collect now, for example, will be useful if you write the exploratory paper taught in Chapter 4 or the researched position paper taught in Chapter 11.

BEGIN WITH WHAT YOU KNOW

Use the following strategies to help you access your ideas and background information for your argument papers and prepare for future research.

Write Down Everything You Now Know about Your Issue. As soon as you have an issue in mind, make some notes. You are often at your most creative when an idea for a paper first occurs to you, so write insights and ideas immediately to use later in your paper. This practice guarantees that some of the material in your paper will be your original ideas.

Read to Improve Your Background Information. Do some broad reading to find out who else is interested in your issue and what positions they take. Try the encyclopedia, books, or the Internet. Use a search engine like *Google* or *Yahoo!* and enter a keyword that is related to your issue to help you find some basic information online. Detailed information on how to conduct more thorough online research appears later in this chapter (pages 49–53). At this point, write notes on the ideas that strike you, and write your original reactions to these ideas as they occur to you. If you find material you want to read and note further, record where you found it so that you can go back and read it more thoroughly later.

Use Critical Thinking Prompts. Get additional insights and ideas about your issue by using some well-established lines of thought that stimulate critical thinking. The fifteen prompts in Box 3.1 (page 47) will help you think about your issue in some new ways. First, write what you now think you want to prove about your issue, and then write your responses to the critical thinking prompts that push your thinking. You will be pleased by the quantity of new information these questions generate for your paper. Here is an example to get you started.

Example of How to Use Critical Thinking Prompts

1. *What is your issue?* My issue is old-growth forests. I want to preserve those on the western coast of the United States.

2. *Associate it.* This is an enduring environmental issue. It is associated with other environmental issues, including reducing greenhouse gases that cause global warming and saving wildlife like the spotted owl, deer, and the other animals that live in these forests. It is also associated with preserving natural beauty and the history of these areas.

3. *Describe it.* These trees are as much as 3200 years old. The giant sequoias in California, for example, are huge, majestic trees that can reach heights of 325 feet. People standing among them appear to be very small, and when they look up, they can barely see the tops. Even the sky seems farther away than usual. It is awe-inspiring to walk among these trees because of their size, their age, and their beauty.

4. *Compare it.* Saving these forests from logging is similar to preserving natural lakes, national parks and forests, and other wilderness areas from commercial interests.

These responses will give you the idea. As you work through all the prompts, you will find that some are more productive than others for a particular issue. Use as many as you can. If you do not yet know enough to respond to some prompts, add information later when you have done more reading.

Talk with Others to Clarify Your Ideas. Many people find it easier to speak the first words than to write them. Typical audiences for an initial talk-through may include the other students in your argument class or a peer group made up of four or five students in your class. Your instructor, in conference, may also ask a few

---

| BOX 3.1 | Use These Prompts to Help You Think Critically about Your Issue. |

Critical Thinking Prompts

What is your issue? _____

Use some, but not all, of these prompts to help you think about it.

1. **Associate it.** Consider other related issues, big issues, or enduring issues. Associate your issue with familiar subjects and ideas.

2. **Describe it.** Use detail. Make the description visual if you can.

3. **Compare it.** Think about items in the same or different categories. Compare it with things you know or understand well. Compare what you used to think about the issue and what you think now. Give reasons for your change of mind.

4. **Apply it.** Show practical uses or applications. Show how it can be used in a specific setting.

5. **Divide it.** Get insight into your issue by dividing it into related issues or into parts of the issue.

6. **Agree and disagree with it.** Identify the extreme pro and con positions and reasons for holding them. List other approaches and perspectives. Say why each position, including your own, might be plausible and in what circumstances.

7. **Consider it as it is, right now.** Think about your issue as it exists, right now, in contemporary time. What is its nature? What are its special characteristics?

8. **Consider it over a period of time.** Think about it in the past and how it might present itself in the future. Does it change? How? Why?

9. **Decide what it is a part of.** Put it in a larger category and consider the insights you gain as a result.

10. **Analyze it.** Break the issue into parts and get insight into each of its parts.

11. **Synthesize it.** Put it back together in new ways so that the new whole is different, and perhaps clearer and better, than the old whole.

12. **Evaluate it.** Decide whether it is good or bad, valuable or not valuable, moral or immoral. Give evidence to support your evaluation.

13. **Elaborate on it.** Add and continue to add explanation until you can understand the issue more easily. Give some examples to provide further elaboration.

14. **Project and predict.** Answer the question "What would happen if . . . ?" Think about further possibilities.

15. **Ask why, and keep on asking why.** Examine every aspect of your issue by asking why.

---

questions and then just listen to you explore your ideas. A writing center tutor can do the same for you, as can friends or family members. End such sessions with some rapid freewriting (writing without paying attention to sentence structure, grammar, or punctuation), listing, or outlining to preserve the good ideas that have surfaced.

Develop a Research Plan for Your Issue and Enter It in Your File or Notebook. Make your research as efficient as possible. You may spend some of your time "just reading" about the issue as you look for background information. Most of the time, however, you will want to do directed reading that will fill in specific parts of your paper. The following suggestions will organize your reading and note taking so that you maintain your focus and avoid wasting time with aimless reading. You may not know much, and the issue may shift or change as you learn more, but you need a place to start.

1. When you have made a few notes, then write a claim plus reasons. Make a statement that you want to prove. Pose it as an answer to an issue question. Then list reasons to support your claim.

   ### EXAMPLE OF A CLAIM WITH REASONS

   Your issue question: To what extent should the Internet be censored?
   Your claim: The Internet should never be censored at all.
   Your reasons:

   > . . . because the Internet is a free speech arena that has its own internal organization, and censorship could alter its most basic nature.
   > . . . because censorship violates the First Amendment of the Constitution, which guarantees the right to free speech.
   > . . . because monitoring and filtering software is being improved and can protect children from accessing certain sites.
   > . . . because parents can and should supervise their children's use of the Internet.

   You now have the beginning of an outline or a list of possible ideas that reflect what may become the main sections of your paper. Once you begin research, you may find you need to narrow your topic and write on only one aspect of it, add additional reasons as support, or even change to another topic or pattern of organization entirely. Stay flexible and adjust your original outline or list as you go along so that it continues to focus and guide your research. Each piece of research material that you gather should be related to an item on your list or outline. When you read creatively and generate ideas of your own, write them in also. You do not need to make an elaborate outline, but you will need some kind of list or brief outline to help you decide on content and an order for your ideas.

2. Make a list of words associated with your issue that will help you locate sources both in the library and online. For example, if you are writing about college entrance tests, you could list terms like *testing, standardized testing, college entrance tests, standardized college entrance tests,* or *tests and college admission.* To focus your search more specifically, you might want to add *SAT* or *ACT.* Keyword searches will help you find both relevant and irrelevant information. Refine and narrow them by trying different combinations of the words from your list.

3. Think about what you have learned about your audience and write out what your audience needs as background. Jot down some reasons and other types of information the audience might find particularly convincing.

4. Identify at least three different perspectives or ways of looking at your issue, yours and two others, and be prepared to add to them or change them as you read more. In this way you will learn who else is interested in your issue, including what they think, want, and believe, along with some of the reasons they have for the perspectives they take.

5. List the types of research materials you will seek and where you will seek them. Books and articles will be high on your list, but you may also want to use other sources such as personal interviews, speeches, television programs, radio programs, advertisements, song lyrics, graphs, photographs, drawings or paintings, maps, letters, or any other types of material that would help you write an argument that is convincing to your audience.

A research plan (see Worksheet 3 on page 66) can save you considerable time and frustration when you begin your actual research, as can a knowledge of where to find research materials, which is the subject of the next section.

LOCATING SOURCES FOR RESEARCH

Begin your research by getting acquainted with the general layout of your library. Locate the library's online catalog, which indexes all its holdings; find out where the books, magazines, and journals are located; and then find the microforms, the government documents, the reference books, and the media section that houses video and audio materials. In addition, search where the copy center or copy machines are located as well as the reference desk and the reference librarians who will help you when you get stuck.

Learn to Use the Library's Online Catalog. Most libraries now store information about all of their holdings, including their books and periodicals (magazines, journals, and newspapers), in an online index. Note that only the periodicals are indexed in the online catalog and not the articles themselves. You will learn how to use library online databases to find articles in the section on this subject below.

Any computer with access to the Internet will allow you to search your library's online catalog. Search for a book by entering the author's name, the title, or the subject, and look for a particular magazine or journal by entering the title or the subject. Online catalogs also permit you to search by keyword. The keyword search is a powerful and effective research tool that can help you find mainly books but also other materials relevant to your topic, such as reference books, government documents, and various magazines and newspapers that have been reduced in size and preserved on microfilm. Start with a keyword that represents your topic, such as *clear-cutting*, and the computer will display all titles of the books and other holdings in the library that contain that word. Read the titles as they appear on the screen and identify those that might be useful. When you have found a title that looks promising, move to the screen that gives complete information about that book. There you will find all of the other subject headings under which that book is listed in the index. Use those subject headings, or keywords extracted from them, to expand your search. For instance, you might move from the original keyword, *clear-cutting*, to a new keyword, *erosion*, in order to access more varied material. Online catalogs are user-friendly and will tell you on the screen how to use them. Follow the directions exactly, and ask for help if you get frustrated.

Learn to Find a Library Book. To locate the actual books or other research materials you want to use, copy the *call number* listed with the title in the online catalog. Copy it exactly; find out where the source is located by consulting a directory, which is usually in plain sight in the lobby of the library, and go to the shelf where the source belongs. If you cannot find that title, look at the other books and resources on the shelf. They will often be on the same or a similar subject, and one of them may serve you just as well as the one you cannot find. Some libraries allow you to click on the call number of a book in the online catalog to find a list of the volumes that are shelved in close proximity. Books often contain bibliographies, or lists of related books and articles, which can lead you to additional sources.

Use Library Online Databases to Find Articles. Most libraries now subscribe to huge licensed online databases that allow you, with a single command, to search through several years' worth of articles from a large number of different print periodicals for information. All of these databases provide full publishing information about the articles they index, including the author, title, and time and place of publication. Some of the databases also provide either abstracts or full-text versions of the articles themselves. Since the library pays for these databases, you will need to obtain a password to use them. A librarian can help you. When you have the password, you will be able to search for articles related to your research project with any computer linked to the Internet. Many students now conduct at least some of their research on their home computers, printing copies of selected material at home. Alternatively, most of these databases allow the user to forward either article information or an entire article to your e-mail account to be read later.

Verify which database services your library subscribes to before you begin. Here are a few of the most common ones: *Academic Search Complete* describes itself as the "world's largest scholarly, multi-discipline, full text database" with peer-reviewed articles from more than four thousand periodical titles; *CQResearcher* provides full-text articles on topics of current interest that include a wide range of issues; *LexisNexis Academic* indexes six thousand international titles, including national and international newspapers, plus it provides full text and is updated hourly; and EBSCO*host* allows you to search multiple databases at the same time. Some databases specialize in particular areas of research and list journals, magazines, newspapers, books, and other media related to that area. Check each database you use to see how far back in time it goes. Some cover only the last twenty to twenty-five years, while others go back one hundred years or more.

Use databases by typing in subjects or keywords and executing a search. A list of associated articles in periodicals and scholarly journals will be displayed on the screen, with the most current appearing first. Read the title and, if there is one, the brief annotation of what the article is about to help you decide which articles to locate and read.

Learn to Find a Printed Journal or Magazine Article. If the database does not provide you with the full text of an article, you will have to find it in the printed

periodical in which it first appeared. Look up the name of the periodical, including the issue and date, in the online catalog and copy the call number. Then look
for it in the same way you would a book. You can find additional information
about the magazine or journal itself, including who publishes it and why, the
types of material it publishes, and its overall quality by visiting the periodical's
Web site and reading about it. Scholarly journals, for example, are often
described as "refereed," which means the articles in them are read by several
expert reviewers before they are accepted for publication and appear in print.
Such articles are usually very reliable sources.

Be forewarned—some issues of a periodical may be in bound volumes in the
book stacks, some may be on microfilm, and the newest issues may be stacked on
shelves in the current periodicals section of the library. You may have to search
to find what you want. Ask a librarian to help you. If you discover that your
library does not own the journal in which your article appears, it is usually possible for you to order it through an Interlibrary Loan system and have a copy from
another library mailed directly to you.

Learn to Find Newspaper Articles. The databases we have just described will lead
you to newspaper articles as well as journal and magazine articles, and many of
them are full text. When they are not, you may be able to find the newspaper in
which the article appeared in the microfilm section of the library. Newspapers
such as the *New York Times*, the *Wall Street Journal*, the *Christian Science Monitor*,
and the *London Times*, along with newsmagazines like *Time* and *Newsweek*, are
kept in this special section of the library. Some books and many other journals
are kept in this form also. When you encounter the abbreviations *mic, mf, cm,* or
mfc as part of the catalog information for a book or magazine, you will need to
find these sources in the microfilm section of the library. Machines are available
there that enlarge the tiny images so that you can read them. Other machines
enable you to print copies of microfilm material. Indexes to newspapers and
some magazines are available in the microfilm section as well.

Learn to Find Reference Materials and Government Documents. Two other areas of
the library can be useful for research. The reference area contains a variety of
volumes that provide factual, historical, and biographical information. Government documents contain data and other factual information that is also useful for
argument. Indexes, such as the *Public Affairs Information Bulletin,* which your
library may have online, show you the types of information you can expect to
find in documents printed by the government. Your librarian will help you locate
the actual documents themselves.

Make Appropriate Use of the World Wide Web. The World Wide Web, unlike library
databases that you access with a password, is free and available to everyone. Not
all of the materials on the Web are quality sources, however. Unlike the sources
indexed in library databases that have also appeared in print, not all of the material you find on the World Wide Web goes through a publisher or editor. In fact,
anyone familiar with computers can set up a Web site and put articles or other
documents on it. To maintain your own credibility with your audience, a good

rule of thumb is that no source from the Internet or in print should be used unless it has gone through a submission process and has been selected for publication by an editor of a reputable publication. While finding sources from well-known magazines and journals or professional organizations is generally safe, selecting sources from second-rate publications or from individuals lacking credentials reflects negatively on your credibility. Consequently, it is wise to use online articles and information sparingly unless directed otherwise by your instructor. Your paper will benefit from your using a variety of sources.

Use Web Browsers and Search Engines. Use a browser such as Safari, Firefox, or Microsoft Internet Explorer to gain access to the World Wide Web. You can then surf the Internet to find information for your paper by using search engines like *Google* at www.google.com, *Yahoo!* at www.yahoo.com, or *Firefox* at www.firefox .com. These search engines take the search terms (keywords) that you enter, comb the Net, and give you a search report, which is a list of titles and descriptions along with hypertext links that take you directly to the documents. Look through several of those that come up to judge which are most relevant for your purpose.

Vary Keyword Searches. Some engines allow you to use operators like *and, or*, and *not* to combine your search terms in a more focused way so that the results can be more relevant. By using specific keywords and their grammatical variations and synonyms along with these operators, you can find more particular information.

Use Wikipedia, Blogs, E-mail, and Chat Rooms Carefully. *Wikipedia*, the free, online encyclopedia that is open to anyone who has information to contribute, can be a good source of background information when you begin to think about your topic. Some of the entries, for example, are accompanied by useful bibliographies that can lead you to additional sources. Be cautious, however, about quoting *Wikipedia* in your paper. Some schools have policies that discourage the use of *Wikipedia* as a source for a scholarly paper because the entries have not been refereed by panels of experts and because anyone can write or edit material on this site at any time. Ask about the policy at your school. If you do use *Wikipedia* as a source, use it in a limited way just as you would any encyclopedia, to provide a few basic facts or definitions. Do cite it as a source for any information you use from it that is not general knowledge.

Blogs are virtual journals that may be written by anyone who wants to do this type of writing on the Internet. Blogs are personal, opinionated, and idiosyncratic. Explain exactly why you are quoting a blog. For example, you might quote a sampling of opinions on an issue from a few blogs. If you do, make your sources of information clear, explain how they contribute to your paper, and say why you have used them. Follow this same general advice for material you quote from e-mail, chat rooms, or personal sites like MySpace or Facebook.

The Internet also offers a forum for you to discuss your issue with other interested people: you can send e-mail to addresses made available on Web sites, and you can take part in "live" chats in discussion rooms. Remember that e-mail and chatting are potential sources for your paper, so always generate a print copy of any exchanges you think are particularly interesting or pertinent. Your instructor may in fact want you to submit print copies of all electronic material you quote or paraphrase in your final paper, so it is best to keep print copies of everything you use from the Internet.

EVALUATE ALL SOURCES AND SELECT THE BEST

As you locate the sources you think you will use for your paper, take a few minutes to evaluate each of them and discard those that do not meet your standards. Good, reliable sources that you find both in print and online add to your credibility as an author, making your argument more convincing. In the same way, bad sources reflect poorly on your judgment and detract from your credibility. You will need to evaluate every source you use in your paper, whether it is a printed or an online source. Printed sources that are also to be found online, such as those you access through the library's databases, should be evaluated as you would print sources.

Recognize Purpose in Written Argument. Recognizing different purposes in written argument, whether in print or online, will help you evaluate your sources. Some texts and Web sites are obviously intended as argument, and others conceal their purpose, making it more difficult to recognize argumentation in the material. Think of a continuum of types of writing that ranges from obvious argument at one extreme to objective writing at the other. Each type exhibits not only a different authorial intention but also a different relationship between the author and the audience. By noticing these differences, you will become more aware of the rhetorical situation for each source you read, and you will be able to represent it more accurately if you decide to summarize, paraphrase, or quote parts of it in your paper.

■ *Obvious argument.* The author's purpose is clearly and obviously to take a position and to change minds or to convince others. The author's point of view and purpose are clearly expressed along with reasons and supporting details that appeal to a wide audience.

■ *Extremist argument.* Authors who hold fast to prejudiced beliefs and stereotypes about various people, causes, or special projects sometimes rely on strongly held values and emotional language to appeal to specific audiences who may already share their views. The aim is to strengthen these views and motivate people to act. Think of an animal rights activist writing for print or a Web site to convince others to join this cause.

■ *Hidden argument.* Some texts seem to be written to inform but, on closer reading, actually favor one position over another but not in an obvious manner. Supporting material may be carefully selected to favor a particular view. Also, emotional language, vivid description, or emotional examples can be other signs that the author has strong opinions and intends not only to inform but also to convince. For example, in an article about college financial aid, all of the examples are about students who failed to pay their loans, and none are about responsible students who did pay. It is obvious from what is left out that the author has a position that manifests itself in biased reporting. The intention, even though concealed, is to convince people to question current financial aid practices.

■ *Unconscious argument.* Some authors who try to write objectively are influenced unconsciously by strong personal opinions, and the result is an unconscious intent to change people's minds. Imagine a journalist who strongly opposes war being sent to write an objective article about an active war zone. Negative perceptions can enter even as this writer presents the facts. Stacked or selected evidence, emotional language, quotations from authorities who agree with the author, or pictures with an outright point of view may attest to an argument purpose even while the author is unaware of it.

■ *Exploratory argument.* In exploratory essays the author lays out and explains three or more of the major positions on a controversial issue. The reader is invited to view an issue from several perspectives and to understand all of them better. If the author has a position, it may or may not be revealed.

■ *Objective reporting.* The author reports facts and ideas that may be accepted by everyone without controversy. The author's own point of view, opinions, or interpretations are deliberately omitted. You might find such writing in almanacs, data lists, weather reports, some news stories, and government, business, science, and technical reports. The audience reads this type of material to get information. Read this material as carefully, however, as any other information source because sometimes the author's opinion creeps in even in this type of writing.

Collect sources that represent different argumentation purposes and that also provide as many different perspectives or positions on an issue as possible. You will then be in a better position to examine individuals' reasons for holding these positions.

Analyze Web Address Extensions to Determine the Purpose of Web Sites. Web sites can have a variety of purposes. A site may be created to sell a product, persuade the reader to vote for a political candidate, provide entertainment, or offer educational information. Understanding how to read a Web site address can provide valuable clues to help you determine the purpose of a site. The following examples demonstrate common Web site extensions that provide information about the general category of a Web site and an indication of its basic purpose:

- The *.gov* extension means the Web site was created by a government agency. An example is *irs.gov*.
- The *.edu* extension means an educational institution produced the Web site. An example is *stanford.edu*.
- The *.mil* extension means the site is produced by the military. An example is *army.mil*.
- The *.com* extension means the Web site has a commercial purpose. An example is *honda.com*. The most common Web extension on the Internet is *.com*.
- The *.org* extension means the Web site was produced by a nonprofit organization. An example is *npr.org*.

- The *.net* extension stands for network. An example is *asp.net*.
- The *.int* extension stands for international. An example is *who.int*, the address of the World Health Organization.
- The *.us* extension stands for the United States, and *.uk* for the United Kingdom. Every country (and in the United States every state) has its own extension. An example is *lib.ks.us*, the Kansas State Library.

It is difficult to generalize about the reliability of the different types of sites. Consider, however, that *.gov*, *.edu*, *.lib*, and *.mil* sites are created by established institutions with stated public purposes, and *.com*, *.net*, and *.org* can be set up by any person or group with a particular self-interest. Knowing you are on a commercial or special interest site can be useful when you are trying to access reliable information for a research paper.

Analyze the Rhetorical Situation of Your Sources. This will help you gain even more insight into them. Remember TRACE. Consider the *text:* analyze its point of view on the issue, compare it with other sources on the same subject, analyze the values implicit in it, look at the types of support it contains, and examine its conclusion. Then ask, Who is the intended *reader*? Notice, for example, the nationality of the publication and the date of publication. Is the source intended for a particular category of readers or for a universal audience? Would you classify yourself as an intended reader?

Learn more about the *author*. Read the preface of a book or the beginning or end of an article for author information (if there is any). Use the Internet for additional information by accessing *Google* and entering the author's name as a keyword in the "Search" box. Many authors have Web sites on which you can learn more about their interests, associations, and other publications. Commercial book-shopping sites such as Amazon, found at www.amazon.com, list other available books authors have written as well as some descriptive or review material on them.

Imagine each source in a context, and think about the *constraints* that may have influenced the author to write about this issue in a certain way and also about the constraints that might influence you as you read it. Try to understand the author's motivation or *exigence* for writing on the issue.

Evaluate the Credibility of Your Sources. To help you determine the credibility of all sources, but particularly online sources, ask the following questions:

1. *Is the source associated with an organization that is recognized in the field?* For example, an American Civil Liberties Union Web site on capital punishment is credible because the ACLU is a nationally known organization that deals with issues of civil rights.
2. *Is the source listed under a reputable domain?* Look at what comes after "www" in the online address or URL. For example, information found at www.stanford.edu has some credibility because it is associated with a university. Universities are considered reliable sources of information. Of course, any Stanford student, faculty member, or staff member could publish material online. The material would not necessarily be credible, so you have to review it carefully.

3. *Is the source published in a print or online journal that is peer-reviewed?* Check the journal's Web site or look at a print copy. The journal will usually advertise this on its front page. For example, *Modern Language Notes*, published by Johns Hopkins University Press, is credible because everything written in it has been reviewed by a panel of experts to ensure that it meets a high standard of scholarship.

4. *Is the online source duplicated in print?* For example, material appearing on www.nytimes.com is credible because the *New York Times*, a nationally respected newspaper, sponsors it.

5. *Is the source accessed by a large number of people?* For example, a daily updated news site, www.cnn.com, is read and talked about across the country.

6. *Is the source directed mainly to extremists?* You will recognize such sources by their emotional language, extreme examples, and implicit value systems that are associated with extremist rather than mainstream groups. Learn what you can about such groups, and try to determine whether or not they have a wide appeal. Your goal should be to find information with sufficiently wide appeal so that it might be acceptable to a universal audience.

7. *Is the evidence in the source stacked to represent one point of view?* Again, an unusual amount of emotional language, carefully selected or stacked evidence, and quotations from biased sources and authorities characterize this material. You can attack the obvious bias in this material if you want to refute it.

8. *Is the source current?* Check to see when a Web site was published and last updated. Many topics are time sensitive. A Web site that discusses foreign policy in the Middle East, but is dated before 2001 (especially before 9/11), might have limited value unless you are examining the history of American foreign policy in this area. If you are looking for the latest ideas about global warming or immigration, check the date of the Web site, which is sometimes at the bottom of the document or on the home page.

9. *Is the source sloppily edited, undocumented, or unreasonable?* Material that is poorly edited, infrequently updated, or old may be untrustworthy. Other red flags are inflammatory language and no identified author. Sweeping generalizations made without evidence, undocumented statistics, or unreasonable arguments indicate questionable sources for research.

10. *Is the source moral or immoral, ethical or unethical according to your values?* This is a bottom-line question that will help you differentiate credible from noncredible sources for research.

CREATE A BIBLIOGRAPHY

The bibliography is the alphabetically arranged list of evaluated sources you have decided are credible, related to your issue, and potentially valuable to your research. You will begin by reading them. You may not use all of them, and some of them may lead you to other sources that you will add later. You will either enter these items directly into a computer or write them on note cards to be typed later.

Using a Computer

Copy and paste bibliographical information for each of your sources into a computer file. Use the journalist's questions to help you get the basic information you will need: *who* is the author, *what* is the title, *where* was the source published, *when* was it published, *which* medium of publication is it,[1] and *why* would I use it? For each source, add a note to suggest why you might use it in your paper. You will need this information later when you assemble the bibliography or list of works cited in your paper, so write or type all of it out accurately. You will not want to have to find a source again later. Here are some examples in MLA style.

In examples 2 and 3, a search by author and title on a search engine such as *Google* or a database such as *JSTOR* locates the source, and no URL is necessary. In the notecard example on page 58 the URL is needed to locate that specific source.[2]

- *Bibliographical information for a book* must include the author, the title italicized (underlined in handwritten notes),[3] the place of publication, publisher, date of publication, and medium of publication. To help you, add the call number so that you can find it later in the library.

  EXAMPLE: Book
  Stock, Gregory. *Redesigning Humans: Our Inevitable Genetic Future*. Boston: Houghton, 2002. Print.
  [Call number in stacks, QH438.7 S764]

- *Bibliographical information for a printed article* must include the author's name (if there is one); title of the article (in quotation marks); name of the publication (italicized); Volume, issue number (year) for journals, or date-of-publication for magazines, page numbers, and medium of publication. Add the call number or a location.

  EXAMPLE: Magazine Article
  Sandel, Michael J. "The Case Against Perfection: What's Wrong with Designer Children, Bionic Athletes, and Genetic Engineering." *Atlantic Monthly* Apr. 2004: 51–62. Print.
  [photocopied article; in research file folder]

- *Bibliographical information for online material accessed on the Web or a database* must include as many of the following elements as are available or needed for the type of source: author's (editor's, etc.) name; title of article (in quotation marks); title of the magazine, journal, or book

---

[1] The medium of publication is required for all bibliography entries in MLA style. The medium is listed after the other publication information. Examples include Print, Web, E-mail, DVD, Radio, Performance, and so on. For a list of mediums, see Appendix 1 (page 266).
[2] This is an MLA documentation standard, published in 2008. For more complete information, see Appendix 1, pages 266–267.
[3] Italicize the titles of books and journals in your bibliography when following both MLA style and APA style. Underlining in written notes is understood to mean "place in italics." See additional MLA and APA information and examples in Appendix 1, pages 259–301.

(italicized); Volume.Issue numbers: (date of publication or last update); page or paragraph numbers (N. pag. when unpaged) for articles; name of the Web site or database (italicized); sponsor, owner, or publisher of the site (or N.p. if not available), date of sponsorship, publication, or update (use n.d. when unavailable); medium; access date; and the URL (for MLA following the access date within angle brackets) when an author-title search does not locate the source.

EXAMPLE: Magazine Article Located in Database
Hayden, Thomas. "The Irrelevant Man." *US News & World Report* 3 May 2004. *Academic Search Complete.* Web. 15 May 2010.

Using Note Cards

Another way to record bibliographical information should you not be recording directly into a computer file is on 3 by 5 inch index cards. Write out a bibliography card for each separate source you are likely to utilize and include the same items of information you have just been advised to include in a computer file. Figure 3.1 shows an example of a bibliography card for an online article. Notice that the card provides publication information, a brief statement of use, and some specific quoted material that can later incorporated into the paper. Underlining is used to represent italics. Additional information on how to format bibliographical sources appears in Appendix 1 (pages 259–301).

McVay, Douglas A.,ed. "Drug War Facts." 6th ed.

Common Sense for Drug Policy. Jan. 2008. Web. 21 Apr. 2010.
<http://www.drugwarfacts.org/index2.htm>.

Use for statistics to support more treatment and less imprisonment. Click on entries under "Prisons" and "Treatment" in list of Chapters.

1. "Treatment is 10 times more cost effective than interdiction in reducing the use of cocaine in the United States."

2. "Over 80% of the increase in the federal prison population from 1985–1995 was due to drug convictions."

FIGURE 3.1   Bibliography Card for an Online Article.

SURVEY, READ, AND ADD ANNOTATIONS TO YOUR BIBLIOGRAPHY

Survey and Skim. A stack of books, a file of articles, and other materials that you have gathered for research may seem daunting if you are not sure where to start. A good way to begin is to *survey and skim* to save yourself some time. Survey a book or an article before you read it or take information from it. This critical reading practice helps you understand the type of work it is and also find the major ideas and a few of the supporting details to make an initial assessment of relevance. Surveying helps you decide which articles or books you will want to read more carefully. Box 3.2 below lays out the steps for surveying both books and chapters or articles.

BOX 3.2	How to Survey.

Steps for Surveying Books, Articles, and Chapters

Survey a book or an article before you read it to get an introduction to the major ideas and a few of the supporting details.

Books. To survey a book (not a novel), follow these six steps in the order given.

1. Read the *title* and focus on what it tells you about the contents of the book.
2. Read the *table of contents.* Notice how the content has been divided and organized into chapters.
3. Read the *introduction.* Look for background information about the subject and author and for any other information that will help you read the book.
4. Examine the special *features* of the book. Are there headings and subheadings in bold-face type that highlight major ideas? Is there a glossary? An index? A bibliography? Are there charts? Other visuals?
5. Read the title and first paragraph of the *first* and *last chapters* to see how the book begins and ends.
6. Read the title and first paragraph of the *other chapters* to get a sense of the flow of ideas.

   This procedure should take about half an hour. It will introduce you to the main issue and approaches in a book, and reading it will then be much easier.

Articles and Chapters. To survey an article or a chapter in a book, follow these six steps in this order.

1. Read the *title* and focus on the information in it.
2. Read the *introduction,* which is usually the first paragraph but can be several paragraphs long. Look for a claim and any forecasts of what is to come.
3. Read the *last paragraph* and look for the claim.
4. Read the *headings* and *subheadings,* if there are any, to get a sense of the ideas and their sequence. If there are no headings, read the first sentence of each paragraph to accomplish the same goal.
5. Study the *visuals:* pictures, charts, graphs. Read their captions. They often illustrate major ideas.
6. Identify the *key words* that represent the main concepts.

   Surveying an article or chapter takes ten to fifteen minutes. It introduces you to the issue, the claim, and some of the support.

It is especially important to read the preface of a book to learn the author's position on the issue. Then use the table of contents and index to find specific information. After you have surveyed, you can skim relevant parts to find the specific information you need. To skim, read every fourth or fifth line quickly, or sweep your eyes across the page. If you know what you are looking for and you are concentrating on finding it, you will be able to locate information by skimming.

Read to Understand the Author. If you survey and skim and the material looks promising, eventually you will want to slow down and read. Here is what you can expect if you are reading written argument. All arguments have the structural components you are familiar with from other kinds of reading and writing. The main difference is their names. The special characteristics of the components of argument will be described when the Toulmin model is discussed in Chapter 5. We start using Toulmin's terms here, however, to help you get used to them.

The thesis of an argument, which shapes the thinking of the entire text and states what the author finally expects you to accept or believe, is called the *claim*. Look for it at the beginning or end of a book or in the first or last paragraph of an article. The main ideas or *subclaims* are assertions, reasons, or supporting arguments that develop the claim. They are in themselves almost meaningless without further explanation. *Support* in the form of facts, opinions, evidence, and examples is the more specific material that provides additional information and further explanation about the claim and the subclaims. Support makes the claim and subclaims clear, vivid, memorable, and believable. *Transitions* lead the reader from one idea to another and also sometimes state the relationships among ideas. Furthermore, there is a constant movement between general and specific material in all texts, including argumentation texts, and this movement becomes apparent when the ideas are presented in various types of outline form. You can improve your comprehension of an argument essay by identifying some of these elements and characteristics as you read.

Read Creatively to Get Ideas and Form Your Responses. As you work to understand the source you are reading, add some creative reading strategies to help you think about your audience and generate additional ideas for your paper. Creative reading enables you to form original ideas and think critically. Here are some questions that you can keep in mind to guide creative reading.

- What strikes me in this text? What interests me? Why? Will these same ideas interest my audience?
- What new ideas and answers are occurring to me as I read? Will my audience accept them?
- Do these new ideas challenge any of my existing ideas or the existing ideas of my audience? How?
- Do I basically agree or disagree with these ideas? Do I find them convincing? Will my audience be convinced?
- What can I use from my reading that will appeal to my audience?

Answers to these questions will help you write the responses for your annotated bibliography, which are explained in the next section. They will also preserve your ideas so that you can use them later in your paper. Other suggestions to help you read argument critically and creatively appear in Chapters 5 through 7.

Add Annotations to Your Bibliography. Your instructor may ask you to add annotations to your bibliography in the form of summaries and responses, or you may decide to do this on your own. Summaries show you understood each source, and responses show you thought about and reacted to the ideas. An *annotated bibliography* helps you visualize your sources, their basic content, and your reactions to them as a unit of information, gathered together in one place. As you read through this material, you will gain insights into how to use the sources in your paper. Some of the ideas and even the phrasing in summaries and responses can also be incorporated into your paper later when you write it.

Write summaries in your own words. Answer these questions:

1. *What is this about?* to identify the issue, the claim, and some of the sub-claims; and
2. *What did the author say about the claim?* to understand the main points the author makes about the claim.

An example of an annotated bibliography appears on pages 67–70. Note that the first sample annotation includes a summary, a response, and a statement of how it could be used in an argument paper.

The first entry is labelled. Use it as an example.

DEVELOP A SYSTEM FOR TAKING AND ORGANIZING YOUR NOTES

You may want to open a file in your computer where you will enter your own ideas and also enter various types of reading notes, including material you *quote* word for word, the material you *paraphrase* or rephrase in your own words, and the material you *summarize*. You can, if you prefer, keep your notes in a research notebook, in a paper folder, or on note cards. A combination of these possibilities may work best for you. **The cardinal principle in whatever note-taking system you use is to clearly indicate on every note which ideas and language belong to other authors and which of them are your own.** Add the author's name and the page number to all quoted, paraphrased, or summarized material, place direct quotations in quotation marks, and set off your own ideas and comments in square brackets [ ], place them in a different font or color in your computer files, or label them "mine."

Using a Computer

Use your research plan (pages 48–49) both to guide your research and to help you organize your notes and ideas. Arrange your notes as you go along and enter them under appropriate headings either in a computer file like those on your research plan (see Worksheet 3, page 66) or on the list or outline that you have prepared to guide your research. Add additional headings to this plan when you need them. One way to accomplish this on a computer is to open two windows side by side. One window displays the headings from your research plan that may become major sections in your paper, and the other window displays an online article you are reading and noting. Copy the material from the article you want to quote and paste it into your tentative outline. Always enclose such material in quotation marks, and then add the name of the author at the end. Add the page number (if there is one) as well. Many online sources do not have page (or paragraph) numbers. You do not need at this point to add the title, place, or date of publication of each source since that information is available in your bibliography. However, if you are using more than one book by the same author, write both the author's name and a short version of the title at the end of the citation.

When you are taking notes, you may omit words in a direct quotation to make it shorter and more to the point; indicate where words have been omitted with three spaced periods, known as an *ellipsis*. If the omitted material occurs at the end of a sentence, add a period immediately after the last quoted word, followed by the three spaced periods. Add the page number after the closing quotation mark. The quotation in Figure 3.2 below provides an example of ellipsis.

If your research leads you to a new source and you want to use it, add full information about it to your bibliography. Every source you quote should be represented in your bibliography. Conversely, you should not have any items in your bibliography that you do not quote, paraphrase, or summarize in your paper.

Clearly distinguish paraphrased and summarized material from your own ideas, just as you would quoted material. Introduce each paraphrase or summary that you enter into your document with a phrase that attributes it to its original author. "According to Scott . . . ," or "Jones points out . . . ," will make it clear who is responsible for the material that follows even if it has been reworded and does not appear in quotation marks. Add a page number at the end, if it is from a paged source.

Using Note Cards

You may prefer to take notes on 3 by 5 index cards. When using cards you must also be careful to differentiate among the material you quote, the material you write in your own words (paraphrase), the material you summarize, and your own ideas. Code the different types of information by using different colors of cards, by

Problems—current system

Gray

"Not only has America nothing to show . . . , but the failed attempt has clearly made everything worse. After blowing hundreds of billions of dollars and tens of thousands of lives, the drugs on the street today are stronger, cheaper, more pure, and more widely available. . . ." (189)

FIGURE 3.2   Note Card with Quoted Material.

writing with different colors of pens, or by labeling each type of information. When you intersperse your own insights with material quoted from others, place your ideas in brackets [ ] to set them off or label them "mine." Always indicate directly quoted material by placing it in quotation marks. See Figure 3.2 (page 62) for an example of a note card with a direct quotation using ellipses and a page number.

Indicate at the top of the card where you intend to use the source in your paper. Use a brief heading from your list of ideas, outline, or research plan for this cross-referencing. The example in Figure 3.2 shows one way to do this.

Paraphrased or summarized material should also be recorded carefully and accurately with the page number at the end. Since you are condensing or changing the wording of this material, do not place it in quotation marks. You still must let your reader know where you got the material when you write your paper, so include on the card the author's name and the page number. Also indicate where you will use it in your paper.

Arrange these cards as you go along according to the categories that are written at the top. Then place the categories in the sequence you think you will follow in your paper. The cards are now ready to work into your paper when you write the first draft.

AVOID PLAGIARISM

If you follow the advice on taking notes in the previous section, you will have no problem with plagiarism. Just in case you are still unclear about what plagiarism is exactly, here is a statement made by the Council of Writing Program Administrators that will help you: "In an instructional setting, plagiarism occurs when a writer deliberately uses someone else's language, ideas, or other original (not common-knowledge) material without acknowledging its source. This definition applies to texts published in print or online, to manuscripts, and to the work of other student writers."[4] Plagiarism is regarded as an extremely serious personal and academic violation because it negates the purpose of education, which is to encourage original and analytical thinking in a community in which expression of thought is both respected and protected.

Online research seems to have increased the incidence of plagiarism in student work. Some students find it tempting to copy and paste information from online articles into their own papers without documenting the source. Sometimes students mix their words in with the words of the quoted author and neglect to put these quoted words in quotation marks. The result is a strange mix of styles and voices that creates a problem for the reader, who cannot easily sort out the students' words from those of the person being quoted.

Lynne McTaggart, a professional writer whose work was plagiarized by a well-known author and commentator, explains plagiarism in this way:

> Plagiarism is the dishonorable act of passing someone else's words off as your own, whether or not the material is published. . . .Writers don't own facts. Writers don't

---

[4]From "Defining and Avoiding Plagiarism: The WPA Statement on Best Practices." The full statement can be accessed at www.wpacouncil.org/positions/plagiarism.html.

own ideas. All that we own is the way we express our thoughts. Plagiarism pillages unique expressions, specific turns of phrase, the unusual colors a writer chooses to use from a personal literary palette. . . . In this age of clever electronic tools, writing can easily turn into a process of pressing the cut-and-paste buttons, . . . rather than the long and lonely slog of placing one word after another in a new and arresting way.[5]

McTaggart was shocked to read a book by a best-selling author that included material from her book, exactly as she had worded it, in passage after passage throughout the work without proper acknowledgment.

Here is another example of this error. The late Stephen E. Ambrose, an author of popular history books, was accused of plagiarism when his book *The Wild Blue* was published in 2001.[6] Both professional historians and the media criticized him publicly, and he suffered considerable embarrassment. Figure 3.3 reproduces two of several illustrations of the plagiarized passages along with the original passages as they were presented in the *New York Times*. Compare the passages in the two columns until you understand why those in the right-hand column present a problem. This will help you avoid making the same mistake yourself.

Note that Ambrose added footnotes in his book to show in general where the material came from, but he did not place quotation marks around the material that he copied directly nor did he introduce the quoted author's name to the reader. Kirkpatrick, the *New York Times* critic, reflects the opinions of several professional historians when he explains, "Mr. Ambrose should have marked direct quotations in the text, or at the very least noted the closeness of his paraphrase in his footnotes, historians say. College students caught employing the same practices would be in trouble."[7] When criticized, Ambrose admitted his mistake, and he was quoted as saying, "I wish I had put the quotation marks in, but I didn't."[8] He said he would do things differently in future books: "I am sure going to put quotes around anything that comes out of a secondary work, always."[9]

You can avoid plagiarism by differentiating between your ideas and those of others at all stages of the paper-writing process. This is why you are advised to enclose all direct quotations in quotation marks in your notes, to introduce paraphrases and summaries drawn from other people's works with the names of the authors in your notes, and to keep your own ideas separate from those of others by placing them in brackets or a different font. You may safely and responsibly use other people's ideas and words in your paper, but you must always acknowledge that they are theirs. More instruction on how to separate your words from those of others when you incorporate source material into your paper occurs on pages 246–248. More detailed information on how to cite many different types of sources appears in Appendix 1 (pages 259–301).

---

[5]Lynne McTaggart, "Fame Can't Excuse a Plagiarist," *New York Times*, March 16, 2002, p. A27.
[6]David D. Kirkpatrick, "As Historian's Fame Grows, So Do Questions on Methods," *New York Times*, January 11, 2002, pp. A1, A19.
[7]Ibid, p. A19.
[8]Ibid, p. A1.
[9]Ibid, p. A19.

EXCERPTS

ECHOES IN PRINT
Stephen E. Ambrose, the author of historical best-sellers, appears to have reused words and phrases from other works, though passages are attributed in footnotes to original authors.

From *The Rise of American Air Power*, 1987, by Michael S. Sherry.

From *The Wild Blue*, 2001, by Stephen E. Ambrose.

ON JOHN STEINBECK'S WORK WRITING PROPAGANDA ABOUT AIRMEN

"Crewmen supposedly sprang from the frontier tradition of the 'Kentucky hunter and the Western Indian fighter.'... Like Lindbergh 15 years earlier, the airman was presented as both individualist and joiner, relic of the past and harbinger of the new era, free spirit and disciplined technician, democrat and superman, 'Dan'l Boone and Henry Ford.'"

"Steinbeck wrote that the men of the AAF sprang from the frontier tradition of the 'Kentucky hunter and the Western Indian fighter.' He presented the airman as both individualist and a joiner, a relic of the past and a harbinger of a new era, a free spirit and a disciplined technician, a democrat and a superman, 'Dan'l Boone and Henry Ford.'"

ON THE DANGERS OF ANOXIA (DEPRIVATION OF OXYGEN)

"Anoxia from shortages of oxygen both compounded the perils of frostbite and posed a serious danger in and of itself."

"Anoxia from shortages of oxygen compounded the threat of frostbite and posed a serious danger in and of itself."

FIGURE 3.3 Examples of Plagiarism.

SOURCE: David D. Kirkpatrick, "As Historian's Fame Grows, So Do Questions on Methods," *New York Times*, January 11, 2002, p. A19.

If the passages you have drawn from outside sources are reasonably short, support your own ideas, and clearly indicate where you found them, then you have done the right thing. If the passages are copied into your paper as though you had written them yourself, then you could receive a poor grade in the course or even be expelled from college. Understand too that you fail to link reading to thinking when you are reading to copy. It is a theft from someone else, but also from yourself. And, of course, you don't learn to improve your own writing when you copy other people's words instead of writing your own.

REVIEW QUESTIONS

1. What is the difference between library subscription databases, such as *Academic Search Complete* and *LexisNexis*, and the World Wide Web? What types of material might you find by using each of them?
2. What is a bibliography? What is an annotated bibliography? How might writing an annotated bibliography help you research and write your paper?
3. Name some of the characteristics of a credible source.

4. Why would you create a research plan to guide your research?

5. What is plagiarism? How can you avoid it?

CLASS ACTIVITIES AND WRITING ASSIGNMENTS

1. **Create Peer Writing Groups**

   a. *List and briefly discuss the issues that class members have selected for research.* Place related issues in categories. Use these categories to form groups of four or five students each for future group work.

2. **Start Thinking and Writing about Your Issue**

   a. *Freewrite what you know about your issue.* Write rapidly, do not bother about exact phrasing or punctuation, and include details, descriptions, and examples. Explain the position you think you will take.

   b. *Apply the critical thinking prompts to your issue and write out the results.* Keep these to use later in your argument papers.

   c. *Develop a tentative research plan using the following worksheet.*

WORKSHEET 3: RESEARCH PLAN

Claim Plus Reasons

Write your claim, write the word *because* after the claim, and list three to five possible reasons or subclaims that you might develop in your paper.

Research Needs

Anticipate your research needs: What parts of your paper can you develop with your present knowledge and information? What parts will you need to think about and research further? Can you learn enough to develop the claim, or should you simplify it? What types of research materials will you seek, and where will you seek them?
Make a list of key words related to your issue to help you search.
How much preliminary background reading do you need to do, and where should you do it?

Plan for Your First Draft

How much background information will you need to provide your readers?
What terms will you need to define?
What are your strongest opinions? Your best reasons?
What is a reasoned way to begin your paper? What is a reasoned way to end it?
What original examples, descriptions, or comparisons occur to you now?

◆ **3. Write an Annotated Bibliography**

    a. *Collect ten quality sources about your issue.* Make certain that your sources express several different perspectives or ways of thinking about this issue. Copy all the publisher's information needed to cite your sources in MLA or APA format, and assemble your bibliography in alphabetical order. See Appendix 1 (pages 259–301), especially the examples of formatted papers on pages 276–286 and 300–301 to help you. Notice that the following example of an annotated bibliography includes both print and online sources and that more than two perspectives on the issue are represented in these bibliographical items. Your bibliography should include the same range, unless your instructor indicates otherwise.

    b. *Survey, skim, and read selected parts of each source.*

    c. *Write a summary, a response, and an indication of how you might use each source in your paper after each item.* The following example provides selected items from a student's annotated bibliography and demonstrates how to record information from different types of sources, how to summarize, how to respond to the sources, and how to indicate where you might use them in your paper.

Student Paper 1

Angela A. Boatwright
Annotated Bibliography
Professor Thorne
English 1302
15 March 2010

Human Cloning: An Annotated Bibliography

Online journal (appeared earlier in print)

1 Bailey, Ronald. "The Twin Paradox: What Exactly Is Wrong with Cloning People?" *Reason* May 1997. *Reasononline.* Web. 12 Mar. 2010.

2   This article explains simply, in nonscientific terms, exactly what was done to clone Dolly the sheep. The author briefly explains the legislation that has resulted from the first asexual reproduction of a mammal. Bailey explains what a clone would be (Summary) and discusses the reasons why human clones could in no way be exact copies of their predecessors. Clones would have different personalities and would be as different as identical twins. He doesn't feel it is unethical to clone humans because they would be treated with the same moral status as any identical twins or triplets. He states that as long as we treat cloned individuals as we would treat any other human being, all other ethical problems we have concerning cloning would essentially disappear.

3   This article answers the questions I had regarding exactly (Response) what a clone would be like in relation to the "original model." It reinforces the belief I had that clones would be different people because of different social influences and environmental factors that have so much to do with the personality of an individual.

(statement of use)   4   I will use information about Dolly and the uniqueness of clones in my discussion about the feasibility of cloning people.

Web site (online publication)   5   U.S. Dept. of Energy Office of Science, "Cloning Fact Sheet." *Genomics.energy.gov*. Human Genome Project Information, 11 May 2009. Web. 14 Feb. 2010.

6   According to this government Web site, which is maintained by the Human Genome Project, both scientists and physicians at present advise against cloning humans. When the first cloned animal, Dolly, died in 2003, she had developed both arthritis and cancer. Since that time, animal cloning has been very difficult. Only one or two tries out of one hundred are successful with animals. Also, many cloned animals are born with "large offspring syndrome" and other birth defects. They often die prematurely. There is fear that cloning humans could lead to similar problems. For these reasons, human cloning at this time is considered unethical and dangerous.

7   This Web site also provides links to anti-cloning legislation information and answers many other questions about all types of cloning issues. It is a credible Web site.

8   I will draw some information from this Web site to use in the introduction to my paper; and I will also use the information about the dangers of human cloning in my conclusion.

Magazine article (print)   9   Mann, Charles C. "The First Cloning Superpower." *Wired* (Jan. 2003): 116+. Print.

10   The author has interviewed a number of scientists in China who are working on therapeutic cloning techniques that employ stem cell research with the ultimate end of growing human replacement organs and tissues. China does not have as many regulations against experimenting with human stem cells as do the United States and other Western countries. China allows almost complete freedom to scientists in this field, disallowing only human reproductive cloning experiments. This means that scientists can experiment with embryonic stem cells to clone spare human parts, to regenerate damaged nerve and other tissue, and to find cures for diseases that have had no cures in the past. The author gives several examples of Chinese scientists who received their education in the United States but could not conduct stem cell research there because of bans on such research, and who have now returned to China where they have the freedom and access to funding and materials to conduct such research. The Chinese government hopes to win a Nobel Prize for China's work with therapeutic cloning.

11   While the United States debates the morality of this technology, China, with a different set of values, pursues it. Stem cell research and therapeutic cloning will be carried on in other

parts of the world as well, even while being banned in the United States. This science is not likely to go away, and it is potentially extremely valuable to humans.

12   I will use this article to develop my section on the feasibility of therapeutic cloning.

Book (print)   13   Pence, Gregory E. *Who's Afraid of Human Cloning?* Lanham: Rowman, 1998. Print.

14   This is a comprehensive source of information on cloning. The book provides a complete overview, including discussions on the misconceptions, ethics, regulations, and arguments regarding human cloning. This author is most definitely an advocate of human cloning technology. He feels the discussion of this issue to date has been horribly one-sided. He states that never in the history of modern science has the world seen such an instant, overwhelming condemnation of an application to humanity of a scientific breakthrough. His aim is to correct this problem of a one-sided debate over the issue.

15   I will probably cite this book because of the wealth of information it contains. Although the author advocates human cloning, his book is a fairly good source of material for arguing against human cloning.

16   I will use ideas from this book in my introduction to show how some people are in favor of cloning and how some are not. I will also make the distinction between cloning humans and therapeutic cloning, both of which are controversial.

Article in print and online (accessed on database)   17   Wilson, Jim. "Cloning Humans." *Popular Mechanics* June 2002: 42-44. *Academic Search Complete*, Web. 11 Mar. 2010.

18   This article discusses the technological progress of cloning and the "inevitability" that humans will soon be cloned. Wilson begins by showing that cloning humans is not different from the procedure used for in vitro fertilization (IVF). For IVF, a human conception (the union of a male sperm and female egg) takes place in a glass lab dish, grows into an embryo, and is then implanted in a human uterus. Human clones will go through the same process, Wilson tells us. The difference between IVF and cloned embryos is that the genetic blueprint for IVF cases comes from two parents, whereas clones require only one. Wilson traces the potential for human cloning back to 1997 and shows that while the world marveled at the cloning of Dolly the sheep, the scientific community marveled that researchers from Duke University Medical Center had learned that cloning humans would be simpler than cloning sheep.

19   Once this discovery was made, Italian researcher Severino Antinori argued that the genetic pattern of sterile males could be passed on via clones. Antinori, who successfully performed IVF for a woman 62 years of age, presented his findings at the

International Cloning Consortium in Rome in 2001. His case was taken quite seriously by the scientific community, and since then a number of cloning projects have emerged. A major market for this process is fertility clinics.

20   This article shows how the technology for cloning may be used in a way that is more insidious than many may have previously thought. Combining cloning with fertility treatment to allow couples and individuals to pass along their genetic traits may be a way for cloning to become silently mainstreamed.

21   I will use this material at the end of my paper to suggest what could happen if this technology is not carefully monitored.

---

4. **Write Summary-Response Papers**

If you are reading essays in a reader or a packet of materials supplied by the professor, write a one-page summary-response paper, in your own words, for each of the essays you have been assigned to read. Divide a piece of paper in half, and write a summary on the top half and your response on the bottom half. The summary should answer the questions, *What is this essay about?* and *What did the author say about it*? The response should include answers to such questions as the following: *Do you agree or disagree with the author? Why? What examples, suggestions, or other ideas of your own can you add that the essay made you think about? Whether you agree with the author or not, is the essay convincing? Why or why not?* Refer to the examples of summaries and responses in the annotated bibliography on pages 67–70 to help you.

◆   5. **Evaluate Your Research**

Look back over your bibliography and the other research and ideas you have gathered and complete the following worksheet. Make certain all of the information you want to use is complete and that you have the information you need to cite all sources. Add, correct, or eliminate any material that might weaken your argument.

WORKSHEET 4: RESEARCH EVALUATION

Examine the research you have done so far.

a. Do I have enough information to be convincing? What can I add?

b. Is my information reliable and convincing? How can I make it more so?

c. Is anything exaggerated or oversimplified? How can I be more accurate?

d. Do I rely too much on my own authority ("This is true because I say so") instead of giving support? Can I add opinions of other authorities to be more convincing?

e. Am I weakening this argument with too much emotional material? Should any of it be eliminated?

Writing
the Exploratory Paper

This chapter describes the exploratory paper and provides general strategies for academic writing that will help you write this paper as well as the argument papers assigned in Chapters 8, 10, and 11.

WHAT IS AN EXPLORATORY PAPER?

You were introduced to the concept of the exploratory paper[1] on page 54. In an exploratory paper, the arguer identifies as many of the major positions on an issue as possible, both past and present, and explains them through summaries and an analysis of the overall rhetorical situation for the issue. The analysis of the rhetorical situation in this kind of paper includes an explanation of what happened to cause the issue to surface in the first place and may also identify who is interested in the issue and what each of these groups of individuals wants, thinks, or believes in regard to it. The summaries of the different positions in exploratory papers not only explain each of the different perspectives on the issue but also provide the usual reasons cited to establish the validity of each perspective. The writer's own opinions are not expressed at all or are withheld until later in the paper. The reader either may or may not identify a personal favored position.

Here are some examples of issues that lend themselves to multiple perspectives: The issue of *how to finance universal health care in the United States* is not limited to spending more than the country can afford versus abandoning the whole idea because it is too expensive. Other positions, among many, include creating health insurance that most people can afford, placing limits

---

[1] I am indebted to the late Professor James Kinneavy at the University of Texas at Austin for the basic notion of the exploratory paper.

on the cost of certain medical treatments, limiting medical malpractice costs through tort reform, providing public subsidies for people who can't afford insurance, and denying medical care to illegal immigrants who seek it in emergency and charity hospitals. The issue of *what to do with convicted criminals* is not limited to putting criminals in jail or putting them to death. Other positions might include sending them to various types of rehabilitation programs, releasing elderly inmates to their families when they are too old or too feeble to be a threat to society, or segregating different types of offenders in correctional institutions. The *immigration issue in the United States and other countries* also invites more perspectives than either letting all foreigners in or keeping them all out. Other possibilities include issuing green cards to certain categories of immigrants or providing temporary work permits for immigrant workers for a limited period of time.

There are a number of advantages to writing and reading exploratory papers about issues such as these. When writers and readers view an issue from many perspectives, they acquire a greater depth of understanding of it and the various views taken.

They also learn to expose and avoid the fallacy that there are only two sides to an issue, and that one side can ultimately be declared "the winner." (See Plates 2–3 and 4–5 in the Color Portfolio for examples of issues explored through images.)

Exploratory papers help establish common ground between writers and readers. Writers, by restating several opposing positions along with the usual reasons for accepting them, are forced to understand that opposing views have commonalities that permit not only qualified but also multiple perspectives. The reader is interested because the exploratory paper explains several views, which usually include or inform the reader's. The reader is consequently more willing to learn about the other positions on the issue. Exploratory papers can provide mutual understanding and common ground for what may become the next stage in argument, the presentation of the writer's position and reasons for holding it. You are taught to write a position paper of this sort in Chapter 11.

If you have identified yourself as a consensual arguer (see pages 7–8 and 23), you will probably be drawn to exploratory argument for a number of reasons: it does not polarize issues by identifying them as either right or wrong, or desirable or undesirable, and it is, thus, rarely adversarial; and it helps arguing parties find common ground and reach favorable conclusions that most people can either partially or totally agree to. If you have identified yourself as an adversarial arguer, exploratory papers can help you identify and understand positions on your issue that you may want to refute. You will encounter exploratory arguments in newspapers, newsmagazines, other popular magazines of opinion, and scholarly journals. You will find examples of the exploratory paper at the end of this chapter (pages 86–88 and 89–91).

Before you try writing an exploratory paper of your own, let's first examine your current writing process and think about how you can further develop it so that you will be able to write any paper you are assigned with expertise, confidence, and motivation. Additional specific advice or how to write an exploratory paper appears on pages 83–85. The assignment for the exploratory paper is on page 92.

HOW DO YOU WRITE NOW?

You already have a writing process, and to make it useful for writing argument papers, you will need to adapt it to that purpose. Begin by thinking first about what you do when you write argument.

What do you do . . .

- Before you write the draft of an argument paper?
- While you are writing the draft of an argument paper?
- When you get stuck?
- When you revise the draft of an argument paper?

Not all students answer those questions in the same way. Some students say they "just write" and turn in their first effort. Others describe their writing as a cyclical process that involves reading, thinking, and drafting, over and over again, until a complete draft emerges that they can revise and turn in. Still other students describe their writing as a discovery process. They start writing and figure out what they have to say as they go along. They find their outline as they write. Finally, there are students who say they like to begin by organizing their ideas before they write. They are more comfortable with an outline or a list of ideas to guide their writing. All of these approaches, with the exception of the first approach, can result in good papers. Very few people can "just write" and turn out a good paper without rereading and revising it.

If you have developed a writing process that works for you, you will be reluctant to give it up. You don't have to, but you can consider what you might add to your present process that will improve your ability to write argument papers. This chapter invites you to think about what you can add before you write a draft (prewriting), while you write (drafting), when you are stuck (writer's block), and when you are working to finish your paper (revising). You do not have to follow these ideas in the order in which they are presented. Most people do not. For example, many people write major chunks of a paper before they put a complete draft together, others revise constantly as they go along, and still others just start writing. Then they go back to find the ideas, put them in order, and work with them until they represent what they want to say.

PREWRITING STRATEGIES

Prewriting is creative, and creativity is delicate to teach because it is individual. Still, like most writers, you will need directed prewriting strategies from time to time, either to help you begin writing or to help you break through writer's block. Prewriting strategies help you get organized, access what you already know, think about it, and plan what more you need to learn. Here are some suggestions to get you started.

Get Organized to Write

Some people develop elaborate rituals like cleaning house, sharpening pencils, laying out special pens, putting on comfortable clothes, chewing a special flavor of gum, or making a cup of coffee to help them get ready to write. These rituals help them concentrate on the writing task, improve their motivation to write, and avoid procrastination and writer's block. A professional writer, describing what she does, says she takes a few moments before she writes to imagine her work as a completed and successful project. She visualizes it as finished, and she thinks about how she will feel at that time.[2]

Creating a place to write is an essential part of getting organized to write. A desk and a quiet place at home or in the library work best for most students. Other quiet places will work as well, including computer labs on campus or even an empty classroom. You also should gather the materials you will need, including books, articles, idea notes, research notes, lists and outlines, and drafts at various stages of completion. Develop a system to keep these writing materials organized so that you can quickly spread them out each time you write. Finally, make a decision about the writing equipment you will use. Most students now prefer using computers to writing by hand for the same reasons that many professional writers like using them: typing is faster, and the copy is easier to read and revise. A disadvantage of using computers is that some people write too much. They literally write everything that occurs to them, and some of it is undeveloped, poorly organized, or off the subject. If you tend to write too much, you will need to concentrate on cutting when you revise or doing part of your writing by hand.

Analyze the Assignment and Allocate Time

You will need to analyze the writing assignment and find time to do it. Divide the assignment into small, manageable parts, assign a sufficient amount of time for each part, set deadlines for completing each part, and use the time when it becomes available. Below is an example.

Assignment. Write a five- to six-page, typed, double-spaced argument paper in which you identify an issue of your choice, take a position, make a claim, and support it so that it is convincing to an audience of your peers. Do as much reading as you need to do, but plan to draw material from at least five sources when you write your paper. Use MLA style (detailed in Appendix 1) to document your sources and prepare your bibliography.

---

[2]Barbara Neely, "Tools for the Part-Time Novelist," *Writer*, June 1993, p. 17.

Analysis of Assignment

WEEK 1

Select an issue and write down some ideas.	2 hours Tuesday night
Read some articles on the issue, think, and take notes; write a first draft.	3 hours Thursday night
Read the draft to a peer group in class to get ideas for additional research.	Friday's class
Do research in the library and online to fill in the needs of the first draft.	3 hours Saturday

WEEK 2

Incorporate research and write a second draft.	3 hours Thursday night
Read it to the peer editing group in class.	Friday's class

WEEK 3

Rewrite, revise, and prepare final copy.	4 hours Tuesday night
	Hand in on Wednesday

Notice that the work on this paper has been spread out over three weeks and is divided into manageable units. If this schedule were followed, a student would be able to complete this paper successfully, on time, and without panic and discomfort. A total of fifteen hours have been set aside for the various stages. The time is available even though the student may not need all of it. The student's focus should be, however, on finishing the paper as quickly as possible, not on simply using all of this time.

Here is a professional writer who cautions about the importance of working to finish rather than working to put in time: "Don't set your goal as minutes or hours spent working; it's too easy to waste that time looking up one last fact, changing your margins, or, when desperate, searching for a new pen." Instead, she advises, set a realistic writing goal for each day and work until you complete it.[3] Another author advises that you avoid creating units of work that are so large or unmanageable that you won't want to do them, such as writing an entire paper in one day. It may sound good or efficient on the surface to write a whole paper in one day or one night, "but you'll soon feel overwhelmed," and "you'll start avoiding the work and won't get *anything* done." Remember, she says, "it's persistence that counts" in completing writing projects.[4]

Identify an Issue and Do Some Reading and Writing

In the last two chapters you were presented with a number of strategies for combining reading, thinking, and writing to help you gather ideas and research materials, put them in a logical order, and prepare to write a draft of your paper. These prewriting strategies included identifying an issue, doing some initial reading, writing an issue proposal, and freewriting about what you already know.

---

[3]Peggy Rynk, "Waiting for Inspiration," *Writer*, September 1992, p. 10.
[4]Sue Grafton, "How to Find Time to Write When You Don't Have Time to Write," *The Writer's Handbook*, ed. Sylvia K. Burack (Boston: Writer, 1991), p. 22.

You also learned to analyze the rhetorical situation and the audience's knowledge and interest in your issue. You may have used critical thinking prompts, talked with others about your ideas, and developed a research plan for your issue that included a claim plus some reasons. Finally, you now know how to conduct research on your issue, how to put together a bibliography, and how to survey, summarize, and write responses to sources, which, in turn, will help you develop quoted, paraphrased, or summarized notes to include in your paper.

Notice that most of these strategies include writing. Be prepared to jot down ideas at any time during the writing process. Once your reading and thinking are under way, your subconscious mind takes over. At odd times you may suddenly see new connections or think of a new example, a new idea, a beginning sentence, or a good organizational sequence for the main ideas. Insights like these often come to writers when they first wake up. Plan to keep paper and pencil available so that you can take notes when good ideas occur to you. Here is one way to do that.

Keep a Journal, Notebook, or Folder of Ideas

Many writers keep a journal or notebook, or they simply write on pieces of paper and keep them in a folder. To help you gather material for an argument paper, you may clip or print articles, write summaries, and write out ideas and observations about your issue as they come to you. These materials will provide you with an excellent source of information for your paper when it is time to write it.

A professional writer describes this type of writing as a tool that helps one think. This author sets out some suggestions that could be particularly useful for the writer of argument.

> Write quickly, so you don't know what's coming next.
> Turn off the censor in your head.
> Write from different points of view to broaden your sympathies.
> Collect quotations that inspire you and jot down a few notes on why they do.
> Write with a nonjudgmental friend in mind to listen to your angry or confused thoughts.
> When words won't come, draw something—anything.
> Don't worry about being nice, fair, or objective. Be selfish and biased; give your side of the story from the heart.
> Write even what frightens you, *especially* what frightens you. It is the thought denied that is dangerous.
> Don't worry about being consistent. You are large; you contain multitudes.[5]

Make an Extended List or Outline to Guide Your Writing

A written outline helps many people see the organization of ideas before they begin to write. Other people seem to be able to make a list or even work from a mental outline. Still others "just write" and move ideas around later to create order. There is, however, an implicit outline in most good writing. The outline is

---

[5]Marjorie Pellegrino, "Keeping a Writer's Journal," *Writer*, June 1992, p. 27.

often referred to metaphorically as the skeleton or bare bones of the paper because it provides the internal structure that holds the paper together. An outline can be simple—a list of words written on a piece of scrap paper—or it can be elaborate, with essentially all major ideas, supporting details, major transitions, and even some of the sections written out in full. Some outlines actually end up looking like partial, sketchy manuscripts.

If you have never made outlines, try making one. Outlining requires intensive thinking and decision making. When it is finished, however, you will be able to turn your full attention to writing, and you will never have to stop to figure out what to write about next. Your outline will tell you what you have already decided to do, and it will ultimately save you time and reduce much of the difficulty and frustration you would experience without it.

Now let's consider what you can do to help you write the first draft.

WRITING THE FIRST DRAFT

The objective of writing the first draft is to get your ideas in some kind of written form so that you can see them and work with them. Include quoted, paraphrased, and summarized material in your draft as you write. Here is how a professional writer explains the drafting process.

> Writing a first draft should be easy because, in a sense, you can't get it wrong. You are bringing something completely new and strange into the world, something that did not exist before. You have nothing to prove in the first draft, nothing to defend, everything to imagine. And the first draft is yours alone, no one else sees it. You are not writing for an audience. Not yet. You write the draft in order to read what you have written and to determine what you still have to say.[6]

This author advises further that you "not even consider technical problems at this early stage." Nor should you "let your critical self sit at your desk with your creative self. The critic will stifle the writer within." The purpose, he says, is "not to get it right, but to get it written."[7]

Here is another writer, Stephen King, who advises putting aside reference books and dictionaries when concentrating on writing the first draft.

> Put away your dictionary. . . . You think you might have misspelled a word? O.K., so here is your choice: either look it up in the dictionary, thereby making sure you have it right—and breaking your train of thought and the writer's trance in the bargain—or just spell it phonetically and correct it later. Why not? Did you think it was going to go somewhere? And if you need to know the largest city in Brazil and you find you don't have it in your head, why not write in Miami or Cleveland? You can check it . . . but *later*. When you sit down to write, *write*. Don't do anything else except go to the bathroom, and only do that if it absolutely cannot be put off.[8]

---

[6]John Dufresne, "That Crucial First Draft," *Writer*, October 1992, p. 9.
[7]Ibid., pp. 10–11.
[8]Stephen King, "Everything You Need to Know about Writing Successfully—in Ten Minutes," *The Writer's Handbook*, ed. Sylvia K. Burack (Boston: Writer, 1991), p. 33.

You will be able to follow this advice if the materials you have gathered during prewriting are available to guide you and keep you on track. If you occasionally get stuck, you can write some phrases, freewrite, or even skip a section that you cannot easily put into words. You will have another chance at your draft later. Right now, work only to capture the flow of ideas, either as they are written on an outline or as they are organized in your mind. You will discover, as you write, that many of the ideas that were only half formed before you began to write will now become clear and complete as you get insight from writing.

BREAK THROUGH WRITER'S BLOCK

Most writers suffer from writer's block from time to time, and there are a number of ways to get going again if you find that you are stuck while writing your first draft.

- *Read what you have written so far.* Concentrate on the ideas, think about what you need to write next, and jot down a few notes to remind yourself what you want to do. Then get back to writing.
- *Read more about your issue.* If you don't have enough material, take notes on additional sources. Place limits by doing directed reading to meet specific needs.
- *Reread your outline, lists, and other idea notes.* Add new ideas that occur to you as you read, and rearrange ideas into new combinations.
- *Freewrite, read some more, and freewrite again.* Write fast, in phrases or sentences, on your topic without imposing any structure or order. Go through it later, crossing out what you cannot use, changing phrases to sentences, adding material in places, and soon you will find that you are started again.
- *Use critical thinking prompts.* Revisit these prompts (page 47). They will help you think in new ways about your topic and generate new ideas and information.
- *Talk about your ideas with someone else.* Or ask someone else to read the draft as it now is and write some comments on it.
- *Give yourself permission to write a less than perfect first draft.* You can paralyze yourself by trying to produce a finished draft on the first try. Lower your expectations for the first draft, and remind yourself that you can always go back later and fix it.

REVISE THE DRAFT

Resist the temptation to put your paper aside when you have finished drafting and declare it "finished." Now is your opportunity to improve it in significant ways. Working with a rough draft is easier than outlining or drafting. It is, in fact, creative and fun to revise because you begin to see your work take shape and become more readable. Skillfully revised material, incidentally, makes a good impression on the reader. It is worthwhile to finish your draft early enough so that you will have several hours or even a full day to read and revise before you submit it in its final form to a reader.

Look at Your Draft as a Whole

When you have a draft, print it and lay it out in front of you so that you can see it as a whole. Look at organization first. How does your paper begin? Have you written an introduction that informs your audience about the subject of your paper? What are your main points? Where does each of them begin and end? Have you used enough transitional material to make your ideas stand out. Do you have enough support to make each of your main points believable to your audience? Think about your audience and decide whether you need to add information to make your paper more persuasive. How do you conclude your paper? Is your ending strong and memorable?

If you cannot answer these questions about your paper, try making a list or an outline of the most important ideas in it. Apply this test: Can you state the claim or the main point of your paper and list the parts that develop it? Take a good look at these parts, rearrange them if necessary and make them clearer and more complete.

Now read paragraph by paragraph. Do you make links between the end of one paragraph and the beginning of another so that the ideas in them flow and appear to be clearly related to each other? Is most of each paragraph about one idea? Is that idea developed with sufficient supporting detail?

Check your sentences. Is each a complete thought? Do they all make sense? Rewrite problem sentences or sentence fragments. As a final check, read your entire paper aloud and listen for problems. Correct with pencil as you go along. You can enter corrections into the computer later.

Ask Revision Questions to Help You Locate Other Problems

Most writers have some ideas and rules about writing that come to their aid, from an inner voice, when it is time to revise. Listen to this inner voice or sensibility so that you will know what to look for and what to change. If you do not have a strongly developed inner writer's voice, you can strengthen it by learning to ask the following questions. Notice that these questions direct your attention to global revisions for improved clarity and organization as well as to surface revisions for details.

1. *Is it clear?* If you cannot understand your own writing, other people will not understand it either. Be critical as you read your draft. Ask yourself whether what you have written really says what you understand. If you encounter confusing passages, stop and analyze why they are confusing and then rewrite them until the words represent what you want to say.

2. *What should I add?* Sometimes in writing the first draft you will write such a sketchy version of an idea that it does not explain what you want to say. Add fuller explanations and examples, or do some extra research to improve the skimpy parts of your paper.

3. *What should I cut?* Extra words, repeated ideas, and unnecessary material find their way into a typical first draft. Every writer cuts during revision. Stephen King, who earns millions of dollars each year as a professional writer, describes how he learned to cut the extra words. His teacher was the newspaper editor John Gould, who dealt with King's first feature article as follows:

> He started in on the feature piece with a large black pen and taught me all I ever needed to know about my craft. I wish I still had the piece—it deserves to be framed, editorial corrections and all—but I can remember pretty well how it looked when he had finished with it. Here's an example:

Last night, in the ~~well-loved~~ gymnasium ~~of~~ Lisbon High School, partisans and Jay Hills fans alike were stunned by an athletic performance unequalled in school history: Bob Ransom, ~~known as "Bullet" Bob for both his size and accuracy,~~ scored thirty-seven points. He did it with grace and speed . . . and he did it with an odd courtesy as well, committing only two personal fouls in his ~~knight-like~~ quest for a record which has eluded Lisbon's ~~thinclads~~ basketball team since 1953 . . .

When Gould finished marking up my copy in the manner I have indicated above, he looked up and must have seen something on my face. I think he must have thought it was horror, but it was not: it was revelation.

"I only took out the bad parts, you know," he said. "Most of it's pretty good."

"I know," I said, meaning both things: yes, most of it was good, and yes, he had only taken out the bad parts. "I won't do it again."

"If that's true," he said, "you'll never have to work again. You can do *this* for a living." Then he threw back his head and laughed.

And he was right: I *am* doing this for a living, and as long as I can keep on, I don't expect ever to have to work again.[9]

4. *Are the language and style consistent and appropriate throughout?* Edit out all words that create a conversational or too informal tone in your paper. For example:

Change: And as for target shooting, well go purchase a BB gun or a set of darts.[10]

---

[9]King, pp. 30–31.
[10]From a student paper by Blake Decker; used with permission.

> *To Read:*   For target shooting, a BB gun or a set of darts serves just as well as a handgun.

Also, edit out all cheerleading, slogans, clichés, needless repetition, and exhortations. You are not writing a political speech.

You will learn more about language and style in Chapter 7. In general, use a formal, rational style in an argument paper unless you have a good reason to do otherwise. Use emotional language and examples that arouse feelings only where appropriate with a particular audience to back up logical argument.

5. *Is there enough variety?* Use some variety in the way you write sentences by beginning some with clauses and others with a subject or even a verb. Vary the length of your sentences. Try to write not only simple sentences but also compound and complex sentences. You can vary the length of your paragraphs as well. The general rule is to begin a new paragraph every time you change the subject. Variety in sentences and paragraphs makes your writing more interesting to read. Do not sacrifice clarity for variety, however, by writing odd or unclear sentences.

6. *Have I used the active voice most of the time?* The active voice is more direct, energetic, and interesting than the passive voice. Try to use it most of the time. Here is a sentence written in the active voice; it starts with the subject.

> Robotics is an exciting new technology that could enhance nearly every aspect of our lives.[11]

Notice how it loses its directness and punch when it is written in the passive voice.

> Nearly every aspect of our lives could be enhanced by robotics, an exciting new technology.

7. *Have I avoided sexist language?* Avoid referring to people in your paper as though they were either all male or all female. However, using such expressions as "he or she" or "himself or herself" sounds inclusive but comes across as awkward. Solve this problem by using plural nouns (*students* instead of *student*) and pronouns (*they* instead of *he or she*) Occasionally, you may need to rewrite a sentence in the passive voice. It is better to write, "The U.S. Constitution is often used as the guide when making new laws," than to write, "He or she often uses the U.S. Constitution as a guide when making new laws."

Avoid the Seven Most Common Errors Students Make. Learn the rules for grammar, usage, and punctuation. You will avoid the most common errors made by student writers if you make the following rules a part of that inner writer's voice that guides your revision.

1. Write three or more similar items in a *series,* separated by commas, and finally connected by *and* or *or.*

   EXAMPLE: The National Rifle Association, firearms manufacturers, and common citizens are all interested in gun control.[12]

---

[11]From a student paper by Greg Mathios; used with permission.
[12]The examples presented here are drawn from a student paper by Blake Decker. I have revised his sentences for the sake of illustration.

2. Use *parallel construction* for longer, more complicated elements that have a similar function in the sentence.

   EXAMPLE: Parents who fear for their children's safety at school, passengers who ride on urban public transit systems, clerks who work at convenience stores and gas stations, and police officers who try to carry out their jobs safely are all affected by national policy on gun control.

3. Keep everything in the same *tense* throughout. Use the present tense to introduce quotations.

   EXAMPLE: As Sherrill *states,* "The United States is said to be the greatest gun-toting nation in the world." Millions of guns create problems in this country.

4. Observe *sentence boundaries.* Start sentences with a capital letter, and end them with a period or question mark. Make certain they express complete thoughts. Do not punctuate a clause as a sentence. In the following sentence, the "because" clause is incorrectly punctuated as a sentence.

   EXAMPLE (INCORRECT): Because criminals, including terrorists, can buy guns easily in this country. There should be a system for checking the background of everyone who purchases a gun.

   The clause is actually a part of the rest of the sentence. Change the period to a comma to correct this common error.

   EXAMPLE (CORRECT): Because criminals, including terrorists, can buy guns easily in this country, there should be a system for checking the background of everyone who purchases a gun.

5. Make *subjects agree* with *verbs.*

   EXAMPLE: *Restrictions* on gun control *interfere* [not *interferes*] with people's rights.

6. Use *clear and appropriate pronoun referents.*

   EXAMPLE: The *group* is strongly in favor of gun control, and little is needed to convince *it* [not *them*] of the importance of this issue.

7. Use *commas* to set off long initial clauses, to separate two independent clauses, and to separate words in a series.

   EXAMPLE: When one realizes that the authors of the Constitution could not look into the future and imagine current events, one can see how irrational and irresponsible it is to believe that the right to bear arms should in these times still be considered a constitutional right, and according to Smith, the groups that do so "are shortsighted, mistaken, and ignorant."

Check for Final Errors, Add or Adjust the Title, and Type or Print Your Paper

Just before you submit your paper, check the spelling of every word you are not absolutely sure you know. If spelling is a problem for you, buy a small spelling dictionary that contains only words and no meanings. Also, use the spell-checker on the computer. If you use a spell-checker, you should still read your paper one last time since the computer might not find every error. At this point you should format your paper and correct all the typographical errors that remain. Now add a title or adjust your existing title, if necessary. Be sure that your title provides information that will help the reader understand the topic or focus of your paper.

Complete your revision process by reading your paper aloud one more time. Read slowly and listen. The number of problems that bother your ears but were not noticeable to your eyes will surprise you. Make these corrections, and your paper should be ready now to submit for evaluation. Print it so that it is easy to read.

HOW TO WRITE AN EXPLORATORY PAPER

Now plan and write an exploratory paper of your own. Look at your issue from several angles in order to decide which position you prefer. If you are later given the assignment to write a position paper on your issue, you may have discovered your own position along with some of the other views that you will want to refute. The exploratory paper assignment appears on page 92. To complete it successfully, follow these general suggestions.

1. *Select an issue, do some research and reading, and identify three or more perspectives.* If you have worked your way through the first three chapters, you may have an issue to write about, one that invites several perspectives. You may also have written an issue proposal (pages 43–44), and an annotated bibliography (pages 67–70) or several summary-response papers (pages 61 and 70). If you do not have an issue, select one now that interests you. Next, read about the issue on the Internet and in the library until you are acquainted with several different ways of looking at it. Either take notes on these different perspectives or make copies of the reading materials you locate so that you can quote them later in your paper if you decide to do so.

An example of an issue that invites several perspectives is handgun control: some people believe there should be no restrictions on personal handgun ownership; other people believe possession of handguns should be banned for everyone except police officers and military personnel; a third group believes people have a right to own handguns but with restrictions, including background checks, special training, and licensing. Notice that these are three positions on this issue, not merely three separate ideas about the issue. As you plan the perspectives for your paper, you can think about perspectives that are for, against, or somewhere else on the spectrum of possibilities; perspectives that represent three (or more) possible approaches to an issue; perspectives that describe three (or more) possible ways to solve an issue; perspectives that provide three (or more) ways of interpreting an issue; and so on. These perspectives may be yours or other people's. You may actually find four or five different approaches that different groups of people hold.

2. *Analyze the rhetorical situation.* Sketch out answers to the three parts of the rhetorical situation for your issue that are already in place before you begin to write: the exigence, the reading audience, and the constraints. To establish exigence, ask, What happened to arouse people's interest in this issue in the first place? To establish audience, ask, Who shares my position on the issue, and who takes other positions? To establish constraints, ask, What do each of these groups or individuals value, want, and believe?

3. *Write a draft, and include transitions.* Draw on some of the ideas for drafting a paper that are discussed in this chapter (pages 77–78). As you write your draft, include transitions to separate and emphasize the different perspectives on your issue. You might use transitions like "some people believe," "others believe," and "still others believe"; "one perspective on this issue is," "another perspective is," and "a final perspective is"; or "one way to look at this issue is," "another way is," and "a third way is."

Here is an example of how Jacob Weisberg uses transitional phrases to separate and emphasize the ideas he will explore in an essay titled "Dubious New Models for News."

> The sorry predicament of the newspaper industry has given rise to a testy argument about journalism's future. In one corner are editors who believe news organizations committed a fatal mistake by giving their content away for free on the Internet. These people think that a successful digital business model demands revenue from users as well as from advertisers. Another camp favors philanthropic support. Newspapers, these establishment types think, should be more like universities, with their independence underwritten by charitable endowments. A third faction, which includes most Web journalists, doubts both those models and looks to online advertising for sole support.[13]

4. *Work summarized ideas and quotes from your research into your draft.* In an exploratory paper, you mainly summarize, in your own words, the positions you describe. If you decide to add direct quotations to make these summaries clearer or more interesting, work the quotations smoothly into your draft so that they make sense in context and are easy to read. Tell your reader where the summarized, paraphrased, and quoted material came from by introducing them with the author's names and citing the page numbers of the original sources in parentheses at the end of the citations in the text. The student exploratory paper on pages 89–91 provides examples of such materials that have been smoothly incorporated into the text to the paper.

For further information on how to incorporate source material into your draft, see pages 259–265 in Appendix 1. For an further advice on how to cite these sources in the text itself, see pages 265–275 in Appendix 1. For an additional example of citing and documenting sources, look at the student paper that appears, in MLA style, on pages 276–286. This student paper provides examples of source material that has been worked into the text smoothly and clearly so that the reader always knows which parts of the text are supplied by the student author and which represent outside sources.

5. *Revise your paper, and include a list of works cited or references at the end.* Follow the suggestions for revision that appear on pages 78–82. At the end of your paper, list the works you have quoted in the text of your paper so that your

---

[13]*Newsweek*, March 2, 2009, p. 51.

reader can see where your citations came from. Refer to Appendix 1 for help with this. Look also at the student examples on pages 285–286, and 301.

SUBMITTING YOUR PAPER FOR PEER REVIEW

If you can, put the draft of your exploratory paper aside for twenty-four hours, then read it critically and make changes to improve it. It helps to read the paper aloud at this point to get an even better idea about what can be improved. Then seek the opinion of other students in a class peer review session. Peer review sessions may include only three or four of your fellow students. You may be asked to provide each member of the review group with a photocopy of your paper so that, as you read your paper aloud to them, they can follow along and begin to mark problem areas to discuss later. Or you may participate in a round-robin reading session, in which group members read all of the papers silently and make some notes before they discuss the papers one by one. In some cases, your instructor may join the group as an equal member and participate with the students in asking questions that call your attention to areas that could be improved. Still another way of conducting peer reviews is for pairs of students to exchange papers to take home and read before the next class. This provides each student with time to read another student's paper more than once, if necessary, to locate areas for improvement.

There are several advantages to submitting your paper for review. No matter how well you write, revise, and edit a paper, another reader is almost always likely to have suggestions that can make your final paper better. Peer groups also make the writing task more sociable and provide immediate feedback from a real audience. They help you become a more sensitive critic of your own and others' work. Most professional writers rely heavily on other people's opinions at various stages of writing. Look at the prefaces of some of the books you are using this semester. Most authors acknowledge the help of several people who read their manuscript and made suggestions for improvement.

If peer review groups are not conducted in your writing class, try to find someone else, such as a writing center tutor or another student, to read your draft. Most writers need someone to read their work as they continue to refine it.

REVIEW QUESTIONS

1. Describe the exploratory argument paper along with some of the benefits for writing it.
2. Briefly describe a process for producing an argument paper.
3. What are the advantages of outlining your ideas before you write a draft?
4. Name at least three specific suggestions for revision made in this chapter and describe in detail how you could use each of them.
5. What are some possible ways of conducting peer review? What are the advantages of peer review?

CLASS ACTIVITIES AND WRITING ASSIGNMENTS

1.   **Analyze an Exploratory Paper from a Newspaper**

Analyze the exploratory paper "Kids and Chores: All Work and No Pay?" that follows.

BEFORE YOU READ: Have you been paid to do chores at home? What is your present position on paying children to do family chores?

Essay 1

KIDS AND CHORES: ALL WORK AND NO PAY?*

Jeff D. Opdyke

Opdyke covers personal finance for the *Wall Street Journal* and writes the column "Love and Money."

What is the rhetorical situation? 1 A few nights ago I asked my seven-year-old son to help set the table for dinner. His reply: "Can I have two dollars?"

2 Several weeks earlier, he wanted a quarter for helping fold some clothes. And when my wife, Amy, asked him to complete a chore he had already agreed to do, he tried to renegotiate so he could get a dollar for it.

3 We didn't pay him for any of it, and generally don't for most chores. As I've told him, he has reached an age where he has no choice but to pitch in and contribute to the family's upkeep.

What is the issue? 4 Still, Amy and I are trying to formulate a philosophy on what we will and won't pay for when it comes to housework. It isn't easy. On one hand, there's no reason he should be paid for chores like setting the table or cleaning his room. Then again, some chores *do* deserve extra rewards—and paying for them also can help us encourage our son's entrepreneurial spirit.

5 But the distinction between paying and nonpaying chores is both hard for us to make and hard for him to understand.

6 If you pay for too much, kids begin to assume you should pay for everything—and they'll figure they have the power to reject the work if they think the price is too low. But if you don't pay for anything, you get nothing but resentment.

7 Thus, we're learning that when it comes to kids and their chores, managing expectations is as important as the chore itself.

---

*Wall Street Journal. Reprinted in *Fort Worth Star-Telegram*, February 1, 2004, p. 4F.

8   Just as there is a wide disparity in allowance programs among parents, moms and dads tackle this issue in numerous ways.

What are the three perspectives?

9   Some get in the habit early on of paying for just about any chore, and the pattern sticks as the kids grow older. Others pay for no chores, expecting that as a member of the family a kid is required to perform certain tasks. And many parents, like me and Amy, are somewhere in between, trying to navigate a fuzzy line between expectation and encouragement.

Describe the common ground.

10   The common denominator is that all parents face this at some point, usually around first or second grade—roughly the stage when kids begin to understand the significance of money and the frustrations of not having enough to buy what Mom and Dad won't.

What is Grace's perspective?

11   My friend Grace went through this with her seven-year-old not long ago.

12   He went through a phase, she says, "when he was asking to get paid to do anything around the house." Grace generally told him "no."

13   One day, Grace told her son to pick up his toys. When he asked what the assignment was worth, Grace realized she'd had enough with the constant request for money for simple chores around the house.

14   "I put a stop to that impertinence right then and there," Grace says. "I told him that if I paid him to pick up his toys, then he needs to pay me for his food, his clothes, his toys, rent, etc." The message sunk in; he stowed his toys without seeking remuneration.

What was the author's grandfather's perspective?

15   Now, when I was a kid I didn't get paid for many things. My grandfather would tell me to cut the grass, so I cut the grass. My grandmother would ask me to straighten up the disaster in my bedroom, so I cleaned my room. They didn't offer money as an enticement; the work was simply expected.

16   My friend at the office grew up similarly, responsible for working outside after school every day. He had to cut the grass and weed in the spring and summer, rake leaves in the fall and shovel snow in the winter. Thirty minutes pretty much every day—after which he could play with his friends.

17   In retrospect, he says, he learned a lot about outdoor work— about planting shrubs, for instance, and building walks—that has served him well as an adult with his own house. But what stuck with him even more was how much he disliked it.

What is the perspective of the friend at the office?

18   "It was part of my job in the house and I pretty much hated most of it," my friend says. "It was torture because all I wanted to do was play baseball. But I had to get the chores done first."

19   So my friend did what many people do: He went the other direction when he had his own kids, and rarely asked them to do anything. And he looks back on raising his son and daughter, now in their late teens, and says, "I think I made a mistake."

20   The problem, he says, is that he "set the bar too low on the required things. We expected them to do stuff like clear the table. But anything above and beyond, I offered to pay."

21   In the end, he says, "that backfired. When they got older, they didn't really want to do the work, even for money. That was partly because they had outside jobs. But it was mainly because I had undermined the expectation that they *must* work in the house. I had set it up so these jobs were optional—they could turn them down if they wanted to. So I ended up having to do all the stuff as an adult that I hated as a kid because my kids didn't want to do it."

22   Basically, my friend says he learned, as I'm learning now, "that I should have set a much higher minimum expectation for being a family member."

23   He's now applying that lesson to his preteen daughter. "She's expected to do much more around the house, like cleaning or helping cook or keeping her room straight," he says. "She's too young still, but I won't be paying for folding clothes or cutting the grass or raking leaves."

24   Speaking of leaves . . . over the fall I was raking the blanket of foliage that covers our yard every year when my son came wandering up from the tool shed with a kid-sized rake I had bought him last year at Home Depot.

What is this author's perspective?

25   "If I help you rake, Dad, can I have a dollar?"

26   Now, I knew his efforts would be short-lived and that, more than likely, I'd have to rake over his tracks. But to have your son willingly volunteer to help is a heartwarming feeling and a bonding experience.

27   "Sure, buddy."

28   I was right; he lasted about 10 minutes before he decided to play in the leaves instead of rake them. Still, I paid him his dollar and thanked him for taking the initiative to help around the house.

29   Then, I took the opportunity to lay some groundwork: "You know, one day you're going to be old enough where Mommy and I are going to expect you to rake the leaves without getting paid— and that day is getting closer."

30   "OK," he replied. "Maybe we can start when I'm your age."

For Discussion:

What is the issue? Describe the rhetorical situation that motivated the author to write this essay. How do you think this author imagines his audience? What are the different perspectives on the issue? Locate some transitional words and phrases that separate and emphasize the different perspectives. What is the author's perspective? What common ground, if any, exists between you and this author? What is your perspective, and is it mentioned in this article?

2. **Analyze a Student's Exploratory Paper**

The following is an example of an exploratory paper written by Prisna Virasin, a student in an argument class. Her issue proposal on this subject appears on pages 43–44, and her position paper on pages 276–286. Take a few minutes to read Prisna's paper. Then work in pairs to answer the following questions. Report your answers to the class.

1. What is the issue?
2. Describe the parts of the rhetorical situation that were in place when Prisna started to write. What is the exigence? Who are the groups of people interested in this issue? What are their positions? What are some of the constraints of these groups?
3. What are the perspectives on the issue that the author identifies? Make a list.
4. What transitions does the author use? Underline them.
5. What is the author's perspective? Why does she hold it?

You may want to use Prisna's paper as a model for your own exploratory paper.*

| **BEFORE YOU READ:** | What do you know about Barbie dolls? |

Student Paper 1

Prisna Virasin
Exploratory Paper
Prof. Wood
English 1302
1 March 2010

The Controversy behind Barbie

Explain the issue. 1

The Barbie doll was created in 1959 by Ruth Handler, the cofounder of Mattel. Handler created the doll after seeing her daughter, whose nickname was Barbie, and her daughter's friends play with their paper dolls. According to Gaby Wood and Frances Stonor Saunders, Handler realized that little girls wanted a doll "they could aspire to be like, not aspire to look after" (38). This was a revolutionary idea because before the creation of Barbie, the toy store doll selection mainly consisted of baby dolls, which encouraged girls to pretend to be mothers. For Handler, according to Wood and Saunders, Barbie "has always represented the fact that a woman has choices" (39).

Describe the rhetorical situation.
■ Exigence
■ Interested parties
■ Constraints

2

The Barbie doll has been a commercial success since the toy was first introduced on March 9, 1959. The lead story of March 9, 2009, on the History.com Web site is entitled "Barbie Makes Her Debut," and

---

*See the Appendix to Chapter 13 for the actual MLA format guidelines for student papers.

it provides some of the highlights of Barbie's 50-year history. By 1993, the doll and related merchandise was earning more than a billion dollars annually. By the time Barbie turned 50 years old, this article reports, "more than 800 million dolls in the Barbie family have been sold around the world and Barbie is now a bona fide global icon."

What is the first perspective?

3   The fact that Handler created Barbie as a challenge to the ideology that the proper role for women was that of a mother has become ironic in light of the subsequent feminist protest against the Barbie doll. The Barbie protesters have stated that Barbie is responsible for the development of poor body image in girls. They believe that the Barbie's proportions create impossible images of beauty that girls will strive toward. It has been "estimated that if she were a real woman, her measurements would be 36-18-38," and this has "led many to the claim that Barbie provided little girls with an unrealistic and harmful example and fostered negative body image" ("Barbie Makes Her Debut").

4   In addition to protests of the Barbie's physical appearance, there is also the issue of the doll's intellectual image. Barbie detractors have criticized the Barbie lifestyle, which seems to center around clothes, cars, dream homes, and other material possessions. Protests followed the release of the talking Barbie that localized such expressions as "Math is hard" and "Let's go shopping." Parents feared that the first sentence would reinforce the stereotype that girls were less skilled at math than boys. The second sentence seemed to reinforce the importance of clothes, physical appearance, and material goods.

What is the second perspective?

5   Supporters of the Barbie doll state that the toy is a fun part of growing up. They refer to the simple fun of playing with Barbie dolls. They believe that Barbie as a figure is a tool in building girls' imaginations. They also maintain that Barbie as a figure is a positive role model because she is able to do almost anything. Barbie was an astronaut before the first woman went into space. Barbie has been a veterinarian, a doctor, a businesswoman, and to top it all off, a presidential candidate.

6   In February 2010 Mattel, the creator of Barbie dolls, came out with a new Barbie: Computer Engineer Barbie. This doll "wears a neon-colored T-shirt with a binary code pattern and carries a smartphone and a Bluetooth headset. Her hot pink glasses will come in handy during late nights coding on her hot pink laptop" (Miller). Miller adds that Mattel asked people to vote for this most recent Barbie's career, and the idea of a Computer Engineer career doll won the vote. Few women choose computer engineering as a career, and it is hoped that this new Barbie doll may have a positive influence on attracting young women to this field. Since members of the Society of Women Engineers and the National Academy of Engineering were consulted in the creation of this doll, this doll's creators predict a more positive image for this Barbie doll than for the Barbie dolls of the early 1990s who complained that math was too hard.

What is the third
perspective?

7   Between the anti-Barbie camp and the pro-Barbie camp, there are the Barbie moderates. The Barbie moderates do not completely agree with how Mattel chooses to portray the "ideal American woman," nor do they view the doll as all evil. They see the positive aspects of the Barbie (the many professions, the ability to foster imaginative play, and the message that girls can choose to be whomever they want) and the negative aspects of the Barbie as a figure (a materialistic nature, a focus on outward appearance, and the vapid blond stereotype). The moderates state that by banning Barbie dolls, we will not be solving the problem of poor body image. They believe that Barbie is a scapegoat—the figure (or doll) to blame for all the negative feelings that children develop about themselves. Although the moderates do not agree with the image of women that Barbie seems to sustain, they also do not believe that this doll (or figure) is the source of the problem.

What is the author's
perspective? Why
does she hold it?

8   As a twenty-something female who grew up in America, I am very interested in the Barbie debate. I played with Barbie dolls almost obsessively from first to third grade. I designed clothes for them out of handkerchiefs and tissues and dreamed about becoming a fashion designer. I remember envying the girls who had Barbie Ferraris and dream houses. I looked on in horror as my little sister cut Barbie's hair short and colored it hot pink with a marker. In college, when I was introduced to feminism, I tried to deny any past connection to Barbie. I was ashamed to have ever associated with this figure. I felt sorry for the girls who looked like walking Barbie dolls, always worried about looking perfect. I realize now that I cannot blame thoughts of being fat, short, or out of style on a doll or girls that look like dolls. I agree with the Barbie moderates. As simple as the Barbie looks, it seems that the Barbie issue is more complicated than "Barbie good" or "Barbie bad." The debate encompasses many interesting and controversial issues concerning how we view beauty and how we view ourselves. In my eyes, Barbie is a scapegoat. We, as an entire culture, need to look at our ideas about beauty and what we are teaching children about themselves.

Works Cited

"Barbie Makes Her Debut." *History.com*, 9 Mar, 2009. Web. 15 Feb. 2010.

Miller, Claire Cain. "Barbie's Next Career? Computer Engineer." *bits.blogs.nytimes.com*, 12 Feb. 2010. Web. 17 Feb. 2010.

Wood, Gaby, and Frances Stonor Saunders. "Dream Doll." *New Statesman* 15 Apr. 2002: 38–40. *Academic Search Complete*. Web. 18 Feb. 2010.

FOR DISCUSSION:

Did you ever play with a Barbie or G.I. Joe? If not those, what were your favorite childhood toys? How did they affect your imagination and self-image? Have they had any lasting effects on you?

3. **Find Three Positions in the Annotated Bibliography**

   Reread the summaries and responses in the annotated bibliography about cloning on pages 67–70, and identify at least three different perspectives on the cloning issue.

◆ 4. **Writing Assignment: Review Your Annotated Bibliography, Identify Three or More Perspectives, and Write an Exploratory Paper**

   Review "How to Write an Exploratory Paper" (pages 83–85) to help you complete this assignment. Then write a 750- to 1000-word exploratory paper. Use the worksheet on this page to help you plan your exploratory paper. Follow MLA style as explained in Appendix 1.

WORKSHEET 5: EXPLORATORY PAPER

1. Write your issue in a complete sentence. Explain it, and include the information that provides background and makes the issue interesting to your readers.

2. Explain the parts of the rhetorical situation that are already in place as you begin to write. Describe the exigence or context for your issue, including what happened to make people interested in it. Identify the individuals or groups of people interested in this issue, with a brief introduction to their positions. Mention some of the constraints of these groups: for example, What do they think, value, and believe?

3. Describe at least three different positions on your issue, state who holds them, and give some of their reasons for holding them. You may explain more than three positions, if you want or need to do so. Jot down the positions.

   a. Position 1: _____

   b. Position 2: _____

   c. Position 3: _____

   _____

4. Explain your personal interest in the issue and the position you favor.

USING ARGUMENT THEORY FOR READING AND WRITING

Part II

The purpose of the next four chapters is to explain the essential component parts of an argument and show how they operate together to convince an audience. Chapter 5 identifies the parts of an argument as explained by Stephen Toulmin in what has come to be known as the Toulmin model. Chapter 6 describes the types of claims and purposes in argument. Chapter 7 describes how support and warrants combine to provide proof for argument and also discusses language and style, fallacies, and ethical argument. Chapter 8 teaches you to apply what you have learned as you analyze a classic argument and write an argument analysis paper. When you finish reading Part Two:

- You will understand and be able to identify the essential parts of an argument.

- You will know the key questions that arguments attempt to answer.

- You will be able to identify types of claims and purposes in argument.

- You will understand how argument employs proof, language, and style to appeal to your reason, your emotions, and your sense of values about people's character. You will also learn to recognize fallacies and expose unethical argument.

- You will know how to develop the parts of your argument, establish the purpose of your argument, plan effective proofs, avoid common fallacies, and write with appropriate language and style.

- You will know how to write an argument analysis paper.

The Toulmin Model of Argument: Understanding the Parts

The purpose of this chapter and the two that follow is to present ideas from argument theory that will help you add strategies for reading and writing argument. This chapter will introduce you to the component parts of argument as they are described by Stephen Toulmin in his model of argument. When you have read these three chapters, you will have additional information and expertise to draw on as you prepare the papers and projects presented in the last four chapters.

THE PARTS OF AN ARGUMENT ACCORDING TO THE TOULMIN MODEL

Stephen Toulmin, a modern English philosopher, developed a six-part model of argument in his book *The Uses of Argument*; this model will help you understand the parts of any argument, whether you are analyzing it or creating it.[1] You will find that you can employ the model to help you read and write college papers, reports, letters of application, proposals, legal memos, or any other document intended to convince others. The Toulmin model is also useful in designing or interpreting visual argument, such as photos, television, or motion pictures, and in writing or analyzing persuasive speeches. This model is a very natural and practical model because it follows normal human thought processes. You have had experience with all its parts either in the everyday arguments you carry on with your friends and family, in the arguments that you see on television, or in the arguments you encounter in your college classes and reading material.

The first three parts of the Toulmin model are present in every argument, including both traditional and consensual argument. They are (1) the *claim*, (2) the *data*,

---

[1]Stephen Toulmin, *The Uses of Argument* (Cambridge: Cambridge University Press, 1958). I have adapted and added applications of the model to make it more useful for reading and writing.

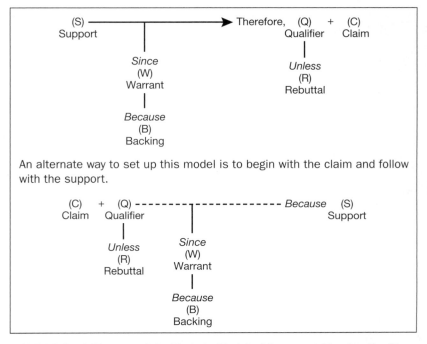

An alternate way to set up this model is to begin with the claim and follow with the support.

FIGURE 5.1   A Diagram of the Toulmin Model of Argument Showing the Six Parts: Claim, Support, Warrant, Backing, Rebuttal, and Qualifier. Note that an argument can be configured either as "support *therefore* claim" or as "claim *because* support."

SOURCE: Adapted from Stephen Toulmin, *The Uses of Argument* (Cambridge: Cambridge University Press, 1958), p. 104.

encompassing subclaims and specific supporting details, which we are calling *support*; and (3) the *warrant*. The other three parts are used as needed to strengthen an argument and adapt it to the needs and beliefs of a particular audience. These parts are (4) the *backing*, (5) the *rebuttal*, and (6) the *qualifier*. Figure 5.1 shows Toulmin's diagram of these six parts of the model.

Here is an example to illustrate how these parts work together in an actual argument: The narrator of a television program makes the *claim* that critical thinking is more important now than it was seventy-five years ago. This is followed by *support* that includes pictures of modern scientists launching space shuttles and air traffic controllers directing airplanes to land. These individuals seem intent and busy. It appears to be clear that if they do not think critically, there will be trouble. Then the camera switches to children riding on an old-fashioned school bus of seventy-five years ago. One boy is saying that he wants to grow up and be a farmer like his dad. This youngster is relaxed and bouncing along on the bus. He doesn't look like he is thinking critically or that he will ever need to do so. The unspoken part of this argument—the assumption that the author of this program hopes the audience will share—is the *warrant*. The author hopes the audience will agree, even though it is not explicitly stated, that farmers of seventy-five years ago did not have to think critically, that modern scientists and engineers do have to think critically, and that critical thinking was not so important then as now. The author wants the audience to look at the two bits of support, the scientist and the farmer's son, and make the leap necessary to accept the claim.The author hopes the audience will think, "That's right, those scientists and that young boy don't seem to share the same demands for critical thinking. Times have changed. Critical thinking is more important now than it was seventy-five years ago." Those three parts, the *claim*, the *support*, and the *warrant*, are the three parts you will find present in any argument.

Suppose, at this point, however, that some members of the audience do not accept the claim. An additional three parts of the model are available to make the argument stronger. Here is how these parts could be incorporated into the argument. It might be presented like this: The camera then shifts to an elderly man, who says, "Wait a minute. What makes you assume farmers didn't think? My daddy was a farmer, and he was the best critical thinker I ever knew. He had to think about weather, crops, growing seasons, fertilizer, finances, harvesting, and selling the crops. The thinking he had to do was as sophisticated as that of any modern scientist." This speaker is indicating that he does not share the unstated warrant that farmers of seventy-five years ago had fewer demands on their thinking processes than modern scientists. In response to this rejoinder, the author, to make the argument convincing, provides *backing for the warrant*. This backing takes the form of additional support. The camera cuts to the narrator of the program: "At least two out of three of the farmers of seventy-five years ago had small farms. They grew food for their families and traded or sold the rest for whatever else they needed. The thinking and decision making required of them was not as complicated and demanding as that required by modern scientists. Your father was an exception."

Notice that this backing takes the form of a smaller unit of argument within the argument. It is linked to the main argument, and it is used to back up the weakest part of the main argument. Furthermore, this smaller argument has a claim-support-warrant structure of its own: (1) the *claim* is that most farmers did not have to think; (2) the *support* is that two out of three did not have to think and that the man's father was an exception; and (3) the *warrant*, again unstated, is that the man will believe the statistics and accept the idea that his father was an exception. If he resists this backing for the new warrant by asking, "Hey, where did you get those statistics? They're not like any I ever heard," then another argument would need to be developed to cite the source of the figures and to convince the old man of their reliability. As you can see, the requests for backing, for more information to serve as further proof, can go on and on. However, let's leave the man and the narrator and look at what else might appear in this argument.

Suppose the camera now shifts to a modern science professor who wants to take exception with the claim itself by making a *rebuttal*. She makes her own claim: "The critical thinking required seventy-five years ago was demanding and sophisticated. Critical thinkers of that time had to figure out how to get the country out of a severe recession, and they had to develop the technology to win World War II." These opinions are then supported with factual evidence that includes pictures of individuals thinking.

After all of these challenges, exceptions, and requests for more information, the author at this point finds it necessary to *qualify* the original claim in order to make it acceptable to more of the audience members. Qualifying involves adding

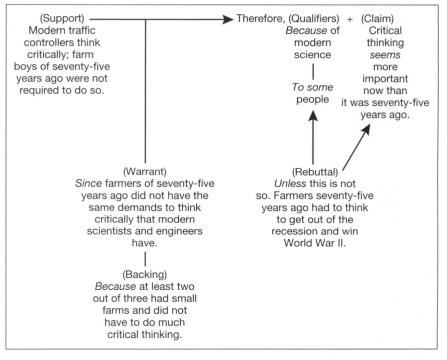

FIGURE 5.2   An Example of the Six Elements in the Toulmin Model.

words and phrases to the claim like *sometimes, seems to be, may be*, or *possibly* to make it more acceptable to the audience. In this case, the narrator now restates the qualified claim: "Critical thinking, because of modern science, seems to some people to be more important now than it was seventy-five years ago." Compare this with the original claim that critical thinking *is* more important now than it was seventy-five years ago. Figure 5.2 diagrams this argument according to the Toulmin model.

You have probably never systematically used this or any other model to read or write argument. The model can serve as a guide for reading and analyzing arguments and also for writing them. Authors do not usually use the model as an exact formula for writing, however. Rather, it describes what can be but is not necessarily always present in an argument. Consequently, when you read argument, you will at times easily recognize parts of the model and at other times you will not. Some arguments, in fact, may not contain one or more of the parts at all, such as a rebuttal, for example. You are not getting it wrong if you read and do not find all of the parts. When you write, you do not need to make all parts explicit either. The following sections about each of the six parts will help you recognize and use them better.

Claim

Discover the claim of an argument by asking, "What is the author trying to prove?" Or plan a claim of your own by asking, "What do I want to prove?" The claim is the main point of the argument. Identifying the claim as soon as possible helps you focus on what the argument is all about.

Synonyms for *claim* are *thesis, proposition, conclusion,* and *main point.* Sometimes an author of an argument in a newspaper or magazine will refer to the "proposition," or an individual arguing on television will ask, "What is your point?" Both are referring to the claim. When someone refers to the claim as the conclusion, don't confuse it with the idea at the end of an argument. The claim can appear at the end, but it can also appear at other places in the argument. The claim is sometimes stated in a sentence or sentences called the *statement of claim.* This sentence can also be called the *thesis statement,* the *purpose sentence,* the *statement of focus,* or the *statement of proposition.*

The terms used in this text to describe the main elements in argument, along with some of their synonyms, appear in Box 5.1. Become familiar with them so that you will understand other writers on the same subject who may vary the terminology.

BOX 5.1	Argument Terminology: Terms Used in This Book and Some of Their Synonyms.

What Terms Are Used in Argument?		
TERMS	**SYNONYMS**	
Claim	Thesis	Main point
	Proposition	Macro-argument
	Conclusion	Controlling idea
Statement of claim	Thesis statement	Statement of focus
	Purpose sentence	Statement of proposition
Subclaims	Reasons	Lines of argument
	Main ideas	Supporting arguments
	Micro-arguments	Specific issues
	Arguments	
Support	Evidence	Proof
	Opinions	Premise
	Reasons	Statistics
	Examples	Explanations
	Facts	Information
	Data	Personal narratives
	Grounds	Interviews
Warrants	Assumptions	Cultural values
	General principles	Presuppositions
	Widely held values	Unstated premises
	Commonly accepted beliefs	Generally accepted truths
	Appeals to human motives	Underlying logic

To locate the claim, what should you look for? The claim may be explicitly stated at the beginning of an argument, at the end, or somewhere in the middle. Or it may not be stated anywhere. It is sometimes *implied*, in which case you will be expected to *infer* it. To infer an implicit claim, you will need to use what you already know about the subject along with what you have just read to formulate your own statement of it. In this case, the author is paying you a kind of compliment in assuming that you are smart enough to figure out the claim for yourself. You should probably make your own claims in your written arguments clear and explicit, however, at least at first.

Delaying the claim pulls the audience in and increases interest and attention. "What is this author after?" the audience wonders, and reads to find out. The end of an essay is the most emphatic and memorable place for a claim. Many authors prefer to put the claim there to give it as much force as possible. There is some risk involved in putting the claim at the end. Students who use this strategy must be careful to insert cues along the way so that readers understand where the argument is headed and do not feel they are being led through a random chain of topics.

The claim, whether implied or explicitly stated, organizes the entire argument, and everything else in the argument is related to it. The best way to identify it, if it is not obvious or easy to locate, is to complete the following statement as soon as you have finished reading: "This author wants me to believe that . . ." When you have finished that statement, you have the claim. As a writer, you can check your own claim during revision by completing this statement: "I want my audience to agree that . . . " Can you do it? If you can, you understand the concept of the claim, and you will be able to recognize the main point in the arguments you read and to use a claim to articulate the main point in any argument you write.

Support

Discover the support in an argument by asking, "What additional information does the author supply to convince me of this claim?" Or if you are the author, ask, "What information do I need to supply to convince my audience?" Most arguments contain two levels of support: *subclaims* and *specific support*. Check Box 5.1 (page 99) for synonyms for these terms.

Subclaims. At the first level of support are the *subclaims*, which are the supporting arguments or reasons for the claim. Here is an example that illustrates the relationships among an issue area, at the most general level in the example, a specific related issue that represents an idea about the general issue area, a claim that is made in response to the specific related issue, and four subclaims that are used to support the claim. The subclaims are at the most specific level in this example because they represent ideas about the claim.

Issue Area: The Environment
  Specific related issue: How serious are the world's environmental problems?

> **Claim:** The environment is the single-most serious problem the world faces today.
> **Subclaims:**
> 1. The rain forests are being destroyed, causing global warming.
> 2. Increasing population is depleting resources in some parts of the world.
> 3. Many important water sources are being polluted by industry.
> 4. The ozone layer, which protects us from harmful sun rays, is being destroyed by chemicals.

Specific Support. The second level of support is the *specific support*. Specific support provides the evidence, opinions, reasoning, examples, and factual information about a claim or subclaim that make it possible for us to accept it. Look back at the claim and subclaims in the example above. If you are to take this claim seriously, you will want some additional specific support to make it convincing.

To locate such support, what should you look for? One bit of good news: support is always explicitly stated, so you will not have to infer it as you sometimes have to infer the claim. Thus an understanding of the types of support is all you really need to help you recognize it. Let us look at some of the most common types.

Facts. In a court of law, factual support (the murder weapon, for example) is laid out on the table. In written argument, it must be described. Factual support can include detailed reports of *observed events*; specific *examples* of real happenings; references to *events*, either *historical* or *recent*; and *statistical reports*. Factual support is vivid, real, and verifiable. Two people looking at it together would agree on its existence and on what it looks like. They might not agree on what it *means* to each of them—that is, they might interpret it differently. However, essentially, they would agree on the facts themselves.

Opinions. When people start interpreting the facts and events, opinion enters the picture. Opinions may be the personal opinions of the author or the opinions of experts the author selects to quote. The author can use direct quotations, set off in quotation marks, or summaries or paraphrases of what someone else thinks or reports. Furthermore, opinions may be informed, based on considerable knowledge and excellent judgment, or they may be ill-founded, based on hearsay and gossip. The most convincing opinions are those of experts, whether they be those of the author or of another person. Experts possess superior background, education, and experience on an issue. Contrast in your own mind the opinions of experts with the uninformed opinions of people on the evening news who are surprised in the streets by reporters and asked to give their opinions. Ill-founded, baseless opinion is boring and rarely convincing. In contrast, *informed personal opinions and the opinions of experts can be more interesting and convincing than the facts themselves.*

Examples. Examples can be real or made up, long or short. They are used to clarify, to make material more memorable and interesting, and in argument particularly, to prove. Examples that are real, such as instances of actual events or references to particular individuals, function in the same way that fact does in an argument. They are convincing because they are grounded in reality. Made-up or hypothetical examples are invented by the writer and, like opinions, can only demonstrate what may be the case. Personal experience is one type of example that is frequently used in argument. Writers often go into considerable detail about the experiences that have influenced them to think and behave as they do. Combining personal experience with the opinions and reasoning derived from it is a common way to develop a claim.

Different authors manage support in different ways depending on the requirements of the subject, their purpose, and their audience. When the issue is an abstract idea and the audience is informed, the author may present mainly opinions and few, if any, facts or examples. Such arguments include a claim and blocks of logical reasoning organized around subclaims to develop and prove the claim. If you were to outline the argument, you might not need more than two levels, as in the claim and subclaim example on pages 100–101. When the subject requires more specific support or the audience needs more information to be convinced, specific materials at lower levels on an outline are required to ground the subclaims in facts, figures, images, quotations from others, or author opinions. The next example expands on the example on page 101 by adding specific support.[2]

Issue Area: The Environment

Specific related issue: How serious are the world's environmental problems?

Claim: The environment is the single-most serious problem the world faces today.

Subclaim: The rain forests are being destroyed, causing global warming.

Support: Global warming could cause the oceans to rise, the number of storms to increase, and more droughts. (*opinion*)

Subclaim: Increasing population is depleting resources in some parts of the world.

Support: One-third of the world does not have enough food and is in danger of starvation. (*fact*)

Subclaim: Many important water sources are being polluted by industry.

Support: By 2025, two-thirds of the world's population may live in areas where there is a serious water shortage. (*opinion*)

Subclaim: The ozone layer, which protects us from harmful sun rays, is being destroyed by chemicals.

Support: It was widely reported in the fall of 2003 that the hole in the ozone layer was significantly larger than it had been the previous year. (*fact*)

---

[2]The support in the example is drawn from Jeffrey Kluger and Andrea Dorfman, "The Challenges We Face," *Time*, August 26, 2002, pp. A7+.

Quality support helps build common ground between the arguer and the audience. Rantings, unfounded personal opinions that no one else accepts, or feeble reasons like "because I said so" or "because everyone does it" are not effective support. Audiences usually do not believe such statements, they do not share experiences or ideas suggested by them, and they lose common ground with the arguer when they read or hear them.

When reading argument, to help you focus on and recognize the support, complete this sentence as soon as you finish: "The author wants me to believe that . . . [the claim] because . . . [list the support]." When you read to revise your own writing, you can complete this statement: "I have convinced my audience to believe [the claim] because [list your support]."

Warrants

Warrants are the assumptions, general principles, conventions of specific disciplines, widely held values, commonly accepted beliefs, and appeals to human motives that are an important part of any argument.[3] Even though they can be spelled out as part of the written argument, usually they are not. In many instances it would be redundant and boring if they were. For example, an argument might go as follows: *Claim*: The president of the United States is doing a poor job. *Support*: The economy is the worst it has been in ten years. The unstated *warrants* in this argument might include the following *generally accepted beliefs*: the president is responsible for the economy; when the economy is weak, it is a sign that the president is doing a poor job; or even though the president may be doing well in other areas, a robust economy is the main index to overall performance. You may think of other ways of expressing the warrants in this argument. Since individual audience members vary in their backgrounds and perspectives, not everyone will state the warrants in exactly the same way.

Here is another example, and this one relies on a *value warrant*. *Claim:* Business profits are adversely affected by environmental protection laws. *Support:* Obeying environmental protection laws that call for clean air, for example, costs industry money that could otherwise be realized as profit. The unstated *warrants* in this argument involve the relative value that individuals place on the environment and on business profit and might be stated in this way: profit is more important than clean air; businesses must make a profit to survive; or environmental protection laws are threatening the capitalist system.

Finally, here is an example of a warrant that relies on a *commonly accepted convention* of a specific discipline, which in this case is the discipline of writing. *Claim:* You have received a failing grade on this paper. *Support:* You have many sentence fragments and subject-verb agreement errors in your paper. The unstated *warrants* could be stated as follows: these kinds of errors result in a poor or failing grade in college papers, or the conventions of writing college papers do not allow

---

[3]Toulmin's warrants are somewhat similar to Bitzer's constraints in the rhetorical situation. Bitzer, however, extends the concept of constraints to also include the resources available to the writer and the type of text being produced, whether written, spoken, or visual. Thus constraints is a broader concept than warrants.

fragments and subject-verb agreement problems. When you encounter argument in your other college courses, try to identify the warrants that are implicit in them and that are also part of the generally accepted knowledge or conventions that inform these particular disciplines. Such warrants could include laws in physics, equations in mathematics, or theories in philosophy. This underlying or foundational information is not always spelled out in every argument, particularly if the people who are arguing share the same background information about these conventions, laws, equations, or theories.

Warrants originate with the arguer. Note, however, that the warrants also exist in the minds of the audience. They can be *shared* by the arguer and the audience, or they can be *in conflict*. Furthermore, if the audience shares the warrants with the arguer, the audience will accept them, and the argument is convincing. If the warrants are in conflict and the audience does not accept them (they believe private enterprise, not the president, is responsible for improving the economy, or they believe sentence fragments are acceptable in academic writing because many widely admired writers have used them), the argument is not convincing to them.

Warrants provide critical links in argument. For instance, they link the support to the claim by enabling an audience to accept particular support as proof of a particular claim. Without the linking warrant, the support may not be convincing. Here is an example.

Claim:	The appeal process for criminals should be shortened . . .
Support:	because the appeals for criminals on death row can cost millions of dollars per criminal.
Expected warrant:	Spending several million dollars to keep a convicted criminal alive a little longer is a waste of money. (*This individual shares the author's warrant, the link is made, and the argument is convincing.*)
Alternative warrant:	We are dealing with human life here, and we should spend whatever is necessary to make certain we have a fair conviction. (*This individual supplies an opposing warrant, the link between claim and support is not made, and the argument is not convincing.*)

Besides being related to what people commonly believe, value, want, or accept as background knowledge in a discipline, warrants are also culture-bound. Since values, beliefs, and training vary from culture to culture, the warrants associated with them also differ from culture to culture. Tension between Japan and the United States was caused by a Japanese official's claim that American workers are lazy and do not work hard enough. American workers were angry and countered with a rebuttal about how hard they think they work. Japanese and American workers have different work schedules, attitudes, and experience with leisure and work time. Consequently, the part of both arguments that was unstated, the warrant, described hard work in different ways for each culture. The lack of a shared warrant caused the tension. Furthermore, neither side was convinced by the other's argument. When American workers argued with the Japanese about whether they are lazy or hardworking, a shared warrant was missing.

Japanese claim:	American workers are lazy . . .
Support:	because they work only 40 hours a week.
Japanese warrant:	People who work only 40 hours a week are lazy.
American rebuttal:	American workers are hardworking . . .
Support:	because they work 40 hours a week.
American warrant:	People who put in 40 hours a week are industrious and hardworking.

Perhaps now you have begun to appreciate the importance of shared warrants in argument. Shared warrants are crucial to the success of an argument because they are the most significant way to establish common ground between reader and writer in argument. Shared warrants and common ground, as you can imagine, are particularly important in international negotiations. Skillful negotiators take time to analyze warrants and to determine whether or not both parties are on common ground. If they are not, communication breaks down and argument fails.

At this point, you may wonder why authors do not spell out the warrants, since they are so essential to the success of the argument. There are two reasons for usually leaving warrants unstated, so that the audience has to supply them. First, an audience who supplies the warrant is more likely to buy in to the argument through a sense of participation. If there is potential for agreement and common ground, it will be strengthened by the audience's supplying the warrant. Second, remember that audiences differ and that their views of the warrant also vary somewhat, depending on their past experiences and present perceptions. A stated warrant negates the rich and varied perceptions and responses of the audience by providing only the author's interpretation and articulation of the warrant. Less active participation is then required from the audience, and the argument is less powerful and convincing to them.

To help you discover warrants, ask questions like the following:

What is left out here?
What does this author value? Do I share those values?
What is causing this author to say these things?
Do I believe that this evidence supports this claim? Why or why not?

As the author of argument, you should consider your audience and whether or not they will or can accept your warrants.

Let's turn now to the other three parts of the Toulmin model that an arguer can use to adapt an argument to a particular audience. All or none might appear in a written argument.

Backing

You should have a sense by now that warrants themselves may require their own support to make them more acceptable to an audience, particularly if the audience does not happen to share them with the author. An author may provide backing, or additional evidence and ideas to "back up" a warrant, whenever the audience is in danger of rejecting it. When you are the author, you should provide backing also.

Backing sometimes appears as appeals to generally accepted knowledge and beliefs that are held by most individuals or groups of people who belong to a specific discipline or culture. Certain cable news stations, radio commentary, magazines or newspapers, and affiliations with political parties or interest groups can also contribute to an individual's belief system. These beliefs are sometimes spelled out explicitly as backing for a warrant, and at other times they are implied and the audience has to supply them by examining the logic of the argument and making inferences.

Here is an example of backing for a warrant.

Claim: Immigrants should be allowed to come into the United States . . .

Support: because immigration has benefited the U.S. economy in the past.

Warrant: Current economic conditions are similar to past conditions.

Backing: Now, as in the past, immigrants are willing to perform necessary low-paying jobs that American citizens do not want, particularly in the service areas. Furthermore, immigrants perform these jobs better than citizens and for less pay.

Look for backing in an argument by identifying the warrant and then determining whether or not you accept it. If you do not, try to anticipate additional information that would make it more acceptable. Then examine whether the author supplied that or similar additional support. When you are the writer, consider your audience. Will they accept your warrant, or can you strengthen it by supplying additional information or by appealing to common values and beliefs that will help justify your claim?

Rebuttal

A rebuttal establishes what is wrong, invalid, or unacceptable about an argument and may also present counterarguments or new arguments that represent entirely different perspectives or points of view on the issue. To attack the validity of the claim, an author may demonstrate that the support is faulty or that the warrants are faulty or unbelievable. Counterarguments start all over again, with a new set of claims, support, and warrants.

Here is an example of a rebuttal for the argument about immigration.

Rebuttal 1:   Immigrants actually drain more resources in schooling, medical care, and other social services than they contribute in taxes and productivity.

Rebuttal 2:   Modern immigrants are not so willing to perform menial, low-skilled jobs as they were in past generations.

Here is an example of a counterargument for the immigration argument.

Claim: Laws should be passed to limit immigration . . .

Support: because we have our own unskilled laborers who need those jobs.

Warrant: These laborers are willing to hold these jobs.

Backing: The recession has caused many citizens to lose their jobs, and they need access to all types of work.

Rebuttals may appear as answers to arguments that have already been stated, or the author may anticipate the reader's rebuttal and include answers to possible objections that might be raised. Thus an author might write a rebuttal to the claim that we should censor television by saying such a practice would violate the First Amendment. Or, if no claim has been made, the arguer could anticipate what the objections to television violence might be (violence breeds violence, children who see violence become frightened, etc.) and refute them, usually early in the essay, before spelling out the reasons for leaving television alone.

Look for a rebuttal or plan for it in your own writing by asking, "What are the other possible views on this issue?" When reading, ask, "Are other views represented here along with reasons?" Or, when writing, ask, "How can I answer other views?" Phrases that might introduce refutation include *some may disagree, others may think*, or *other commonly held opinions are*, followed by the opposing ideas and your reasons and evidence for rejecting them.

Qualifiers

The outcomes of argument are usually not described as establishing certainty or truth in the same sense that mathematics and science seek to establish certainty and truth. We do not argue about the fact that $2 + 3 = 5$ or that the area of a circle is πr^2. Mathematical proofs seek to establish such truths. Argument seeks to establish what is probably true as well as what might be expedient or desirable for the future. Arguers tell you what they think for now along with what they think should be done, given their present information. On that basis, you decide what you think for now, given your present information.

Consequently, the language of certainty (*always, never, the best, the worst*, and so on) promises too much when used in claims or in other parts of the argument. It is not uncommon for an author to make a claim and in the midst of writing to begin revising and qualifying it to meet the anticipated objections of an audience. Thus words like *always* and *never* change to *sometimes; is* or *are* change to *may be* or *might; all* changes to *many* or *some; none* changes to *a few*; and *absolutely* changes to *probably* or *possibly*. Qualified language is safer for demonstrating the probabilities of an argument. Look to see how the author has stated the claim in other parts of the argument, either in probable or absolute terms, and then read the entire argument to figure out why.

The following is a qualified version of the claim that all immigrants should be allowed to come into the United States. These qualifications would make the original claim more acceptable to the people who offered the rebuttals and counterargument.

> Immigrants should be allowed to enter the United States only if they can prove that they already have jobs yielding sufficient income to offset social services and that no American citizens are currently available to perform these jobs.

VALUE OF THE TOULMIN MODEL FOR READING AND WRITING ARGUMENT

The Toulmin model has some advantages that make it an excellent model for both reading and writing argument. Its most essential advantage is that it invites common ground and audience participation in the form of shared warrants, increasing the possibility of interaction between author and audience. Backing, rebuttals, and qualifiers also encourage an exchange of views and common ground because they require an arguer both to anticipate other perspectives and views and, at times, to acknowledge and answer them directly. The backing, for instance, requires additional evidence and reference to common cultural values and beliefs to satisfy audience concerns. The rebuttal requires answers to different or opposing views. The qualifier requires a modification of the claim to gain audience acceptance. The backing, rebuttal, and qualifier in the Toulmin model invite the audience to participate. They encourage dialogue, understanding, and agreement as argument outcomes. These features make the model valuable for examining the multiple perspectives likely to be expressed in response to complex modern issues.

The model works for reading or writing not only in traditional argument, including debate and single-perspective argument, but also in academic inquiry, negotiation, dialectic, Rogerian argument (explained in Chapter 10), or any other form of argument that requires exchange and attempts to reach agreement. It can even be a useful tool for one-on-one argument or personal decision making.

Writers of argument find the Toulmin model useful as both an invention strategy and a revision strategy. It can be used to help an author come up with the essential parts of an argument in the first place, and later it can be used to check and evaluate the parts of a newly written argument.

Readers of argument find the model useful for analyzing, describing, and summarizing the essential parts of a written argument. Listeners find it just as useful for analyzing and describing the essential parts of an argumentation speech. Viewers find they can use the model to analyze visual argument, whether it appears on television, in film, or in photographs, charts, graphs, and drawings accompanying printed text. It can be used to write or to analyze both consensual and adversarial arguments. It accommodates all of the various forms of arguments. The model is summarized in a handy chart for quick reference for the use of both readers and writers in the Summary Charts (page 304) in Appendix 2.

REVIEW QUESTIONS

1. Name and describe the six parts of the Toulmin model. Which parts, stated or inferred, can be found in any argument? Which parts are used, as needed, to make an argument more convincing to a particular audience?
2. What are some synonyms for each of the three essential parts of the Toulmin model? Consult Box 5.1 (page 99).
3. What are subclaims? What are some types of specific support?
4. Define warrants. Why does argument work better when warrants are shared by the arguer and the audience?
5. Give some examples of qualifiers.

CLASS ACTIVITIES AND WRITING ASSIGNMENTS

1. **Use the Toulmin Model to Analyze an Advertisement**

   Study the advertisement that appears on the next page. Answer the following questions. *The first three parts will be present.*

   1. *What is the claim?* Complete the sentence, "The author wants me to believe that . . ." Is the claim stated or implied?
   2. *What is the support?* Complete the sentence, "The author wants me to believe that . . . [the claim] because . . . [support]." Look for subclaims (*reasons*) and specific support (e.g., *facts, opinions, examples*).
   3. *What are the warrants?* Ask, "What does this author value or believe regarding the claim? Are these values or beliefs stated or implied? Do I agree or disagree with them?" Recall, also, that the warrants supply a link between support and claim. Ask, "Can I accept this evidence as support for this claim? Why or why not?" If you do not see how the evidence supports the claim, the argument will not be convincing to you.

   The next three parts may or may not be present.

   4. *Is there backing for any of the warrants?* Ask, "Does the author supply any additional information that would make it easier for me to accept the warrants, whether they are stated or implied? What is it?"
   5. *Is there a rebuttal?* Ask, "Are other views on the issue represented here along with reasons? What are they?"
   6. *Is there a qualifier?* Ask, "Is the claim stated in absolute terms (e.g., *always, never, the best, the worst*) or in probable terms (e.g., *sometimes, probably, often, possibly*)?"
   7. *Do you find this ad convincing?* Why or why not?

2. **Use the Toulmin Model to Analyze a Cartoon**

   Analyze the cartoon on page 111 and discuss the answers to these questions:

   a. What is the claim?
   b. What is the support?
   c. What are the warrants?
   d. Are backing, rebuttals, or qualifiers present? Describe them.

3. **Use the Toulmin Model to Read and Analyze a Short Editorial**

   Read the editorial on pages 111–112. Then answer the questions on page 112 and discuss your answers with the class. You can expect some disagreement because of your differing backgrounds and experiences. If you disagree on some of these answers, try to figure out what is causing your differences.

   a. What is the claim? Is it explicitly stated, or did you have to infer it?
   b. What are some examples of support?
   c. What are the author's warrants? Does the author supply backing for the warrants? If yes, how?
   d. Do you share the author's warrants, or do you have conflicting warrants? If you have conflicting warrants, what are they?

(Continued on page 111.)

SOURCE: *New Yorker*, January 26, 2004, p. 33.

SOURCE: Jeff Stale: © Columbus Dispatch/Dist. by *Newspaper Enterprise Association, Inc.*

(Continued from page 109, Activity 3.)

      e. Is there a rebuttal in the article? If yes, what is it?

      f. Is the claim qualified? How?

      g. Do you find this argument convincing? Why or why not?

BEFORE YOU READ: How many people do you think are hungry on a daily basis in America?

Essay 1

BROTHER, CAN YOU SPARE A WORD?*

Editorial

1   First the good news: the government's annual hunger report shows a slight decline last year in the number of citizens in need of food. Now the bad news: the annual hunger report has dropped the word "hunger."

*New York Times, November 20, 2006, A26.

2   Instead, there were 35 million Americans last year suffering from "low food security," meaning they chronically lacked the resources to be able to eat enough food. Of these, 10.8 million lived with "very low food security," meaning they were the hungriest among the hungry, so to speak.

3   Bureaucratic terminology about food security has always been a part of the hunger report, but so was the plain word "hunger." The Agriculture Department decided that variations of "hungry" are not scientifically accurate, following the advice of the Committee on National Statistics of the National Academies. The specialists advised that being hungry was too amorphous a way to refer to "a potential consequence of food insecurity that, because of prolonged, involuntary lack of food, results in discomfort, illness, weakness or pain that goes beyond the usual uneasy sensation."

4   The government insists that no Orwellian plot is in the works to mask a national blight. The goal has been to cut what we'll call the hungry households to no more than 6 percent of the population. But hungry people persist at nearly twice that rate, despite the slight drop last year. To the extent that more public empathy is needed to prod a stronger attack on low food security, we opt for "hunger" as a most stirring word.

For Discussion:

Why is this author arguing that the word *hunger* should be used in the government's annual hunger report instead of the term "very low food security"? Why do you think government writers made this substitution? Which of these choices do you think best describes the condition of the millions of Americans who never have enough food to eat?

---

4.   **Write a Toulmin Analysis and Report on It in Class**

a. Clip a short article, an advertisement, a cartoon, or a letter to the editor and use the Toulmin model to analyze it.

b. Write a 250- to 300-word paper in which you identify and explain the claim, support, and warrants in your example. Provide further information about backing, rebuttals, or qualifiers, if they are present.

c. In class, circulate the item you clipped among your classmates. Either read your paper or give a two- to three-minute oral report in which you describe the parts of the argument to the class.

A student-written analysis of the cartoon about the price of oranges follows. Reading this student paper should help you write your Toulmin analysis paper. Also, discuss whether you and your classmates agree with this analysis. Everyone does not apply the Toulmin model in exactly the same way. There are no absolutely correct answers because different readers' interpretations vary.*

---

*See Appendix 1 for the actual format guidelines for student papers.

Student	Mohamed T. Diaby Jr.
Paper	Toulmin Analysis
1	English 1302
	February 12, 2010

Toulmin Analysis of the Price of Oranges Cartoon[†]

Identifies claim and support   1   The reader has to infer the claim of this cartoon since it is not directly stated. The claim is that the price of oranges will go way up in the United States if they are picked by legal U.S. workers. The support is provided by the shopper, who is considering buying the oranges, and the sign that says they are handpicked by U.S. workers but their price is 3 for $20 dollars, a prohibitively high price for oranges.

Analyzes warrant   2   The implied warrant is that illegal immigrants will work for lower wages than legal workers, which keeps the price of oranges low.

Identifies backing   3   The backing is also implied and reinforced by the picture. It suggests that oranges are a staple and are purchased frequently by family shoppers. It also reinforces the common belief that many people will not be able to buy oranges that are handpicked by U.S. workers because they will be too expensive.

Infers rebuttal   4   No direct rebuttal or qualifier appears in this cartoon. I think, however, that this cartoon could be considered as a rebuttal to those who think illegal immigrants should be sent home and no longer allowed to work in the United States. As a rebuttal, this cartoon suggests the consequences of that popular position if it were enforced.

◆ **5. Prewriting: Use the Toulmin Model to Get Ideas for a Future Argument Paper**

You have used the Toulmin model in the previous exercises to analyze other people's argument. Now use it to identify the main parts of an argument you will write. If you have already selected an arguable issue, written an issue proposal, analyzed the rhetorical situation and your audience, conducted some research, assembled an annotated bibliography, and written an exploratory paper to help you understand some of the positions people take on your issue, you may now use the Toulmin model as a prewriting exercise to help you develop ideas for the researched position paper. Full instructions for writing this paper appear in Chapter 11.

Toulmin Prewriting Prompts

1. Write a claim. All of the rest of your paper will support this claim.
2. Write the support. Write two or three subclaims that you could develop in the paper. To help you do this, write the word *because* after your claim, and list reasons that support it. Also jot down ideas for specific support for these

---

[†] This paper is modeled on a paper done by Mohamed Diaby Jr. in an argument class.

subclaims, such as examples, facts, and opinions, that come from your reading of the essays in your bibliography or from your own experience.

3. Write the warrants. Decide whether to spell out the warrants in your paper or to leave them implicit so that the reading audience will have to infer them.

4. Decide on the backing. Assume that your classmates are your audience. They may be reading drafts of your paper. In your judgment, will some of them require backing for any of your warrants because they will not agree with them otherwise? If so, how can you back these warrants? Write out your ideas.

5. Plan rebuttal. Think about the positions others may hold on this issue. You identified some of these positions in your exploratory paper. Write out some strategies for weakening these arguments.

6. Decide whether to qualify your claim to make it more convincing to more people. Write one or more qualifiers that might work.

Read what you have written, and make a note about additional information you will need to locate for your paper. Save what you have written in a folder. You will use it later when you complete your planning and write your researched position paper.

6.   Understand Value Warrants

Often, both the warrants and the backing for warrants come from the systems of values that people hold. The values will not be spelled out in an argument, yet they will still influence the arguer and make an argument more convincing to an audience who happens to share them. The following essay describes six American value systems. These systems are somewhat oversimplified, and they do not identify all American value systems. They are useful, however, to help you understand some of the values that people hold. Read the essay, and then answer the questions for discussion at the end.

BEFORE YOU READ: What values are important to you? How would you describe core American values?

Essay 2

AMERICAN VALUE SYSTEMS*

Richard D. Rieke and Malcolm O. Sillars

Rieke and Sillars are speech communication professors whose most recent book is *Argumentation and Critical Decision Making.*

1   By careful analysis individual values can be discovered in the arguments of ourselves and others. There is a difficulty, however, in attempting to define a whole system of values for a person or a group. And as difficult as that is, each of

---

*Richard D. Rieke and Malcolm O. Sillars, *Argumentation and the Decision Making Process*, 2nd ed. (Boston: Allyn & Bacon, 1984), 118–24, Copyright © 1984 by Pearson Education. Reprinted with permission of the publisher.

us, as a participant in argumentation, should have some concept of the broad systems that most frequently bring together certain values. For this purpose, it is useful for you to have an idea of some of the most commonly acknowledged value systems.

2   You must approach this study with a great deal of care, however, because even though the six basic value systems we are about to define provide a fair view of the standard American value systems, they do not provide convenient pigeonholes into which individuals can be placed. They represent broad social categories. Some individuals (even groups) will be found outside these systems. Many individuals and groups will cross over value systems, picking and choosing from several. Note how certain words appear as value terms in more than one value system. The purpose of this survey is to provide a beginning understanding of standard American values, not a complete catalog.[1]

The Puritan-Pioneer-Peasant Value System

3   This value system has been identified frequently as the *puritan morality* or the *Protestant ethic*. It also has been miscast frequently because of the excessive emphasis placed, by some of its adherents, on restrictions of personal acts such as smoking and consuming alcohol.[2] Consequently, over the years, this value system has come to stand for a narrow-minded attempt to interfere in other people's business, particularly if those people are having fun. However, large numbers of people who do not share such beliefs follow this value system.

4   We have taken the liberty of expanding beyond the strong and perhaps too obvious religious implications of the terms *puritan* and *Protestant*. This value system is what most Americans refer to when they speak of the "pioneer spirit," which was not necessarily religious. It also extends, we are convinced, to a strain of values brought to this country by Southern and Eastern European Catholics, Greek Orthodox, and Jews who could hardly be held responsible for John Calvin's theory or even the term *Protestant ethic*. Thus, we have the added word *peasant*, which may not be particularly accurate. Despite the great friction that existed between these foreign-speaking immigrants from other religions and their native Protestant counterparts, they had a great deal in common as do their ideological descendants today. On many occasions after describing the puritan morality we have heard a Jewish student say, "That's the way my father thinks," or had a student of Italian or Polish descent say, "My grandmother talks that way all the time."

5   The Puritan-Pioneer-Peasant value system is rooted in the idea that persons have an obligation to themselves and those around them, and in some cases to their God, to work hard at whatever they do. In this system, people are limited in their abilities and must be prepared to fail. The great benefit is in the striving against an unknowable and frequently hostile universe. They have an obligation to others, must be selfless, and must not waste. Some believe this is the only way to gain happiness and success. Others see it as a means to salvation. In all cases it takes on a moral orientation. Obviously, one might work hard for a summer in order to buy a new car and not be labeled a "puritan." Frequently, in this value system, the instrumental values of selflessness, thrift, and hard work become terminal values where the work has value beyond the other benefits it can bring

one. People who come from this value system often have difficulty with retirement, because their meaning in life, indeed their pleasure, came from work.

6   Likewise, because work, selflessness, and thrift are positive value terms in this value system, laziness, selfishness, and waste are negative value terms. One can see how some adherents to this value system object to smoking, drinking, dancing, or cardplaying. These activities are frivolous; they take one's mind off more serious matters and waste time.

7   Some of the words that are associated with the Puritan-Pioneer-Peasant value system are:

Positive: activity, work, thrift, morality, dedication, selflessness, virtue, righteousness, duty, dependability, temperance, sobriety, savings, dignity

Negative: waste, immorality, dereliction, dissipation, infidelity, theft, vandalism, hunger, poverty, disgrace, vanity

The Enlightenment Value System

8   America became a nation in the period of the Enlightenment. It happened when a new intellectual era based on the scientific findings of men like Sir Isaac Newton and the philosophical systems of men like John Locke were dominant. The founders of our nation were particularly influenced by such men. The Declaration of Independence is the epitome of an Enlightenment document. In many ways America is an Enlightenment nation, and if Enlightenment is not the predominant value system, it is surely first among equals.

9   The Enlightenment position stems from the belief that we live in an ordered world in which all activity is governed by laws similar to the laws of physics. These "natural laws" may or may not come from God, depending on the particular orientation of the person examining them; but unlike many adherents to the Puritan value system just discussed, Enlightenment persons theorized that people could discover these laws by themselves. Thus, they may worship God for God's greatness, even acknowledge that God created the universe and natural laws, but they find out about the universe because they have the power of reason. The laws of nature are harmonious, and one can use reason to discover them all. They can also be used to provide for a better life.

10   Because humans are basically good and capable of finding answers, restraints on them must be limited. Occasionally, people do foolish things and must be restrained by society. However, a person should never be restrained in matters of the mind. Reason must be free. Thus, government is an agreement among individuals to assist the society to protect rights. That government is a democracy. Certain rights are inalienable, and they may not be abridged; "among these are life, liberty and the pursuit of happiness." Arguments for academic freedom, against wiretaps, and for scientific inquiry come from this value system.

11   Some of the words associated with the Enlightenment value system are:

Positive: freedom, science, nature, rationality, democracy, fact, liberty, individualism, knowledge, intelligence, reason, natural rights, natural laws, progress

Negative: ignorance, inattention, thoughtlessness, error, indecision, irra-
tionality, dictatorship, fascism, bookburning, falsehood, regression

The Progressive Value System

12   Progress was a natural handmaiden of the Enlightenment. If these laws were
available and if humans had the tool, reason, to discover them and use them to
advantage, then progress would result. Things would continually get better. But
although progress is probably a historical spin-off of the Enlightenment, it has
become so important on its own that it deserves at times to be seen quite separate from the Enlightenment.

13   Richard Weaver, in 1953, found that "one would not go far wrong in naming
progress" the "god term" of that age. It is, he said, the "expression about which
all other expressions are ranked as subordinate... . Its force imparts to the others
their lesser degrees of force, and fixes the scale by which degrees of comparison
are understood."[3]

14   Today, the unmediated use of the progressive value system is questioned, but
progress is still a fundamental value in America. Most arguments against progress
are usually arguments about the definition of progress. They are about what
"true progress is."

15   Some of the key words of the Progressive value system are:

Positive: practicality, efficiency, change, improvement, science, future, modern, progress, evolution
Negative: old-fashioned,[4] regressive, impossible, backward

The Transcendental Value System

16   Another historical spin-off of the Enlightenment system was the development
of the transcendental movement of the early nineteenth century. It took from
the Enlightenment all its optimism about people, freedom, and democracy, but
rejected the emphasis on reason. It argued idealistically that there was a faculty
higher than reason; let us call it, as many transcendentalists did, intuition. Thus,
for the transcendentalist, there is a way of knowing that is better than reason, a
way which *transcends* reason. Consequently, what might seem like the obvious
solution to problems is not necessarily so. One must look, on important matters
at least, to the intuition, to the feelings. Like the Enlightenment thinker, the
transcendentalist believes in a unified universe governed by natural laws. Thus,
all persons, by following their intuition, will discover these laws, and universal
harmony will take place. And, of course, little or no government will be necessary. The original American transcendentalists of the early nineteenth century
drew their inspiration from Platonism, German idealism, and Oriental mysticism. The idea was also fairly well limited to the intellectuals. By and large, transcendentalism has been the view of a rather small group of people throughout
our history, but at times it has been very important. It has always been somewhat more influential among younger people. James Truslow Adams once
wrote that everyone should read Ralph Waldo Emerson at sixteen because his

writings were a marvel for the buoyantly optimistic person of that age but that his transcendental writings did not have the same luster at twenty-one.[5] In the late 1960s and early 1970s, Henry David Thoreau's *Walden* was the popular reading of campus rebels. The emphasis of anti-establishment youth on Oriental mysticism, like Zen, should not be ignored either. The rejection of contemporary society and mores symbolized by what others considered "outlandish dress" and "hippie behavior" with its emphasis on emotional response and "do your own thing" indicated the adoption of a transcendental value system. Communal living is reminiscent of the transcendental "Brook Farm" experiments that were attempted in the early nineteenth century and described by Nathaniel Hawthorne in his novel *The Blithedale Romance.*

17   In all of these movements the emphasis on humanitarian values, the centrality of love for others, and the preference for quiet contemplation over activity has been important. Transcendentalism, however, rejects the common idea of progress. Inner light and knowledge of one's self is more important than material well-being. There is also some tendency to reject physical well-being because it takes one away from intuitive truth.

18   It should be noted that not everyone who argues for change is a transcendentalist. The transcendental white campus agitators of the late 1960s discovered that, despite all their concern for replacing racism and war with love and peace, their black counterparts were highly pragmatic and rationalistic about objectives and means. Black agitators and demonstrators were never "doing their thing" in the intuitive way of many whites.

19   It should also be noted that while a full adherence to transcendentalism has been limited to small groups, particularly among intellectuals and youth, many of the ideas are not limited to such persons. One can surely find strains of what we have labeled, for convenience, transcendentalism in the mysticism of some very devout older Roman Catholics, for instance. And perhaps many Americans become transcendental on particular issues, about the value to be derived from hiking in the mountains, for example.

20   Here are some of the terms that are characteristic of the Transcendental value system:

> *Positive:*   humanitarian, individualism, respect, intuition, truth, equality, sympathetic, affection, feeling, love, sensitivity, emotion, personal kindness, compassion, brotherhood, friendship, mysticism
>
> *Negative:*   science,[6] reason, mechanical, hate, war, anger, insensitive, coldness, unemotional

The Personal Success Value System

21   The least social of the major American value systems is the one that moves people toward personal achievement and success. It can be related as a part of the Enlightenment value system, but it is more than that because it involves a highly pragmatic concern for the material happiness of the individual. To call it selfish would be to load the terms against it, although there would be some who accept this value system who would say, "Yes, I'm selfish." "The Lord helps those who

help themselves" has always been an acceptable adage by some of the most devout in our nation.

22   You might note that the Gallup poll . . . is very heavily weighted toward personal values. Even "good family life" rated as the top value can be seen as an item of personal success. This survey includes only a few social values like "helping needy people" and "helping better America," and even those are phrased in personal terms. That is, the respondents were asked "how important you feel each of these is to you." The personal orientation of the survey may represent a bias of the Gallup poll, but we suspect it reflects much of American society. We are personal success–oriented in an individual way which would not be found in some other cultures (e.g., in the Japanese culture).

23   Here are some of the terms that tend to be characteristic of the Personal Success value system:

> *Positive:*   career, family, friends, recreation, economic security, identity, health, individualism, affection, respect, enjoyment, dignity, consideration, fair play, personal
> *Negative:*   dullness, routine, hunger, poverty, disgrace, coercion, disease

The Collectivist Value System

24 Although there are few actual members of various socialist and communist groups in the United States, one cannot ignore the strong attachment among some people for collective action. This is, in part, a product of the influx of social theories from Europe in the nineteenth century. It is also a natural outgrowth of a perceived need to control the excesses of freedom in a mass society. Its legitimacy is not limited to current history, however. There has always been a value placed on cooperative action. The same people today who would condemn welfare payments to unwed mothers would undoubtedly praise their ancestors for barnraising and taking care of the widow in a frontier community. Much rhetoric about our "pioneer ancestors" has to do with their cooperative action. And anticollectivist presidents and evangelists talk about "the team." At the same time many fervent advocates of collective action in the society argue vehemently for their freedom and independence. Certainly the civil rights movement constituted a collective action for freedom. Remember the link in Martin Luther King, Jr.'s speech between "freedom" and "brotherhood"?

25   But whether the Collectivist value system is used to defend socialist proposals or promote "law and order," there is no doubt that collectivism is a strong value system in this nation. Like transcendentalism, however, it is probably a value system that, at least in this day, cannot work alone.

26   Here are some of the terms that tend to characterize the Collectivist value system:

> *Positive:*   cooperation, joint action, unity, brotherhood, together, social good, order, humanitarian aid and comfort, equality
> *Negative:*   disorganization, selfishness, personal greed, inequality

27   Clearly, these six do not constitute a complete catalog of all American value systems. Combinations and reorderings produce different systems. Two values deserve special attention because they are common in these systems and sometimes operate alone: *nature* and *patriotism*. Since the beginning of our nation the idea has prevailed that the natural is good and there for our use and preservation. Also, since John Winthrop first proclaimed that the New England Puritans would build "a city on the hill" for all the world to see and emulate, the idea has endured that America is a fundamentally great nation, perhaps God-chosen, to lead the world to a better life. This idea may be somewhat tarnished in some quarters today, but there is no doubt that it will revive as it has in the past. Linked to other value systems we have discussed, it will once more be a theme that will draw the adherence of others to arguments.

NOTES

1. The following material draws from a wide variety of sources. The following is an illustrative cross-section of sources from a variety of disciplines: Virgil I. Baker and Ralph T. Eubanks, *Speech in Personal and Public Affairs* (New York: David McKay, 1965), pp. 95–102; Clyde Kluckhohn, "An Anthropologist Looks at the United States," *Mirror for Man* (New York: McGraw-Hill, 1949), pp. 228–261; Stow Persons, *American Minds* (New York: Holt, Rinehart and Winston, 1958); Jurgen Ruesch, "Communication and American Values; A Psychological Approach," in *Communication: The Social Matrix of Psychiatry*, eds. Jurgen Ruesch and Gregory Bateson (New York: W. W. Norton, 1951), pp. 94–134; Edward D. Steele and W. Charles Redding, "The American Value System: Premises for Persuasion," *Western Speech*, 26 (Spring 1962), pp. 83–91; Richard Weaver, "Ultimate Terms in Contemporary Rhetoric," in *The Ethics of Rhetoric* (Chicago: Henry Regnery, 1953), pp. 211–232; Robin M. Williams, Jr., *American Society*, 3rd ed. (New York: Alfred A. Knopf, 1970), pp. 438–504.
2. It is ironic that the original American Puritans did not have clear injunctions against such activity.
3. Weaver, p. 212.
4. Note that "old-fashioned" is frequently positive when we speak of morality and charm but not when we speak of our taste in music.
5. James Truslow Adams, "Emerson Re-read," in *The Transcendental Revolt,* ed. George F. Whicher (Boston: D. C. Heath, 1949), pp. 31–39.
6. It is interesting to note, however, that one of the major organizations in the United States with transcendental origins, the Christian Science Church, combines transcendentalism with science.

For Discussion:

1. Can you find your own system of values in this article? Of the six value systems described, with which of them do you most closely identify?
2. Look back at the positive words associated with each system of values. Describe a visual image that could be used to depict each system. Use your imagination and describe what you see in your mind that would help readers visualize and understand each of these systems of values.
3. Which value systems do you find operating in the selections listed below that you have analyzed in this and earlier chapters? What value warrants are implicit in each of these selections? Provide reasons for your answers. There

are no correct answers. Use your imagination and have some fun with this exercise.

> The "Sense of Community" ad (page 110)
> The "Price of Oranges" cartoon (page 111)
> "Kids and Chores: All Work and No Pay?" (pages 86–88)
> "Brother, Can You Spare a Word?" (pages 111–112)
> "'A' is for 'Absent'" (pages 25–26)

4. When your system of values does not match the system of values implicit in an argument essay, what happens? How does a difference in value systems influence your acceptance of the author's argument?

Chapter

6

The Types of Claims: Establishing Purpose and Organization

This chapter and the one that follows it expand on and develop some of the ideas in Chapter 5. The claim, the support, and the warrants were identified in Chapter 5 as the three parts that are present in every argument. This chapter, along with Chapter 7, provides additional information about these three parts. Claims are the subject of this chapter. Support and warrants, which constitute the proofs of an argument, are the subject of the next chapter.

Argument theorists categorize claims according to types, and these types suggest the fundamental purposes of given arguments. Becoming aware of these categories for claims and the special characteristics associated with each of them will help you understand more fully the purposes and special features of the arguments you read and will also improve your writing of them.

FIVE TYPES OF CLAIMS

Virtually all arguments can be categorized according to one of five types of claims. You can identify each argument type by identifying the questions the argument answers. Here are the five categories of claims, along with the main questions that they answer.

1. *Claims of fact:* Did it happen? Does it exist?
2. *Claims of definition:* What is it? How should we define it?
3. *Claims of cause:* What caused it? Or, what are its effects?
4. *Claims of value:* Is it good or bad? What criteria will help us decide?
5. *Claims of policy:* What should we do about it? What should be our future course of action?

Notice how these questions all invite different purposes and different points of view. Furthermore, they all lead to argument. Let's look at some examples and descriptions of each of these types of claims, along with some brief examples of the patterns of organization and types of support that are typically used to develop them.

Claims of Fact

When you claim that you turned a paper in on time even if the professor cannot find it, or that you were not exceeding the speed limit when a police officer claims that you were, you are making claims of fact. Claims of fact are often central to the argument in courtroom debate since lawyers argue about what happened in order to prove innocence or guilt. Historians also argue about what happened as they sort through historical evidence to try to establish historical fact. Here are some additional examples of claims of fact: women are as effective as men in combat; the ozone layer is becoming depleted; increasing population threatens the environment; Bigfoot exists in certain remote areas; men need women to civilize them.

Notice that all of these claims are apparent statements of fact, but not everyone would agree with them. They are all controversial. Consequently, the "facts" in these claims need to be proved as either absolutely or probably true in order to be acceptable to an audience.

The following selection is the first paragraph in a longer article that argues that the "digital divide," a concept that predicted computer use would be unevenly distributed between the rich and the poor, did not, in fact, take place, and that the opposite has occurred. This article aims to disprove one fact and establish a more accurate one in its place. The claim for this article appears in the first sentence and is underlined.

| Example 1 | ### DEBUNKING THE DIGITAL DIVIDE
Robert Samuelson |

Samuelson, a contributing editor to *Newsweek* magazine, often writes about socio-economic issues in his biweekly column for that magazine.

1   It may turn out that the "digital divide"—one of the most fashionable political slogans of recent years—is largely fiction. As you will recall, the argument went well beyond the unsurprising notion that the rich would own more computers than the poor. The disturbing part of the theory was that society was dividing itself into groups of technology "haves" and "have nots" and that this segregation would, in turn, worsen already large economic inequalities. It's this argument that's either untrue or wildly exaggerated.[1]

Chronological order, which traces what has occurred over a period of time, usually in the order in which it occurred, can be used to develop claims of fact. For

---

[1]*Newsweek,* March 25, 2002, p. 37.

example, the history of the increase in population might be provided to show how it has happened over a period of time. Or a *claim with reasons* may be used to organize a fact paper. The claim above about the digital divide could be developed by adding several reasons for looking at actual computer use in a more accurate way.

The claim of fact itself is often stated at or near the beginning of the argument, unless there is a psychological advantage for stating it at the end. Most authors make claims of fact clear from the outset, revealing early what they seek to establish. Factual support, as you might guess, is especially appropriate for claims of fact. Such support includes both past and present *facts, statistics, real examples,* and *quotations from reliable authorities.* When reliable authorities are used, the quotations are usually based on fact and less on opinion.

Claims of Definition

Entire arguments can center around the definition of a term. When you claim that an athlete who receives compensation for playing a sport is "professional," and thereby loses "amateur" status, you are making a claim of definition. Note that here we are looking at definition claims that dominate the argument in the essay as a whole. Definition is also used as a type of support, often at the beginning, to establish the meaning of one or more key terms.

Here are some additional examples of claims of definition: marriage as an institution needs to be redefined to include modern variations on the traditional family; some so-called art exhibits could more accurately be described as pornography exhibits; the fetus is a human being, not just a group of cells; wars in the modern era can all be defined as "just" rather than "unjust" wars; sexual harassment is defined in terms of behavior and not sexual desire. Notice that the arguments introduced by these claims will focus on the definitions of family, art, fetus, just war, and sexual harassment. If you agree with the definition presented, you agree with the claim. If you do not, you may want to argue.

The following is an example of a claim of definition that appears in an article written by a scientist who was assigned to a bioethics panel to consider the future of cloning. The claim is underlined.

| Example 2 | ZYGOTES AND PEOPLE AREN'T QUITE THE SAME |

Michael S. Gazzaniga

Gazzaniga is the director of the Center for Cognitive Neuroscience at Dartmouth College.

1   Most people are now aware that medical scientists put cloning in two different categories. Biomedical cloning is distinct from reproductive cloning, the process by which a new human being might be grown from the genetic material of a single individual. At this point, no scientist or ethicist I know supports reproductive cloning of human beings. <u>The debate is solely about biomedical cloning for lifesaving medical research.</u>

2   Scientists prefer to call biomedical cloning somatic cell nuclear transfer, because that is what it is. Any cell from an adult can be placed in an egg whose own nucleus has been removed and given a jolt of electricity. This all takes place in a lab dish, and the hope is that this transfer will allow the adult cell to be re-programmed so that it will form a clump of approximately 150 cells called a blas-tocyst. This will be harvested for the stem cells it contains.[2]

Compare-and-contrast organization can dominate the development of a claim of definition and serve as the main structure. In this structure two or more objects are compared and contrasted throughout. In the essay above, comparison and contrast are used to show how cloning of stem cells differs from cloning people. In another example, a claim that expands the notion of crime to include white-collar crime, conventional crime would be compared with white-collar crime to prove that they are similar.

Topical organization may also be used. Several special qualities, characteristics, or features of the word or concept are identified and explained as discrete topics. Thus in an essay defining a criminal as mentally competent, the characteristics of mental competence would be explained as separate topics and applied to the criminal. Another strategy is to *explain the controversy* over the term and *give reasons* for accepting one view over another.

The main types of support used to prove claims of definition are *references to reliable authorities and accepted sources* that can be used to establish clear definitions and meanings, such as the dictionary or a well-known work. Also useful are *analogies* and other comparisons, especially to other words or situations that are clearly understood and that can consequently be used to shed some light on what is being defined. *Examples*, both real and hypothetical, and *signs* can also be used to clarify or develop definitions.

Claims of Cause

When you claim that staying up late at a party caused you to fail your exam the next day or that your paper is late because the library closed too early, you are making claims of cause. People often disagree about what causes something to happen, and they also disagree about the effects. Here are some other examples of claims of cause which you may or may not agree with: obesity can cause dis-ease and early death; a poor economy causes people to lose faith in their political leaders; comprehensive health care reform in the United States could lower the quality of health care for everyone; inadequate funding for AIDS victims in Africa could cause a serious resurgence of the disease; a lack of family values can lead to crime. The cause-effect relationship is at issue in these statements.

The following excerpt is from an article about conflicting views on whether or not antidepressants cause dangerous side effects in children. The claim is underlined.

---

[2]*New York Times* op-ed, April 25, 2002, p. A35.

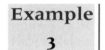

ANTIDEPRESSANTS: TWO COUNTRIES, TWO VIEWS

Sally Satel, M.D.

The author is a practicing psychiatrist and a resident scholar at the American Enterprise Institute. She also writes articles for magazines and newspapers.

1   "**W**here you stand depends on where you sit."

2   This saying usually applies to political issues, but it is also relevant to medicine. Consider the current controversy over the prescription of antidepressants to children, and the different reactions of British and American regulators and physicians.

3   After examining a series of 13 clinical trials including more than 2,300 children and adolescents, drug regulators in Britain strongly urged doctors not to use certain antidepressants, among them Paxil, Luvox, and Zoloft, for childhood depression because the risk of self-harm and suicidal thoughts was judged to be too great.

4   In the United States, however, officials at the Food and Drug Administration, relying on the same clinical data, have yet to make up their minds on the safety issue, and doctors here continue to prescribe antidepressants to children in volume. . . .

5   The important issue, then, is whether antidepressants truly worsen the potential for suicide.[3]

You can see from this example how causes and their effects can become a subject for controversy.

An organizational strategy commonly used for cause papers is to *describe causes and then effects.* Thus clear-cutting would be described as a cause that would lead to the ultimate destruction of the forests, which would be the effect. Or *effects* may be *described and then the cause or causes.* The effects of global climate change may be described before the possible causes that contribute to such change. You may also encounter refutation of other actual or possible causes or effects.

The best type of support for establishing a cause-and-effect relationship is *factual data,* including *real examples* and *statistics* that are used to prove a cause or an effect. You can also use various types of *comparison,* including parallel cases in past history to show that the cause of one event could also be the cause of another similar event. *Signs* of certain causes and effects can also be used as well as *hypothetical examples* that project possible results.

---

[3]*New York Times,* May 25, 2004, p. D6.

Claims of Value

When you claim that sororities and fraternities are the best extracurricular organizations for college students to join, you are making a claim of value. Claims of value, as their name implies, aim at establishing whether the item being discussed is either good or bad, valuable or not valuable, desirable or not desirable. It is often necessary to establish criteria for goodness or badness in these arguments and then to apply them to the subject to show why something should be regarded as either good or bad. Here are some additional examples of claims of value: public schools are better than private schools; science fiction novels are more interesting to read than romance novels; dogs make the best pets; marijuana has positive medicinal values; Facebook is better than e-mail for communicating with one's friends; viewing television is a wasteful activity; the contributions of homemakers are as valuable as those of professional women; animal rights are as important as human rights.

The following is drawn from an article about sport-utility vehicles (S.U.V.s). You can guess from the title that this author will be making a value judgment about these automobiles. The claim is underlined.

Example **4**	**BIG AND BAD** *Malcolm Gladwell*

Malcolm Gladwell has been a staff writer for *The New Yorker* magazine since 1996. He is the author of the book, *The Tipping Point*.

1   In the history of the automotive industry, few things have been quite as unexpected as the rise of the S.U.V. <u>Detroit is a town of engineers, and engineers like to believe that there is some connection between the success of a vehicle and its technical merits</u>. But the S.U.V. boom was like Apple's bringing back the Macintosh, dressing it up in colorful plastic, and suddenly creating a new market. It made no sense to them. Consumers said they liked four-wheel drive. But the overwhelming majority of consumers don't need four-wheel drive. S.U.V. buyers said they liked the elevated driving position. But when, in focus groups, industry marketers probed further, they heard things that left them rolling their eyes. As Keith Bradsher writes in *High and Mighty*—perhaps the most important book about Detroit since Ralph Nader's *Unsafe at Any Speed*—what consumers said was "If the vehicle is up high, it's easier to see if something is hiding underneath or lurking behind it." Bradsher brilliantly captures the mixture of bafflement and contempt that many auto executives feel toward the customers who buy their S.U.V.s. Fred J. Schaafsma, a top engineer for General Motors, says, "Sport-utility owners tend to be more like 'I wonder how people view me,' and are more willing to trade off flexibility or functionality to get that."[4]

---

[4]*The New Yorker*, January 12, 2004, p. 29.

Applied criteria, like "flexibility" and "functionality" in the S.U.V. example, can be used to develop a claim of value. Criteria for evaluation are established and then applied to the subject that is at issue. For example, in arguing that a particular television series is the best on television, criteria for what makes a superior series (sympathetic characters, original plots, etc.) would be identified and then applied to the series to defend it as best. The audience would have to agree with the criteria to make the argument effective. Or suppose that the claim is that toxic waste is the worst threat to the environment. A list of criteria for evaluating threats to the environment would be established and applied to toxic waste to show that it is the worst of all.

Another possibility for organizing papers that make a claim of value is to *make the claim and add a list of reasons* about why something is good or bad. Actual *cases* and *examples* can be added as support. You may also expect that *narrative* structure will sometimes be used to develop a claim of value. Narratives are real or made-up stories that can illustrate values in action, with morals or generalizations noted explicitly or implicitly along the way. An example of a narrative used to support a claim of value is the New Testament parable of the good Samaritan who helped a fellow traveler. The claim is that helping one another in such circumstances is valued and desirable behavior.

Appeals to values are important in developing claims of value. The arguer thus appeals to what the audience is expected to value. A sense of a common, shared system of values between the arguer and the audience is important for the argument to be convincing. These shared values must be established either explicitly or implicitly in the argument. *Motivational appeals* that suggest what the audience wants are also important in establishing claims of value. People place value on the things that they work to achieve. Other types of support used to establish claims of value include various types of *comparisons* that establish links with other good or bad objects or qualities. Also, *quotations from authorities* who are admired help establish both expert criteria and judgments of good or bad, right or wrong. *Examples* can also be used to demonstrate that something is good or bad. *Signs* that something is good or bad are sometimes cited; and *definitions* are used to clarify criteria for evaluation.

Claims of Policy

When you claim that all new students should attend orientation or that all students who graduate should participate in graduation ceremonies, you are making claims of policy. A claim of policy often describes a problem and then suggests ways to solve it. Here are some additional examples of policy claims: we should stop spending so much on war and start spending more on education; parents should have the right to choose the schools their children attend; small business loans should be available during a recession to help small businesses remain successful; social security should be distributed on the basis of need rather than as an entitlement; every person in the United States should have access to health care; filmmakers and recording groups should make objectionable language and subject matter known to prospective consumers.

Deciding what to do in the face of problems has always been one of the major purposes of argument. Here are selections drawn from an article in which the author, the former director of mental health for a major prison system, describes the problems created by prisons and describes his solution for these problems. His policy claim is underlined.

Example 5	**REFLECTIONS FROM A LIFE BEHIND BARS: BUILD COLLEGES, NOT PRISONS**

James Gilligan

The author directed mental health services for the Massachusetts prison system for many years. He is a faculty member in the Department of Psychiatry at the Harvard Medical School.

1   **N**either words nor pictures, no matter how vivid, can do more than give a faint suggestion of the horror, brutalization, and degradation of the prisons of this country. I speak from extensive personal knowledge of this subject, for I have spent 25 years of my professional life behind bars—not as an inmate, but as a prison psychiatrist. . . .

2   It is too late now to even begin to attempt to "reform" prisons. The only thing that can be done with them is to tear them all down, for their architecture alone renders them unfit for human beings. . . . <u>It would benefit every man, woman, and child in this country, and it would hurt no one, to demolish the prisons and replace them with much smaller, locked, secure residential schools and colleges in which the residents could acquire as much education as their intelligence and curiosity would permit.</u>[5]

The *problem–solution organization* is typical of policy claims. The problem is first described in sufficient detail so that the audience will want a solution. Then the solution is spelled out. Furthermore, the solution suggested is usually shown to be superior to other solutions by anticipating and showing what is wrong with each of the others. Sometimes the problem and solution sections are followed by a *visualization* of how matters will be improved if the proposed solution is accepted and followed. Sometimes problem–solution arguments end with an *action* step that directs the audience to take a particular course of action (vote, buy, etc.).

Data and *statistics* are used to support a policy claim, but so are moral and commonsense appeals to what people value and want. *Motivational appeals* are especially important for policy claims. The audience needs to become sufficiently motivated to think or even act in a different way. To accomplish this degree of motivation, the arguer must convince the audience that it wants to change. *Appeals to values* are also used for motivation. The audience becomes convinced it should follow a policy to achieve important values. *Comparisons* are sometimes used to support policy claims. The arguer establishes what other similar people or groups have done and suggests the same thing can work in this case also. Or a successful effort is described, and the claim is made that it would work even

---

[5]*Chronicle of Higher Education*, October 16, 1998, pp. B7–B9.

better on a broader scale. This is another type of comparison, because it compares a small-scale effort to a large-scale, expanded effort. *Quotations from authorities* are also often used to establish claims of policy. The authorities quoted, however, must be trusted and must have good credibility. Effort is usually made to establish their credentials. *Cause* can be used to establish the origin of the problem, and *definition* can be used to clarify it. *Examples* are useful to show both the extent of the problem and how things might turn out if the proposed solution is accepted.

MIXED CLAIMS

In argument, one type of claim may predominate, but other types may be present as supporting arguments or subclaims. It is not always easy to establish the predominant claim in an argument, but close reading will usually reveal a predominant type, with one or more of the other types serving as subclaims. For example, a value claim that the popular press does harm by prying into the private lives of public figures may establish the fact that this is a pervasive practice, may define what should be public and what should not be public information, may examine the causes or, more likely, the effects of this type of reporting, and may suggest future policy for dealing with this problem. All may occur in the same article. Still, the dominant claim is one of value, namely, that this practice of newswriters is a bad one. By identifying the dominant claim, you also identify the main purpose of the argument.

When planning and writing argument, you will more easily focus on the main purpose for your argument when you have established the predominant claim and have identified its type. You can use other types as subclaims if you need to do so. When you know your purpose, you can then plan appropriate organization and support for your paper, depending on the type of claim that dominates your paper. The organizational patterns and the types of support that are particularly appropriate for developing different types of claims have been introduced in this chapter and are organized in tables on pages 243 and 244. A summary of the information in this chapter about types of claims appears in Appendix 2 on pages 305–306.

CLAIMS AND ARGUMENT IN REAL LIFE SITUATIONS

As you read and write argument, you will also notice that claims follow a predictable sequence when they originate in real-life situations. In fact, argument appears most vigorous in dramatic, life-and-death situations or when a person's character is called into question. We see claims and rebuttals, many kinds of support, and every conceivable organizational strategy in these instances. For example, as juvenile crime in this country increased in recent years, the issues that emerged included these: What is causing young people to commit crimes? What can be done to protect the family unit? Is the educational system adequate? Should the criminal justice system treat young offenders differently from older criminals? Does racial discrimination contribute to juvenile crime? How can we make inner cities more livable? How can we improve social programs?

Such real-life situations, particularly when they are life-threatening as juvenile crime often is, not only generate issues; they also usually generate many arguments. Interestingly, the types of arguments usually appear in a fairly predictable order. The first arguments made in response to a new issue-generating situation usually involve claims of fact and definition. People first have to come to terms with the fact that something significant has happened. Then they need to define what happened so that they can understand it better.

The next group of arguments that appear after fact and definition often inquire into cause. People need to figure out why the event happened. Multiple causes are often considered and debated. Next, people begin to evaluate the goodness or badness of what has happened. It is usually after all of these other matters have been dealt with that people turn their attention to future policy and how to solve problems.

The issues and claims that emerged from the September 11, 2001, terrorist attacks on the World Trade Center in New York City follow this pattern. Again, people were caught off guard, and the first questions that emerged as people watched their television sets were questions of fact. "What is happening? Is this a bomb? Are we being attacked?" Definition arguments followed. The issue was how to define what had happened, which would help determine the country's response. The president and his advisers defined the situation as an act of terrorism and then declared a war on terrorism.

Causal arguments engaged people for a long time after the initial event. Possible causes of the attacks included the presence of evil in the world, the terrorists' desire for power, religious conflicts, the uneven opportunities between developed and developing nations, hatred of America, even biblical prophecy. At the same time many value arguments appeared in the media. The questions were, "How bad is this?" and "Can any good be discovered?" Pictures of grieving survivors and of the excavation work at Ground Zero, along with obituaries of the dead, forcefully demonstrated the bad effects. Some good was found in the heroic efforts of passengers on one of the planes who attacked the terrorists and died with them as well as in the selfless efforts of New York police officers and firefighters, many of whom died in the rescue effort in the buildings.

Deliberations about policy followed. Many American citizens, on their own intitiative, decided to fly the American flag and to donate money to the survivors. Government officials set policy on how to conduct a war on terrorism. Many additional arguments about policy followed about how to get the donated money to the deserving victims; how to identify the terrorists and then how to find, try them in court, and convict them; how to know when the war was over; and how best to protect the country from future attack.

VALUE OF THE CLAIMS AND THE CLAIM QUESTIONS FOR READING AND WRITING ARGUMENT

Readers of argument find the list of the five types of claims and the questions that accompany them useful for identifying the claim and the main purpose in an argument: to establish fact, to define, to establish cause, to assign value, or to propose a solution. Claims and claim questions can also help readers identify minor purposes in an argument, those that are developed as subclaims. When a reader is able to discover the overall purpose of an argument, it is much easier to make predictions and to follow the argument.

Writers of argument find the list of the five types of claims and the questions that accompany them useful for analyzing an issue, writing a claim about it, and identifying both the controlling purpose for a paper and additional ideas that can be developed in the paper. Here is an example of how this can work. The author writes the issue in the form of a question, as in the example "Should high schools be safer places?" Then the author asks the claim questions about this issue and writes a paragraph in response to each of them: Is it a fact that high schools are unsafe places? How should we define *unsafe*? What causes a lack of safety in high schools, and what are its effects? Is a lack of safety good or bad? What criteria could be established to judge the goodness or badness of safety in high schools? What can be done to make high schools safer places?

Finally, the author reads the paragraphs and selects the one that is most promising to form the major claim and purpose in the paper. For example, suppose the author decides to write a policy paper, and the claim becomes "Parents, students, teachers, and administrators all need to cooperate to make high schools safer places." To show how that can be done becomes the main purpose of the paper. The information generated by asking the other claim questions, however, can also be used in the paper to provide reasons and evidence. The claim questions, used in this way as part of the prewriting process, can generate considerable information and ideas for a paper.

SOME OTHER PRELIMINARY QUESTIONS TO HELP YOU DEVELOP YOUR CLAIM

In addition to the claim questions, you can also ask the following questions to clarify and develop your claim. Some tentative answers to these questions now can help you stay on track and avoid problems with the development of your paper later.

Is the Claim Narrow and Focused? You may have started with a broad issue area, such as technology or education, that suggests many related specific issues. You may have participated in brainstorming sessions in class to discover some of the specific issues related to an issue area, and this work may have helped you narrow your issue. You may now need to narrow the issue even further by focusing on one prong or aspect of it. Here is an example.

Issue area: The environment

> *Related specific issue:*
> What problems are associated with nuclear energy?
> *Aspects of that issue:*
> What should be done with nuclear waste?
> How hazardous is nuclear energy, and how can we control the hazards?
> What are the alternatives to nuclear energy?

In selecting a narrowed issue to write about, you may want to focus on only one of the three listed aspects of the nuclear energy problem. You might, for instance, decide to make this claim: *Solar power is better than nuclear energy.* Later, as you write, you may need to narrow this topic even further and revise your claim: *Solar power is better than nuclear energy for certain specified purposes.* Any topic can turn out to be too broad or complicated when you begin to write about it.

You could also need to change your focus or perspective to narrow your claim. You may, for example, begin to research the claim you have made in response to your issue but discover along the way that the real issue is something else. As a result, you decide to change your claim. For example, suppose you decide to write a policy paper about freedom of speech. Your claim is, *Freedom of speech should be protected in all situations.* As you read and research, however, you discover that an issue for many people is a narrower one related to freedom of speech, specifically as it relates to violence on television and children's behavior. In fact, you encounter an article that claims that television violence should be censored even if doing so violates free speech rights. You decide to refocus your paper and write a value paper that claims, *Television violence is harmful and not subject to the protection of free speech rights.*

Which Controversial Words in Your Claim Will You Need to Define? Identify the words in your claim that may need to be defined. In the example just used, you would need to be clear about what you mean by *television violence, censorship,* and *free speech rights.*

Can You Learn Enough to Cover the Claim Fully? If the information for an effective paper is unavailable or too complicated, write another claim, one that you know more about and can research more successfully. Or, narrow the claim further to an aspect that you can understand and develop.

How Can You Make Your Claim Both Interesting and Compelling to Yourself and Your Audience? Develop a fresh perspective on your issue when writing your claim. Suppose you are writing a policy paper that claims public education should be changed. You get bored with it. You keep running into old reasons that everyone already knows. Then you discover a couple of new aspects of the issue that you could cover with more original ideas and material. You learn that some people think parents should be able to choose their children's school, and you learn that competition among schools might lead to improvement. You also learn that contractors can take over schools and manage them in order to improve them. You refocus your issue and your perspective. Your new fact claim is, *Competition among schools, like competition in business, leads to improvement.* The issue and your claim now have new interest for you and your audience because you are looking at them in a whole new way.

At What Point Are You and the Audience Entering the Conversation on the Issue? Consider your audience's background and initial views on the issue to decide how to write a claim about it. If both you and your audience are new to the issue, you may decide to stick with claims of fact and definition. If your audience understands it to some extent but needs more analysis, you may decide on claims of cause or value. If both you and your audience have adequate background on the issue, you may want to write a policy claim and try to solve the problems associated with it. Keep in mind also that issues and audiences are dynamic. As soon as audiences engage with issues, both begin to change. So you need to be constantly aware of the current status of the issue and the audience's current stand on it.

REVIEW QUESTIONS

1. What are the five types of claims?
2. What are the questions associated with each type?
3. What is a predictable sequence that claims follow when they originate in a dramatic, real-life situation?
4. How do claims typically appear in written argument? That is, do writers usually limit themselves to a single purpose and claim or not? Discuss.
5. What events have occurred in the past few months either on campus or on the national or international level that have generated issues? What are some of these issues? What types of claims have been made in response to these issues?

CLASS ACTIVITIES AND WRITING ASSIGNMENTS

1. **Analyze the Types of Claims**
    a. Refer to the essays and advertisement listed below. What purpose and type of claim predominates in each item? Here are the types again: *fact, definition, cause, value,* and *policy.* In each item, underline a sentence that might best serve as the claim, and provide additional evidence from the text to support your designation.
       1. "'A' Is for 'Absent,'" pages 25–26.
       2. "Welcome to the Club," pages 39–40.
       3. "American Value Systems," pages 114–120.
       4. Sense of Community advertisement, page 110.
       5. "Brother, Can You Spare a Word," pages 111–112.
    b. Bring in the front page of a current newspaper. Identify headlines for stories that probably deal with controversial topics. Predict from each headline, and the first paragraph if you need it, the type of claim that will be made in the story.

2. **Read the Following Essay and Analyze the Claim**
    This essay will raise most of the claim questions in your mind about the subject of adultolescents, the trend for college graduates to return home after college for a period of time before they become independent of their parents. More than one type of claim is made. What do you think is the predominant type of claim?

BEFORE YOU READ: Do you know any individuals who have returned home to live with their parents after they had been gone for a time? What were the circumstances?

Essay 1	

BRINGING UP ADULTOLESCENTS*

Peg Tyre

Tyre, a former CNN reporter, now writes freelance articles about various public issues.

1 When Silvia Geraci goes out to dinner with friends, she has a flash of anxiety when the check comes. She can pay her share—her parents give her enough money to cover all her expenses. It's just that others in her circle make their own money now. "I know I haven't earned what I have. It's been given to me," says Geraci, 22, who returned to her childhood home in suburban New York after graduating from college last year. "It's like I'm stuck in an in-between spot. Sometimes I wonder if I'm getting left behind." Poised on the brink of what should be a bright future, Geraci and millions like her face a thoroughly modern truth: it's hard to feel like a Master of the Universe when you're sleeping in your old twin bed.

2 Whether it's reconverting the guest room back into a bedroom, paying for graduate school, writing a blizzard of small checks to cover rent and health-insurance premiums or acting as career counselors, parents across the country are trying to provide their twentysomethings with the tools they'll need to be self-sufficient—someday. In the process, they have created a whole new breed of child—the adultolescent.

3 For their part, these overgrown kids seem content to enjoy the protection of their parents as they drift from adolescence to early adulthood. Relying on your folks to light the shadowy path to the future has become so accepted that even the ultimate loser move—returning home to live with your parents—has lost its stigma. According to the 2000 Census, nearly 4 million people between the ages of 25 and 34 live with their parents. And there are signs that even more moms and dads will be welcoming their not-so-little-ones back home. Last week, in an online survey by MonsterTRAK.com, a job-search firm, 60 percent of college students reported that they planned to live at home after graduation—and 21 percent said they planned to remain there for more than a year.

4 Unlike their counterparts in the early '90s, adultolescents aren't demoralized slackers lining up for the bathroom with their longing-to-be-empty-nester parents. Iris and Andrew Aronson, two doctors in Chicago, were happy when their daughter, Elena, 24, a Smith graduate, got a modest-paying job and moved back home last year. It seemed a natural extension of their parenting philosophy—make the children feel secure enough and they'll eventually strike out on their own. "When she was an infant, the so-called experts said letting babies cry

*Newsweek, March 25, 2002, 38–40.

themselves to sleep was the only way to teach them to sleep independent of their mother," says Iris. "But I never did that either." Come fall, Elena is heading off to graduate school. Her sister, who will graduate from Stanford University this spring, is moving in. Living at home works, Elena explains, because she knows she's leaving. "Otherwise, it'll feel too much like high school," says Elena. "As it is, sometimes I look around and think, 'OK, now it's time to start my homework.'"

5   Most adultolescents no longer hope, or even desire, to hit the traditional benchmarks of independence—marriage, kids, owning a home, financial autonomy—in the years following college. The average age for a first marriage is now 26, four years later than it was in 1970, and childbearing is often postponed for a decade or more after that. Jobs are scarce, and increasingly, high-paying careers require a graduate degree. The decades-long run-up in the housing market has made a starter home a pipe dream for most people under 30. "The conveyor belt that transported adolescents into adulthood has broken down," says Dr. Frank Furstenberg, who heads up a $3.4 million project by the MacArthur Foundation studying the adultolescent phenomenon.

6   Beyond the economic realities, there are some complicated psychological bonds that keep able-bodied college graduates on their parents' payroll. Unlike the Woodstock generation, this current crop of twentysomethings aren't building their adult identity in reaction to their parents' way of life. In the 1960's, kids crowed about not trusting anyone over 30; these days, they can't live without them. "We are seeing a closer relationship between generations than we have seen since World War II," says University of Maryland psychologist Jeffrey Jensen Arnett. "These young people genuinely like and respect their parents."

7   To some, all this support and protection—known as "scaffolding" among the experts—looks like an insidious form of codependence. Psychiatrist Alvin Rosenfeld says these are the same hyperinvolved parents who got minivan fatigue from ferrying their kids to extracurricular activities and turned college admission into a competitive sport. "They've convinced themselves they know how to lead a good life, and they want to get that for their kids, no matter what," says Rosenfeld.

8   By the time those children reach their 20s, says market researcher Neil Howe, their desires for the future are often indistinguishable from the desires of their parents. "The Me Generation," says Howe, "has simply turned into the Mini-Me Generation."

9   Trying to guarantee your children the Good Life, though, can sometimes backfire. A few years ago, Janice Charlton of Philadelphia pressured her daughter, Mary, then 26, to get a master's degree, even agreeing to cosign two $17,000 school loans if she did. Mary dropped out, Janice says, and the loans went into default. "I'm sorry I ever suggested it," says Janice. "We're still close but it's a sticky issue between us."

10   Many parents say they're simply ensuring that their kids have an edge in an increasingly competitive world. When Tom D'Agnes's daughter, Heather, 26, told him she was thinking about graduate school, D'Agnes, 52, flew from their home in Hawaii to San Francisco to help her find one. He edited the essay section of her application and vetted her letters of recommendation, too. While Tom's wife, Leona, worried about creating a "dependency mentality," Tom was adamant about giving his daughter a leg up.

11   Parents aren't waiting to get involved. Campus career counselors report being flooded with calls from parents anxious to participate in their college senior's job search. Last fall the U.S. Navy began sending letters describing their programs to potential recruits—and their parents. "Parents are becoming actively involved in the career decisions of their children," says Cmdr. Steven Lowry, public-affairs officer for Navy recruiting. "We don't recruit the individual anymore. We recruit the whole family."

12   The steady flow of cash from one generation of active consumers to another has marketers salivating. These twenty-somethings are adventuresome, will try new products and have a hefty amount of discretionary money. "They're willing to spend it on computers and big-screen TVs, travel and sports cars, things that other generations would consider frivolous," says David Morrison, whose firm, Twentysomething Inc., probes adultolescents for companies like Coca-Cola and Nokia.

13   Jimmy Finn, 24, a paralegal at the Manhattan-based law firm of Sullivan & Cromwell, made the most of his $66,000 annual income by moving back to his childhood home in nearby Staten Island. While his other friends paid exorbitant rents, Finn bought a new car and plane tickets to Florida so he could see his girl-friend on the weekends. He had ample spending money for restaurants and cabs, and began paying down his student loans. "New York is a great young person's city but you can't beat home for the meals," says Finn.

14   With adultolescents all but begging for years of support after college, many parents admit they're not sure when a safety net becomes a suffocating blanket. "I've seen parents willing to destroy themselves financially," says financial plan-ner Bill Mahoney of Oxford, Mass. "They're giving their college graduates $20,000, $30,000, even $40,000—money they should be plowing into retire-ment." And it might only buy them added years of frustration. Psychiatrists say it's tough to convince a parent that self-sufficiency is the one thing they can't give their children.

15   No matter how loving the parent-child bond, parents inevitably heave a sigh of relief when their adult kids finally start paying their own way. Seven months ago, when Finn's paralegal job moved to Washington, D.C., he left home and got an apartment there. The transition, he said, was hard on his mother, Margie. Mom, though, reports that she's doing just fine. She's stopped making plates of ziti and meatballs for her boy and has more time for her friends. "The idea all along was that he should be self-sufficient," she says. It just took a little while.

For Discussion:

This article will raise most of the claim questions in your mind: What are adulto-lescents? Do they really exist? What has caused this situation? How good or bad is it? What should we do about it? The author deals with all these questions. Which of these questions, however, seems to dominate the article? What are your experiences with the trend described in this article? Compare your experi-ences with those of your classmates.

3. **Writing Assignment: Types of Claims**

   Write a 250- to 300-word paper that is organized around a single type of claim. Use the following claims about campus issues as starter sentences for your paper. Before you write, spend a few minutes with classmates to brainstorm some ideas for each of the papers. If you need more information, go to the Financial Aid Office for topic *a*, the Office of Student Affairs for topics *b* or *d*, to the Registrar's Office for topic *e*, and the Office of Institutional Studies or the Registrar for topic *c*. You might also interview students and faculty or consult the Internet. Use some of the ideas about organizational patterns and support described in this chapter to help you think about and develop your ideas.

   a. Is it true? Does it exist? *Claim of fact:* <u>Financial aid for students (is or is not) readily available on our campus</u>.
      Hint: Try a claim with reasons or a topical pattern of organization. Add facts, statistics, and real examples.
   b. How should we define it? *Claim of definition:* <u>A dangerous level of alcohol consumption is not defined by everyone in exactly the same way</u>.
      Hint: Explain the controversy over what is considered a dangerous level. Quote an authoritative source that defines the term "dangerous level." Compare definitions of dangerous and not-dangerous levels and use examples and statistics as support.
   c. What caused it? What are the effects? *Claim of cause:* <u>Various causes contribute to the student dropout problem in colleges</u>.
      Hint: Describe the major causes for students leaving college before they graduate. Use factual data, including statistics and examples as support. Describe the effects on the students themselves.
   d. Is it good or bad? *Claim of value:* <u>Student organizations (do or do not) contribute significant positive value to the college experience</u>.
      Hint: Make a list of the positive values that student organizations provide students, or, make a list of negative values that show students should not join these organizations. Apply them to one or more student organizations. Since you are not writing a personal values paper, create broad interest by appealing to what you think most students would value or want.
   e. What is the problem and what should we do to solve it? *Claim of policy:* <u>Students do not always know their academic standing in all of their courses during a semester, and measures should (or should not) be taken to correct this lack of information</u>.
      Hint: Try a problem–solution pattern of organization. Use examples, comparisons, quotes from authorities, and appeals to values and motives. Consider identifying several solutions followed by the one(s) you consider best, and say why.

   ◆ 4. **Prewriting: Develop Your Claim for a Future Position Paper**

   Complete the following worksheet by writing answers to the questions. They will help you focus on your claim and ways to develop it. Discuss your answers with the other members in your writing group, or discuss some of your answers with the whole class.

WORKSHEET 6: CLAIM DEVELOPMENT

1. Write an issue question to focus your issue.
2. Freewrite in response to the claim questions. They are as follows:
   Fact: Did it happen? Does it exist?
   Definition: What is it? How can I define it?
   Cause: What caused it? What are the effects?
   Value: Is it good or bad? Who agrees and who disagrees? What do they value? What criteria will help us decide the potential value or lack of value?
   Policy: What should we do about it? What should be our future course of action? Consider several possible courses of action; if appropriate, identify the one you think is best, and say why.
3. Read what you have written and decide on a purpose. Write your claim as a complete sentence.
4. Which will be your predominant argumentation purpose in developing the claim: fact, definition, cause, value, or policy?
5. What is your original slant on the issue, and is it evident in the claim?
6. Is the claim too broad, too narrow, or manageable for now? Elaborate.
7. How will you define the controversial words in your claim?
8. Do you predict at this point that you may have to qualify your claim to make it acceptable to the audience? How?

Chapter

7

The Types of Proof: Supporting the Claim

You learned in Chapter 5 that the claim, the support, and the warrants are the three parts that are present in any argument. Chapter 6 helped you understand claims. This chapter will help you understand the support and warrants that provide proofs for the claim. You are reading this chapter because it will help you plan effective and convincing proof for the papers you write for your college classes. The success of an argument with an audience depends on the proofs, and they include all types of evidence and support for a claim. Academic writing, in particular, requires skillful use of evidence and proofs to make a claim convincing to an expert and educated audience.

You will be introduced first to the different types of proof, and then to the language and style associated with each of them. Fallacies or pseudoproofs will next be identified so that you can expose them as false proofs and avoid using them yourself. Finally, you will be provided with a list of criteria to help you recognize ethical argument and learn to distinguish it from unethical argument.

As you begin to work with the proofs, you will discover that they are not simple uniform patterns that are obvious and easy to recognize. Rather, slippery and imperfect as they are, they represent an attempt to describe what goes on in the world of argument, both inside and outside the classroom, and in the minds of writers and readers of argument. Understanding them can put you closer to an author so that you can better understand how that individual thought about, interpreted, and developed a particular subject. When you switch roles and become the author yourself, your knowledge of what can happen in argument will help you develop your own thoughts and create your own effective arguments.

THE TRADITIONAL CATEGORIES OF PROOF

The traditional categories of proof, like much of our most fundamental argument theory, were first articulated by classical theorists, and they are still useful for describing what goes on in argument today. Aristotle's *Rhetoric*, written somewhere between 360 and 334 B.C., is a key text in the history of argument theory. Its purpose is to train persuasive speakers to be convincing to audiences. Aristotle says in the *Rhetoric* that an arguer must state a claim (or a proposition) and prove it. He goes into detail about the broad categories of proof that can be used to establish the probability of a claim. Aristotle's categories of proof are still useful because they accurately describe what classical arguers did then, and what modern arguers still do, and because they have become such an accepted part of our intellectual heritage. Like generations before us, we learn these methods and use them to observe, think about, and interpret reality. Aristotle's ideas and observations continue to provide accurate descriptions of what goes on in argument.

Aristotle distinguishes between proofs that can be produced and laid on the table, so to speak, like a murder weapon, fingerprints, or a written contract, and proofs that are invented and represent the creative thinking and insights of clever and intelligent people.

Aristotle divides this second category of proof into three subcategories: proofs that appeal to logic and reason, proofs that establish the credibility of the source, and proofs that appeal to the emotions. The Greek words used to refer to the proofs are *logos* (logic), *ethos* (credibility), and *pathos* (emotion).

Logical proof appeals to people's reason, understanding, and common sense. It is consistent with what we know and believe, and it gives us fresh insight and ideas about issues. As proof, it relies mainly on such support as reasoned opinion and factual data as well as on warrants that suggest the soundness and truth of such support. Aristotle declared that logical proof is the most important kind of proof in argument, and most modern theorists agree with him. Richard M. Weaver, a well-known modern rhetorician, for example, says that argument has its primary basis in reasoning and that it appeals primarily to the rational part of humans. Logical proof, he says, provides the "plot" of argument.[1] The other two types of proof are also present and important, however.

Proof that establishes ethos appeals to the audience's impressions, opinions, and judgments about the individual stating the argument. An arguer who demonstrates competence, good character, fair-mindedness, and goodwill toward the audience is more convincing than the arguer who lacks these qualities. Those who project such favorable qualities to an audience have established good *ethos*. Audiences are more likely to trust and believe individuals with good *ethos* than those without it. At times, arguers also need to establish the *ethos* of the experts whom they quote in their arguments. They usually accomplish this purpose by providing information about these authorities so that audiences will appreciate their mastery or expertise and consequently be more willing to accept what they say.

---

[1]Richard M. Weaver, "Language Is Sermonic," in Richard L. Johannesen, ed., *Contemporary Theories of Rhetoric: Selected Readings* (New York: Harper & Row, 1971), pp. 163–79.

Emotional proof is used to appeal to and arouse the feelings of the audience. The audience's feelings are aroused primarily through emotional language, examples, personal narratives, and vivid descriptions of events that contain emotional elements and that provoke strong feelings in other people. Emotional proof is appropriate in an argument when it is used to develop the claim and when it contributes to the sense of logical conviction and agreement that are argument's intended outcomes. A well-reasoned set of logical proofs contributes to such outcomes. Emotion contributes as well to the strength of the acceptance of a logical conclusion. Imagine, for example, an argument in favor of increasing taxes to build housing for homeless people. The logical argument would describe reasons for these taxes, methods for levying them, and recommendations for spending them. The argument would be strengthened, however, by one or more vivid and emotional examples of homeless people who lead miserable lives. Visual argument, as you will learn in Chapter 9, also relies on these same proofs to strengthen its claims.

The next three sections will introduce you to seven types of logical proof, one type of proof that builds *ethos,* and two types of emotional proof. All are commonly used in argument. The number and variety of logical proofs is greater because logical thinking dominates and provides the "plot" for most argument. However, *most arguments rely on a variety of proofs because offering several types of proof usually makes a stronger argument than relying on only one.*[2]

Each type of proof will be explained briefly. The proofs are summarized in Appendix 2 (pages 307–312) where you will also find an additional example and some critical questions you can ask to test the reliability and validity of each proof. The test of validity questions can also help you locate the weaknesses in an argument, which will help you plan rebuttal and formulate arguments of your own.

TYPES OF LOGICAL PROOF: *LOGOS*

Logical proofs (also called substantive proofs) include facts, reasons, and opinions that are based on reality. Such proofs rely on factual information, statistics, and accounts of actual events, past and present. The support used in logical proof is real and drawn from experience. Logical (or substantive) warrants guarantee the reliability and relevance of this support. Logical proofs represent common ways of thinking about and perceiving relationships among the events and data of the real world and offer those ideas and relationships as support for a line of argument.

A Mnemonic Device

It is helpful to be able to remember the full range of logical proofs both when you are reading and when you are developing a paper so that you can use them more readily. Figure 7.1 provides a mnemonic device that will help you remember

---

[2]In this chapter I have drawn on some of Wayne Brockriede and Douglas Ehninger's ideas in "Toulmin on Argument: An Interpretation and Application." *Quarterly Journal of Speech* 46 (1969): 44–53. I have expanded and adapted these authors' analysis of proofs to make it apply to the reading and writing of argument as explained in this book.

Sign
Induction
Cause
Deduction
Analogies (historical, literal, figurative)
Definition
Statistics

"SICDADS" refuted by logical proof

FIGURE 7.1   The Seven Logical Proofs: Their Initials Spell Out SICDADS.

them. It shows the first letter of each proof rearranged to make a nonsense word, SICDADS, and a picture to help you remember it. You can run through this mnemonic mentally when you are thinking about ways to develop the ideas in argument you create.

Now let us consider the seven logical proofs in the order created by the mnemonic SICDADS.

Argument from Sign

A *specific visible sign* is sometimes used to prove a claim. A sign can be used to prove with *certainty:* someone breaks out in chicken pox, and the claim, based on that certain sign, is that the person has chicken pox. Or, a sign can be used to prove the *probability* of a claim: a race riot, someone argues, is probably a sign of the claim that people think they are treated unfairly. Or, the sign may turn out to be a pseudoproof, the "proof" of a false claim: a child asks, "Why should I believe in Santa Claus?" and the parent answers, "Look at all the toys under the tree that weren't there yesterday." That support is used as a sign for the claim that Santa Claus exists. The rumbling in the streets of San Francisco, described in the first paragraph of "Undocumented, Indispensable" by Anna Quindlen (page 161), is caused by thousands of people marching, which, in this case, is a sign of significant public unrest.

Sign Warrants. You are expected to assume that the sign is actually a sign of what the author claims it to be.

Argument from Induction

Inductive argument provides a number of examples and draws a claim, in the form of a conclusion, from them. For example, four different people take their cars to the same car repair shop and are overcharged. The claim is then made that anyone who takes a car to that repair shop will probably be overcharged. The audience is expected to accept the group of examples as adequate and accurate enough to make the inductive leap to the claim. Inductive argument is also called *argument from generalization* or *argument from example* because the claim is a generalization made on the basis of the examples. To help you remember the special features of inductive argument, learn its prefix *in-*, which means "in" or "into," and the root *duc*, which means "lead." *An inductive argument uses examples to lead into a claim or generalization about the examples.*

In the Declaration of Independence, Thomas Jefferson listed several examples of "repeated injuries" that the king of Great Britain was guilty of in dealing with the United States. From these examples, Jefferson drew the conclusion that the United States was justified in declaring the United States free and independent of Great Britain. This is another example of argument from induction.

Inductive reasoning is the basis of the scientific method. Most scientific conclusions are reached inductively. When a sufficient number of phenomena are observed repeatedly, a generalization is made to explain them. Induction demonstrates *probability* rather than truth when there is the possibility of even a single example that would prove an exception. For instance, an unpromising student *may* become an unpromising adult. But an apple *always* falls from the tree, thereby demonstrating gravity, and the sun *always* comes up, demonstrating that law of nature. No one has been able to find exceptions to disprove these last two generalizations.

Look back at the third paragraph of Sally Satel's article "Antidepressants: Two Countries, Two Views" (page 126). The author refers to 13 clinical trials that examined the effects of antidepressants on more than 2,300 children and adolescents. The conclusion drawn from these examples is that these medicines should not be used for children and adolescents because of the risk of self-harm or suicide. This is an example of inductive reasoning: the multiple examples led to the final conclusion.

Inductive Warrants. You are expected to assume that the list of examples is representative and that it shows a definite trend. You are also expected to assume that if you added more examples of the same general type, the conclusion would not change.

Argument from Cause

Argument from cause places the subject of the argument in a *cause-and-effect relationship* to show that it is either the cause of an effect or the effect of a cause. Thus the argument might aim to prove that violent video games cause children to become violent; or, conversely, violent children become that way as a result of playing violent video games. It is very common in argument to explain or to justify a claim with cause-and-effect reasoning. Cause and effect can serve as an organizational pattern for the whole essay, or it can serve as a proof to develop one aspect or idea in an essay.

Historians frequently use argument from cause. When they ask why a certain historical event occurred, they are seeking the cause, though they do not always agree on the same causes. For example, several causes have been given for the most recent war on Iraq, including the existence of weapons of mass destruction, threatened U.S. oil interests, and the need to liberate the Iraqi people. There has been considerable disagreement about which of these are the actual causes for that war. There has also been disagreement about the immediate and long-term effects that each of these causes may eventually have on the history of that country. "Bringing Up Adultolescents" (pages 135–137) provides another example of argument from cause. This article claims that parents, in their efforts to help their adult children get good jobs and become as successful as they are, are causing these children to become "adultolescents," a term for the educated young in their twenties who are postponing the responsibilities of an independent adulthood by living at home.

Causal Warrants. You are expected to assume that the causes really do create the identified effects or that the effects really are the results of the named causes.

Argument from Deduction

Deductive argument is also called *argument from principle* because its warrant is a general principle. Remember that the warrant may or may not be stated explicitly in an argument. Etymology can help you remember the special features of deductive argument. The prefix *de-* means "from" and the root *duc* means "lead." *A deductive argument leads from a general principle*, which is the warrant, applies it to an example or specific case, which is described in the support, and draws a conclusion, which is the claim. For example, a general principle (warrant) might be: families cannot be happy when the mother works outside the home. The specific case would be an example of a family in which the mother works and the children spend hours at home alone in front of television. The conclusion would be that this is an unhappy family.

Here is another example of deductive argument. The author of "'A' Is for 'Absent'" (pages 25–26) states the general principle for his argument as follows: Students with high test scores and excessive absences should receive grades based only on the test scores and not the absences. The supporting example is the author himself who has good test scores but also excessive absences. The conclusion is that the author should receive grades based only on the test scores and not the absences.

Deductive Warrants. You are expected to assume that a general principle about a whole category of phenomena (people, places, events, and so forth) has been stated or implied in the argument and that it is accurate and acceptable. You are expected to decide that since the general principle, or warrant, and the support for the specific case are both accurate and acceptable, the conclusion is also acceptable and probably true. If you have a problem with either the warrant or the example in a deductive argument, you will find the conclusion unacceptable also.

Argument from Historical, Literal, or Figurative Analogy

Historical and literal analogies explore *similarities and differences* between items in the same general category, and *figurative analogies* do the same, only with items in very different categories. In drawing analogies, we show how something we may not know much about is like something we know in greater detail. *In other words, we interpret what we do not know in the light of what we do know*. We then supply the warrant that what happened in one case will happen in the other, we draw conclusions, and we make a claim based on the comparisons in the analogy.

Historical Analogies. These explain what is going on *now* in terms of what went on in similar cases *in the past*. Future outcomes are also often projected from past cases. The idea is that what happened in the past will probably repeat itself in the present. Also, the two events are so similar that the results of the former will surely be the end result of the latter. The argument that since U.S. citizens lost faith in the Vietnam war, they will probably also lose faith in the war in Afghanistan, is an historical analogy. Anyone wishing to refute this argument could point out that the differences in the two wars make this claim unlikely or too imprecise.

Literal Analogies. These compare two items in the *same category:* two school systems, two governments, two religions, two individuals. Outcomes are described as in historical analogies—that is, what happened in one case will happen in the other because of the similarities or the differences. An author argues that standardized tests in one school system will lower the quality of education because students who strive for higher scores on these tests neglect to learn the important material that is never tested, and students in other schools will repeat this pattern because of the similarity among students.

Figurative Analogies. These compare items from *two different categories*, as in metaphor, but the points of comparison in a figurative analogy are usually spelled out in more detail than they are in a metaphor. Many figurative analogies appeal to the emotions rather than to reason. Figurative analogies are effective as logical proof only when they are used to identify *real qualities* that are shared by both items and that can then be applied to help prove the claim logically. When the items in a figurative analogy are compared either to add ornament or to stir up an emotional response, the analogy functions as emotional proof. It engages the emotions rather than the reason. The author of the argument about S.U.V.s (page 127) uses a figurative analogy when he says, "the S.U.V. boom was like Apple's bringing back the Macintosh, dressing it up in colorful plastic, and suddenly creating a new market." This analogy is used to suggest that neither of these products were sensible additions to the market.

Analogy Warrants. You are expected to assume that the items being compared are similar as described and that what happens in one case will probably occur in the other. For figurative analogies you are expected to assume that the qualities of the two items are similar and significant enough so that reference to one will help explain the other and will serve as convincing proof.

Argument from Definition

Definition is extremely important in argument. It is difficult to argue about any subject unless there is general agreement about the meanings of the *key terms*. This is especially true when they are part of the claim. Sometimes an entire argument is based on the audience's acceptance of a certain meaning of a key term. If the audience accepts the definition, the arguer says that the claim should be accepted "by definition."

For example, if the law defines marriage as joining only a man and a woman, and a gay couple wants to get married, that act, because of the definition, is against the law. The way to change that outcome is to change the definition of marriage. Argument by definition takes the form of deductive argument. It is listed separately here to emphasize the important function of definition in arguments that depend on it as major proof.

Here is a second example. The author of the essay "Zygotes and People Aren't Quite the Same" (pages 124–125) defines *zygotes* as "not human beings." He goes on to say that biomedical cloning conducts experiments with zygotes. The claim drawn from these statements is that biomedical cloning does not experiment with human beings. We will accept the claim that biomedical cloning, by definition, does not experiment with human beings only if we also accept the definition that the clumps of cells known as zygotes are not embryonic human beings.

Definition Warrants. You are expected to assume that the definition describes the fundamental properties and qualities of the term accurately so that it can be used to prove the claim.

Argument from Statistics

Like other forms of logical proof, statistics describe *relationships* among data, people, occurrences, and events in the real world, only they do so in *quantitative* terms. An example of statistics used as proof appears in paragraph 3 on page 135 of the essay "Bringing Up Adultolescents." Here, numbers and percentages are given to demonstrate the extent of the problem of adult children living with their parents, which is the subject of the essay.

Read statistical proofs carefully to determine where they come from and how reliable, accurate, and relevant they are. Note also whether the original figures have been altered or interpreted in some way. Figures are often rounded off or stated in different terms, such as percentages or plots on a graph. They are also sometimes compared to other material that is familiar to the audience to make them more interesting or memorable.[3] Various types of graphs or charts also make data and statistics visual and easier to grasp and remember.

Statistical Warrants. You are expected to assume that the data have been gathered and reported accurately by competent people, that they are representative and complete unless stated otherwise, and that they have been interpreted fairly and truthfully.

---

[3]James Wood, *Speaking Effectively* (New York: Random House, 1988), pp. 121–27.

PROOF THAT BUILDS CREDIBILITY: *ETHOS*

The materials provided in argument that help the audience gain a favorable impression of the arguer, the group the arguer represents, or the authorities and experts the arguer cites or quotes help create *ethos*, or the credibility of the author. The author may build credibility by referring to experience and credentials that establish his or her own expertise. Another way is to quote others or to use arguments from authority.

Argument from Authority

We are usually inclined to accept the opinions and factual evidence of people who are authorities and experts in their fields. For example, in an article that claims California will have another earthquake, the author describes and provides the credentials for several professors of geology from the major universities in Southern California as well as scientists from the U.S. Geological Survey Office before quoting their opinions as support. Authors themselves sometimes establish their own credentials by making references to various types of past experience that qualify them to write about their subject. Note how James Gilligan provides his own credentials in the first paragraph of his essay "Reflections from a Life Behind Bars: Build Colleges, Not Prisons," on page 129. Authors also sometimes establish the *ethos* of the group they represent, such as writing "the great Republican Party" rather than "the Republicans."

Authoritative Warrants. You are expected to assume that the information provided about the author, the group, or the expert is accurate, that these authorities are honorable, fair, reliable, knowledgeable, and experienced, and that they also exhibit goodwill toward the audience.

TYPES OF EMOTIONAL PROOF: *PATHOS*

Some argument theorists would say that there should be no appeals to emotion or attempts to arouse the emotions of the audience in argument. The idea is that an argument should appeal only to reason. Emotion, they claim, clouds reasoning and judgment and gets the argument off course. Richard M. Weaver, quoted earlier in this chapter, would disagree. Weaver points out that people are not just austerely unemotional logic machines who are interested only in deduction, induction, and cause-and-effect reasoning. People also use language to communicate feelings, values, and motives.[4]

Furthermore, when we consider that the source of much argument lies in the dramatic, emotionally laden occurrences of everyday life, we realize how impossible it is to eliminate all emotion from argument. As you read the many

---

[4]Weaver elaborates on some of the distinctions between logic and emotion in "Language Is Sermonic."

argument essays in this book, study the emotional material that professional writers use. Try to develop a sense of when emotion contributes to argument in effective and appropriate ways and when it does not.

In general, emotional proofs are appropriate in argument when the subject itself is emotional and when it creates strong feelings in both the writer and the reader. For writers of argument, emotion leads to positions on issues, influences the tone of the writing, and informs some of the interpretations. For readers, emotion leads to a stronger engagement with the issue and influences the final outcomes. Emotional proof is appropriate when the occasion justifies it and when it strengthens logical conviction. It is inappropriate when it merely ventilates feelings, serves as an ornament, or distracts the audience from the logical conclusion of the argument. Types of emotional proof focus on *motivation*, or what all people want, and on *values*, or what we consider good or bad, favorable or unfavorable, acceptable or unacceptable.

Motivational Proofs

Some proofs appeal explicitly to what all audiences are supposed to want, such as food, drink, warmth and shelter, sex, security, belongingness, self-esteem, and creativity or self-expression. Authors also sometimes appeal to the opposites of these needs and values, including hunger, cold, fear, self-doubt, boredom, or other kinds of dissatisfaction, to motivate people to change their behavior and restore themselves to a more positive state of being. Advertisements aimed at convincing young people that they should avoid taking illegal drugs often show the negative effects of drugs to appeal to people's sense of fear.

The purpose of motivational proof is to urge the audience to take prescribed steps to meet an identified need. For example, advertisements and speeches by political candidates provide obvious examples of motivational proof. Drink a certain beer or buy a brand of blue jeans, and you will be irresistible to others. Or, support a particular candidate, and you will gain job security and safe neighborhoods. Charles M. Blow in "Welcome to the Club" (pages 39–40) appeals to the insecurity and fear black people experience when they are unfairly profiled by police officers.

Motivational Warrants. Look for references to items or qualities that you might need, want, or fear and assume you need or fear them.

Value Proofs

Some proofs appeal to what all audiences are expected to value, such as fairness, reliability, honesty, loyalty, industry, patriotism, courage, integrity, conviction, faithfulness, dependability, creativity, freedom, equality, and devotion to duty. For example, an author who argues for policies and laws that protect the environment is assuming that you value the environment and think it might be in danger. Jeff Opdyke in his essay "Kids and Chores: All Work and No Pay" (see pages 86–88) appeals to the values that influence parents when they are training their children to do chores, which in this case include a sense of community, fairness, reliability, and industry.

Value Warrants. You are expected to assume that you share the author's values and that they are as important as the author says they are.

A Mnemonic Device

The mnemonic VAM (for *value, authority,* and *motivation*) may help you remember and use the proofs involving *ethos* and *pathos.*

VALUE OF THE PROOFS FOR READING AND WRITING ARGUMENT

Analyzing the proofs in an argument focuses a reader's attention on the author's reasoning, use of evidence and other supporting detail, and warrants. These are the elements in an argument that convince an audience.

Writers of argument can use the proofs to help them think of ways to develop a claim. By running through the list of proofs and asking relevant questions—What do I need to define? Should I use statistics? Can I generalize from some examples? What caused this? What can I compare this to in the past or present? Whom should I quote? What audience values and motives can I appeal to on this issue?—authors invent ideas and locate material that can be used at a specific level in a paper. The specific material is what makes a paper both interesting and convincing.

Work to create a mix of proofs in your writing. They are separated out here for explanation only. In the context of actual argument quoting a particularly reliable authority can function as both *ethos* and *logos.* Or, *ethos* and *logos* can also function as *pathos,* as they do in the essay "Welcome to the Club" (pages 39–40). Arguments that rely on personal conviction only or on an overly simple line of argument that is not well supported with evidence do not qualify as strong argumentation in an academic context.

LOGOS, ETHOS, AND *PATHOS* COMMUNICATED THROUGH LANGUAGE AND STYLE

You can learn to recognize logic, *ethos,* and emotion in argument not only by the proofs in an argument but also by the language and style associated with each of these types of appeal. Actually, you will not often encounter pure examples of one of these styles; most often, you will encounter a mix, with one of the styles predominating. The same is true of writing. You may plan to write in a logical style, but emotion and *ethos* creep in and actually help you create a richer and more varied style for your argument.

Language That Appeals to Logic

The language of logical argument, which is the language associated with reason, is sometimes called rational style. Words that carry mainly denotative meaning are favored in rational style over connotative and emotionally loaded language.

The denotative meaning of a word is the commonly held meaning that most people would agree on and also the one found in the dictionary. Examples of words that have predominantly denotative meanings and that are emotionally neutral include *introduction, facts, information,* and *literal meaning.* Most people would agree on the meanings of those words and could produce synonyms. Words with strong connotative meaning may have many extra, unique, and personal meanings or associations attached to them that vary from person to person. Examples of words with connotative meaning include *rock star, politician, mugger, family values,* and *human rights.* Asked to define such words, different people would provide personal meanings and examples that would not be exactly alike or match the denotative meanings of these words in a dictionary.

For support, rational style relies on opinion in the form of reasons, literal or historical analogies, explanations, and definitions and also on factual data, quotations, and citations from experts and authorities. Furthermore, the reader is usually not required to make as many inferences as for other, more informal styles of writing. Most parts of the argument are spelled out explicitly for the sake of agreement and a better adherence of minds.

Statements or slogans that elicit emotional response, such as "Yes, we can," "We want our country back," or "Now is the time for change," are also usually omitted in rational style. Slogans of this type substitute for logical thinking. Readers think better and draw better conclusions when provided with well-reasoned opinion, quotations from authorities, and facts.

For example, in the opening paragraph of an essay titled "The Lost Art of Political Argument," Christopher Lasch argues in favor of argument and debate.

> Let us begin with a simple proposition: What democracy requires is public debate, not information. Of course it needs information too, but the kind of information it needs can be generated only by vigorous popular debate. We do not know what we need to know until we ask the right questions, and we can identify the right questions only by subjecting our own ideas about the world to the test of public controversy. Information, usually seen as the precondition of debate, is better understood as its by-product. When we get into arguments that focus and fully engage our attention, we become avid seekers of relevant information. Otherwise, we take in information passively—if we take it in at all.[5]

Rational style, you can see, evokes mainly a cognitive, rational response from its readers.

Language That Develops *Ethos*

Authors who seek to establish their own credentials and good character use language to provide a fair-minded view of reality, one that is restrained and accurate rather than exaggerated or overly opinionated. When language is used to create positive *ethos,* an audience will trust the author as a credible source of information and opinion.

Language that develops *ethos* has several specific characteristics. To begin with, the writer exhibits a consistent awareness of the audience's background

---

[5]Christopher Lasch, "The Lost Art of Political Argument," *Harper's,* September 1990, p. 17.

and values by adopting a vocabulary level that is appropriate for the topic and the audience. The writer does not talk down, use technical jargon for an audience unfamiliar with it, or use slang or colloquial language, unless the context allows for that. Rap music, for example, invites a different vocabulary level than does a scholarly paper.

Writers intent on establishing *ethos* are sensitive to different audiences and what they will admire, trust, and accept. They try to use language precisely and to say exactly what they mean. They project an honest desire to communicate by avoiding ranting, filler material that gets off the subject, or anything that the audience would perceive as offensive or repugnant.

As you have probably already concluded, an author can destroy *ethos* and alter an audience's favorable impression by changing the language. A student who uses colloquial, everyday expressions in a formal essay written for a professor, a commencement speaker who shouts obscenities at the audience, a father who uses formal, abstract language to talk to his five-year-old—all have made inappropriate language choices for their particular audiences, thereby damaging their *ethos* with those audiences.

When you read argument, notice how an author uses language to build connections and trust and also to establish reliability with the audience. When you write argument, use language that will help your audience regard you as sincere and trustworthy. Appropriate language is important when you write a college paper. The use of slang, slogans, and street language and expressions in otherwise formal writing damages your credibility as a serious thinker. Writing errors, including mistakes in spelling, punctuation, and grammar, also destroy *ethos* because they indicate a lack of concern and goodwill for your readers.

Look back at "'A' Is for 'Absent'" (pages 25–26) and notice the language, values, and examples that this author uses to build *ethos* with a certain type of student audience. He describes a "dreaded" course, refers to the class absence policy as "allotted 'freebies,'" says that attendance policies "subvert the value of learning and education," and suggests that, since tuition pays for the professor, students should be able to make their own rules about attending class. The same language could destroy his *ethos* with readers who disagree with him.

Language That Appeals to Emotion

References to values and motives evoke feelings about what people regard as good and bad and about what they want, and authors use the language associated with emotional style in a variety of ways to express and evoke feelings about these matters. The following paragraphs describe a few special techniques that are characteristic of emotional style. Examples of each are drawn from "Bringing Up Adultolescents" (pages 135–137).

Emotionally loaded language evokes connotative meanings and causes the audience to experience feelings and associations at a personal level that are not described in dictionaries. Here is an example: "It's hard to feel like a Master of the Universe when you're sleeping in your old twin bed." Underline the words and phrases in this passage that evoke your emotions.

Emotional examples engage the emotions, as in this example: "When Silvia Geraci goes out to dinner with friends, she has a flash of anxiety when the check comes. She can pay her share—her parents give her enough money to cover all her expenses. It's just that others in her circle make their own money now." Most readers can share this type of anxiety.

Vivid description of an emotional scene creates an emotional reader response, as in this example: "Jimmy Finn, 24, a paralegal at the Manhattan-based law firm of Sullivan & Cromwell, made the most of his $66,000 annual income by moving back to his childhood home in nearby Staten Island. While his other friends paid exorbitant rents, Finn bought a new car and plane tickets to Florida so he could see his girlfriend on the weekends. He had ample spending money for restaurants and cabs, and began paying down his student loans." Notice how this description brings you into the scene, causing you to imagine the daily life of Jimmy Finn.

Narratives of emotional events draw readers into a scene just as vivid description does. Here is a story about a mother and her daughter: "A few years ago, Janice Charlton of Philadelphia pressured her daughter, Mary, then 26, to get a master's degree, even agreeing to cosign two $17,000 school loans if she did. Mary dropped out, Janice says, and the loans went into default. 'I'm sorry I ever suggested it,' says Janice. 'We're still close but it's a sticky issue between us.'" By describing the emotions of the mother, the author invites the reader to share them also.

Emotional tone, created by emotional language and examples, indicates that the author has a strong feeling about the subject and wants the audience to share that feeling. Here is an example: "No matter how loving the parent-child bond, parents inevitably heave a sigh of relief when their adult kids finally start paying their own way. Seven months ago, when Finn's paralegal job moved to Washington, D.C., he left home and got an apartment there. The transition, he said, was hard on his mother, Margie. Mom, though, reports that she's doing just fine." Also, irony and sarcasm should always be viewed as examples of emotional tone. They indicate strong feeling and a desire for change.

Figurative analogies contribute to emotion in an argument, particularly when two emotional subjects are compared and the resulting effect appeals more to emotion than to reason. For example, a researcher who is studying the adultolescent phenomenon states, "The conveyor belt that transported adolescents into adulthood has broken down." The comparison of an operational and a broken conveyor belt, particularly in their relationship to moving students toward adulthood, is supposed to have an emotional effect on the reader.

Emotional style is the easiest of all the styles to recognize because it is emotionally charged and is often close to our own experiences. Do not become distracted by emotional material or use it excessively in your own arguments. Remember, in argument, logic is the plot, and emotion and *ethos* add support. Box 7.1 on page 154 provides a summary of the characteristics of language used to appeal to reason, to establish *ethos*, and to appeal to emotion.

Now let's consider how the proofs and the language associated with them can be misused by arguers, and how this can discredit them with their audiences.

BOX 7.1	A Summary of Language and Style in Argument.

How Do You Make Appeals in Argument?

TO APPEAL TO LOGIC	TO DEVELOP *ETHOS*	TO APPEAL TO EMOTION
Style		
Theoretical abstract language	Language appropriate to audience and subject	Vivid, concrete language
Denotative meanings		Emotionally loaded language
Reasons	Restrained, sincere, fair-minded presentation	
Literal and historical analogies		Connotative meanings
Explanations	Appropriate level of vocabulary	Emotional examples
Definitions	Correct grammar	Vivid descriptions
Factual data and statistics		Narratives of emotional events
Quotations		Emotional tone
Citations from experts and authorities		Figurative analogies
Informed opinion		
Effect		
Evokes a cognitive, rational response	Demonstrates author's reliability, competence, and respect for audience's ideas and values through reliable and appropriate use of support and general accuracy	Evokes an emotional response

HOW TO RECOGNIZE FALLACIES

Authors sometimes resort to using misleading evidence and faulty reasoning when they try to be convincing. Such ineffective proofs are called *fallacies.* You will sometimes encounter fallacies in advertisements, letters to the editor, and other argumentation writing that you find both in print and online. Avoid quoting sources that contain fallacies, and avoid using them in your own writing. Fallacies in your writing, whether created by you or by the authors you choose to quote, weaken your argument and damage your *ethos.*

Fallacies can seem convincing when they appear to support what an audience already believes or wants to believe. Warrants that few people would find convincing can create the common ground necessary for argument if they hold an emotional appeal to someone's deep prejudices, unreasonable biases, or irrational beliefs, fears, or wishes. You may have encountered Web sites on the Internet, like those supported by hate groups, for example, that present support and warrants that you would never find acceptable. As you analyze the reasoning on these sites, you discover that much of it is extremist and that it supports only one narrow view. The support is often distorted, insufficient, unreliable, exaggerated, or oversimplified. Furthermore, the warrants are untrue, and emotional material is used to stir up excessive feelings rather than to prove a rational point. You can also often identify a number of specific fallacies on such sites.

When you are tempted to believe an argument that does not seem logical to you or seems to have something wrong with it, consider why you are tempted to believe it. If fallacies and unacceptable reasoning are weakening the claim or proving the argument false, analyze it and expose these problems. This will be comparatively easy to do if you already strongly disagree with the ideas and harder to do if, for some reason, you are tempted to accept them.

Recognize fallacies by asking, "Is this material relevant? Is it adequate? Do I agree? Does it support the claim?" Learning the common types of fallacies will also help you recognize and avoid them. Described here are the most common ones in the same categories we have used for genuine proofs: logic, character (*ethos*), and emotion.

Fallacies in Logic

Fallacies pose as logical proof, but you will see that they actually prove nothing at all. You may have trouble remembering all of their names; many people do. Concentrate instead on the fallacious thinking, characterized by each of them, such as introducing irrelevant material; exaggerating; providing wrong, unfair, inadequate, or even no support; harboring unacceptable warrants; drawing inappropriate conclusions; and oversimplifying the choices.

Begging the Question. No support is provided by the arguer who begs the question, and the claim is simply restated, over and over again, in one form or another. For example, "Climate change does not exist because the climate is not really changing" simply restates the same idea in other words. Here are other familiar examples: "Why is this true? It's true because I know it's true." "Everyone knows that the president of the United States has done his best for the environment because he said so" or "because he's the president."

You can remember the name of this fallacy, begging the question, by recalling that the arguer, when asked for support, begs off and simply restates the claim in the same or different words.

Red Herring. A red herring provides irrelevant and misleading support that pulls the audience away from the real argument. For example, "I don't believe we should elect this candidate because she would have to put her kids in day care" is a red herring; qualifications to hold office have nothing to do with household arrangements. Citing the existence of weapons of mass destruction as a reason for starting the war with Iraq in 2003 turned out to be a red herring when it became evident that the weapons did not exist. Authors of detective fiction sometimes use red herrings in their plots as false clues to divert the reader's attention from the real murderer.

To remember the red herring fallacy, recall that the fish, the red herring, was at one time used to train hunting dogs to follow a scent. It was not a true scent, however. The herring scent was irrelevant to the real smells of the real hunt, and the fallacy, the red herring, is irrelevant to an argument when it introduces such unrelated support. To argue that a person's parental responsibilities is a factor in the person's qualifications for a job or whether nonexistent weapons of mass destruction justify a preemptive war is to use this "fishy fallacy."

Non Sequitur. *Non sequitur* is Latin for "it does not follow." In this type of fallacy, the conclusion does not follow from the evidence and the warrant. Here are some examples: the professor in the Hawaiian shirt and gold chains must be an easy grader; the self-consciously beautiful woman who has applied for a job as a secretary would not do the job well; that man with the powerful new computer must be highly skilled in the use of computer technology. The warrants for these three examples are that the professor's clothes indicate how he will grade, beautiful women cannot be good secretaries, and owning powerful equipment implies the ability to use it. You can probably sense the problems with these warrants. They are so difficult for most people to accept that none of these examples come across as convincing arguments. Here is another example of a non sequitur: women should not be placed in executive positions because they cannot drive cars as well as men.

Straw Man. A straw man involves attributing an argument to an opponent that the opponent never made and then refuting it in a devastating way. The arguer sets up an idea, refutes it, and appears to win, even though the idea may be unrelated to the issue being discussed. For example, a political candidate might set up a straw man by claiming that his opponent has said he is too old to do the job, when in fact the opponent has never mentioned age as an issue. Then the candidate refutes the age issue by detailing the advantages of age and appears to win the argument even though this is not an issue at all. In fact, by refuting this false issue, the candidate may give the impression that he could refute any other arguments put forth by the opposition as well. The use of a straw man suggests competence where it might not actually exist.

Misusing Evidence. Stacking evidence to represent only one side of an issue that clearly has two sides gives a distorted impression of the issue. For example, to prove that television is an inspiring and uplifting medium, the only evidence given is that PBS nature shows are educational, *Friends* promotes personal bonds, and news programs and documentaries keep audiences informed. The sex and violence programming and the commercials are never mentioned. Evidence can be misused in other ways, including providing unreliable or insufficient evidence, using distorted or made-up evidence, or manipulating statistics to make them serve as false proof.

Either-Or. Some arguments are oversimplified by the arguer and presented as black-or-white, either-or choices when there are actually other alternatives. Some examples are, "This country can either have a strong defense program or a strong social welfare program," "We can develop either a strong space program or an urban development program," "A woman can either be a mother or have a career," and "A man can either go to graduate school or become a company man." No alternative, middle-ground, or compromise positions are acknowledged.

Post Hoc. This is short for *post hoc, ergo propter hoc*, a Latin phrase that translates as "after this, therefore because of this." To put it more simply, post hoc is the *fallacy of faulty cause*. For example, it is fallacious to claim in an advertisement that people will be more attractive and more popular if they drink a certain brand of cola. Look at other advertisements on television or in magazines, and you will easily find other examples of post hoc, the claim that one thing causes another when there is actually no causal relationship between them. Think of the fun-loving guys in beer advertisements, for example, and the suggestion that they got that way by drinking beer. Another example is the person who finds romance by serving a particular spaghetti sauce or using a specific cologne.

Hasty Generalization. Sometimes arguers "jump to conclusions" by basing a conclusion on too few examples. For example, someone may conclude that the justice system is hopelessly flawed because a man is sent to jail by mistake or that since some students in urban schools belong to gangs, most students in those schools belong to gangs. Hasty generalizations often contribute to stereotyping.

Fallacies That Affect Character or *Ethos*

Fallacies that are aimed at attacking character or at using character instead of evidence for proof are misleading and can damage *ethos*.

Ad Hominem. *Ad hominem* means "to the man" in Latin. An ad hominem argument attacks a person's character rather than a person's ideas. The press is notorious for such attacks during political campaigns, and so are some of the candidates themselves. The "character issue," for example, may receive more attention than more serious, substantive issues. Thus negative information is provided about the candidates' personal lives rather than about their ideas and the issues that concern them. The purpose of ad hominem arguments is to discredit these individuals with the public. Here is another example of an ad hominem attack: piety is said to have no value or validity because of the careless personal and financial habits of a television evangelist. This *ad hominem* argument directs attention away from the issue (here, the value of religious piety) and toward the person as bad. As a result we become prejudiced and biased against both an individual personally and an institution generally instead of evaluating facts or ideas when ad hominem exchange predominates.

Guilt by Association. The fallacy of guilt by association suggests that people's character can be judged by examining the character of their associates. For example, an employee in a company that defrauds the government is declared dishonest because of his association with the company, even though he may have known nothing of the fraud. Or, an observer is thrown into jail along with some political protesters simply because she was in the wrong place at the wrong time. Political figures are often judged as morally defective if they associate with people with questionable values and reputations. It is assumed that these individuals are members of these groups and guilty by association.

Using Authority Instead of Evidence. This is a variation of begging the question. The arguer relies on personal authority to prove a point rather than on evidence. For example, a salesman tells you to buy the used car because he is honest and trustworthy and he knows your neighbor.

Emotional Fallacies

Irrelevant, unrelated, and distracting emotional materials are often introduced into argument to try to convince the audience. Here are some examples.

Bandwagon Appeal. The argument is that since everyone is doing a particular thing, you should too. For example, everyone is watching reality TV, so you should jump on the bandwagon and watch it. Political and other public opinion polls are sometimes used to promote the bandwagon appeal. The suggestion is that since a majority of the people polled hold a certain opinion, you should adopt it also. Evaluate the ideas or actions being recommended before you accept them.

Slippery Slope. The slippery-slope fallacy is a scare tactic that suggests that if we allow one thing to happen, we will immediately be sliding down the slippery slope to disaster. This fallacy is sometimes introduced into environmental and abortion issues. If we allow loggers to cut a few trees, we will soon lose all the forests. Or, if a woman is required to wait twenty-four hours to consider her decision to have an abortion, soon there will be so many restrictions that no one will be able to have an abortion. This fallacy is similar to the saying about the camel that gets its nose into the tent. If we permit the nose today, we have the whole camel to deal with tomorrow. It is better not to start because disaster may result.

Creating False Needs. Emotional proofs, as you have learned, appeal to what people value and think they need. Sometimes an arguer will create a false sense of need where none exists or will unrealistically heighten an existing need. The intent is to make the argument more convincing. Advertising provides excellent examples. The housewife is told she needs a shining kitchen floor with a high gloss that only a certain wax can provide. Parents are reminded that they want smart, successful children, so they should buy a computer for each of them.

These examples of fallacies provide you with a good sense of what constitutes fallacious reasoning. Armed with this list and with the tests of validity for genuine proofs listed under "Tests of Validity" in the Summary Charts (pages 307–312), you now have what you need to evaluate the strength and validity of the proofs in an argument. This information will help you make evaluations, form rebuttals to challenge weak arguments, and create arguments of your own that rely on genuine proofs instead of fallacies. We now leave unethical argument with its fallacies and faulty evidence and turn to the subject of ethics and morality in argument.

ETHICS AND MORALITY IN ARGUMENT

A person's ability to argue persuasively has been recognized as a potentially powerful influence over other people for centuries. Thus the classical argument theorists, Aristotle, Cicero, and Quintilian, all recognized that citizens should be schooled in argumentation so that they could argue for the causes that would benefit society. They also argued that society needed moral arguers because, without them, immoral arguers would gain too much power. Plato criticized arguers who used their persuasive powers to manipulate people to achieve their own selfish ends. Basic standards that include skill in argumentation coupled with good judgment and common honesty have always been critical to ethical argument, both in classical times and in the present.

Ethical arguers must have the courage and willingness to argue logically and honestly from a strong sense of personal integrity and values. They should also have a strong sense of responsibility and feel obliged to come forward and advocate for what they believe is right. Emotional and motivational appeals should be consistent with positive value systems that will benefit not just one individual but all of society. Using emotions that cloud judgment or persuade individuals to accept ideas that the arguer does not really believe is clearly unethical.

Unethical individuals who argue mainly to manipulate public opinion often resort to fallacies and use other unethical tactics to influence and gain adherence to their points of view. Such tactics include opinion polls that push for particular points of view, exaggerated or manipulated statistics, manufactured evidence, outright lies, and deliberately fallacious reasoning. Other tactics include recasting or redefining issues to make them easier to argue, as in some of the arguments about global warming that minimize its potential dangers to the planet. Language can also be manipulated to change audience perceptions. For example, in "Brother, Can You Spare a Word?" (pages 111–112) the government's annual hunger report in 2006 was criticized for substituting the terms "low food security" and "very low food security" for the word *hunger*. It would seem that some people thought that changing the word *hunger*, with its strong negative connotations, to vague multiword terms with weaker connotations might subtly minimize the sting of the problems of poverty and starvation in the country. All of these techniques can be very effective in changing audience opinion, even when they are based on false values and motives.

People were struck by some letters discovered in Germany a few years ago that were perfect examples of excellent argumentation, but whose subject matter was totally immoral. These letters were the written orders for exterminating the Jews during World War II. Although Hitler was a convincing arguer, his values and his claims were immoral. In more recent years a political consultant working for the president of the United States was exposed as a person who had no core system of values and who was more interested in manipulating public opinion than in determining what was the best political course for the country. This individual was accused by the analysts at the time of believing in nothing.

It is important that you learn to recognize the differences between ethical and unethical argument. You can begin by asking the questions that follow and then searching for information that will help you answer them. Discussing these questions with others will help you achieve a sense of whether an argument is ethical or unethical. Also, gathering additional information about the issue and the arguer can help. Read reviews, editorials, commentaries, and look up biographical information about the author on the Internet. Inform yourself about the author's affiliations and background to help you discover his or her true purpose and motives, point of view, and values. Look for additional information on these matters, whether stated explicitly or implicitly, in the argument itself. Also, gather information on the rhetorical situation and understand some of the perspectives and positions held by others.

Ask These Questions to Help You Determine if an Argument Is Ethical or Unethical

1. Has the arguer made an adequate effort to understand the issue and its consequences and to present this information in a fair and unbiased way? Does the arguer also understand the positions held by other people? Does the arguer describe these differing positions accurately and without obvious bias or prejudice?
2. Is the arguer just and fair-minded? Is the support fair, accurate, and convincing? Can I accept the warrants? Should the claim be qualified, if it is not already?
3. Does the arguer sincerely believe that the position he or she is proposing is in the best interests both of the audience and of the larger society?
4. *Is* the position being proposed actually in the best interests of the audience and the larger society? Ask, Who is benefited and who is burdened or hurt?
5. Does the arguer seem to be manipulating the audience by hiding the real purpose of the argument, by resorting to fallacies, by using inappropriate emotional appeals, by over-simplifying or manufacturing evidence, by using inaccurate evidence, exaggerating, or telling lies?
6. Is the arguer changing the definition of words or substituting unusual words for commonly used words to cloud people's perceptions of the issue?
7. Is the arguer recasting or rewording an issue to reduce its threat when it actually represents a significant threat?
8. Do images that accompany the argument distort or exaggerate, or do they present the individual or situation accurately? (See examples on pages 205 and 206 in Chapter 9.) Do they function as reliable support that enhances the argument, or are they irrelevant, inaccurate, or insulting so that they weaken the argument?

Use this list of criteria to judge the ethical and moral qualities of the argumentation you read or view and let them also guide you when you write. You will be more convincing to your audience.

REVIEW QUESTIONS

1. Describe logical proofs, and name the seven types of logical proof. Describe proofs that build *ethos*, or credibility, and name one type of proof that builds *ethos*. Describe the emotional proofs, and name two types of emotional proofs. Use the mnemonics SICDADS and VAM to help you remember the proofs.
2. Describe some of the features of the language and style associated with each of the three types of proof.
3. What are fallacies? What are some of the qualities that characterize fallacious thinking? Under what circumstances might you be tempted to believe a fallacy?
4. Describe three characteristics of ethical argument.
5. What is the difference between *ethos* in argument and ethics in argument?

CLASS ACTIVITIES AND WRITING ASSIGNMENTS

1. **Analyze *Logos*, *Ethos*, and *Pathos* in an Advertisement**

   Study the advertisement on page 110 and identify the logical proofs, the proofs that establish *ethos*, and the emotional proofs. Which type of proof is strongest in this ad, in your opinion? Can you identify any fallacies? If so, describe them. How effective is the ad? Why do you think so?

2. **Analyze the Proofs in an Essay**

   Analyze the proofs in the essay below. Underline the material in each paragraph that helps you answer the questions in the margin. Then answer the questions that follow the essay.

BEFORE YOU READ: What are your present opinions about illegal immigration and undocumented workers in the United States?

Essay
1

UNDOCUMENTED, INDISPENSABLE*

Anna Quindlen

Anna Quindlen is a best-selling author of novels, nonfiction books, and children's books. She wrote the column Public and Private for the *New York Times* for many years. The column won a Pulitzer Prize in 1992. This essay originally appeared in *Newsweek* magazine.

What is taking place?   1   **O**n May Day a persistent rumble came from Market Street in San Francisco, but it was not the oft-predicted earthquake, or

---

*Newsweek, May 15, 2006, p. 78.

What is it a *sign* of?

at least not in the geologic sense. Thousands of people were marching down the thoroughfare, from the Embarcadero to city hall, holding signs. No HUMAN BEING IS ILLEGAL. I AM A WORKER, NOT A CRIMINAL. TODAY I MARCH, TOMORROW I VOTE. I PAY TAXES.

What *historical analogy* is made?

What result from the past will be repeated in the present?

2   The polyglot city by the bay is so familiar with the protest march that longtime citizens say it handles the inconveniences better than anyplace else. Some of them remember the Vietnam War marches, the feminist rallies. The May Day demonstration bore some resemblance to both, which was not surprising. Immigration is the leading edge of a deep and wide sea change in the United States today, just as those issues were in their own time.

What is the *effect* of new residents on established residents?

What *causes* this effect?

3   Of course, this is not a new issue. The Founding Fathers started out with a glut of land and a deficit of warm bodies. But over its history America's more-established residents have always found ways to demonize the newcomers to the nation needed to fill it and till it. It was only human, the contempt for the different, the shock of the new.

How does "conventional wisdom" *define* immigrants? What *definition* is more accurate?

4   Today, because so many immigrants have entered the country illegally or are living here on visas that expired long ago, the demagoguery has been amped up full throttle. Although the conventional wisdom is that immigrants are civic freeloaders, the woman with a sign that said I PAY TAXES was reflecting the truth. Millions of undocumented immigrants pay income taxes using a special identification number the IRS provides. They pay into the Social Security system, too, even though they're not eligible to collect benefits. In fact, they may be helping to keep the system afloat, with $7 billion currently in a designated suspense file, much of which is believed to have come from undocumented workers.

What are these *statistics* used to prove?

5   A man carrying a sign saying I AM A WORKER, NOT A CRIMINAL said he pays taxes, too, through his construction job. All three of his children were born in the United States. Although he said he had a hard time deciphering government forms—and don't we all?—he had applied for a green card and had been waiting for four years. In 2004 there was a backlog of more than 6 million unprocessed immigration petitions, a record high. So much for suggestions that immigrants are lax about regularizing their status. Clearly the laxity is at least partly federal.

What are these *statistics* used to prove?

What *general principles* are stated here?

6   It's true that immigrants use government services: schools, public hospitals. It's also true that many pay their way through income and sales taxes. Despite the rhetoric, no one really knows whether they wind up being a loss or a gain for the economy. Certainly lots of them work. A state like Arizona, for instance, could not keep pace with the demand for new homes at reasonable cost without immigrant workers, many of them undocumented.

What is the *example*?

What is the *conclusion*?

7   The counterargument is that that drives down the wages of American citizens. It's galling to hear that argument from members of Congress, who have not raised the federal minimum wage for

What do some members of Congress say *causes* low wages? What does the author say is the real *cause*?

8   Americans who are really incensed by millions of undocumented immigrants can take action, just as those marching in the streets did. They can refuse to eat fruits and vegetables picked by those immigrants. They can refuse to buy homes on which they worked. After all, if a migrant worker like Cesar Chavez could organize a national boycott of grapes, then opponents of immigration could surely organize something similar. But they won't. We like our cheap houses and our fresh fruit. And our government likes the bait-and-switch, taking taxes from workers whose existence it will not recognize. The borders are most porous in Washington, D.C.

almost a decade. Most of those politicians blame the workers for their willingness to accept low wages. Don't hold your breath waiting for significant sanctions against those companies that shut their eyes to the immigration status of their employees—and that also make large political contributions.

What *historical analogy* is drawn here? What does the author say the result would be?

What are the author's unique *credentials* for writing on this subject? How does this effect her *ethos*?

9   Full disclosure: I'm the granddaughter of immigrants, and I know how much of the melting pot is a myth. My grandparents always referred to my father as "an American boy," which meant he was not from Italy. It was not a compliment. They didn't melt; their daughter did, although one of the only times I ever saw her bitter was when she explained what the word "dago" meant.

What *motives* and *values* are appealed to in this paragraph?

Underline examples of *emotionally loaded language.*

10   There are big decisions to be made about the vast wave of undocumented workers in this country, issues that go beyond slogans and placards. But there's no premium in discussing those issues in xenophobic half-truths, in talking about what undocumented immigrants cost the country without talking about what they contribute, in talking about them as illegals when they are nannies, waiters, roofers and the parents of American citizens. One fact is indisputable: the essence of America is free enterprise and human rights. It's why people come here in the first place. WE ARE ALL IMMIGRANTS, read signs on Market Street. Some of us just got here sooner.

FOR DISCUSSION:

Read the title and the final paragraph of the essay. Then state the claim of this essay: This author wants me to believe . . .

What logical proofs does the author use to prove her claim? Which are most effective and why? How does she engage your emotions? What values and motives are present in this argument? Do you share them? How does she build *ethos*? Describe an audience who might be sympathetic to her *ethos* and her claim. Is this essay convincing to you? Why or why not? Apply the questions on page 160 and decide whether you think this is an ethical or an unethical argument. Why do you think so?

3. **Analyze the Fallacies in an Essay**

The next argument is written by an author who holds strong opinions about the subject of sexual harassment. As you read the essay, focus on specific statements with which you agree or cannot agree. Then explain why you agree or do not agree. Evaluate the evidence. Identify what you consider strengths and weaknesses in the argument. Then discuss your findings with the class.

BEFORE YOU READ: What do you associate with feminism? How do you define sexual harassment?

Essay 2

THE LATEST FROM THE FEMINIST "FRONT"*

Rush Limbaugh

The following is excerpted from the book *See, I Told You So*. The author is well known for his widely aired radio show.

1   Few of my "Thirty-five Undeniable Truths of Life" have stirred as much controversy and outrage as Number Twenty-four: "Feminism was established so that unattractive women could have easier access to the mainstream of society."

2   Many have suggested that this statement is too rough, insensitive, cruel, and unnecessarily provocative. However, there is one absolute defense of this statement. It's called truth. Sometimes the truth hurts. Sometimes the truth is jarring. Sometimes the truth is the most provocative thing you can tell someone. But the truth is still the truth. And it needs to be heard.

3   Likewise, for years I've been telling you that the feminist leadership is basically anti-male. I've said this in many different ways on many different occasions. But no matter how many times I have said it and no matter how cleverly I have rephrased this message, skeptics abound.

4   "Oh, Rush," people say, "aren't you going a little too far? Aren't you overstating your case?"

5   Well, folks, once again, I have to say it. The evidence that I was right all along about feminism—as with so many other things—is now overwhelming. [. . .]

6   The people who define modern feminism are saying that normal male deportment is harassment, near rape, abuse, and disrespect. These extremists, who make up the intellectual leadership of the modern feminist movement, are attempting to make the case that any expression of interest by a man in a woman is harassment. Inevitably, this is going to lead to several serious problems.

7   First among those is that men will become fearful about making any advances. This attitude will confuse men about what is right and what kind of behavior is acceptable. If no approach is welcome, then women will, by necessity, have to become the aggressors. Men will be afraid of crossing the line.

---

*Rush H. Limbaugh III, *See, I Told You So* (New York: Simon & Schuster, 1993), 221–23, 225–27.

8   The second major problem with this trend is that it trivializes real sexual harassment, real rape. When people are labeling everyday, normal, male-female conduct as sexual harassment, we not only obliterate relations between the sexes, but we greatly trivialize true sexual harassment. Harassment is now being so broadly defined by some that it entails behavior that offends or annoys or interrupts your life.

9   The fact of the matter is that women have far more power than most of them realize. It's a biological fact that males are the aggressors. We all know this is true. That means that the ultimate power—the power to say yes or no—lies with women.

10   If consent is denied and the aggressive male physically forces himself on the woman to the point of penetration, then you have rape—real rape. But this is the exception. Most men are not rapists. But militant feminists seek to blur the distinctions. Let's look at date rape, for example. I have a problem with feminists seeking to expand the concept of rape by adding such adjectives as *date* and *acquaintance*. Words mean things. . . . Especially in these times of hypersensitivity, it is very important that we are clear in our word usage. This is even more the case when the word in question represents criminal behavior, in some cases punishable by life imprisonment. This is dead-serious, folks. Rape means rape. It either is, or it isn't. It matters not whether it occurs on a date or on Mars. It is my belief that the date-rape concept has been promoted by those whose agenda it is to blur these distinctions. By calling it "date rape," the intent is to expand the scope of the very serious crime of rape, and to include within the category of "rape" behavior that certainly is not rape. Please don't misinterpret my meaning. As a firm believer that words have meaning, I'm very careful to use mine precisely. I condemn the act of rape as much as any other human being would. It is inexcusable. Confusing its definition by trying to expand its scope deceitfully will only redound to the detriment of real rape victims. That is unconscionable.

11   Some militant feminists apparently harbor such animosity for the opposite sex that they want to criminalize the process of courtship—the old-fashioned "chase." I have news for these people: It's normal for boys to pursue girls. It's natural for men to pursue women. This normal and natural process, once called the fine art of seduction, is being confused with harassment. What was once considered an important part of the process of finding a mate is being mischaracterized as rape.

12   How should you channel normal masculinity and the aggressive nature of the male? Would these women prefer men as husbands, or leaders of marauding gangs? That is basically the choice. Because women can be—and need to be—a great civilizing influence over men.

13   Do you realize that in some cities today men can be arrested for making a wolf whistle at a comely woman? Now, I'm not suggesting this is the kind of behavior we should encourage, but should it be criminalized? And what are the consequences of this sort of overreaction? The consequences are manifold. It's no wonder so many men and women have problems interacting. Rules and regulations like these are presumably meant to foster improved relations between men and women, but their effect is just the opposite. What is being fostered is an adversarial relationship between the sexes.

14   Take, for instance, the young star of "The Wonder Years," Fred Savage. The then sixteen-year-old was hit with a sexual-harassment suit by a former staffer of the show, Monique Long, who claimed that Savage repeatedly asked her to have an affair with him and—egads!—touched her by holding her hand. The lawsuit also charged that Jason Hervey, another actor on the show, harassed Long during her two years on the show as a costume designer, at one point touching her "in a sexual way." Long, thirty-two, claimed she was asked not to return to the show because of her complaints about the actors.

15   Have things gotten to the point where a man, or boy, can't ask a woman out? Can't flirt? Is it a crime to hold somebody's hand? Wouldn't a more appropriate response to questionable behavior have been for this thirty-two-year-old woman to call the teenager's parents? Or even slap him in the face? Is our society so confused now about relations between men and women that a mature adult doesn't know how to deal with a flirtatious sixteen-year-old?

FOR DISCUSSION:

What strengthens this argument? What weakens it? How could the author have made it a stronger argument?

◆   4.   **Prewriting: Plan the Proofs and Language for a Future Position Paper**

Use the mnemonics SICDADS and VAM to help you plan some proofs for a future paper. Think about the language and style you will use as well. Ask the following questions and write out answers for those that are most promising. Remember, a variety of proofs and types of language and style will make your paper more convincing to an audience.

WORKSHEET 7: PROOFS AND LANGUAGE DEVELOPMENT

Write your claim: _____

a. *Signs:* What symptoms or signs will demonstrate that this might be true?

b. *Induction:* What examples can I use? What conclusions can I draw from the examples? Can my readers make the "inductive leap" from the examples to an acceptance of the conclusion?

c. *Cause:* What is the main cause of the controversy? What are the effects?

d. *Deduction:* What conclusions will I draw? On what general principles, warrants, and examples are they based?

e. *Analogies:* What comparisons can I make? Can I show that what happened in the past might happen again or that what happened in one case might happen in another? Can I use a figurative analogy to compare items from different categories?

f. *Definition:* What words or concepts will I need to define?

(Continued)

g. *Statistics:* What statistics can I use? How should I present them? Would they be more convincing in graph form? (If yes, see examples of graphs in Chapter 9, pages 210–212.)

h. *Values:* What values can I appeal to? Should I spell them out or leave them unstated? What emotional narratives, examples, descriptions, and emotional language would make my appeals to values stronger?

i. *Authority:* Whom should I quote? What background information should I supply both for myself and for those I quote to establish our expertise? How can I use language to create common ground and establish *ethos*?

j. *Motives:* What do my readers need and want in regard to my issue? How can I appeal to those needs? What emotional material might help?

k. *Language:* What type of language do I want to predominate in my paper: the language of reason? emotional language? language that establishes *ethos*? a mix of styles? Make a few notes to help you plan language.

Chapter

8

Writing the Argument Analysis Paper: Review and Synthesis

The purpose of this chapter is to provide you with the opportunity to review and synthesize what you have learned about reading and writing argument in the first seven chapters of this book. You will apply argument theory as you read and analyze two letters. The first, "A Call for Unity: A Letter from Eight White Clergymen" was published in a Birmingham, Alabama, newspaper in April 1963. The second, "A Letter from Birmingham Jail," was written shortly thereafter by Martin Luther King Jr. in response to the clergymen's letter. These are classic, historic arguments that were written during the civil rights movement in the United States. They have been selected for analysis here because they provide clear examples of the argumentation strategies that are discussed in the first seven chapters of this book. In addition, they shed light on racial issues that persist today.

As you read these letters, you will analyze the rhetorical situation, notice the positions both parties take on the issue, and identify the claims, support, warrants, and backing for the warrants in both letters. You will also analyze fallacies and refutation. You will make a final evaluation and decide whether each letter is primarily ethical or unethical. You will formulate reasons and evidence for your final evaluation. Plan to make some notes on these matters as you read.

Then you will apply your understanding to write an argument analysis paper in which you explain the results of your reading and analysis. In this paper you will not be criticizing or showing what is wrong with the letters; you will not be arguing with the ideas or attempting to refute them. Instead, your purpose will be to explain the argumentation methods that these authors use to make their arguments. You will rely on information about argument theory that you have learned in earlier chapters in this book to help you make your analysis and write your paper. A side benefit of this assignment is that you will learn to write a type of paper that is sometimes required in other classes.

READING FOR THE ARGUMENT ANALYSIS PAPER

Use the following information to help you read and analyze the letters:

1. The rhetorical situation for the letters is explained on pages 170–172. Read this first to help you situate these letters in their historical context.
2. Focus topics that identify relevant argument theory are listed along with directed questions on pages 172–173. Page numbers for each topic are provided, if you need to review. When you finish reading the letters, you should be able to answer the questions that accompany each of the topics.
3. Questions appear in the margins of the letters that will direct your attention to various argumentation techniques and methods that the clergymen and King have used. Answer these questions as you read. Your answers will help you understand the letters, respond to the questions that accompany the topics, and gather the information you will need to write your paper. Underline the information in the letters that answers the questions in the margins. Write your own insights and thoughts in the margins. These activities will help you generate plenty of material for your paper.

WRITING THE ARGUMENT ANALYSIS PAPER

The complete assignment for the argument analysis paper appears at the end of this chapter on pages 189–190. You may want to read it now so that you will know what you will finally be asked to do. Here are some ideas to help you write this paper.

1. Create a structure for your essay, even if it is little more than a list of your main points. Or, you may prefer to make an outline. Place your ideas in an order that makes sense to you. Since you will be comparing and contrasting the two letters in this paper, you may want to write first about the clergymen's letter and then about King's letter and draw conclusions about both of them last. Or, you may want to set up topics, such as *emotional proof* or *writing style,* and then describe how each author, in turn, employs each technique in their letters.

2. You will be asked to explain the rhetorical situation. Be sure to place each letter in historical context and to describe the audiences each addresses. Then explain the issue from both points of view and summarize the authors' positions. An example of a summary appears on page 67. Your summaries should be no longer than this example. You may be able to make them shorter, but plan to include enough detail to help your reader understand the ideas in each letter and how each is organized. Make a brief outline of each letter to guide your summary writing.

3. You will be asked to state the claims and describe the support in both letters. The following example, written about Anna Quindlen's claim and support in "Undocumented, Indispensable" on pages 161–163, provides one way to do this.

The following sentence not only states the claim but also lists the types of support Quindlen uses. More information about the support can be provided in the paragraphs that follow.

> In her essay "Undocumented, Indispensable," Anna Quindlen uses all three kinds of proof—*logos, ethos,* and *pathos*—to support her claim that many undocumented workers in America are valuable and contributing members of society and that decisions made about their future should be influenced by the same American values that have driven immigration policy in earlier centuries, including the values of free enterprise and human rights.

4. Include summarized, paraphrased, or quoted material from the letters to provide evidence to support your main points. Here is an example, again using Quindlen, that illustrates how a summary and a direct quote could provide support.

> Quindlen uses an historical analogy to suggest that protest marches in the past, including those associated with the Vietnam war and feminism, are similar to the protest marches associated with the treatment of undocumented workers today. All of these protests result in change. "Immigration," she says, "is the leading edge of a deep and wide sea change in the United States today, just as those issues were in their own time" (162).

Place page numbers in parentheses at the end of each summarized, paraphrased, or quoted passage to show where you found it in this textbook, as in the example above.

5. Write a conclusion in which you evaluate these letters. Are they ethical or unethical? Is one more effective and convincing than the other? Why? Write a final evaluative claim about the letters that is based on the ideas and evidence in your paper. At this point, decide whether you want to leave your claim at the end of your paper or to move it to an earlier position in your paper. Where would it be most effective?

6. Read your draft, revise it, and submit it.

RHETORICAL SITUATION FOR "A CALL FOR UNITY: A LETTER FROM EIGHT WHITE CLERGYMEN" AND MARTIN LUTHER KING JR.'S "LETTER FROM BIRMINGHAM JAIL"

Birmingham, Alabama, was a very strange place in 1963. Black people were allowed to sit only in certain parts of buses and restaurants, they were required to drink out of separate water fountains, and they were not allowed in white churches, schools, or various other public places. The Reverend Martin Luther King Jr. was a black Baptist minister who was a leader in the civil rights movement at that time. The purpose of the movement was to end segregation and discrimination and to obtain equal rights and access for African Americans.

King and others carefully prepared for demonstrations that would take place in Birmingham in the spring of 1963. The demonstrators began by "sitting in" at lunch counters that had never served blacks before and by picketing stores. Twenty people were arrested the first day on charges of trespassing. Next, the civil rights leaders applied for permits to picket and hold parades against the in-justices of discrimination and segregation. They were refused permission, but they demonstrated and picketed anyway. King was served with an injunction granted by a circuit judge. It said civil rights leaders could not protest, demon-strate, boycott, or sit in at any facilities. King and others decided that this was an unfair and unjust application of the law, and they decided to break it.

Dr. Martin Luther King Jr. was jailed more than once during the civil rights movement. In this 1960 photo, police in Atlanta, Georgia, are taking him to court in handcuffs for participating in a sit-in at a segregated lunch counter in a department store. He was sentenced in this in-stance to four months of hard labor and was released on bail pending appeal only after Bobby Kennedy[1] phoned the judge.

SOURCE: From *Life in the '60s*, ed. Doris C. O'Neil (New York: Little, Brown & Co., 1989), 3. Copyright © 1989 by The Time Inc. Magazine Company.

---

[1]Bobby Kennedy, brother of President John F. Kennedy, was Attorney General at this time.

King himself decided to march on Good Friday, and he expected to go to jail. Indeed, before he had walked half a mile, he was arrested and jailed, along with fifty other people. King stayed in jail for eight days. During that time he wrote his famous letter. It was written in response to a letter signed by eight white clergymen that had been published in a local newspaper.

After King left jail, there were further protests and some violence. Thousands of people demonstrated, and thousands were jailed. Finally, black and white leaders began to negotiate, and some final terms were announced on May 10, 1963. All lunch counters, restrooms, fitting rooms, and drinking fountains in downtown stores were to be desegregated within ninety days; blacks were to be hired in clerical and sales jobs in stores within sixty days; the many people arrested during the demonstrations were to be released on low bail; and permanent lines of communication were to be established between black and white leaders. The demonstrations ended then, and the city settled down and began to implement the agreements.[2]

FOCUS TOPICS TO HELP YOU ANALYZE THE LETTERS

Answer the questions that accompany the eight focus topics listed below. Use the questions in the margins of the letters to help you locate the information you need to answer the questions.

1. *Rhetorical situation (pages 27–30).* Answer these questions.

    a. What is the *exigence* for these two letters? What caused the authors to write them? What was the problem? Was it a new or recurring problem?

    b. Who is the *audience* for the clergymen's letter? For King's letter? What is the nature of these audiences? Can they be convinced? What are the expected outcomes?

    c. What are the *constraints*? Speculate about the beliefs, attitudes, habits, and traditions that were in place that limited or constrained both the clergymen and King. How did these constraining circumstances influence the audience at that time?

    d. Think about the *authors* of both letters. Who are they? Speculate about their background, experience, affiliations, and values. What motivated them to write?

    e. What kind of *text* is this? What effect do its special qualities and features have on the audience?

    f. Think about *yourself as the reader.* What is your position on the issue? Do you experience constraints as you read? Do you perceive common ground with either the clergymen or King, or both? Describe it. Are you influenced by these letters? How?

---

[2]This account is drawn from Lee E. Bains Jr., "Birmingham, 1963: Confrontation over Civil Rights," in *Birmingham, Alabama, 1956–1963: The Black Struggle for Civil Rights,* ed. David J. Garrow (Brooklyn: Carlson, 1989), 175–83.

2. *Organization and claims (pages 122–130).* Divide each letter into its main parts. What is the subject of each part? Why have the parts been placed in this particular order? What is the relationship between them? What is the main claim in each letter? What types of claims are they? What are some of the subclaims? What types of claims are they?

3. *Logical proofs and style (pages 142–147, 150–151, and 154).* Analyze the use of logical proof in each of the letters. Provide examples. Describe their effect on the audience. Provide an example of the language of rational style in one of the letters.

4. *Emotional proofs and style (pages 148–150 and 152–154).* Analyze the use of emotional proof in each of the letters. Provide examples. Describe their effect on the audience. Provide an example of the language of emotional style in one of the letters.

5. *Proofs and style that establish ethos (pages 148, 151–152 and 154).* Analyze the use of proofs that establish *ethos* or credibility in the letters. Provide examples. Describe their effect on the audience. Provide an example of language that establishes *ethos* in one of the letters.

6. *Warrants and Backing (pages 103–106).* Identify the warrants in each of the letters. What appeals to community values provide backing for the warrants? How much common ground do you think exists between the authors of the letters? How much common ground do you share with the authors? As a result, which letter do you find more convincing? Why?

7. *Fallacious thinking and rebuttals (pages 154–159 and 106–107).* Provide examples of reasoning that is considered fallacious or wrongheaded by the opposing parties in each of the letters. What rebuttals are made in response to these? How effective are they?

8. *Ethical or Unethical (pages 159–160).* Do the clergymen and King both make an adequate effort to understand the issue and its consequences? Does each also understand the position held by the other? How just and fair-minded are both parties? Is their support fair, accurate, and/or convincing? Can you, as the reader, accept their warrants? Can you accept the references to community values that serve as backing for these warrants? Should the claims be qualified, if they are not already? Do the clergymen and King sincerely believe their positions are in the best interests of the people in Birmingham as well as in the larger society? Do you agree with them? Who is benefited, and who is burdened by their positions? Do you find evidence that either the clergymen or King are trying to manipulate their audience by hiding their real purpose, using inappropriate emotional appeals, manufacturing evidence, using inaccurate evidence, or telling lies? Do either of the arguers change the usual definitions of words to cloud perceptions, or do they minimize issues to trivialize them? What do you conclude about the ethical and unethical qualities of the letters?

Essay 1

A CALL FOR UNITY: A LETTER FROM EIGHT WHITE CLERGYMEN

The eight white Alabama clergymen who wrote this letter to the editor of a Birmingham, Alabama, newspaper represent various churches or religious denominations.

What is the issue?

1   We the undersigned clergymen are among those who, in January, issued "An Appeal for Law and Order and Common Sense," in dealing with racial problems in Alabama. We expressed understanding that honest convictions in racial matters could properly be pursued in the courts, but urged that decisions of those courts should in the meantime be peacefully obeyed.

What is the clergymen's position?

What is the claim?

2   Since that time there had been some evidence of increased forebearance and a willingness to face facts. Responsible citizens have undertaken to work on various problems which cause racial friction and unrest. In Birmingham, recent public events have given indication that we all have opportunity for a new constructive and realistic approach to racial problems.

What type of claim is it?

3   However, we are now confronted by a series of demonstrations by some of our Negro citizens, directed and led in part by outsiders. We recognize the natural impatience of people who feel that their hopes are slow in being realized. But we are convinced that these demonstrations are unwise and untimely.

What are the rebuttals?

How do the authors build *ethos*?

4   We agree rather with certain local Negro leadership which has called for honest and open negotiation of racial issues in our area. And we believe this kind of facing of issues can best be accomplished by citizens of our own metropolitan area, white and Negro, meeting with their knowledge and experience of the local situation. All of us need to face that responsibility and find proper channels for its accomplishment.

How do they appeal to logic?

5   Just as we formerly pointed out that "hatred and violence have no sanction in our religious and political traditions," we also point out that such actions as incite to hatred and violence, however technically peaceful those actions may be, have not contributed to the resolution of our local problems. We do not believe that these days of new hope are days when extreme measures are justified in Birmingham.

6   We commend the community as a whole, and the local news media and law enforcement officials in particular, on the calm manner in which these demonstrations have been handled. We urge the public to continue to show restraint should the demonstrations continue, and the law enforcement officials to remain calm and continue to protect our city from violence.

How do they appeal to emotion?

What are the warrants?

Describe the predominant style.

7   We further strongly urge our own Negro community to withdraw support from these demonstrations, and to unite locally in working peacefully for a better Birmingham. When rights are

Describe the backing
for the warrants.

consistently denied, a cause should be pressed in the courts and in negotiations among local leaders, and not in the streets. We appeal to both our white and Negro citizenry to observe the principles of law and order and common sense.

(Signed)

C.C.J. Carpenter, D.D., L.L.D., Bishop of Alabama; Joseph A. Durick, D.D., Auxiliary Bishop, Diocese Mobile-Birmingham; Rabbi Milton L. Grafman, Temple Emanu-El, Birmingham, Alabama; Bishop Paul Hardin, Bishop of the Alabama–West Florida Conference of the Methodist Church; Bishop Nolan B. Harmon, Bishop of the North Alabama Conference of the Methodist Church; George M. Murray, D.D., L.L.D., Bishop Coadjutor, Episcopal Diocese of Alabama; Edward V. Ramage, Moderator, Synod of the Alabama Presbyterian Church in the United States; Earl Stallings, Pastor, First Baptist Church, Birmingham

---

Essay 2

LETTER FROM BIRMINGHAM JAIL*

Martin Luther King Jr.

Martin Luther King Jr. was a Baptist minister who preached nonviolence. He was also a pivotal leader in the civil rights movement of the 1960s.

April 16, 1963

My Dear Fellow Clergymen:

1   While confined here in the Birmingham city jail, I came across your recent statement calling my present activities "unwise and untimely." Seldom do I pause to answer criticism of my work and ideas. If I sought to answer all the criticisms that cross my desk, my secretaries would have little time for anything other than such correspondence in the course of the day, and I would have no time for constructive work. But since I feel that you are men of genuine good will and that your criticisms are sincerely set forth, I want to try to answer your statement in what I hope will be patient and reasonable terms.

What is the issue?
What is King's
position?

Identify and describe
the Rogerian elements
and efforts to establish
common ground
throughout this letter.
(see Chapter 10,
Exercise 1b, page 230)

---

*Author's Note: This response to a published statement by eight fellow clergymen from Alabama (Bishop C.C.J. Carpenter, Bishop Joseph A. Durick, Rabbi Milton L. Grafman, Bishop Paul Hardin, Bishop Nolan B. Harmon, the Reverend George M. Murray, the Reverend Edward V. Ramage, and the Reverend Earl Stallings) was composed under somewhat constricting circumstances. Begun on the margins of the newspaper in which the statement appeared while I was in jail, the letter was continued on scraps of writing paper supplied by a friendly Negro trusty, and concluded on a pad my attorneys were eventually permitted to leave me. Although the text remains in substance unaltered, I have indulged in the author's prerogative of polishing it for publication.

2   I think I should indicate why I am here in Birmingham, since you have been influenced by the view which argues against "outsiders coming in." I have the honor of serving as president of the Southern Christian Leadership Conference, an organization operating in every southern state, with headquarters in Atlanta, Georgia. We have some eighty-five affiliated organizations across the South, and one of them is the Alabama Christian Movement for Human Rights. Frequently we share staff, educational and financial resources with our affiliates. Several months ago the affiliate here in Birmingham asked us to be on call to engage in a nonviolent direct-action program if such were deemed necessary. We readily consented, and when the hour came we lived up to our promise. So I, along with several members of my staff, am here because I was invited here. I am here because I have organizational ties here.

How does King build ethos?

What is the effect of the comparison with Paul?

Draw a line at the end of the introduction.

3   But more basically, I am in Birmingham because injustice is here. Just as the prophets of the eighth century B.C. left their villages and carried their "thus saith the Lord" far beyond the boundaries of their home towns, and just as the Apostle Paul left his village of Tarsus and carried the gospel of Jesus Christ to the far corners of the Greco-Roman world, so am I compelled to carry the gospel of freedom beyond my own home town. Like Paul, I must constantly respond to the Macedonian call for aid.

Draw a line at the end of each of the other major sections of material. Label the subject of each section in the margin.

4   Moreover, I am cognizant of the interrelatedness of all communities and states. I cannot sit idly by in Atlanta and not be concerned about what happens in Birmingham. Injustice anywhere is a threat to justice everywhere. We are caught in an inescapable network of mutuality, tied in a single garment of destiny. Whatever affects one directly, affects all indirectly. Never again can we afford to live with the narrow, provincial "outside agitator" idea. Anyone who lives inside the United States can never be considered an outsider anywhere within its bounds.

What is the subject of this first section?

What is the claim?

What type of claim is it?

Is it qualified?

5   You deplore the demonstrations taking place in Birmingham. But your statement, I am sorry to say, fails to express a similar concern for the conditions that brought about the demonstrations. I am sure that none of you would want to rest content with the superficial kind of social analysis that deals merely with effects and does not grapple with underlying causes. It is unfortunate that demonstrations are taking place in Birmingham, but it is even more unfortunate that the city's white power structure left the Negro community with no alternative.

Identify and analyze the effect of the emotional appeals.

6   In any nonviolent campaign there are four basic steps: collection of the facts to determine whether injustices exist; negotiation; self-purification; and direct action. We have gone through all these steps in Birmingham. There can be no gain-saying the fact that racial injustice engulfs this community. Birmingham is probably the most thoroughly segregated city in the United States. Its ugly record of brutality is widely known. Negroes have experienced grossly

unjust treatment in the courts. There have been more unsolved bombings of Negro homes and churches in Birmingham than in any other city in the nation. These are the hard, brutal facts of the case. On the basis of these conditions, Negro leaders sought to negotiate with the city fathers. But the latter consistently refused to engage in good-faith negotiation.

7   Then, last September, came the opportunity to talk with leaders of Birmingham's economic community. In the course of the negotiations, certain promises were made by the merchants—for example, to remove the stores' humiliating racial signs. On the basis of these promises, the Reverend Fred Shuttlesworth and the leaders of the Alabama Christian Movement for Human Rights agreed to a moratorium on all demonstrations. As the weeks and months went by, we realized that we were the victims of a broken promise. A few signs, briefly removed, returned; the others remained.

8   As in so many past experiences, our hopes had been blasted, and the shadow of deep disappointment settled upon us. We had no alternative except to prepare for direct action, whereby we would present our very bodies as a means of laying our case before the conscience of the local and the national community. Mindful of the difficulties involved, we decided to undertake a process of self-purification. We began a series of workshops on nonviolence, and we repeatedly asked ourselves: "Are you able to accept blows without retaliating?" "Are you able to endure the ordeal of jail?" We decided to schedule our direct-action program for the Easter season, realizing that except for Christmas, this is the main shopping period of the year. Knowing that a strong economic-withdrawal program would be the by-product of direct action, we felt that this would be the best time to bring pressure to bear on the merchants for the needed change.

What are some of the values expressed in this argument?

Identify and describe the rebuttals.

9   Then it occurred to us that Birmingham's mayoral election was coming up in March, and we speedily decided to postpone action until after election day. When we discovered that the Commissioner of Public Safety, Eugene "Bull" Connor, had piled up enough votes to be in the runoff, we decided again to postpone action until the day after the runoff so that the demonstrations could not be used to cloud the issues. Like many others, we waited to see Mr. Connor defeated, and to this end we endured postponement after postponement. Having aided in this community need, we felt that our direct-action program could be delayed no longer.

10   You may well ask: "Why direct action? Why sit-ins, marches and so forth? Isn't negotiation a better path?" You are quite right in calling for negotiation. Indeed, this is the very purpose of direct action. Nonviolent direct action seeks to create such a crisis and foster such a tension that a community which has constantly refused to negotiate is forced to confront the issue. It seeks so to dramatize the issue that it

What is the effect
of the comparison
with Socrates?

can no longer be ignored. My citing the creation of tension as part of the work of the nonviolent-resister may sound rather shocking. But I must confess that I am not afraid of the word "tension." I have earnestly opposed violent tension, but there is a type of constructive, nonviolent tension which is necessary for growth. Just as Socrates felt that it was necessary to create a tension in the mind so that individuals could rise from the bondage of myths and half-truths to the unfettered realm of creative analysis and objective appraisal, so must we see the need for nonviolent gadflies to create the kind of tension in society that will help men rise from the dark depths of prejudice and racism to the majestic heights of understanding and brotherhood.

What is King's
planned
argumentation
strategy?

11   The purpose of our direct-action program is to create a situation so crisis-packed that it will inevitably open the door to negotiation. I therefore concur with you in your call for negotiation. Too long has our beloved Southland been bogged down in a tragic effort to live in monologue rather than dialogue.

12   One of the basic points in your statement is that the action that I and my associates have taken in Birmingham is untimely. Some have asked: "Why didn't you give the new city administration time to act?" The only answer that I can give to this query is that the new Birmingham administration must be prodded about as much as the outgoing one, before it will act. We are sadly mistaken if we feel that the election of Albert Boutwell as mayor will bring the millennium to Birmingham. While Mr. Boutwell is a much more gentle person than Mr. Connor, they are both segregationists, dedicated to the maintenance of the status quo. I have hope that

Why does King refer
to history?

Mr. Boutwell will be reasonable enough to see the futility of massive resistance to desegregation. But he will not see this without pressure from devotees of civil rights. My friends, I must say to you that we have not made a single gain in civil rights without determined legal and nonviolent pressure. Lamentably, it is a historical fact that privileged groups seldom give up their privileges voluntarily. Individuals may see the moral light and voluntarily give up their unjust posture; but, as Reinhold Niebuhr has reminded us, groups tend to be more immoral than individuals.

Why does he refer
to Niebuhr?

13   We know through painful experience that freedom is never voluntarily given up by the oppressor; it must be demanded by the oppressed. Frankly, I have yet to engage in a direct-action campaign that was "well-timed" in the view of those who have not suffered unduly from the disease of segregation. For years now I have heard the word "Wait!" It rings in the ear of every Negro with piercing familiarity. This "Wait" has almost always meant "Never." We must come to see, with one of our distinguished jurists, that "justice too long delayed is justice denied."

Identify and analyze
the emotional proof.

To what human
motives and values
does King appeal?

14   We have waited for more than 340 years for our constitutional and God-given rights. The nations of Asia and Africa are moving with jetlike speed toward gaining political independence, but we

Identify emotional
language, examples,
and vivid description.

still creep at horse-and-buggy pace toward gaining a cup of coffee at a lunch counter. Perhaps it is easy for those who have never felt the stinging darts of segregation to say, "Wait." But when you have seen vicious mobs lynch your mothers and fathers at will and drown your sisters and brothers at whim; when you have seen hate-filled policemen curse, kick and even kill your black brothers and sisters; when you see the vast majority of your twenty million Negro brothers smothering in an airtight cage of poverty in the midst of an affluent society; when you suddenly find your tongue twisted and your speech stammering as you seek to explain to your six-year-old daughter why she can't go to the public amusement park that has just been advertised on television, and see tears welling up in her eyes when she is told that Fun-town is closed to colored children, and see ominous clouds of inferiority beginning to form in her little mental sky, and see her beginning to distort her personality by developing an unconscious bitterness toward white people; when you have to concoct an answer for a five-year-old son who is asking, "Daddy, why do white people treat colored people so mean?"; when you take a cross-country drive and find it necessary to sleep night after night in the uncomfortable corners of your automobile because no motel will accept you; when you are humiliated day in and day out by nagging signs reading "white" and "colored"; when your first name becomes "nigger," your middle name becomes "boy" (however old you are) and your last name becomes "John," and your wife and mother are never given the respected title "Mrs."; when you are harried by day and haunted by night by the fact that you are a Negro, living constantly at tiptoe stance, never quite knowing what to expect next, and are plagued with inner fears and outer resentments; when you are forever fighting a degenerating sense of "nobodiness"—then you will understand why we find it difficult to wait. There comes a time when the cup of endurance runs over, and men are no longer willing to be plunged into the abyss of despair. I hope, sirs, you can understand our legitimate and unavoidable impatience.

15   You express a great deal of anxiety over our willingness to break laws. This is certainly a legitimate concern. Since we so diligently urge people to obey the Supreme Court's decision of 1954 outlawing segregation in the public schools, at first glance it may seem rather paradoxical for us consciously to break laws. One may well ask: "How can you advocate breaking some laws and obeying others?" The answer lies in the fact that there are two types of laws: just and unjust. I would be the first to advocate obeying just laws. Conversely, one has a moral responsibility to disobey unjust laws. I would agree with St. Augustine that "an unjust law is no law at all."

16   Now, what is the difference between the two? How does one determine whether a law is just or unjust? A just law is a man-made code that squares with the moral law or the law of God. An unjust

---

Sidebar notes:

What is the effect of the emotional proof?

What is the predominant type of proof in the first section of the letter?

Draw a line where the subject changes. What is the subject of the second section?

How and why does King use definition?

How does he
support the
definition?

law is a code that is out of harmony with the moral law. To put it in the terms of St. Thomas Aquinas: An unjust law is a human law that is not rooted in eternal law and natural law. Any law that uplifts human personality is just. Any law that degrades human personality is unjust. All segregation statutes are unjust because segregation distorts the soul and damages the personality. It gives the segregator a false sense of superiority and the segregated a false sense of inferiority. Segregation, to use the terminology of the Jewish philosopher Martin Buber, substitutes an "I-it" relationship for an "I-thou" relationship and ends up relegating persons to the status of things.

What is the effect of
the support?

Hence segregation is not only politically, economically, and sociologically unsound, it is morally wrong and sinful. Paul Tillich has said that sin is separation. Is not segregation an existential expression of man's tragic separation, his awful estrangement, his terrible sinfulness? Thus it is that I can urge men to obey the 1954 decision of the Supreme Court, for it is morally right; and I can urge them to disobey segregation ordinances, for they are morally wrong.

17   Let us consider a more concrete example of just and unjust laws. An unjust law is a code that a numerical or power majority group compels a minority group to obey but does not make binding on itself. This is *difference* made legal. By the same token, a just law is a code that a majority compels a minority to follow and that it is willing to follow itself. This is *sameness* made legal.

Explain the example
of just and unjust
laws.

18   Let me give another explanation. A law is unjust if it is inflicted on a minority that, as a result of being denied the right to vote, had no part in enacting or devising the law. Who can say that the legislature of Alabama which set up the state's segregation laws was democratically elected? Throughout Alabama all sorts of devious methods are used to prevent Negroes from becoming registered voters, and there are some counties in which, even though Negroes constitute a majority of the population, not a single Negro is registered. Can any law enactment under such circumstances be considered democratically structured?

How does King
further elaborate on
this idea?

19   Sometimes a law is just on its face and unjust in its application. For instance, I have been arrested on a charge of parading without a permit. Now, there is nothing wrong in having an ordinance which requires a permit for a parade. But such an ordinance becomes unjust when it is used to maintain segregation and to deny citizens the First-Amendment privilege of peaceful assembly and protest.

20   I hope you are able to see the distinction I am trying to point out. In no sense do I advocate evading or defying the law, as would the rabid segregationist. That would lead to anarchy. One who breaks an unjust law must do so openly, lovingly, and with a willingness to accept the penalty. I submit that an individual who breaks a law that conscience tells him is unjust, and who willingly accepts the penalty of imprisonment in order to arouse the

Analyze the deductive
reasoning in this
paragraph.

conscience of the community over its injustice, is in reality expressing the highest respect for law.

21

Identify and describe the effect of the historical analogies.

Of course, there is nothing new about this kind of civil disobedience. It was evidenced sublimely in the refusal of Shadrach, Meshach and Abednego to obey the laws of Nebuchadnezzar, on the ground that a higher moral law was at stake. It was practiced superbly by the early Christians, who were willing to face hungry lions and the excruciating pain of chopping blocks rather than submit to certain unjust laws of the Roman Empire. To a degree, academic freedom is a reality today because Socrates practiced civil disobedience. In our own nation, the Boston Tea Party represented a massive act of civil disobedience.

22

What type of proof predominates in the second part of the letter?

Draw a line where the subject changes. What is the subject of the third section?

We should never forget that everything Adolf Hitler did in Germany was "legal" and everything the Hungarian freedom fighters did in Hungary was "illegal." It was "illegal" to aid and comfort a Jew in Hitler's Germany. Even so, I am sure that, had I lived in Germany at the time, I would have aided and comforted my Jewish brothers. If today I lived in a Communist country where certain principles dear to the Christian faith are suppressed, I would openly advocate disobeying that country's antireligious laws.

23

What are King's warrants in this passage?

I must make two honest confessions to you, my Christian and Jewish brothers. First, I must confess that over the past few years I have been gravely disappointed with the white moderate. I have almost reached the regrettable conclusion that the Negro's great stumbling block in his stride toward freedom is not the White Citizen's Councilor or the Ku Klux Klanner, but the white moderate, who is more devoted to "order" than to justice; who prefers a negative peace which is the absence of tension to a positive peace which is the presence of justice; who constantly says: "I agree with you in the goal you seek, but I cannot agree with your methods of direct action"; who paternalistically believes he can set the timetable for another man's freedom; who lives by a mythical concept of time and who constantly advises the Negro to wait for a "more convenient season." Shallow understanding from people of good will is more frustrating than absolute misunderstanding from people of ill will. Lukewarm acceptance is much more bewildering than outright rejection.

What backing does he provide?

24

How do King's warrants differ from the clergymen's?

I had hoped that the white moderate would understand that law and order exist for the purpose of establishing justice and that when they fail in this purpose they become the dangerously structured dams that block the flow of social progress. I had hoped that the white moderate would understand that the present tension in the South is a necessary phase of the transition from an obnoxious negative peace, in which the Negro passively accepted his unjust plight, to a substantive and positive peace, in which all men will respect the dignity and worth of human personality. Actually, we who engage in nonviolent direct action are not the creators of

How and why does King use definition here?

tension. We merely bring to the surface the hidden tension that is already alive. We bring it out in the open, where it can be seen and dealt with. Like a boil that can never be cured so long as it is covered up but must be opened with all its ugliness to the natural medicines of air and light, injustice must be exposed, with all the tension its exposure creates, to the light of human conscience and the air of national opinion before it can be cured.

25

Identify and describe the effects of the analogies in these paragraphs.

In your statements you assert that our actions, even though peaceful, must be condemned because they precipitate violence. But is this a logical assertion? Isn't this like condemning a robbed man because his possession of money precipitated the evil act of robbery? Isn't this like condemning Socrates because his unswerving commitment to truth and his philosophical inquiries precipitated the act by the misguided populace in which they made him drink hemlock? Isn't this like condemning Jesus because his unique God-consciousness and never-ceasing devotion to God's will precipitated the evil act of crucifixion? We must come to see that, as the federal courts have consistently affirmed, it is wrong to urge an individual to cease his efforts to gain his basic constitutional rights because the quest may precipitate violence. Society must protect the robbed and punish the robber.

What is the fallacious thinking King complains of here?

26

Summarize King's reasoning about time.

I had also hoped that the white moderate would reject the myth concerning time in relation to the struggle for freedom. I have just received a letter from a white brother in Texas. He writes: "All Christians know that the colored people will receive equal rights eventually, but it is possible that you are in too great a religious hurry. It has taken Christianity almost two thousand years to accomplish what it has. The teachings of Christ take time to come to earth." Such an attitude stems from a tragic misconception of time, from the strangely irrational notion that there is something in the very flow of time that will inevitably cure all ills. Actually, time itself is neutral; it can be used either destructively or constructively. More and more I feel that the people of ill will have used time much more effectively than have the people of good will. We will have to repent in this generation not merely for the hateful words and actions of the bad people but for the appalling silence of the good people. Human progress never rolls in on wheels of inevitability; it comes through the tireless efforts of men willing to be coworkers with God, and without this hard work, time itself becomes an ally of the forces of social stagnation. We must use time creatively, in the knowledge that the time is always right to do right. Now is the time to make real the promise of democracy and transform our pending national elegy into a creative psalm of brotherhood. Now is the time to lift our national policy from the quicksand of racial injustice to the solid rock of human dignity.

27

Describe the two opposing forces.

You speak of our activity in Birmingham as extreme. At first I was rather disappointed that fellow clergymen would see my nonviolent efforts as those of an extremist. I began thinking about the fact that I stand in the middle of two opposing forces in the Negro community. One is a force of complacency, made up in part of Negroes who, as a result of long years of oppression, are so drained of self-respect and a sense of "somebodiness" that they have adjusted to segregation; and in part of a few middle-class Negroes who, because of a degree of academic and economic security and because in some ways they profit by segregation, have become insensitive to the problems of the masses. The other force is one of bitterness and hatred, and it comes perilously close to advocating violence. It is expressed in the various black nationalist groups that are springing up across the nation, the largest and best-known being Elijah Muhammad's Muslim movement. Nourished by the Negro's frustration over the continued existence of racial discrimination, this movement is made up of people who have lost faith in America, who have absolutely repudiated Christianity, and who have concluded that the white man is an incorrigible "devil."

28

How and why does King attempt to reconcile the opposing forces?

I have tried to stand between these two forces, saying that we need emulate neither the "do-nothingism" of the complacent nor the hatred and despair of the black nationalist. For there is the more excellent way of love and nonviolent protest. I am grateful to God that, through the influence of the Negro church, the way of nonviolence became an integral part of our struggle.

29

Identify and describe the causal proof.

If this philosophy had not emerged, by now many streets of the South would, I am convinced, be flowing with blood. And I am further convinced that if our white brothers dismiss as "rabble-rousers" and "outside agitators" those of us who employ nonviolent direct action, and if they refuse to support our nonviolent efforts, millions of Negroes will, out of frustration and despair, seek solace and security in black-nationalist ideologies—a development that would inevitably lead to a frightening racial nightmare.

30

Summarize King's reasoning about the effects of oppression.

Oppressed people cannot remain oppressed forever. The yearning for freedom eventually manifests itself, and that is what has happened to the American Negro. Something within has reminded him of his birthright of freedom, and something without has reminded him that it can be gained. Consciously or unconsciously, he has been caught up by the *Zeitgeist,* and with his black brothers of Africa and his brown and yellow brothers of Asia, South America and the Caribbean, the United States Negro is moving with a sense of great urgency toward the promised land of racial justice. If one recognizes this vital urge that has engulfed the Negro community, one should readily understand why public demonstrations are taking place. The Negro has many pent-up resentments and latent frustrations, and he must release them. So let him march; let him make prayer pilgrimages to the city hall; let him go on freedom rides—and try to understand why he must do so. If his repressed emotions are not released in nonviolent ways, they will seek expression through violence; this is not a threat but a fact of history. So I have not said to my people: "Get rid of your discontent." Rather, I have tried to say that this normal and healthy discontent can be channeled into the creative outlet of nonviolent direct action. And now this approach is being termed extremist.

31

What is the effect of these comparisons?

But though I was initially disappointed at being categorized as an extremist, as I continued to think about the matter I gradually gained a measure of satisfaction from the label. Was not Jesus an extremist for love: "Love your enemies, bless them that curse you, do good to them that hate you, and pray for them which despitefully use you, and persecute you." Was not Amos an extremist for justice: "Let justice roll down like waters and righteousness like an everflowing stream." Was not Paul an extremist for the Christian gospel: "I bear in my body the marks of the Lord Jesus." Was not Martin Luther an extremist: "Here I stand; I cannot do otherwise, so help me God." And John Bunyan: "I will stay in jail to the end of my days before I make a butchery of my conscience." And Abraham Lincoln: "This nation cannot survive half slave and half free." And Thomas Jefferson: "We hold these truths to be self-evident, that all men are created equal. . . ." So the question is not whether we will be extremists, but what kind of extremists we will be. Will we be extremists for hate or for love? Will we be extremists for the preservation of injustice or for the extension of justice? In that dramatic scene on Calvary's hill three men were crucified. We must never forget that all three were crucified for the same crime—the crime of extremism. Two were extremists for immorality, and thus fell below their environment. The other, Jesus Christ, was an extremist for love, truth and goodness, and thereby rose above his environment. Perhaps the South, the nation and the world are in dire need of creative extremists.

32

Summarize King's description of the oppressor race.

What types of proof are used in this third section?

I had hoped that the white moderate would see this need. Perhaps I was too optimistic; perhaps I expected too much. I suppose I should have realized that few members of the oppressor race can understand the deep groans and passionate yearnings of the oppressed race, and still fewer have the vision to see that injustice must be rooted out by strong, persistent and determined action. I am thankful, however, that some of our white brothers in the South have grasped the meaning of this social revolution and committed themselves to it. They are still all too few in quantity, but they are big in quality. Some—such as Ralph McGill, Lillian Smith, Harry Golden, James McBride Dabbs, Ann Braden and Sarah Patton Boyle—have written about our struggle in eloquent and prophetic terms. Others have marched with us down nameless streets of the South. They have languished in filthy, roach-infested jails, suffering the abuse and brutality of policemen who view them as "dirty nigger-lovers." Unlike so many of their moderate brothers and sisters, they have recognized the urgency of the moment and sensed the need for powerful "action" antidotes to combat the disease of segregation.

33

Draw a line where the subject changes. What is the subject of the fourth section?

Reconsider the rhetorical situations: What went before? What will come later?

Let me take note of my other major disappointment. I have been so greatly disappointed with the white church and its leadership. Of course, there are some notable exceptions. I am not unmindful of the fact that each of you has taken some significant stands on this issue. I commend you, Reverend Stallings, for your Christian stand on this past Sunday, in welcoming Negroes to your worship service on a nonsegregated basis. I commend the Catholic leaders of this state for integrating Spring Hill College several years ago.

34

But despite these notable exceptions, I must honestly reiterate that I have been disappointed with the church. I do not say this as one of those negative critics who can always find something wrong with the church. I say this as a minister of the gospel, who loves the church; who was nurtured in its bosom; who has been sustained by its spiritual blessings and who will remain true to it as long as the cord of life shall lengthen.

35

How does King build ethos *in this fourth section?*

When I was suddenly catapulted into the leadership of the bus protest in Montgomery, Alabama, a few years ago, I felt we would be supported by the white church. I felt that the white ministers, priests and rabbis of the South would be among our strongest allies. Instead, some have been outright opponents, refusing to understand the freedom movement and misrepresenting its leaders; all too many others have been more cautious than courageous and have remained silent behind the anesthetizing security of stained-glass windows.

36

What common ground did King hope for? How was he disappointed?

In spite of my shattered dreams, I came to Birmingham with the hope that the white religious leadership of this community would see the justice of our cause and, with deep moral concern, would serve as the channel through which our just grievances could reach the power structure. I had hoped that each of you would understand. But again I have been disappointed.

37

How and why does King use vivid description?

I have heard numerous southern religious leaders admonish their worshipers to comply with a desegregation decision because it is the law, but I have longed to hear white ministers declare: "Follow this decree because integration is morally right and because the Negro is your brother." In the midst of blatant injustices inflicted upon the Negro, I have watched white churchmen stand on the sideline and mouth pious irrelevancies and sanctimonious trivialities. In the midst of a mighty struggle to rid our nation of racial and economic injustice, I have heard many ministers say: "Those are social issues, with which the gospel has no real concern." And I have watched many churches commit themselves to a completely other-worldly religion which makes a strange, un-Biblical distinction between body and soul, between the sacred and the secular.

38

I have traveled the length and breadth of Alabama, Mississippi and all the other southern states. On sweltering summer days and crisp autumn mornings I have looked at the South's beautiful churches with their lofty spires pointing heavenward. I have beheld the impressive outlines of her massive religious-education buildings. Over and over I have found myself asking: "What kind of people worship here? Who is their God? Where were their voices when the lips of Governor Barnett dripped with words of interposition and nullification? Where were they when Governor Wallace gave a clarion call for defiance and hatred? Where were their voices of support when bruised and weary Negro men and women decided to rise from the dark dungeons of complacency to the bright hills of creative protest?"

39   Yes, these questions are still in my mind. In deep disappointment I have wept over the laxity of the church. But be assured that my tears have been tears of love. There can be no deep disappointment where there is not deep love. Yes, I love the church. How could I do otherwise? I am in the rather unique position of being the son, the grandson and the great-grandson of preachers. Yes, I see the church as the body of Christ. But, oh! How we have blemished and scarred that body through social neglect and through fear of being nonconformists.

40   There was a time when the church was very powerful—in the time when the early Christians rejoiced at being deemed worthy to suffer for what they believed. In those days the church was not merely a thermometer that recorded the ideas and principles of popular opinion; it was a thermostat that transformed the mores of society. Whenever the early Christians entered a town, the people in power became disturbed and immediately sought to convict the Christians for being "disturbers of the peace" and "outside agitators." But the Christians pressed on, in the conviction that they were "a colony of heaven," called to obey God rather than man. Small in number, they were big in commitment. They were too God-intoxicated to be "astronomically intimidated." By their effort and example they brought an end to such ancient evils as infanticide and gladiatorial contests.

What is the effect of the historical analogy?

41   Things are different now. So often the contemporary church is a weak, ineffectual voice with an uncertain sound. So often it is an arch-defender of the status quo. Far from being disturbed by the presence of the church, the power structure of the average community is consoled by the church's silent—and often even vocal—sanction of things as they are.

42   But the judgment of God is upon the church as never before. If today's church does not recapture the sacrificial spirit of the early church, it will lose its authenticity, forfeit the loyalty of millions, and be dismissed as an irrelevant social club with no meaning for the twentieth century. Every day I meet young people whose disappointment with the church has turned into outright disgust.

43   Perhaps I have once again been too optimistic. Is organized religion too inextricably bound to the status quo to save our nation and the world? Perhaps I must turn my faith to the inner spiritual

How does King contrast organized religion and the inner church? What is the effect?

church, the church within the church, as the true *ekklesia* and the hope of the world. But again I am thankful to God that some noble souls from the ranks of organized religion have broken loose from the paralyzing chains of conformity and joined us as active partners in the struggle for freedom. They have left their secure congregations and walked the streets of Albany, Georgia, with us. They have gone down the highways of the South on tortuous rides for freedom. Yes, they have gone to jail with us. Some have been dismissed from their churches, have lost the support of their bishops and fellow ministers. But they have acted in the faith that right defeated is stronger than evil triumphant. Their witness has been the spiritual salt that has preserved the true meaning of the gospel in these troubled times. They have carved a tunnel of hope through the dark mountain of disappointment.

44

Why does King use historical analogies here?

I hope the church as a whole will meet the challenge of this decisive hour. But even if the church does not come to the aid of justice, I have no despair about the future. I have no fear about the outcome of our struggle in Birmingham, even if our motives are at present misunderstood. We will reach the goal of freedom in Birmingham and all over the nation, because the goal of America is freedom. Abused and scorned though we may be, our destiny is tied up with America's destiny. Before the pilgrims landed at Plymouth, we were here. Before the pen of Jefferson etched the majestic words of the Declaration of Independence across the pages of history, we were here. For more than two centuries our forebears labored in this country without wages; they made cotton king; they built the homes of their masters while suffering gross injustice and shameful humiliation—and yet out of a bottomless vitality they continued to thrive and develop. If the inexpressible cruelties of slavery could not stop us, the opposition we now face will surely fail. We will win our freedom because the sacred heritage of our nation and the eternal will of God are embodied in our echoing demands.

What types of proof are used in the fourth section?

Draw a line where the subject changes. What is the subject of the fifth section?

45

Before closing I feel impelled to mention one other point in your statement that has troubled me profoundly. You warmly commended the Birmingham police force for keeping "order" and "preventing violence." I doubt that you would have so warmly commended the police force if you had seen its dogs sinking their teeth into unarmed, nonviolent Negroes. I doubt that you would so quickly commend the policemen if you were to observe their ugly and inhumane treatment of Negroes here in the city jail; if you were to watch them push and curse old Negro women and young Negro girls; if you were to see them slap and kick old Negro men and young boys; if you were to observe them, as they did on two occasions, refuse to give us food because we wanted to sing our grace together. I cannot join you in your praise of the Birmingham police department.

What is the predominant type of proof in this fifth section?

46

It is true that the police have exercised a degree of discipline in handling the demonstrators. In this sense they have conducted themselves rather "nonviolently" in public. But for what purpose?

Provide some
examples.

To preserve the evil system of segregation. Over the past few years I have consistently preached that nonviolence demands that the means we use must be as pure as the ends we seek. I have tried to make clear that it is wrong to use immoral means to attain moral ends. But now I must affirm that it is just as wrong, or perhaps even more so, to use moral means to preserve immoral ends. Perhaps Mr. Connor and his policemen have been rather nonviolent in public, as was Chief Pritchett in Albany, Georgia, but they have used the moral means of nonviolence to maintain the immoral end of racial injustice. As T. S. Eliot has said: "The last temptation is the greatest treason: To do the right deed for the wrong reason."

Describe the effect.

47   I wish you had commended the Negro sit-inners and the demonstrators of Birmingham for their sublime courage, their willingness to suffer and their amazing discipline in the midst of great provocation. One day the South will recognize its real heroes. They will be the James Merediths, with the noble sense of purpose that enables them to face jeering and hostile mobs, and with the agonizing loneliness that characterizes the life of the pioneer. They will be old, oppressed, battered Negro women, symbolized in a seventy-two-year-old woman in Montgomery, Alabama, who rose up with a sense of dignity and with her people decided not to ride segregated buses, and who responded with ungrammatical profundity to one who inquired about her weariness: "My feets is tired, but my soul is at rest." They will be the young high school and college students, the young ministers of the gospel and a host of their elders, courageously and nonviolently sitting in at lunch counters and willingly going to jail for conscience' sake. One day the South will know that when these disinherited children of God sat down at lunch counters, they were in reality standing up for what is best in the American dream and for the most sacred values in our Judaeo-Christian heritage, thereby bringing our nation back to those great wells of democracy which were dug deep by the founding fathers in their formulation of the Constitution and the Declaration of Independence.

48   Never before have I written so long a letter. I'm afraid it is much too long to take your precious time. I can assure you that it would have been much shorter if I had been writing from a comfortable desk, but what else can one do when he is alone in a narrow jail cell, other than write long letters, think long thoughts and pray long prayers?

Draw a line to set off
the conclusion. What
is the concluding idea?

What is King's
purpose in this
conclusion?

49   If I have said anything in this letter that overstates the truth and indicates an unreasonable impatience, I beg you to forgive me. If I have said anything that understates the truth and indicates my having a patience that allows me to settle for anything less than brotherhood, I beg God to forgive me.

Do you find the two
letters convincing?
Why or why not?

50   I hope this letter finds you strong in the faith. I also hope that circumstances will soon make it possible for me to meet each of you, not as an integrationist or a civil-rights leader but as a fellow

clergyman and a Christian brother. Let us all hope that the dark clouds of racial prejudice will soon pass away and the deep fog of misunderstanding will be lifted from our fear-drenched communities, and in some not too distant tomorrow the radiant stars of love and brotherhood will shine over our great nation with all their scintillating beauty.

Are the clergymen's and King's arguments ethical or unethical?

> Yours for the cause of Peace and Brotherhood,
> Martin Luther King, Jr.

REVIEW QUESTIONS

1. Describe the argument analysis paper.
2. What is the purpose of this paper?
3. What do you need to avoid doing in this paper that might be a part of other types of argument papers?
4. Describe the rhetorical situation for the letters by the eight white clergymen and Martin Luther King Jr.
5. What are the focus topics? Provide three examples of them.

CLASS ACTIVITIES AND WRITING ASSIGNMENTS

1. **Form Groups and Discuss the Focus Topics**

   Divide the class into eight groups, and assign each group one of the eight focus topics listed on pages 172–173. Here are the topics: **rhetorical situation; organization and claims; logical proofs and style; emotional proofs and style; proofs and style that establish** *ethos*; **warrants and backing; fallacious thinking and rebuttals; and ethical or unethical qualities**. Utilize the questions that accompany each focus item on the list. To prepare for the group work, all students will read the two letters outside of class and individually make notes on the focus topic assigned to their group. The brief questions in the margins of the letters will facilitate this reading and note taking. In class the groups will meet briefly to consolidate their views on their topic. Each group will then make a brief oral report on their topic, and other class members will discuss the results and take some notes. These notes will be used as prewriting materials for the argument analysis paper.

2. **Write an Argument Analysis Paper**

   Write a four-page double-spaced argument analysis paper of at least 1,000 words in which you analyze the two letters by the clergymen and King. Put the letters in historical context by describing the rhetorical situation, with particular emphasis on the exigence, the audiences, and the constraints. Explain the issue from both points of view. Summarize the positions taken on the issue in both letters. State the claims in both letters. Describe and evaluate the support, warrants, and backing in both. Identify any fallacies and describe how the authors use rebuttal. Finally, evaluate the ethical or unethical qualities that appear in these letters and write a conclusion in which you make a claim about the relative effectiveness of the two letters. Which letter is more effective? Why? Have your own views been modified or changed? How?

WRITING AND PRESENTING ARGUMENTS

The purpose of the next three chapters is to teach you to analyze and present arguments in visual form, and also to write two very different types of argument papers. Chapter 9 alerts you to some special features of visual argument and describes how to present arguments in visual form. Chapter 10 presents Rogerian argument as an alternative strategy to traditional argument. Chapter 11 teaches you to write a traditional argument paper from your own perspective that incorporates research materials from outside sources. Since other professors or even employers may also ask you to produce such papers, this instruction should be useful to you not only now but in the future as well. When you finish reading Part Three:

- You will understand how and why visual argument is used to convince.

- You will know how to write a Rogerian argument paper, an alternative to traditional argument, that aims at consensus.

- You will know how to organize, draft, and prepare the final copy for a researched position paper.

- You will understand how to prepare for and participate in a class symposium on your research topic.

Chapter 9

Analyzing and Creating Visual Argument

You may discover that you spend more time viewing argument than you do reading and writing it. In his article "Rise of the Visual Puts Words on the Defensive," David Carr claims, "In most magazines on today's newsstands, words are increasingly beside the point, mere graphic elements that are generally used to frame pictures."[1] Many of these pictures are used to express perspectives on argument. The same can be said of most advertisements you encounter. They usually contain pictures with comparatively few words of explanation. Textbooks now have more pictures, graphs, tables, maps, and other types of visuals than they did in the past. Add the Internet, movies, and television, and you will discover that much of the material you take in is visual and that it is often used to make or support an argument.

Images, in fact, when viewed from the perspective of argument, frequently take on additional meaning. That is, an image, on close scrutiny, can often be perceived as a visual argument in that it makes a claim about an issue and supports it, just as written argument does. The idea introduced in Chapter 1 that argument is everywhere takes on expanded meaning when you apply it to visual as well as to written argument.

This chapter demonstrates the proposition that the same tools of analysis put forward in earlier chapters that you use to analyze written argument can be successfully applied to analyze visual argument. Visual argument, however, also has certain special characteristics that make it unique. Those characteristics are the subject of this chapter, which teaches you not only to analyze visual argument but also to create it yourself. Instruction and examples appear in the color

---

[1] *New York Times*, April 1, 2002, C8.

portfolio that follows page 224 and the Class Activities and Writing Assignments section at the end of the chapter.

RECOGNIZING VISUAL ARGUMENT

You will need to discover, first, whether you are looking at an argument. Discover this by asking, *Is the visual about an issue that has not been resolved or settled?* and *Does this issue potentially inspire two or more different views?* If your answer to both of these questions is yes, then attempt to describe the issue and the perspective being developed. Next, use two types of information for further analysis. First, analyze the special features of visual argument that are explained later in this chapter to get a sense of how the argument works and how powerful it is. Second, apply argument theory to understand the material better as an argument. You already gained some experience with visual argument when you analyzed the advertisement on page 110. You can extend that experience to analyze other types of visual argument as well.

Review the section "Recognize Purpose in Written Argument" on pages 53–54 to help you recognize and classify types of visual argument. Just like written argument, visual argument can be straightforward, with an obvious purpose and claim; covert, with a hidden claim that you may need to infer; or even unconscious, with the artist advocating a point of view without being fully aware of it. Furthermore, argument expressed through pictures can represent either commonly held or extreme points of view and can present one or several different views on an issue.

You will encounter visual argument both online and in print in a variety of forms, including advertisements, photographs, drawings, illustrations, paintings, sculptures, cartoons, diagrams, flowcharts, various types of graphs, visual demonstrations, tables of numbers, or even maps. Marketers use visual argument on billboards, on signs, and in packaging and other marketing materials such as brochures or various other types of promotional materials. All this visual material, whether in still or moving picture form, can be (and increasingly is) employed to further an argument and convince you of a particular point of view.

Notice how many of these venues for visual argument are a part of the modern media, a particularly potent context for visual argument. A recent study by the Kaiser Family Foundation found that young people ages 8–18 now spend up to six and a half hours a day listening, watching, reading, or interacting with materials that they access through modern media formats. Reflect on the amount of time you spend each day taking in or sending information via new media, and you may be surprised how much your life is impacted. Think also about the number and types of images you encounter in all media forms that can be characterized as visual arguments and that have been constructed to gain profit or power or both. This is a major characteristic of the modern media. Whenever you encounter visual argument in the media or anywhere else, make a point of identifying its purpose because it always has one.

Now let us look at some of the special features of visual argument that make it particularly effective for advancing arguments.

WHY VISUAL ARGUMENT IS CONVINCING: EIGHT SPECIAL FEATURES

The following special features of visual argument will demonstrate how it works and why it is convincing. However, not all visual argument demonstrates all of the special features described in this list, and sometimes these features combine or overlap with one another. They are separated and described here for purposes of instruction. Becoming aware of them will help you look at visuals as potential argument and also understand how images achieve their persuasive effect with an audience. The examples of visual argument in this chapter include classic photographs that illustrate issues associated with dramatic periods in U.S. history, such as World War II, the civil rights movement, and the Vietnam War. Others illustrate contemporary issues. The images in the color portfolio that follows page 224 in this book are additional examples of visual argument.

1. *Visual argument is immediate and tangible and pulls you into the picture.* Visual argument works on a different level of perception than written argument. To use a new media word, it has velocity. It communicates fast and evokes a rich, dense, and immediate response from a viewer. For example, if you are watching a moving picture, you may have the experience of either sharing or even taking part in the action yourself. At the least, you will react in some immediate way to what you are seeing. If the picture is still, you may experience its immediacy and timelessness. A moment has been captured and preserved forever on film. Look at the photograph in Figure 9.1 (page 196). It has been characterized as the most famous picture from the Vietnam War.

2. *Visual argument often establishes common ground and invites viewer identification through shared values and points of view.* You learned in Chapter 1 that common ground is a necessary ingredient of productive argument. Visual argument usually establishes common ground, including a sense of personal identification and shared values with the characters, the action, or the scene, and it does so more quickly than words in print. All viewers, however, may not experience the same degree of common ground or the same type of identification.

Look at the photograph in Figure 9.2 (page 197) taken by American Douglas Martin. This is a picture of Dorothy Counts, an African American girl who enrolled in a newly desegregated high school in Charlotte, North Carolina, during the civil rights movement. Escorted by the individuals on either side of her, she makes her way to her first day of school. Dorothy is being taunted by white students in the background who wanted to keep their school segregated.

Dorothy Counts, now Dot Counts Scoggins, still lives in Charlotte, North Carolina. In 2007 the Charlotte-Mecklenburg Schools community celebrated both the 40th anniversary of the desegregation of the school system and the 50th anniversary of the difficult days that the young Dorothy Counts (she was 15 in 1957) spent in Harding High School in an effort to help desegregate public schools. The school district also invited a couple of the students who were

Street Execution of a Vietcong Prisoner, 1968.
SOURCE: Eddie Adams/AP Wide World Photos.

FIGURE 9.1   Visual argument is immediate and tangible and pulls you into the picture.

In this photograph an officer in the South Vietnamese army is shooting a suspected member of the Vietcong, an armed rebel force supported by North Vietnam, and the photographer has captured the moment when the bullet enters this man's head and kills him. This picture provoked strong antiwar arguments in its time, and it continues to invite responses to issues associated with war. What pulls you into this picture? What issue does it raise for you? What position do you take on the issue?

screaming at her and making faces in this picture to the ceremony. They were present, and they apologized, after all these years.[2]

Attitudes and values have changed radically in the years since this photograph was taken. The picture demonstrates the potential power and influence of visual argument. It memorializes an event that has now become a part of history and that vividly depicts the changed views on school segregation that are recognized now throughout the United States.

3. *Visual argument often evokes an emotional response.* Visual argument operates more directly on the emotions than written argument because images communicate more immediately than words. Visual argument is also less subject to

[2]From information supplied by Professor Andy Brown and student Kristina Wolfe, of the University of North Carolina at Charlotte, and Dave Morris, long-time resident of Charlotte, NC.

Dorothy Counts Entering a Newly Desegregated School, 1957.
SOURCE: © Bettmann/CORBIS.

FIGURE 9.2 Visual argument often establishes common ground and invites viewer identification through shared values and points of view.

This photograph won The Associated Press, World Press Photo of the Year Award in 1957 and remains one of the most famous pictures from the civil rights era. With whom do you identify and experience the greatest amount of common ground in this picture? Do you identify with Dorothy as she moves toward her first experiences in her new school? Do you identify with either of the individuals escorting her? Do you have anything in common with the white students in the background? What values are embedded in this image? What issue does the picture raise for you, and what position would you take on it?

conscious critical awareness and monitoring since most people think less critically about an image than they do a prose piece. You can test this yourself. Imagine reading an unillustrated account of a new car in the automotive section of the newspaper. Compare this with watching a hyped-up color television advertisement about the same car that includes pictures of interesting people driving to exotic locations. You will probably be more likely to think critically and rationally about the written account and more likely to respond emotionally to the visuals in the advertisement. Look for example at the photograph of the child in Figure 9.3 (page 198). This image appeared in *Newsweek* magazine in 2003 and invoked a strong emotional response from many readers who wrote to the editor to express their profound sadness and concern for this child.

A Young Boy Cries When One of Islam's Holiest Shrines Is Destroyed during the War in Iraq, 2003.
SOURCE: Jamal A. Wilson/Landov Media

FIGURE 9.3   Visual argument often evokes an emotional response.

In the photograph the sacred shrine of Imam Ali has just been blown up, and the boy is crying in the midst of the rubble. Would you characterize your response to this picture as primarily rational or emotional? What in the image prompts your response? Describe your response.

4. *Visual argument often relies on the juxtaposition of materials from very different categories, inviting the viewer to make new links and associations.* Use what you learned about figurative analogies in Chapter 7 (page 146) to help you understand the strategy of juxtaposition in visual argument. In placing objects, people, or actions that are not usually associated with each other in a common context, a photographer invites the viewer to establish new associations and to reach new conclusions. Figure 9.4, (page 199), is a well-known photograph of an anti–Vietnam War demonstrator at a march on the Pentagon in 1967. He is placing flowers that symbolize peace in the gun barrels of the troops that have been called in to protect the area.

5. *Visual argument often employs icons to prompt an immediate response from a viewer.* Icons are images that people have seen so often that they respond to them immediately and in predictable ways—or at least, it is on this that people who include iconic references in visual argument rely. The American eagle, for example, is more than a bird to most U.S. citizens. It symbolizes the nation and the values associated with a democratic form of government. Icons appear on computer screens and on the cash registers at McDonald's to prompt quicker responses than the words or numbers they replace. Examples of icons that might appear in visual argument include the villain and the good guy in western

A Vietnam War Protester Placing Flowers in the Rifle Barrels of Troops Guarding the Pentagon during an Antiwar Demonstration, 1967.

SOURCE: Bernie Boston/Getty Images/Washington Post Writers Group

FIGURE 9.4   Visual argument often relies on the juxtaposition of materials from very different categories, inviting the viewer to make new links and associations.

The juxtaposition of flowers and guns in the context of an antiwar demonstration invites the viewer to respond directly to how these different things appear together. What associations do you have with flowers and guns? Think of them separately and then together. How would you state the claim in this picture? Would you accept or argue against this claim?

movies; the sleek, elegantly dressed couple in television car commercials; the cross or the Star of David in religious imagery; or a picture of a starving child in an appeal for money. The photograph on the next page (see Figure 9.5) of Marines raising the U.S. flag on Iwo Jima toward the end of World War II has been printed so many times, including on postage stamps, that it has become a national icon. It has also inspired a famous statue in Arlington Cemetery in Washington D.C. This photograph was staged. The first time these men raised the flag, they decided the flag was too small, so they got a bigger flag and raised it again. The photographer, Joe Rosenthal, took this picture of the second try, and he caught it just at the right time. He won a Pulitzer Prize for photography in 1945 for this image.

In the twenty-first century, the polar bear stranded on a small chunk of ice in a larger ocean of floating ice chunks has become the iconic visual argument for the movement to reduce global climate change.

6. *Visual argument often employs symbols.* You have seen how icons invite viewers to respond with the commonly held, established meanings and feelings,

Marines Raising the Flag on Iwo Jima, 1945.
SOURCE: © CORBIS

FIGURE 9.5   Visual argument often employs icons to prompt an immediate response from a viewer.

What does this photograph, taken toward the end of World War II, communicate to you? What is its purpose? What is the effect of not seeing the faces of the men? Describe the composition, including the focal point of the picture and the arrangement of the different parts. What feelings does it evoke? Why has it become a national icon? Can you think of other examples of iconic images that could be as lasting or become as influential as these Marines raising the flag in commemoration of victory in World War II? Describe them and their significance as icons.

or even to add to those that are usually associated with them. Icons are symbolic since most people look beyond their literal meaning and add the extra meanings they have come to represent. However, of the many symbols used in argument, few are so familiar that they can be classified as icons. Look at the color photograph of the split tree in Figure 9.6, (page 201). This photograph appears in *The Border: Life on the Line* by Douglas Kent Hall. The caption under the picture is "Near El Paso, Texas." El Paso is located on the Texas-Mexico border. This particular tree is a symbol, but not an icon.

   7. *Visual argument is selective.* Whenever you look at a visual argument, it is important to think not only about what is included in the picture but also

Tree Located on the Texas-Mexico Border.
SOURCE: Douglas Kent Hall

FIGURE 9.6   Visual argument often employs symbols.

This quotation by Graham Greene appears in the front of the book in which this picture appears: "How can life on the border be other than reckless? You are pulled by different ties of love and hate." Consider the location of this tree and that it was included in a book describing life on the United States–Mexico border. What symbolic meaning would you assign to it in this border context? How would you describe this meaning? What claim do you infer from looking at this picture? How might someone refute that claim? What type of proof is the tree in this context?

about what is omitted from it. If you could stand back and see more of the entire scene, of which the picture itself is only a small part, your perception of the picture might change a great deal. In any such framed image, you are allowed to see only what the photographer sees or wants you to see. You can infer or imagine what else is there or what else is going on outside the frame of the picture. The power of images often resides in this "edited" quality, but it is also a limit that the viewer must keep in mind.

Look at the photograph in Figure 9.7 (page 202) of a young girl in Afghanistan who is seeking an education. Notice the picture of the young girl provides emotional proof (*pathos*).

8. *Visual argument invites unique interpretations from viewers.* Usually no two people looking at a visual argument will interpret it in exactly the same way since individual viewers bring information and associations from their own past experience and use it to fill in some of the meaning suggested by the picture. Readers do that too, of course, particularly when they infer a claim or supply the warrants in a written argument. When viewers, like readers, draw on their backgrounds to fill out the meaning of a visual argument, they become vested in its message since some of the meaning now belongs to them. As a result, these viewers are more likely to accept the argument.

202   CHAPTER 9   Analyzing and Creating Visual Argument

A Young Girl in Kabul, Afghanistan, Seeks an Education.

SOURCE: Paula Bronstein/Getty Images, Inc.—Getty News

FIGURE 9.7   Visual argument is selective.

What is the main focus of this image? Who are the other figures in the background? The girl is looking up at someone or something. At what or whom do you think she is looking? How would this picture change had the photographer decided to photograph the entire scene in this room, with everyone in the room receiving equal attention? What is the effect of moving in on one individual and making everyone else in the room appear smaller than she? What claim is being made in this image?

Look, for example, at the Plate 4 in the color portfolio that follows page 224. It shows a detail from Michelangelo's scenes of the Creation, which appear on the ceiling of the Sistine Chapel in Rome. Here God is passing life to human beings by stretching out His life-giving finger to the lifeless, limp finger of Adam. Look, for example, at Plate 4 in the color portfolio that follows page 224. In this postcard picture, God is passing a baseball along with the first impulses of human life. One viewer, looking at this picture, says the artist is claiming, "We have had baseball from the beginning of time." Another puts the claim this way: "God is giving baseball to the entire universe." A third viewer has a different idea: "God is playing games with human beings." How would you interpret the meaning of

Animal Rights Activist: Free Hens from Cage! A nude animal rights activist holds a billboard on which is written "Free the hens. Get rid of all cages by 2012!" The activists protested raising hens in the cage, in Berlin, Jan. 16, 2008.

SOURCE: Getty Images

FIGURE 9.8   Visual argument invites unique interpretations from viewers.

The claim of this argument is clear from the writing on these activists' signs. Translated, the signs demand, "Free the hens. Get rid of all cages by 2012!" What is not clear, and therefore open to interpretation, is the significance of the support for the claim. Why do you think these individuals chose to stage their protest in this way? Why is the girl nearly nude, and why is she confined in a wire cage similar to a chicken's? Why is the individual outside of the cage in a chicken suit? What is the meaning of this support? What warrants are you expected to supply that will link this support to the claim? You are expected to make some inferences to understand this argument, and everyone may not make the same inferences.

this picture? How would you argue in favor of your interpretation? Your answer, at least in part, will probably depend on your views about baseball.

Now look at Figure 9.8, which is a visual argument that invites individual interpretations. This is a photograph of two animal rights activists in Germany who have created a tableau with the girl sitting in the cage and the person dressed like a chicken sitting outside of the cage. Both are holding signs, written in German, that state, when translated into English: "Free the hens. Get rid of all cages by 2012!" It is aimed at companies that keep chickens confined and crowded in small wire cages where they lay eggs and are fattened for the market. Many American students are also activists in the free-the-chickens movement, and, in some colleges and universities, they have persuaded their administrations to purchase only cage-free eggs for the student cafeterias. There is no correct interpretation of how the argument in Figure 9.8 is supposed to persuade a viewer to agree with the activists. Your guess may turn out to be as good as the next person's.

So far, the examples of the special features of visual argument have been applied to still images. All of these same features can be applied to motion pictures as well. Many documentaries and mainstream entertainment films take positions on controversial issues and argue for particular points of view. Examples of films that present arguments include documentaries like Michael Moore's *Capitalism: A Love Story* and Al Gore's *An Inconvenient Truth* and fiction films like *Avatar* and *Invincible*.

Motion picture directors and editors can create powerfully persuasive effects through the selection and juxtaposition of shots that lead the audience to see links and make associations that would not otherwise occur to them. Motion pictures also draw in the audience, engage their emotions, establish common ground, invite multiple interpretations, and rely on icons and symbols to create some of their meaning.

Let us turn now to a review of the argument theory you have learned in preceding chapters and consider how it can be used to analyze and critique visual argument.

USING ARGUMENT THEORY TO CRITIQUE VISUAL ARGUMENT

The Summary Charts on pages 302–312 provide a quick review of the argument theory you can use to analyze all types of visual argument in the same way that you would analyze written argument.

Consider the rhetorical situation to gain insight into the context for the argument, including the type of visual argument you are examining, the intended viewers, the artist's background and motivation, the possible constraints of all parties, and the exigence or outside motivation for the argument. Apply the Toulmin model to discover the claim, support, warrants, backing for the warrants, and the presence of a rebuttal or a qualifier.

Learn more about the claim and purpose for the argument by asking the claim questions. Establish which type of claim tends to predominate: a fact claim establishes what happened; a definition claim defines and clarifies what it is; a cause claim looks for causes and sometimes shows effects; a value claim looks at whether it is good or bad; and a policy claim establishes what we should do about it.

Then analyze the proofs. Which are present, *logos, ethos,* and/or *pathos,* and which type of proof predominates in the argument? What is the effect of the proofs? Look next at specific types of proof, including signs, induction, cause, deduction, analogies, definition, statistics, values, authority, and motives. How do those that are present further the argument? Refer to the tests of validity for each of the proofs you identify to judge their effectiveness.

Also, look for fallacies and consider the effect they have on the overall argument. Look for visual fallacies in particular. For example, ask if the image may have been selected or changed to represent a particular point of view. Ask whether a photo or film clip represents a unique or an exaggerated way of viewing a subject or whether it is an accurate picture of what really exists or happened. Consider the photographs taken of disasters, such as major floods, oil spills, earthquakes, or volcanic eruptions: they usually depict the worst, most extreme results of the disaster. You can at least wonder how representative these pictures are of what actually has happened.

Remember, too, that computers can be used to augment or change images. Tabloid newspapers sometimes create humorous composite images by placing one person's head on another person's body. Examine whether there is any evidence that a visual has been changed, doctored, or recreated in any way so that what you see as present in the image is a consequence of manipulation rather than insightful framing. Take time to look at visuals carefully. This helps you understand what is really going on in them and make some judgments about their accuracy and value.

BIAS IN VISUAL ARGUMENT

You will encounter bias in visual argument just as you do in written argument, except that, typically, it is more obvious in visual argument. All argument, by definition, shows bias for a particular point of view or a particular position. When you spot a visual argument that strikes you as biased, identify the source and type of bias being expressed. Here are two examples of biased images of Senator Hillary Clinton of New York when she was running for president of the United States. Figure 9.9 is a caricature of Clinton that appeared with an essay that criticized her idea for government-sponsored preschool for all four-year-old children. The article, which appeared in the conservative magazine *National Review*, opposed her idea as another government program that would be costly for taxpayers.

A caricature of Hillary Clinton.

Source: Roman Genn

FIGURE 9.9 How would you describe the biased point of view in this caricature of Hillary Clinton that appeared in the conservative magazine *National Review* during her campaign for her party's nomination for president?

Worcester, Mass. Senator Hillary Rodham Clinton at Clark University.

SOURCE: Todd Heisler/The New York Times/Redux Pictures

FIGURE 9.10   How would you describe the biased point of view in this photograph of Hillary Clinton that appeared in a liberal newspaper that had also endorsed her nomination for president?

Figure 9.10 is a more flattering photograph of Clinton addressing a large audience. It appeared in the *New York Times*, a liberal newspaper that also had endorsed Clinton's 2008 candidacy for president.

Watching for fallacies, visual distortions, exaggerations, Photoshop changes in original images that have been applied to make them more persuasive, and outright or even less obvious bias in visual argument will help you make fair and objective critiques. In addition, ask these questions to make ethical evaluations of images: Does the arguer understand the issue and its consequences? Is the position proposed in the best interests of the audience? Is the arguer honest and fair-minded? Or, in contrast, is the arguer unethical and manipulative? Refer to page 160 for additional criteria to help you make an ethical evaluation of images. Try to put your own prejudices and favorite ideas aside while you make these objective judgments.

SAMPLE ANALYSIS OF A VISUAL ARGUMENT

The following analysis of the political cartoon in Figure 9.11 on the next page draws on both the special features of visual argument and argument theory.[3]

---

[3]I am indebted to Sandi Hubnik for the cartoon and some of the analysis in this example.

FIGURE 9.11 A political cartoon making a visual argument.

Special Features of Visual Argument Employed in the Cartoon

Visual argument pulls the viewer in, creates common ground, evokes an emotional response, uses juxtaposition, employs icons, uses symbols, is selective, and invites a unique interpretation from the viewer.

1. I am pulled into this picture by the date on the large stocking and by the Christmas setting. Furthermore, common ground is established through the Christmas tree and hearth, which I associate with goodwill toward others and also with giving.

2. The word *Charities*, the date September 11, and the Christmas tree and stockings evoke an emotional response. Also, the juxtaposition of these items causes me to associate Christmas with giving to the victims of September 11 and reminds me of other needy groups, including needy people who live in my area, whom I should remember at Christmastime.

3. The Christmas tree, the stockings, and the date September 11 have been seen so often that they can be considered icons. Thus they communicate quickly and forcefully.

4. The cartoonist, Doug Marlette, has selected what he wants to feature in this picture: the large and the small stockings, the date September 11, and the words *Charities* and *Others*. The fireplace and Christmas tree are only partially depicted, and no presents or people are included. As a result, the focus is on generous giving, as happens at Christmas, but to people outside our immediate families.

5. I interpret this picture by remembering all the people in New York who needed help after September 11, 2001, and I wonder which other charities

were neglected as a result of funneling so much charitable giving to the 9/11 cause. I also remember the Salvation Army volunteers who solicit money for charity at Christmas. To me this picture means I should give more generously, like I would at Christmas, to all groups or persons outside my family that I consider needy and worthwhile.

Argument Theory Used for Analysis of the Cartoon

Useful theory includes applying the rhetorical situation (TRACE), the Toulmin model, the claim questions, and the types of proof, including *logos, ethos,* and *pathos*; identifying fallacies; recognizing bias; and determining whether or not the argument is convincing and ethical.

> *Rhetorical Situation:*
>> *Text:* Political cartoon with an argumentation intent.
>> *Reader/viewer:* People who are able to give to charities.
>> *Author/artist:* Doug Marlette, a Pulitzer Prize–wining political cartoonist for Tribune Media Services.
>> *Constraints:* Some viewers may be wary of giving to charities because they are not sure the money reaches the people who need it; the artist is in favor of giving and thus makes us associate charitable giving with the Christmas spirit of giving.
>> *Exigence:* The destruction of the World Trade Center twin towers by terrorists in New York on September 11, 2001.
>
> *Toulmin Model:*
>> *Claim:* We should give to all charities, not just 9/11 charities.
>> *Support:* The big "September 11" stocking and the small "Other" stockings.
>> *Warrant:* There are "other" charities as important and deserving as the 9/11 charities.
>> *Type of Claim:* This is a policy claim. It suggests what we should do in the future.
>
> *Types of Proof:* (*logos, ethos, pathos*):
>> *Cause:* The problem of uneven giving has been caused by the nature of 9/11.
>> *Analogies:* Stockings are like charities; giving to charities should be like stuffing stockings at Christmas.
>> *Value:* We value Christmas and giving to others. We value fairness.
>> *Motivation:* Christmas stockings should be equal in size because we all want the same amount of rewards or consideration.
>
> *Fallacies:* We could test the validity of the analogy between Christmas stockings and charities. In this case the analogy works because a logical link can be made between Christmas giving and charitable giving, so there is no fallacy.
>
> *Bias:* It is biased in favor of charitable giving.

Ethical Evaluation:

> ***Best interests of society?*** Yes, because giving to 9/11 and other charities is positive and necessary.
>
> ***Ethical?*** Yes, because charitable giving is an ethical activity, and the cartoon argues for equity and against inbalance.

We have described visual argument, explained why it is convincing, and illustrated how you can analyze it by examining its special features and applying argument theory. Let us change the focus now to present some ideas that will help you create visual arguments of your own. Visual argument can be used to provide support for a written argument, or it can stand alone as an independent argument. We will examine both possibilities.

ADD VISUAL ARGUMENT TO SUPPORT WRITTEN ARGUMENT

You may at times decide to add pictures, photographs, drawings, flowcharts, graphs, or other images to your papers as support for your claim. You can see from studying the images presented so far in this chapter that visual argument, when compared to written argument, is immediate and concrete, can appeal powerfully to the emotions, and can enhance an argument's message by making it convincing in ways that words alone cannot do. When an image is used as support, be certain that it functions as support for the specific claim or subclaim you are presenting. You will want your words and your visuals to work together to make your point, just as they do in Figure 9.7 on page 202.

Include images in your argument writing by adding clip art from the Internet or by using various types of printed visual material drawn from books, magazines, and newspapers. Downloaded images from the Internet can be pasted into your paper electronically. You can also use Photoshop to juxtapose or combine images that will invite your viewer to think about your claim in a new way. Printed images or drawings can be photocopied and pasted into your paper. Of course, if you prefer to, draw your own diagrams, flowcharts, or sketches to add visual support for the claim. Also, decide whether or not to add a line or two of explanation under each visual to explain its relationship to the written text. You will need to do that if the relationship between the ideas in the text and the visual support is not immediately clear to the reader. Document all visual sources to show where you obtained them. The MLA and APA sections in Appendix I show how to do that (see pages 257–301).

When you have quantities of numerical data, experimental results, or complex plans that are too cumbersome to describe in the written body of your paper, present it visually. Graphs, charts, tables, and flowcharts are valuable for condensing such material, often making it more easily accessible to the audience.

There are many different types of graphs, but the most commonly used are line, bar, and circle (or pie) graphs. These three kinds of graphs can be generated through common word processing packages such as Microsoft Word or WordPerfect for insertion in a paper. The examples that follow present graphs of data from

The World Almanac and Book of Facts 2010 edition, an excellent source for up-to-date statistics on many subjects.

Bar graphs in particular are used when you want to compare measurements of some kind. The numbers used in the measurements are often large, and the bar graph offers a picture that makes the numbers easily understandable in relation to one another. Figure 9.12 provides an example of a bar graph that shows the most current number of AIDS cases reported in Africa as compared with other parts of the world. There are 22,000,000 cases in Africa compared with 33,000,000 in the world. The graph reports percentages. This graph appears in a paper that argues that AIDS education in Africa has been ineffective.

Line graphs are most often used to show a change in a measurement over time. Some of the different measurements associated with line graphs are temperature, height and weight, test scores, population changes, and profits or deficits. Figure 9.13 shows the changes in the U.S. budget over time. It appears in a paper that argues that the United States needs to reduce its budget deficit.

Circle graphs are ordinarily used to show how something is divided. Figure 9.14 shows a circle graph that sums the percentage of the different sizes of automobiles sold in the United States during a recent year. It appears in a paper that argues that automobiles help deplete the ozone layer in the upper atmosphere.

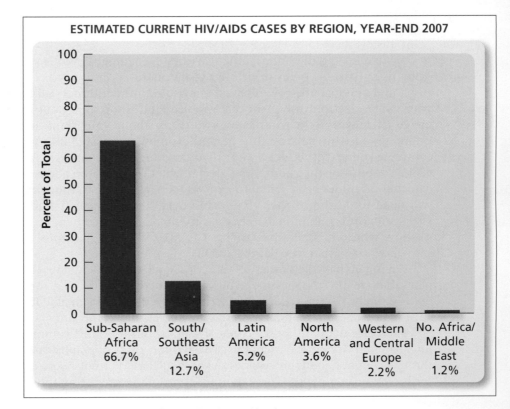

FIGURE 9.12   Bar Graph Comparing Large Numbers.

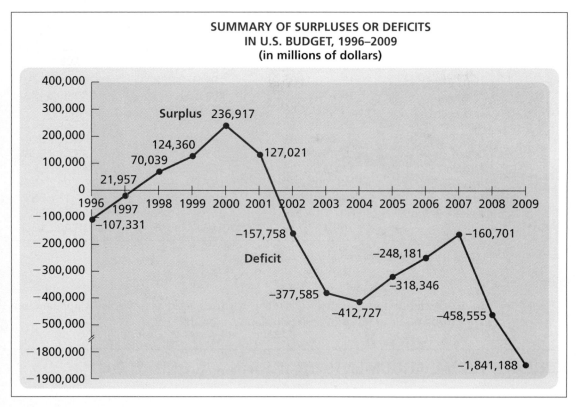

FIGURE 9.13 Line Graph Showing Change Over Time.

Whatever kind of graph you use, you must be sure that it is correctly and clearly titled and labeled, that the units of measurement are noted, and that you report the source of the statistical information used in the graph.

When you find that the statistical information you want to include in a paper is too detailed and lengthy for a graph, a chart or a table is usually recommended. For example, Figure 9.15 on page 212 provides the projected figures for population

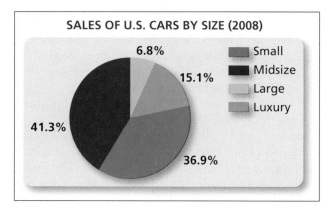

FIGURE 9.14 Circle Graph Showing How a Population or Market Is Divided into Sectors.

Population Projections for Selected Countries and World: 2009, 2025, and 2050			
COUNTRY	**2009**	**2025**	**2050**
Bangladesh	156,050,883	192,976,328	233,587,279
Brazil	198,739,269	231,886,946	260,692,493
China	1,338,612,968	1,453,123,817	1,424,161,948
India	1,156,897,766	1,396,046,308	1,656,553,632
Iraq	28,945,569	40,387,147	56,316,329
Japan	127,078,679	117,816,135	93,673,826
Mexico	111,211,789	130,198,692	147,907,650
Nigeria	149,229,090	197,222,936	264,262,405
Russia	140,041,247	128,180,396	109,187,353
United States	307,212,123	357,451,620	439,010,253
World	6,768,167,712	7,947,310,513	9,318,823,185

FIGURE 9.15   Table Presenting Comparison Data.

growth for ten major countries as well as for the world as a whole. It appears in a paper that argues in favor of zero population growth.

CREATE VISUAL ARGUMENTS THAT STAND ALONE

We have suggested ways to use visual materials as illustrations that support ideas in written arguments. Many visual arguments are, however, quite independent of written text and stand alone as persuasive arguments themselves without the benefit of accompanying verbal explanations. Creating visual arguments of this type requires imagination, creativity, and critical thought. Like other types of argument, you will find visual arguments that stand alone all around you. Look at book covers, bulletin boards and displays, posters, tee shirts, and even your fellow students. Some of your classmates may dress and arrange their hair so that they are walking visual arguments. Figure 9.16 provides two examples.

You can use the same types of images and equipment for all visual argument. These include single or composite images, moving images, photographs, drawings, paintings, or even three-dimensional installations with objects placed in juxtaposition to make a claim. For example, a stack of books and a lightbulb could make the claim that reading helps people think and get ideas. Experiment with stock photography from the Internet, Photoshop or Paint Shop Pro, cameras and camcorders, poster board and markers, scissors and paste.

For visual argument, as with other types of argument, you will need to make a claim about an issue that generates more than one perspective. Select an issue that is important to you and that you can make important to your audience. Reflect on all of the elements in the rhetorical situation as you would in creating a verbal argument. These include the materials and methods you will use; the characteristics and interests of your viewers; your own resources and interests; the constraints, including values, that either pull you and your viewers together

FIGURE 9.16 Clothing Can Make an Argument. (a) Singer, songwriter, and activist Bono, member of the rock group U2, makes a statement with his jacket. (b) Student Daniel Goergen and his message.

SOURCES: WIN MCNAMEE/CORBIS–NY (left); David Scull (right)

or push you apart; and your exigence or motivation for working with this issue in the first place. Use the Toulmin model to set up the main parts of your argument: you will need a claim, support, and warrants that you and your audience can share. Consider also how you can use *logos, ethos,* and *pathos* to create a persuasive and convincing argument.

Think through the **eight special features of visual argument** and how you will employ some of them to make your argument more convincing. You will want to create images that

- Communicate quickly and have immediate and tangible effects on viewers.
- Invite viewer identification and establish common ground through shared values.
- Engage the emotions of the viewers.
- Juxtapose materials from different categories so that the viewer will make new links and associations.
- Employ familiar icons that prompt immediate responses from viewers.
- Present visual symbols that viewers can easily interpret.
- Include only materials that viewers should focus on and omit everything else.
- Invite unique interpretations from viewers through visual subtleties that do not mean the same things to all people.

Consider adding a few words to your visual argument to enhance or extend its meaning. Pete Rearden, an artist who created the visual argument in Figure 9.17 (page 214), suggests limiting word art, if it is used at all, to no more than two or three short sentences. Use minimum punctuation and make the words as immediate and concrete as possible.

In his visual argument, Rearden has photographed an area that a homeless person has established as an outdoor camp. Rearden is deeply concerned with

FIGURE 9.17   Visual Argument That Uses Words to Extend Its Meaning.

SOURCE: Peter K. Rearden

homeless people and the fact that more than half of them are also mentally ill. These individuals have often told him that they are only camping out and will soon be returning to their homes. This rhetorical situation prompted Rearden to create the visual argument reproduced here. Notice that the words superimposed on the photograph add a dimension of meaning to the picture. They do not serve as a photoline that describes the picture. Instead, they create common ground by reminding viewers of going to camp without their parents; they juxtapose Dear Mom (with its immediate links to ideas of home) and the mess of the camp (which is less immediately readable) to invite associations; and they add emotional appeal with the words *mom, camp,* and *fun,* and the question, "Why don't you write me any more?" By adding these words, Rearden invites a more complex and personal interpretation from a viewer than the picture alone could provide. Notice, finally, what is left out of this picture. Consider that for many people, the homeless are the invisible members of society. Not all people would state the claim this picture makes in exactly the same way. How would you state it?

Practice applying the theory explained in this chapter by analyzing and creating visual arguments in the Class Activities and Writing Assignments that follow.

REVIEW QUESTIONS

1. Where are you likely to encounter visual argument? How do you recognize it?
2. What are the eight special features of visual argument that make it convincing?
3. What information about argument theory from earlier chapters in this book might you employ to help you analyze visual argument?

4. Describe some ways that you might use visual argument as support for a written argument.
5. What ideas from this chapter might help you create an effective visual argument that stands alone?

CLASS ACTIVITIES AND WRITING ASSIGNMENTS

Visual Argument

1. Locate a Visual Argument and Analyze It in Class

Find a visual argument in a magazine, newspaper, or on the Internet and bring it to class. Why do you think the item you have selected is a visual argument? Identify the issue. Point out the special features of visual argument that make it convincing. State your interpretation of the claim, even if you have to infer it. What type of claim is being made? (Review pages 122–130 for types of claims.) Point out the support and the warrants. State why you do or do not find the argument convincing. Is the argument you have selected ethical or unethical? Explain why you think so.

2. Analyze a Cartoon

Analyze the cartoon on page 216. What issue is addressed? What position does the artist take? Follow the model on pages 207–209 to analyze this cartoon. Draw on the special features of visual argument and then apply argument theory to help you make your analysis. Describe the rhetorical situation. Employ the Toulmin model. What is the claim? What type of claim is it? How is it supported? State one or more warrants. What is the backing for this cartoon, that is, what is going on in the larger society in respect to this issue that might help you interpret it? Discuss the results with the class.

3. Analyze Visual Arguments in the Color Portfolio

In a small group, analyze one of the pages of the color images that appear in the color portfolio that follows page 224.

a. Read the description of the context for each image. Which images seem to be deliberately staged? Which were caught as they happened? What is the effect?

b. What issues are raised by each image? What positions do the photographers seem to take on these issues? What audiences have the photographers imagined in each case? What are some of the constraints of both the photographer and the potential audiences? What is the exigence that motivated the photographer to take each image?

c. Identify and analyze the special features of visuals that are evident in each image. How and why are they used? Which seem to be particularly effective?

d. Employ the Toulmin model. What is the claim in each picture? What is the support? What are the warrants?

"Get Out!" Source: Cagle Cartoons Inc.

e. What type of claim predominates in each picture? Fact? Definition? Cause? Value? Policy? Why do you think so?

f. Analyze the proofs. Which predominates? *Pathos? Ethos? Logos?* Which types of proof can you identify in each image?

g. What is your final assessment of each image as an argument? Do you find them convincing? Why or why not? Are they ethical or unethical?

4. **Explore an Issue Visually Through Images**

Select an issue and create a visual exploratory essay by gathering three or more images that express different perspectives on the issue. Use the images in the color portfolio on Plates 2 and 3 (walls) and 4 and 5 (hands) as examples. As a class, brainstorm together to generate some ideas that will work for this assignment. Here are a few ideas to get you started: modifying your personal image, embracing new media, selecting a major, planning your career, making a major purchase such as a car or computer. Search for images on the Internet or in magazines or newspapers. Write a title and brief captions to make your essay coherent.

5. Create a Stand-Alone Visual Argument and Write an Analysis of It

This assignment requires you to create a visual argument, to write a paper in which you analyze it, and to present and explain it to the class.

a. Identify an issue that you can make an argument about by using images.
b. Make a claim about the issue.
c. Create a visual argument. Use Worksheet 8, Visual Argument Development, on page 218 to help you plan. See examples on Plate 8 of the color portfolio.
d. Write an analytical paper in which you explain and interpret your visual argument. Describe your own interpretation of your argument. Why did you put it together as you did? What does it mean to you? You may also include an analysis of the special features of visual argument and employ argument theory to analyze your visual argument. An example of a student analysis appears below. It is an analysis of image 2 on Plate 8 of the color portfolio that follows on page 224.

Essay 2

ANALYTICAL ESSAY OF STUDENT VISUAL ARGUMENT 2

NEVER AGAIN

Karen Hernandez

The artist was a student attending the University of Texas at Arlington when she made the sculpture and wrote this essay about it. The graphic novel *Maus* by Art Spiegelman provided the inspiration for this argument. *Maus* had been a reading assignment in her writing class. It tells the story of Spiegelman's parents' experiences during the Holocaust.

1 In 1938 Hitler and the Nazi government began a reign of terror and death that would leave over ten million people dead through pogroms and in prison camps. The book *Maus* tells one survivor's story, and I have tried to speak with this work of art of the horror that these people endured, just as the author of the book does. The skeletal figures of my piece are made of clay because it creates the closest appearance to human bones, and the figures are skeletal because this is the way many of the survivors looked when they were rescued from the camps. I have also left them in various sizes and shapes just as real people are; however, my figures are left incomplete (no hands or feet) because this is how the Germans viewed them, as less than human beings.

2 Even though the figures are skeletal, they have taken on an almost lifelike quality of expression in the way some heads are bowed, while others are held up. Some of the figures lean as if in pain or fatigue, and others seem to look at those standing nearby or into space. The longer I look at them, the more human they become to me, and I hope I have been able to impart this to the viewer as well.

3 I have also included, on the box, pictures of victims and survivors of the Holocaust so that the observer will know that this work is more than just the artist's imagination, and that these horrors really did occur. I also chose to place the title across the front of the piece so that, like the group who first used it in the Holocaust museum, I might impart to the viewer the reminder that those who

died during this terrible time of death and horror will not have done so in vain, and they will be remembered. Something like this will happen NEVER AGAIN.

FOR DISCUSSION:

What do you find most striking about image 2 on Plate 8 of the color portfolio that follows on page 224? What pulls you in as you look at this photograph of it? How is juxtaposition used, and what is the effect? Are the words written on the front of the visual argument sufficient to suggest the claim it is making? How does the analytical essay help you further understand this visual argument?

WORKSHEET 8: VISUAL ARGUMENT DEVELOPMENT

1. Write an issue question to focus your issue. (Example: *How can the unemployed be put back to work?*)

2. Write a claim that answers your issue question. (Example: *The government should create green-collar jobs to help the unemployed and the environment.*) Refer to Worksheet 6: Claim Development, on page 139 to help you get ideas to develop your claim.

3. Check the type of visual argument you will create (check more than one, if necessary):

    _____ stand-alone argument   _____ composite image

    _____ support for my essay   _____ single image

    _____ still image   _____ painting

    _____ moving image   _____ collage of images

    _____ all original   _____ graphic story (comics)

    _____ images from print sources   _____ 3-dimensional installation

    _____ images from Internet   _____ PowerPoint

    _____ photograph   _____ sculpture

    _____ drawing   _____ video

4. Check the materials you will need:

    _____ computer   _____ video camera

    _____ Paint Shop Pro   _____ poster board

    _____ Photoshop   _____ colored markers

    _____ PowerPoint   _____ scissors and paste

    _____ magazines   _____ paints

    _____ newspapers   _____ other art supplies

    _____ still camera   _____ objects for installation

5. Which of the eight special features of visual argument will be evident in my work?

6. What words should I add to make it clear to my audience?

Writing the Rogerian Argument Paper

To this point, you have been studying traditional argument that has its origin in classical sources. It is the form of argument that predominates in American culture, and it is what you are used to when you listen to people argue on television or when you read arguments in current periodicals or books. In traditional argument, the arguer states a claim and proves it by drawing on various types of proofs, including reasoning and evidence. The object is to convince an audience that the claim is valid and that the arguer is right. In this model of argument, the arguer uses the rebuttal to demonstrate how the opposition is wrong and to state why the audience should reject that position. Thus the emphasis in traditional argument is on winning the argument. Debate, with participants on both sides trying to win by convincing a third-party judge, is one form of traditional argument, as is courtroom argument and all other single-perspective argument formats in which one person argues to convince one or more people of a particular point of view.

As you know from your own experience and from reading about argument in this book, traditional argument does not always achieve its aims with the audience. Indeed, in certain situations when strongly held opinions or entire value systems are challenged, traditional argument may not be effective at all. The audience might simply stop listening or walk away. When that happens, it is useful to have another argumentation strategy to turn to, one that might work better in cases in which there seems to be a standoff or a lack of common ground among the arguing parties.

Rogerian argument, so called because it evolved from techniques originally applied by psychotherapist Carl Rogers, is a technique that is particularly useful for reducing conflict and establishing common ground between people who hold divergent positions and may at times express hostility toward each other. Common ground often seems impossible to achieve in such situations, but two opposing parties can almost always find something to agree on if they try hard enough. Here is an anecdote that shows two hostile individuals establishing common ground. This comes from a column titled "In Politics, It Does Help to Be Smart" by Molly Ivins. Ivins claims that this is a true story. (The "Lege" in the passage refers to the Texas legislature.)

> This is the perfect political story and also true, but the names have been changed to protect the players.
>
> Many years ago in the Texas Lege lurked two senators who loathed one another with livid passion. One was conservative, the other liberal; one from a rural area, the other urban; one a mean old bull and the other a witty cosmopolite. We'll call them Bubba and Cary.
>
> One afternoon, Bubba is drinking with a friend in a local dive when in walks Cary. Bubba looks at him and snarls, "You're a sorry ———!"
>
> Cary continues to the bar without comment. But after he gets a drink, he passes Bubba's table again, stops and says: "You think I'm a sorry ———, right?"
>
> "Right," says Bubba.
>
> "Well, I think you're a sorry ———."
>
> Bubba rears back, ready to rise and fight. Cary continues. "But we both *know* Senator Doakes is a sorry ———."
>
> Bubba laughs and says, "I'll drink to that."
>
> They were both smart politicians. And that's what smart politicians do: concentrate on the areas where they can agree, even if there's only one. That's how deals get done, the ball is moved forward, the system works and the people's interest is more or less served.[1]

While establishing common ground in Rogerian argument, as in this example, uncovers what two parties have in common, Rogerian argument also involves more than that. Instead of using rebuttal to show how the opposition is wrong, as in traditional argument, Rogerian argument requires that the arguer spend at least some time at the beginning of the argument not only explaining how the opposition's position is right but also identifying situations in which it might be valid. The arguer cannot do this very successfully without finding some common ground with the opposition. It is almost impossible to show how any part of another individual's opposing position is valid when you disagree with it totally.

Look back at the example in Chapter 1 (page 13) about the two individuals who are seeking common ground on methods for stopping random shooters. One of these individuals advocates that private citizens arm themselves with handguns as a deterrent to shooters. Another believes that the availability of handguns is the problem and advocates that private gun ownership be abolished. Common ground exists between the two parties because of their common concern for personal safety. To use Rogerian argument in this situation, the anti-handgun party would restate the pro-handgun party's position and would emphasize the common concern they both have for protecting their safety, before they search together for a solution on which they can agree.[2]

---

[1] Molly Ivins, "In Politics, It Does Help to Be Smart," *Fort Worth Star-Telegram*. October 28, 1999, p. 9B.
[2] I am indebted to Jenny Edbauer for this example.

Additional descriptions and examples of Rogerian argument in this chapter and in the Class Activities and Writing Assignments at the end of this chapter will demonstrate how various people achieve common ground through restatement and validation of their opponents' positions in Rogerian argument.

If you favor a consensual style of argument (see page 23), Rogerian argument is likely to seem quite natural to you. If, on the other hand, you favor a more adversarial style, you may find Rogerian argument frustrating at first, especially if your ideas and values seem to be under threat. Because Rogerian argument emphasizes making connections with the opposition and reducing hostility in such situations, you will need to curb your instincts to launch your argument by letting the opposition know how wrong you think they are. You can learn to use Rogerian argument, even if it is not your preferred or most natural style of arguing, in situations in which traditional argument is no longer effective. It is a useful strategy when other strategies are failing. Consider the examples in the next section.

ACHIEVING COMMON GROUND IN ROGERIAN ARGUMENT

In 2005, Cal Thomas, a politically conservative newspaper columnist, and Bob Beckel, a liberal political analyst and consultant, began co-authoring their popular column "Common Ground" that appears in the newspaper *USA Today*. In 2007, they published their book *Common Ground: How to Stop the Partisan War That Is Destroying America*, and in it Cal Thomas describes their collaboration.

> We're a good example of how common ground can work. Before we knew each other, we only knew "about" each other. I saw you [Beckel] as a liberal Democrat with "evil" ideas and positions conservatives associate with that label. You saw me as a conservative Republican with similar "evil" ideas and suspect friends. When we got to know each other and talked about politics, as well as personal and family challenges, we stopped seeing each other in stereotype and came first to respect and then (shock, shock) even to admire each other. The politics became less important than the relationship. And, most surprising of all, we found ourselves in agreement about quite a number of things, though we occasionally still differ on the best ways to achieve our common goals.[3]

Their purpose in writing the book, they make clear, is to encourage U.S. politicians to follow their example and make it a rule to seek common ground as part of the political process for resolving difficult and divisive issues. Indeed, Thomas and Beckel claim they are presenting "a plan that makes polarization the issue and common ground the solution." They "believe the time is right to challenge polarization and for common ground to become the next dominant strategic force in national politics."[4] To support this idea, they argue that the public

---

[3]Cal Thomas and Bob Beckel, *Common Ground: How to Stop the Partisan War That Is Destroying America* (New York: Harper-Collins, 2007), 257.
[4]Thomas and Beckel, 12.

prefers this approach: "Surveys conducted over several years have found that Americans believe even the most partisan issues—from abortion to the Iraq war—can be resolved with an honest commitment by elected leaders in Washington to finding consensus."[5]

Rogerian argument, with its emphasis on finding common ground and reaching consensus, can sometimes help people who differ strongly in their views find a bedrock of values and ideas that they can all hold in common. As a result, divided individuals are often able to resolve at least some of their differences. The process of seeking political common ground that Thomas and Beckel believe is beginning to occur in political discussions, and that they hope will occur more often, includes listening, understanding, and accepting points of view different from one's own, recognizing that both positions have some merit, and finally finding a way to resolve some of the differences. This process is at the heart of Rogerian argument strategy.

Let us look at another real-life example of building common ground between disagreeing parties with each side demonstrating an understanding of the other's point of view. Environmentalists, who typically want to protect the environment at all costs, often find themselves in opposition to individuals who make their living by exploiting the environment. Loggers, ranchers, mill owners, and other industrialists, for example, can fall into this second category. Individuals from both groups, stereotyped as "nature haters" and "eco-freaks" by the press, met in Idaho to discuss efforts for protecting endangered wildlife in the area. The environmentalists went to the meeting with some trepidation, but "as they joked and sparred over steak and beer, they discovered that neither side lived up to its stereotype. 'We found that we didn't hate each other,' said Alex Irby, a manager at the Konkolville sawmill. 'Turns out, we all like to do a lot of the same things. We love the outdoors.'" Timothy Egan, who wrote about the details of the meeting, makes this comment: "Loggers in the back country sitting down with environmentalists is an astonishing change."[6] One can infer that the common ground established in this meeting was brought about by each side describing to the other the value it placed on the environment and on outdoor activity in general. In such an exchange, both parties perceived that they had been heard, and further dialogue was then possible.

As you can see from both of these examples, understanding the rhetorical situation in general and the audience in particular by analyzing the thoughts and values of the parties involved is of critical importance in Rogerian argument. In Chapter 2 you learned how to analyze an audience as part of the planning process for writing argument papers. As you read the rest of this chapter, including the examples of Rogerian arguments written by students at the end of the chapter, pay particular attention to how Rogerian arguers analyze their audiences' dissenting opinions and values and then respond to them as part of their overall strategy.

---

[5]Thomas and Beckel, 10.
[6]Timothy Egan, "Look Who's Hugging Trees Now," *New York Times Magazine*, July 7, 1996, p. 28.

ROGERIAN ARGUMENT AS STRATEGY

Carl Rogers was a psychotherapist who was well known for the empathetic listening techniques he used in psychological counseling. Here is how he describes the importance of listening:

> I like to be heard. A number of times in my life I have felt myself bursting with insoluble problems, or going round and round in tormented circles, or during one period, overcome by feelings of worthlessness and despair. I think I have been more fortunate than most in finding at these times individuals who have been able to hear me and thus to rescue me from the chaos of my feelings. I have been able to find individuals who have been able to hear my meanings a little more deeply than I have known them. These individuals have heard me without judging me, diagnosing me, appraising me, evaluating me. They have just listened and clarified and responded to me at all levels at which I was communicating. I can testify that when you are in psychological distress and someone really hears you without passing judgment on you, without trying to take responsibility for you, without trying to mold you, it feels damn good. At these times it has released the tension in me. It has permitted me to bring out the frightening feeling, the guilts, the despair, the confusions that have been a part of my experience. When I have been listened to and when I have been heard, I am able to reperceive my world in a new way and to go on. It is astonishing how elements which seem insoluble become soluble when someone listens. How confusions which seem irremediable turn into relatively clear flowing streams when one is heard. I have deeply appreciated the times that I have experienced this sensitive, empathic, concentrated listening.[7]

Rogers later became interested in how listening techniques could be used to improve communication in other difficult, emotionally charged situations. Richard Young and his colleagues Alton Becker and Kenneth Pike built on Rogers's ideas to formulate Rogerian argument, a method for helping people in difficult situations make connections, create common ground, and understand one another. The object was to avoid undue conflict or, even worse, a mutual standoff.[8]

According to Young, Becker, and Pike, written Rogerian argument reduces the reader's (or listener's) sense of threat and conflict with the writer (or speaker) so that alternatives can be considered. Four goals are met with this strategy.

Goal 1. Writers let readers know they have been understood. To accomplish this purpose, the writer restates the opponent's position in summary form by using dispassionate, neutral language. The writer demonstrates that the reader has been heard and that the writer understands the issue exactly as the reader does. The loggers and the environmentalists listened and understood one another in the example cited earlier.

---

[7]Carl R. Rogers, *A Way of Being* (Boston: Houghton Mifflin, 1980), pp. 12–13. I thank Barbara Ciarello for calling this to my attention.
[8]Richard Young, Alton Becker, and Kenneth Pike, *Rhetoric: Discovery and Change* (New York: Harcourt, Brace, and World, 1970), pp. 7–8, 274–290.

Goal 2. Writers show how readers' positions are valid in certain contexts and under certain conditions. The writer demonstrates to the reader that at least part of the reader's position is both valid and acceptable and thereby makes it easier for the reader to reciprocate and accept part of the writer's position. Both the loggers and the environmentalists discovered validity in each other's positions since neither group wanted to destroy wildlife.

Goal 3. *Writers help readers understand that both of them share the same values, types of experience, attitudes, and perceptions and are thus similar in significant ways.* The loggers and environmentalists made it clear to each other that they both shared a love of the outdoors, held some of the same values, and enjoyed the same types of experience.

Goal 4. Writers propose solutions made up of elements from both sides that can be agreed to by both parties. At this point, environmentalists discovered that loggers were quite willing to pursue ways to preserve wildlife.

The most important feature of Rogerian argument is listening empathetically and nonjudgmentally. Rogers perceived that people usually listen judgmentally and evaluatively. They are eager to jump in, point out what is right or wrong, and make corrections or refutations, whereas Rogerian listening requires that insight into the other's position precede evaluation. Thus a writer of Rogerian argument takes the reader's place, and this is achieved by requiring that the writer provide neutral summaries of the reader's position that show sympathetic understanding of it and its context. In doing this the writer encourages a continued and open exchange of ideas with the reader. In Rogers's words, the writer "listens with" as opposed to "evaluating about."

Beyond empathetic understanding, writers should also show congruence, or genuine agreement, and an unconditional positive regard for the opposition. In communicating these attitudes, Rogerian argument takes the heat out of difficult argument that might otherwise result in a stalemate. Rogerian strategy cools the emotions and makes consensus more likely. The aim of the final reconciliation at the close of Rogerian argument attempts to show that the best solution to the issue may be a combination of what both parties want.

In real life, Rogerian argument is used frequently, particularly in business and politics, where agreement is indispensable. Some people in business claim they could not get anything done if they did not use Rogerian strategies on a daily basis. William L. Ury, one of the founders of the Program on Negotiation at Harvard Law School, claims that in business now, the best way to compete is to be able to cooperate. Cooperation is necessary because of the numerous mergers and cooperative ventures between companies. Many companies now work with the same markets and the same customers, and they cannot compete, as in former times, without weakening themselves as much as their competitors.[9] Some politicians have also resorted to Rogerian strategies to resolve difficult issues like health care and Social Security. Allowing tentative solutions to problems like these to split along party lines and stay that way is not always productive.

---

[9]William L. Ury, "Getting Past No . . . to Yes! The Art of Negotiation." Workshop, Dallas, October 12, 1999.

CONTEXT: These two photos appeared together in *Newsweek* magazine, April 3, 2006. They were accompanied by the following caption: "Crossing Over: Mexicans traverse the U.S. border, protesters rally in D.C."

FOR DISCUSSION: What pulls you, as a viewer, into these photos? Do you experience common ground and identify with the individuals in either photo? Describe it. What is the effect of placing these photos in juxtaposition? What would you identify as symbolic in them? How would you state the claim made by the photos when considered as a unit? What support is included? What is left out? What is the effect? What warrants would you supply? What backing?

FOR WRITING: Compare the fence in this photo with the fences on the next two pages. Some people in the United States advocate building a strong barrier along the U.S.–Mexican border to keep Mexican workers and others from crossing over illegally; other people reject this idea. State your position on this issue along with your reasons for holding it.

Plate 1

Exploring an Issue Through Images.
Walling Off Your Enemies: The Long View

Image 1: The Chinese Perspective.

CONTEXT: The Great Wall of China was first built between the fifth and third centuries B.C. to protect the northern borders of China. It is about 4,000 miles long at present.

Image 2: The German Perspective.

CONTEXT: The Berlin Wall, which separated East Berlin from West Berlin for 28 years, fell in 1989, an event that led to the reunification of Germany in 1990.

Image 3: The Israeli Perspective.

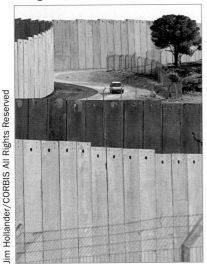

CONTEXT: This wall separates Israelis from Palestinians in the West Bank at the present time.

Image 4: The Iraqi Perspective.

CONTEXT: In Baghdad, Americans have put up walls to secure neighborhoods.

FOR DISCUSSION AND WRITING: These four photographs of walls provide four different perspectives on how governments have coped with perceived enemies by building walls. What do you think about the idea of building walls for protection from enemies? How effective is this solution? What other solutions can you think of that might also work or that might even work better?

Plate 2

Walling Off Your Enemies: The Long View, cont.

Image 5: The Palestinian Perspective.

Goran Tomasevic/CORBIS-NY

CONTEXT: The caption for the photograph above is "Palestinians in ArRam, near Jerusalem, walked yesterday near part of the West Bank barrier built by Israel." The caption for the photograph below is "Mireya Leal shares a picnic lunch through the U.S.-Mexico border fence with her husband Raymundo Orozco, near Tijuana, Mexico."

FOR DISCUSSION: The six images on these facing pages present six different perspectives on an issue. What is the issue? Comment on the special features of visual argument in these images.

FOR WRITING: In the poem "The Mending Wall" by Robert Frost, two men are repairing the rock wall between their farms. One of them makes the statement, "Something there is that doesn't love a wall." His neighbor has a conflicting view. He says, "Good fences make good neighbors." Select one of these statements as your claim, apply it to the six images on these facing pages, and support it. What do you conclude about the final value of walls used as barriers?

Image 6: The Mexican Perspective.

David Maung/AP Wide World Photos

Plate 3

Image (1)

CONTEXT: The work of art above, depicting the creation of Adam, was painted on the ceiling of the Sistine Chapel in Rome by Michelangelo in 1511. The postcard collage below, titled *Play Ball,* adds a baseball being handed to Adam from God.

FOR DISCUSSION: What associations form in your mind with the juxtaposition of the hands in the painting and in the postcard? What additional associations are created by the presence of the baseball?

FOR WRITING: Write a Toulmin analysis of the argument in each of the two pictures: state the claim, the evidence, and the warrants. How are the pictures alike? How are they different? Comment on the effectiveness of these pictures as arguments.

Image (2) **Plate 4**

Image (3)

CONTEXT: The photograph above from the *New York Times* appeared in 2002 over the caption: "A robot with a grappler holding a wounded Palestinian yesterday on a highway in Megiddo, Israel, 12 miles southeast of Haifa. Israeli Radio said the man was a suicide bomber whose explosives detonated prematurely." The 1980 photograph below, titled *Hands,* shows the hands of a Ugandan child and a missionary.

FOR DISCUSSION: How is juxtaposition used in each photograph, and what is the result? What associations are created by each? What is included, what is left out, and what is the effect? Suggest a title for the four images on these facing pages. State a claim. What type of claim is it?

FOR WRITING: Compare the pairs of hands in each of the photographs. How are the hands similar? How are they different? Comment on the effectiveness of these photographs as arguments.

Image (4)   **Plate 5**

Spencer Platt/Getty Images News/Getty Images

Image (1)

CONTEXT: The image above is from an Iraqi war zone and is captioned "A Gruesome Discovery and a Helping Hand." Staff Sgt. Osman Koroma is shown with Ahmed, one of 24 disabled children rescued from a Baghdad orphanage. The image below is taken days after the 2010 earthquake in Haiti that destroyed so much of the country. A child is asking a U.S. army soldier for food.

FOR DISCUSSION: What pulls you into each image? What is the effect of putting them in juxtaposition here? Comment on some of the other special features of visual argument in these images.

FOR WRITING: How do these photographs either confirm or expand your ideas about what U.S. army personnel are called on to do while serving in other countries? Go into detail about how your perceptions have or have not been changed as a result of viewing these images.

Ramon Espinosa/AP Wide World Photos

Image (2)

Plate 6

The Wall Street Journal

Image (1)

CONTEXT: The image above is captioned: "STARTING THE SEASON WITH A BANG: Shoppers hunt for Christmas bargains." The image below is captioned: "Photojournalists surround a Haitian policeman as he aims his rifle at looters in downtown Port-au-Prince Jan. 26, 2010." The photograph was taken shortly after the devastating earthquake in Haiti.

FOR DISCUSSION: These images are stand-alone arguments. What is striking in each of them? How is juxtaposition used in each, and what is the effect? What is the effect of viewing them together? What issues do they raise?

FOR WRITING: State the claims, as you would interpret them, that are made in each of these images and describe some of the evidence for each. Comment on the ethical or unethical messages that may or may not be communicated by each of them.

Rodrigo Abd/AP Wide World Photos

Image (2)

Plate 7

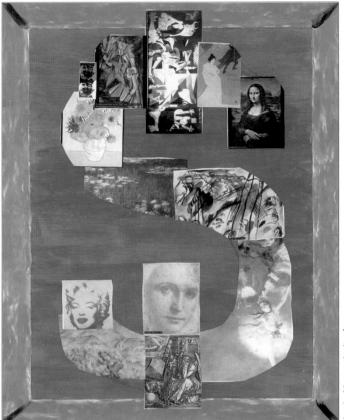

STUDENT VISUAL ARGUMENT 1

Untitled.

Elisabeth Elsberg, a student in a first-year writing class, created this collage from print images that were cut and pasted on to a painted background.

For Discussion: To work with audiences, icons must be immediately recognizable to most people. What parts of this artwork would you classify as iconic? Are they clearly iconic? How does this student use juxtaposition? Comment on the use of selectivity in this piece. What has been selected? What has been left out? How do you interpret this visual argument? How would you state its claim?

Plat

STUDENT VISUAL ARGUMENT 2

Never Again.

Karen Hernandez, the student who made this visual argument, created the figures out of clay. She then installed the clay figures on a platform that displays photographs from the Holocaust, with a title that expresses the claim: "Never Again."

Her written analysis appears on pages 217–2

Karen Hernandez

BOX 10.1	Traditional and Rogerian Argument Compared.

What Is Rogerian Argument?		
	TRADITIONAL ARGUMENT	**ROGERIAN ARGUMENT**
Basic strategy	Writer states the claim and gives reasons to prove it. Writer refutes the opponent by showing what is wrong or invalid.	The writer states opponent's claim to demonstrate understanding and shows how it is valid.
Ethos	Writer establishes own character by demonstrating fair-mindedness, competence, and goodwill.	Writer builds opponent's *ethos* and enhances own character through empathy.
Logos	Writer appeals to reason to establish a claim and refute the opponent's claim.	Writer proceeds in an explanatory fashion to analyze the conditions under which the position of either side is valid.
Pathos	Writer arouses emotions with evocative language to strengthen the claim.	Writer uses descriptive, dispassionate language to cool emotions on both sides.
Goal	Writer seeks to change opponent's mind and thereby win the argument.	The writer creates cooperation, the possibility that both sides might change, and a mutually advantageous outcome.
Use of argument techniques	Writer draws on the conventional structures and techniques taught in Chapters 5–7 of this book.	Writer throws out conventional structures and techniques because they may be threatening and focuses instead on connecting empathetically.

Reaching across the lines to harness the best ideas from both political parties can be much more productive and usually leads to better solutions.

Box 10.1 contrasts Rogerian argument, as explained by Young, Becker, and Pike, with the traditional model of argument.

In Chapter 5 you learned about the Toulmin model for argument. The Toulmin model and Rogerian argument have one extremely important feature in common. Even though the Toulmin model includes rebuttal, it also provides for the creation of common ground in the shared warrants between arguer and audience. Rogerian argument provides for common ground as well, but this is accomplished through the shared values and assumptions established through the summary and restatement of the opponent's position.

WRITING ROGERIAN ARGUMENT

To write Rogerian argument, according to Young, Becker, and Pike, the writer proceeds in phases rather than following set organizational patterns or argumentation strategies. These phases are as follows:

1. The writer introduces the issue and shows that the opponent's position is understood by restating it.
2. The writer shows in which contexts and under what conditions the opponent's position may be valid. Note that the opponent is never made to feel completely wrong.
3. The writer then states his or her own position, including the contexts in which it is valid.
4. The writer states how the opponent's position would benefit if the opponent were to adopt elements of the writer's position. An attempt is finally made to show that the two positions complement each other and that each supplies what the other lacks.

VARIATIONS OF ROGERIAN ARGUMENT

Rogerian argument as described by Young, Becker, and Pike is rarely, if ever, written exactly to their format. You can learn more about Rogerian argument, however, by using their format as practice. The Class Activities and Writing Assignments section of this chapter provides two examples of Rogerian argument papers written by students who followed Young, Becker, and Pike's formulations. You also will be invited to write a Rogerian argument paper by using this format.

As you read professionally written argument, however, you are much more likely to find elements or variations of Rogerian argument rather than arguments that include all of the parts of the Young, Becker, and Pike model. Here are some variations of Rogerian argument that you may encounter in your academic reading.

1. *Report on past research at the beginning of an academic argument.* Authors of academic argument, as a matter of convention, often begin with a review of what previous writers have contributed to the subject. They identify the writers by name and summarize their contributions before identifying and developing their own contribution to the subject. Thus an ongoing chain of conversation is established that acknowledges what has gone before the new material that is the actual subject of the article.
2. *Research proposal.* Research proposals that request funds and resources from granting agencies typically begin with a positive summary of the contributions of past researchers. Only after this former work has been acknowledged does the researcher explain how the new proposed research will build on what has gone before.[10]

---

[10]I am indebted to Mary Stanley for alerting me to this use of Rogerian argument.

3. ***Rogerian response paper.*** This paper is written in response to an essay written by another person with whom the author disagrees. The author of a response paper typically rejects the position that the author of the other essay presents but hopes to create common ground and understanding with that person to keep a dialogue on the issue going. The goal is to make a connection with the author of the other essay and thus create a context of understanding so that both authors can continue exploring the issue. Such papers usually begin with a restatement of the other author's position along with an acknowledgment of what is valuable about that position before the author goes on to present a different view of the matter. You will be invited to try writing a Rogerian response paper yourself in Exercise 2 (page 230).

As you read arguments written by other authors, look for elements of Rogerian argument. The three examples just cited by no means exhaust the possibilities.

THE ADVANTAGES AND DISADVANTAGES OF ROGERIAN ARGUMENT

The advantages of Rogerian argument are clear. Such an approach helps release tension and disagreement and encourages negotiation and cooperation when values and aims are in conflict. Also, Rogerian argument has the potential of leveling or at least controlling uneven power relationships that may interfere with the peaceful resolution of conflicting issues.

There are also perceived disadvantages of Rogerian argument. It is sometimes difficult for the writer to understand and restate the reader's position, particularly when the opponent is not present and no written material is available to explain the opposing position. Then too, connecting with the opponent by restating the opposing position may be extremely difficult, especially if the writer is emotionally involved and strongly dislikes the opposing ideas. It takes courage, Rogers says, to listen to and restate ideas that are strongly antithetical to your own. To succeed, you have to want to make connections. You also have to be willing to risk change. After totally committing yourself to understanding a different viewpoint, your own ideas will almost inevitably shift and change somewhat.[11]

Rogerian argument has also been criticized as annoying to women. Some researchers claim that women have always been expected to understand others, sometimes even at the expense of understanding themselves. As one female critic puts it, Rogerian argument "feels too much like giving in."[12] Another critic finds the advice that the writer should always use unemotional, dispassionate language to restate the opponent's argument unrealistic and constraining. Avoiding

---

[11]I am indebted to Paul Parmeley for this insight.
[12]See Catherine Lamb, "Beyond Argument in Feminist Composition," *College Composition and Communication* (February 1991), pp. 11–24. See also Phyllis Lassner, "Feminist Response to Rogerian Rhetoric," *Rhetoric Review* 8 (1990): 220–32.

rude or insulting language is necessary—a matter of common sense—but to avoid all emotionally connotative language may be impossible.[13]

A final criticism that is sometimes leveled at Rogerian argument when it is first encountered is that it can be perceived to be manipulative. Unethical arguers sometimes exhibit a condescending attitude or a fake sincerity, as they seem to listen to the people who present a view different from their own. Individuals who practice ethical Rogerian argument need to believe that they are involved in an ethical process right from the beginning. Ethical participants need to listen and hear nonjudgmentally; they need to seek genuine agreement with at least part of the opponent's position; and they need to develop some unconditional positive regard for the individuals with whom they are engaged and show that regard in all that they say. Rogerian argument is polite, and it takes the high road in human discourse. It persists as a viable model in spite of some of its shortcomings because its central notion, that it is important to understand and see some validity in other people's opposing positions, is sometimes the only way to create common ground in difficult situations.

REVIEW QUESTIONS

1. What are the four goals of Rogerian argument, and how do they differ from those of traditional argument?
2. What are some of the advantages and disadvantages of Rogerian argument?
3. In what type of argumentation situation do you think you might find Rogerian argument more productive than traditional argument? Describe an issue, along with the rhetorical situation, which might prompt you to resort to Rogerian argument.
4. In what type of argumentation situation do you think you might find traditional argument more productive than Rogerian argument? Describe an issue, along with the rhetorical situation, which might prompt you to use traditional argument instead of Rogerian argument.
5. What difficulties, if any, do you personally contemplate in using Rogerian argument? How do you feel about using this strategy?

CLASS ACTIVITIES AND WRITING ASSIGNMENTS

1. **Class Discussion: Understanding Rogerian Argument as a Strategy**

   a. The excerpt on the next page is taken from Edward O. Wilson's book *The Future of Life*. Read the passage, analyze the Rogerian strategy, and answer the questions at the end.

> **BEFORE YOU READ:** What is your present attitude about preserving the environment? Do you know of anyone who holds a different view? What is it?

---

[13]Doug Brent, "Young, Becker, and Pike's 'Rogerian' Rhetoric: A Twenty-Year Reassessment," *College English* 53 (April 1991): 446–52.

Essay 1	**THE FUTURE OF LIFE***

Edward O. Wilson

Wilson, a well-known scientist and Harvard professor, has been called the father of the modern environmental movement. His book *The Future of Life* provides plans for conserving earth's biodiversity.

1   Everyone has some kind of environmental ethic, even if it somehow makes a virtue of cutting the last ancient forests and damming the last wild rivers. Done, it is said, to grow the economy and save jobs. Done because we are running short of space and fuel. *Hey, listen, people come first!*—and most certainly before beach mice and louseworts. I recall vividly the conversation I had with a cab driver in Key West in 1968 when we touched on the Everglades burning to the north. Too bad, he said. The Everglades are a wonderful place. But wilderness always gives way to civilization, doesn't it? That is progress and the way of the world, and we can't do much about it.

2   Everyone is also an avowed environmentalist. No one says flatly, "To hell with nature." On the other hand, no one says, "Let's give it all back to nature." Rather, when invoking the social contract by which we all live, the typical people-first ethicist thinks about the environment short-term and the typical environmental ethicist thinks about it long-term. Both are sincere and have something true and important to say. The people-first thinker says we need to take a little cut here and there: the environmentalist says nature is dying the death of a thousand cuts. So how do we combine the best of short-term and long-term goals? Perhaps, despite decades of bitter philosophical dispute, an optimum mix of the goals might result in a consensus more satisfactory than either side thought possible from total victory alone. Down deep, I believe, no one wants a total victory. The people-firster likes parks, and the environmentalist rides petroleum-powered vehicles to get there.

FOR DISCUSSION:

What is the issue in this passage? What two groups of people are identified? Why might they feel hostile? What are their differences? How does Wilson create common ground between the two groups? How does Wilson use Rogerian strategy? Summarize the two positions and describe the Rogerian elements in the passages. Why do you think Wilson uses Rogerian strategy in this part of his book? How do you think Wilson might describe his audience for this passage?

---

*From Edward O. Wilson, *The Future of Life* (New York: Knopf, 2002), 151–52.

b. Turn back to Martin Luther King Jr.'s "Letter from Birmingham Jail," (page 190). Has King made any efforts to use Rogerian argument strategies and thereby build common ground by establishing that the opposition may, at times, be correct? If yes, provide some examples and analyze their effects.

2. **Write a Rogerian Response**

Review the following essays that appear in previous chapters. Which one do you disagree with the most? "'A' Is for 'Absent'" (page 25); "Sexual Harassment and the Feminist 'Front'" (page 164); "Brother, Can You Spare a Word?" (page 111). Or, as an option, find a letter to the editor in your local or school newspaper that you disagree with and write a Rogerian response to it. Use either essay or personal letter format. Your paper should be from 300 to 500 words long.

Prewriting

Write a brief summary of the position taken by the author of the essay you have selected. Then write a brief summary of your position. Make certain you understand both positions clearly.

Writing

Do all of the following in your paper:

1. State the opposition's position as presented in the article (or letter) and describe in what instances this position might work or be acceptable. As you write, imagine that the individual who wrote the article or letter will be reading your response. Write so that that person will feel "heard."
2. Write a clear transition to your position on the issue.
3. State how your position would also work or be acceptable.
4. Try to reconcile the two positions.

3. **Writing Assignment: The Rogerian Argument Paper**

You are now going to write a Rogerian argument of around 1,000 words on an issue of your choice. There are two ways to set up this assignment. Read through the following options, select one that appeals to you, and proceed with the rest of the instructions for the assignment. The basic instructions in option 1 apply to both options. Follow MLA or APA guidelines. Student-written examples for option 2 are provided at the end of this exercise.

Option 1

If you wrote an exploratory paper, write a Rogerian argument in response to the position you discovered that is most unlike the position you favor. (You may have already articulated this opposing position in your exploratory paper.) Move this position to the beginning of your Rogerian argument paper, and rewrite it until you believe you have fairly and dispassionately represented that other point of view. People who hold that view need to be able to agree that you have heard and understood them. Look for common ground with that other view and use that common ground to describe contexts and conditions in which the opponent's position might be valid. *Do not show what is wrong with this other position*.

Next, write a transition that changes the subject to your position. Describe your position, and show the contexts in which it is valid. Finally, reconcile the two positions. Show how they can complement each other, how one supplies what the other lacks, and how everyone would benefit if elements of both were finally accepted.

For example, the student who wrote the exploratory paper about Barbie dolls (pages 89–91) might identify the feminist position as the idea she disagrees with most: namely, that Barbie dolls are bad because they create unrealistic expectations for little girls. She will begin her paper with an explanation of that position, show what is valid about it, write a transition to introduce her position that Barbie is neutral and that society needs to face this issue, and, finally, reconcile the two positions by showing that both have common goals, just different ways of meeting them.

Option 2

Select any issue that you understand from at least two opposing points of view. You should feel strongly about your point of view, and you should have strong negative feelings about opposing viewpoints. Write a Rogerian argument in response to an opposing viewpoint. See the Examples section below.

Examples

Here are two examples of Rogerian argument written by students.

Example 1 "Let Those Who Ride Decide!" was written by a student who depends on his motorcycle for all of his transportation. The marginal annotations make it easier for you to distinguish the parts of his paper. Following his paper is a Rogerian argument evaluation sheet that has been filled out to show how this argument conforms to the recommended parts of a Rogerian argument. The requirements for the Rogerian argument paper are described in the left column, and the right column shows how well this paper has met those requirements.

When you have finished reading the paper and evaluation in Example 1, turn to Example 2 (pages 234–236) and see if you can identify and describe the parts of that paper. Complete an evaluation sheet like the sample. These two analyses will help you understand how to write your own Rogerian argument.

Student Paper 1

Eric Hartman
Rogerian Argument Paper
Professor Wood
English 1302
30 April 2010

Let Those Who Ride Decide!

Introduces issue; summarizes rhetorical situation

1   Should the law mandate that motorcyclists wear a helmet? Texas law presently does not require a helmet to be worn by those over twenty-one who have taken a motorcycle safety course or who

have at least $10,000 of health insurance for injuries sustained while operating a motorcycle. In the past, Texas has had a helmet law that was universal, and many neighboring states still do. There are many in Texas who would like to see the old law reinstated so that all motorcyclists, regardless of their age, would be required to wear a helmet at all times.

Explains opposing position to create common ground

2   Proponents of helmet laws are concerned with motorcyclists' safety. Their argument, that one is more likely either to survive a motorcycle wreck or to minimize physical damage if wearing a helmet, is very strong. Thus the value put on safety clearly is significant, especially for those who have lost a loved one in a motorcycle fatality. Similarly, because damage is less likely for helmet wearers, a motorcyclist in an accident is perceived as less likely to become disabled and require monetary support from the government (i.e., the taxpayers). The argument here is that a motorcyclist is potentially not only hurting himself or herself but also those who might have to financially support these unfortunate motorcyclists.

Shows how opposing view is valid

3   It is not too difficult to see why one would be a proponent of mandatory helmet laws. Indeed, it would be unfortunate and unfair for anyone to have to support financially an incapacitated individual who might not be in such a condition had he or she been wearing a helmet. It is also almost inconceivable to argue that one is safer on a motorcycle without a helmet. Certainly the arguments in favor of mandatory helmet laws are so strong that it is difficult to imagine any alternative position.

Transition to preferred view

4   However, there is another position, and one that is held just as passionately by some people as the one just described. As unlikely as it seems, there is a debate about the effectiveness of helmets. Many people who ride motorcycles believe helmet laws should be completely abolished. If that cannot be

Explains preferred view

accomplished, the mandatory age should at least be lowered from twenty-one to eighteen. Individuals who hold this point of view cite studies that suggest helmets have the potential to severely damage the spinal cord and/or vertebrae in an accident,

Evidence for view

causing varying degrees of paralysis and death. Full-face helmets are criticized for obstructing a rider's hearing and vision, especially peripheral vision. Helmets, furthermore, prevent the body's natural process of cooling through the head and can contribute to heat exhaustion or heat stroke (Quigley).

Evidence for view

5   Even the cost notion that is often termed the "social burden" theory is questionable. The famous Harborview Medical Center study showed that injured motorcyclists relied on public funds 63.4 percent of the time, which is significant. But it was later determined that 67 percent of the general population relied on public funding for hospital bills over the same period of time.

Statistically, there does not seem to be any significant distinction between the reliance of motorcyclists and the general public on public funding. Thus the social burden theory seems primarily to be just that, a theory. It sounds good, but it seems to lack statistical validation ("Critics").

Reasons
for view

6   Even though some of the arguments made by the proponents of helmet laws appear to be valid, there is ultimately some question regarding the strength of their arguments, and even some question of whether their arguments address the real issue that is built on a different value altogether, namely freedom. We have certain inalienable rights, rights to life, liberty, and the pursuit of happiness. It seems to many motorcyclists that mandatory helmet laws are in violation of such rights. Governments have a responsibility to protect their inhabitants from being harmed by each other in reasonable situations. It is not necessarily the responsibility of the government to try to prevent people from ever encountering danger. One could die on a plane or in a car or in an electrical fire in one's house, but the government would not think to outlaw airplanes, automobiles, or electricity. The fact that one incurs danger without a helmet is not a sufficient reason to mandate use of a helmet.

Introduces
idea of
reconciliation

7   There is understandably a tension between safety and freedom, and these two values are often in conflict. In many instances people may not be in a position to make an educated decision with regard to their safety, and we understand such decisions being made for them. For example, children are not seen as capable of making certain decisions concerning the use of seat belts in automobiles or watching certain movies. Making those decisions for them seems reasonable as does requiring those under eighteen to wear a helmet. Yet, for those of sound mind who are deemed responsible, it seems unreasonable to strip away their freedom to choose by requiring them to wear a helmet.

Reconciles
positions

8   It is easy to appreciate the care and concern of those proponents of helmet laws and understand their passion, and it seems impossible to be unilaterally against helmets. Still, some riders declare themselves to be pro-choice when it comes to helmets. In other words, the rider should have the right to choose whether or not he or she wants to wear a helmet. Educating and informing riders about helmets should be a part of the licensing process. Then riders are more likely to make the best decision with the best information at their disposal. But the riders themselves should be able to decide whether or not to wear a helmet instead of someone else making that decision for them as if they were children. In short, as many responsible motorcyclists would say, "Let those who ride decide."

Works Cited

"Critics Falsely Claim That Bikers Are a Burden on Society." *Bikers Rights Online!* N.p., 2001. Web. 27 Apr. 2010.

Quigley, Richard. "NHTSA's Safety Standards Are Shown to Be Anything but Safe." *Helmet Law Defense League Report.* 3rd ed. N.p., Mar. 1994. Web. 27 Apr. 2010.

FOR DISCUSSION:

Describe a rhetorical situation in which it would be better to write this paper in this form, using Rogerian strategy, than it would be to write it as a position paper, using traditional strategy. Describe the readers, the constraints, and, in particular, the exigence as you imagine the rhetorical situation that might have prompted this paper.

Example 2 "Dear Boss" was written by a student who worked part-time while going to college and wanted to change her working hours and some of her responsibilities. She had already spoken to her boss about making some changes but ended up with more responsibility instead of less. She was worried that her boss might think she was selfish and unconcerned about the welfare of the company. She was also worried that working too many hours would endanger her scholarship. It was very important to her that she reach a resolution to her problem. She decided to use Rogerian strategy to come to a better resolution of her problem with her boss.

EVALUATION SHEET FOR ROGERIAN ARGUMENT PAPER

REQUIREMENTS OF ROGERIAN ARGUMENT	WHAT THE AUTHOR DID
1. Introduce the issue and state the opposing position to show you understand it.	1. Introduced the issue in paragraph 1 and presented the opposing view accompanied by good reasons in paragraph 2.
2. Show how the opposition might be right.	2. Showed the contexts in which the opposition might be valid in paragraph 3.
3. Write a clear transition from the opposing position to a preferred position.	3. Wrote a transition in the first sentence of paragraph 4 to move from opposing to a preferred position.
4. Explain a preferred position and show how it might be right.	4. Presented preferred position in paragraphs 4, 5, and 6.
5. Reconcile the two positions.	5. Reconciled the two views in paragraphs 7 and 8.

**Student
Paper
2**

Elizabeth Nabhan
Rogerian Argument Paper
Professor Wood
English 1302
30 April 2010

Dear Boss

Dear Boss,

1   I am writing to you in response to our recent conversation regarding my responsibilities as an employee of Smith and Smith. You indicated to me that you felt I had a surplus amount of free time at work and suggested that I was obviously capable of handling a greater workload. Shortly thereafter, you delegated to me several new tasks that are to be performed on a regular basis. I understand that you believe I should pick up the additional workload to ensure that I am performing at a maximum level of output on a day-to-day basis. Also, you think I would complete the tasks more effectively than the individuals previously assigned to them.

2   I understand your reasoning that I should maintain a high level of output on a daily basis. As an employee of the company, it is my obligation to be productive for the duration of my workday. Not producing enough work results in idle time that, in turn, results in a loss to the company. It is intrinsic to the very nature of my role as a corporate auditor to ensure that the company does not engage in wasteful expenditures. If I worked nonstop every workday I would maximize my rate of efficiency and save the company the cost of hiring an additional employee. Additionally, I accept your opinion that I am the employee who could most efficiently handle the new tasks you would like me to take on now. My knowledge and experience with the required tasks puts me at an advantage over the previously delegated employees. Because of this, I would be able to complete the tasks much more quickly than other employees who would likely require more research time. Your perspective is fundamentally valid. However, I would like to introduce several factors that I believe may also bear consideration. In doing so, I believe it will be possible to reach a satisfactory conclusion regarding the issue of my workload and responsibilities.

3   According to the terms of my employment, I am required to complete a minimum of twenty hours per week. It was mutually agreed upon that any time I am not enrolled in school, I am free to work up to forty hours per week. The period during which I had an unusually ample amount of "down time" occurred during the summer months when I was not enrolled in school. As a result, I did briefly have an increased number of work hours. During this interim period I could have easily increased my workload, but I was not assigned any new tasks. In fact, additional duties were

not assigned to me until after I commenced the fall semester. My hours are now reduced by nearly one-half, and, as a result, my idle time has diminished significantly. An increased workload now will limit the time I spend on each project and could result in a decrease in the quality of the work I complete.

4   I do not think there is any great concern as to whether the employees originally assigned to my newest tasks are able to complete them satisfactorily. These employees were hired based on their skills for completing the tasks at hand, and none of these tasks could be considered as falling outside of the scope of their regular duties. Furthermore, I believe it would be counterproductive to reassign their tasks to me, as it would essentially undermine these other employees' expertise. This type of situation can often lead to a decrease in morale, which would in turn affect each employee's total output. Finally, I would like to reconsider the belief that idle time on my part results in decreased productivity. During my free time I am in a position to assist other staff members, as needed. I also utilize this time to observe subordinate employees, which is consistent with my role as the corporate auditor.

5   Our individual points of view share the common purpose of doing what is best for the company as a whole. Therefore, I believe it is possible to accomplish this goal via compromise. According to your perspective, I should take on additional responsibilities to fill gaps in my productivity while relieving less-qualified employees. From my point of view, I feel that my time is already effectively spent. I suggest the following steps be taken in order to ensure that each of our needs are met: First, my reduced hours must be taken into consideration when assigning me work. When I am in a position to take on additional duties, I feel I should be assigned those most compatible with my job description. More general tasks should be delegated to other employees. To alleviate your hesitation regarding their ability to perform these, I accept the responsibility of overseer and will offer them any help they may need. In doing so, I will apply my own expertise to more specific tasks without overburdening myself in such a way as to reduce my overall efficiency. Additionally, this will allow other employees the opportunity to sharpen their skills, while remaining under my observation. I propose this delegation of duties be put into effect under a probationary period, during which time we can observe the success of the program, and, if needed, redelegate tasks. Thank you for your consideration.

Sincerely,
Elizabeth Nabhan

FOR DISCUSSION:

What is the issue? What is the boss's position? What is the student's position? If you were the boss, how would you respond to this letter?

Writing the Researched Position Paper

In this chapter you will learn to write a research paper in which you take a position on your issue, organize the research materials and idea notes that you have collected, and write a paper that is convincing to your audience of readers. You may want to take a look at the assignment for this paper now on pages 253–254 to get a sense of what you will be doing. Instruction in this chapter includes organizing and outlining this paper, incorporating research into your first draft, and revising and preparing the final copy.

Organization, or deciding on a framework of ideas for your paper, will be dealt with first. As you go back and reread the material you have gathered for your paper, you will need to think about (1) how this material can be divided into *parts*, (2) how these parts can be placed in an *order*, and (3) what the logical *relationships* are among the ideas and parts. To help you accomplish this, let's look first at the advice classical rhetoricians give on these matters.

CLASSICAL ORGANIZATION OF ARGUMENTS

In classical times, organization, or *arrangement*, was one of the five canons of rhetoric. These canons identified the important aspects of building an argument to which every orator of the time needed to pay attention. Besides arrangement, the other four canons included: *invention*, or gathering material and creating ideas; *style,* or using appropriate language; *memory,* or speaking without notes; and *delivery,* or making good use of voice and gestures. Three of these canons, invention, style, and arrangement, are topics that are important to writers as well as to speakers of argument. You have already learned to use a number of invention strategies for argument in previous chapters. They are summarized on the

Invention Worksheet on page 253. The second canon, style, is discussed in Chapter 7 (pages 150–154). We now turn to a discussion of arrangement, or ways to organize the ideas, in an argument paper.

Occasional disagreement exists among some of the classical authors regarding the parts and the order of the parts in an argument. In the *Rhetoric* Aristotle complains about earlier writers who present elaborate organizational schemes that he considers unnecessarily complicated. For Aristotle, an argument only has to have two essential parts, the proposition (or claim), which is stated first, and the proof that follows. He allows that an arguer might want to expand on this core structure by adding other parts, including an introduction and a conclusion. He emphasizes, however, that anyone planning an argument needs to remain flexible and consider the purpose, the audience, and the occasion, since any one of these variables could influence the way in which an argument is finally put together. Furthermore, according to Aristotle, if you have no reason to include one of the parts, then leave it out.

After Aristotle, Cicero and other Roman orators made minor modifications to Aristotle's structure. As a result, classical organization is usually explained as having six parts with the following specified functions.

The Six Parts of Classical Organization

1. *Introduction.* Makes the subject and purpose clear at the start. Also, includes information that will interest the audience so that they will want to keep reading.
2. *Statement of proposition and division.* States claim at or near the end of the introduction. Sometimes names the major sections of the paper so that it is easier for readers to follow along.
3. *Narration.* Provides background about the subject and the events that have led to the controversy. Indicates why the subject is important. Gives the author an opportunity to establish *ethos* by offering reasons for an interest in the subject and citing qualifications for writing about it. May describe other positions on the issue or summarize the scholarship to date.
4. *Proof.* Establishes reasons and evidence that are acceptable to the audience to prove the proposition or claim.
5. *Refutation.* Refutes opposing positions. May be placed after the proof, before the proof, or at various points among the items of proof. (According to Aristotle, if the opposition has a lot of objections to your position, it is better to use refutation to remove these objections for the audience early, before you give your reasons. Otherwise, state your position, prove it, and then refute others.)
6. *Conclusion.* Emphasizes the most important point and reminds the audience of the other important points.

You will find classical organization useful when you plan your position paper, particularly if you remain flexible and adapt it to your needs.

CLASSICAL AND MODERN ORGANIZATION

When you look back at the classical structure just described, much of it may seem familiar to you. Did you think of the Toulmin model? Toulmin is a modern writer. Your study of the Toulmin model in Chapter 5 introduced you to the usual parts of an argument. These include a claim, support, warrants and possibly also backing for the warrants, a rebuttal, and a qualifier for the claim. The Toulmin model only identifies parts and does not specify the order in which they should appear, so it is not a model for structuring an argument like classical organization or organizational patterns are. When you begin to think about the claim, the subclaims that represent the major sections of a paper, and the facts, examples, and opinions that support them, then, you also begin to imagine various possibilities for ordering these parts of your paper. You could, for example, easily move the Toulmin model's parts into the classical framework.

You are also probably familiar with the introduction-body-conclusion format that frequently is used to organize modern essays and speeches. These parts have their origin in classical rhetoric. The usual functions mentioned for a modern introduction are to focus and introduce the topic, to provide some background, to get the attention of the audience, and, sometimes, to present the claim. The conclusion either states the claim or refocuses it through restatement and final, compelling reasons.

Concerning *order*, students are often advised to regard the beginning of the paper as a strong position, but the end as even stronger. Thus you would place your strongest material at or near the end, other strong material at the beginning, and the less impressive material in the middle.

Both classical and modern theorists advise you to think about your audience when determining the order of ideas in a paper. For instance, for a hostile audience, consider beginning your paper with material that your readers can agree with so that they will want to continue reading. For a neutral audience, you might want to present strong and interesting examples at the beginning to get their attention and create interest. For a friendly audience, you can show in your introduction how you agree with them and confirm their already favorable opinion about you.

Let's look now at some additional ideas that will help you organize your paper and establish relationships among the ideas and sections in it.

USE ORGANIZATIONAL PATTERNS TO HELP YOU THINK AND ORGANIZE

Organizational patterns represent distinct ways to think about the parts of your paper, the order in which you will place them, and the relationships among the ideas and parts. They can be incorporated into the overall structure of the classical model, particularly in the proof section (body) of the paper. You were introduced to some of the organizational patterns that are particularly useful for argument in Chapter 6 where organizational patterns that work for different types of claims are discussed. This chapter provides additional information about these patterns. These patterns, by the way, can shape your paper as the dominant pattern or be combined as minor patterns within the dominant pattern to organize some of the sections. Use the patterns alone or in combinations accompanied by an introduction and a conclusion. Use these formats both to help you think about your ideas as well as to organize them.

Claim with Reasons (or Reasons Followed by Claim)

This pattern takes the following form:

> Statement of claim
> Reason 1
> Reason 2
> Reason 3, and so forth

Set this pattern up by writing the claim, following it with the word *because*, and listing some reasons. Or, list some reasons, follow them with the word *therefore*, and write the claim. For example, you may present the claim that a national health care program is essential to a society, which is followed by reasons: the unemployed have no insurance, many employed people have no insurance, the elderly cannot afford medicine, many children do not receive adequate health care. The reasons may be distinct and different from one another and set up like separate topics in your paper. Or, you may create a chain of related reasons by asking *why* and answering *because* five or six times. Also, some of your reasons may be used to refute, others to prove, and still others to show how your claim will meet the needs and values of the audience. Support all reasons with facts, examples, and opinions. You can also utilize transitional phrases such as *one reason, another reason, a related reason*, and *a final reason* to emphasize your reasons and make them stand out in your paper.

Cause and Effect (or Effect and Cause)

The cause-and-effect pattern may be used to identify one or more causes followed by one or more effects or results. Or, you may reverse this sequence and describe effects first and then the cause or causes. For example, the causes of water pollution might be followed by its effects on both humans and animals. You can use obvious transitions to clarify cause and effect, such as "What are the results? Here are some of them," or simply the words *cause, effect*, and *result*.

Applied Criteria

This pattern establishes criteria or standards for evaluation and judgment and then shows how the claim meets them. For example, in an argument about children in day care, you might set out physical safety, psychological security, sociability, and creativity as criteria for measuring the success of day care. Then you might claim that day care centers meet those criteria as well as or even better than home care and then provide the support. The applied criteria pattern is obviously useful for value arguments. It is also useful in policy arguments to establish a way of evaluating a proposed solution. You can use the words and phrases *criteria, standards, needs*, and *meets those criteria or needs* to clarify the parts of your paper.

Problem–Solution

The problem–solution pattern is commonly used in policy papers. There are at least three ways to organize these papers. The problem is described, followed by the solution. In this case, the claim is the solution, and it may be stated at the beginning of the solution section or at the end of the paper. An alternative is to propose the solution first and then describe the problems that motivated it. Or, a problem may be followed by several solutions, one of which is selected as the best. When the solution or claim is stated at the end of the paper, the pattern is sometimes called the *delayed proposal*. For a hostile audience, it may be effective to describe the problem, show why other solutions do not work, and finally suggest the favored solution. For example, you may want to claim that labor unions are the best solution for reducing unemployment. First, describe the unemployment problem in vivid detail so that the audience really wants a solution. Next, show that government mandates and individual company initiatives have not worked. Finally, you now show how labor unions protect employment for workers. Use the words *problem* and *solution* if you want to signal the main sections of your paper for your reader.

Chronology or Narrative

Material arranged chronologically is explained as it occurs in time. This pattern may be used to establish what happened for an argument of fact. For example, you may want to give a history of childhood traumas to account for an individual's current criminal behavior. Or, you may want to tell a story to develop one or more points in your argument. Use transitional words such as *then, next*, and *finally* to make the parts of the chronology clear.

Deduction

Recall that deductive reasoning involves reasoning from a generalization, applying it to cases or examples, and drawing a conclusion. For instance, you may generalize that the open land in the West is becoming overgrazed; follow this assertion with examples of erosion, threatened wildlife, and other environmental harms; and conclude that the government must restrict grazing to designated areas. The conclusion is the claim. You can use such transitional phrases as *for instance, for example*, and *to clarify* to set your examples off from the rest of the argument and *therefore, thus, consequently*, or *in conclusion* to lead into your claim.

Induction

The inductive pattern involves citing one or more examples and then making the "inductive leap" to the conclusion. For instance, a number of examples of illegal immigrants who require expensive social services lead some people to conclude that they should be sent home. Other people may add that most immigrants contribute to society and conclude they should be allowed to stay. No matter which claim or conclusion is chosen, it can be stated at the beginning or at the end of the paper. The only requirement is that it be based on the examples. The same transitional words used for the deductive pattern are also useful for the inductive: *for instance, for example*, or *some examples* to emphasize the examples; *therefore, thus*, or *consequently* to lead into the claim.

Compare and Contrast

This pattern is particularly useful in definition arguments and in other arguments that show how a subject is like or unlike similar subjects. It is also often used to demonstrate a variety of similarities or differences. For example, the claim is made that drug abuse is a medical problem instead of a criminal justice problem. The proof consists of literal analogies that compare drug abuse to AIDS, cancer, and heart disease to redefine it as a medical problem. The transitional words *by contrast, in comparison, while, some*, and *others* are sometimes used to clarify the ideas in this pattern.

INCORPORATE IDEAS FROM YOUR EXPLORATORY PAPER

The pattern you used to write your exploratory paper can be expanded for a researched position paper. Recall that you may have explained a variety of positions on an issue, possibly including those in favor of it, those against it, and those with various views in between. Your objective was to explain the range of different perspectives on the issue. Having stated these positions, you can now expand your exploratory paper by refuting some of these positions and by stating and supporting your own. You may want to use another pattern, such as the claim with reasons, to organize your own position on the issue.

As an alternative, you can explain the various positions from your exploratory paper at the beginning of your position paper and show the advantages of each of them; then identify one position as probably best; and, finally, spend the rest of your paper developing that idea. This strategy impresses readers as fair-minded and convincing because each major perspective is acknowledged. To write such a position paper, go to your exploratory paper file in your computer or notebook and build parts of it into your position paper.

HOW TO MATCH PATTERNS AND SUPPORT TO CLAIMS

Some of the organizational patterns are particularly appropriate for specific types of claims. Table 11.1 suggests patterns you might want to consider as promising for particular argumentation purposes. Of course, you can combine more than one pattern to develop a paper. For example, begin with a narrative of what happened, then describe its causes and effects, and, to complete it, propose a solution for dealing with the problems created by the effects.

TABLE 11.1 Appropriate Patterns for Developing Types of Claims (in descending order of suitability)				
CLAIMS OF FACT	**CLAIMS OF DEFINITION**	**CLAIMS OF CAUSE**	**CLAIMS OF VALUE**	**CLAIMS OF POLICY**
Claim with reasons	Deduction	Cause and effect	Applied criteria	Problem–solution
Induction	Claim with reasons	Claim with reasons	Cause and effect	Applied criteria
Chronology or narrative	Compare and contrast	Rogerian argument	Claim with reasons	
Cause and effect	Rogerian argument	Deduction	Chronology or narrative	Cause and effect
Rogerian argument	Exploration	Exploration	Rogerian argument	Claim with reasons
Exploration	Induction		Induction	Rogerian argument
			Deduction	
			Compare and contrast	Exploration
			Exploration	

Use organizational patterns to help you think about and organize your ideas. The patterns may be too constraining if you select only one and try to fill it in before thinking through your material. You may want to work with your ideas first, without the conscious constraints of a pattern to guide you. At some point, however, when you are finished or nearly finished organizing your ideas, move out of the creative mode and into the critical mode to analyze what you have done. You may find that you have arranged your ideas according to one or more of the patterns without being consciously aware of it. This is a common discovery. Now use what you know about the patterns to improve and sharpen the divisions among your ideas and to clarify these ideas with transitions. Ultimately, you will improve the readability of your paper by making it conform more closely to one or more specific patterns of organization.

Some proofs and support work better than others to establish different types of claims.[1] Table 11.2 on the next page offers suggestions, not rules, for you to consider. Remember that a variety of types of proof and a generous amount of specific support create the best, most convincing argument papers.

---

[1] I am indebted to Wayne E. Brockriede and Douglas Ehninger for some of the suggestions in Table 11.2 on page 244. They identify some types of proof as appropriate for different sorts of claims in their article "Toulmin on Argument: An Interpretation and Application," *Quarterly Journal of Speech* 46 (1960): 44–53.

TABLE 11.2   Proofs and Support That Are Particularly Appropriate
for Developing Specific Types of Claims

CLAIMS OF FACT	CLAIMS OF DEFINITION	CLAIMS OF CAUSE	CLAIMS OF VALUE	CLAIMS OF POLICY
Facts	Reliable authorities	Facts	Value proofs	Data
Statistics	Accepted sources	Statistics	Motivational proofs	Motivational proofs
Real examples	Analogies with the familiar	Historical analogies	Literal analogies	Value proofs
Quotations from reliable authorities	Examples (real or made up)	Literal analogies	Figurative analogies	Literal analogies
Induction	Signs	Signs	Quotations from reliable authorities	Reliable authorities
Literal and historical analogies		Induction	Induction	Deduction
Signs		Deduction	Signs	Definition
Informed opinion		Quotations from reliable authorities	Definition	Statistics
			Cause	Cause

OUTLINE YOUR PAPER AND CROSS-REFERENCE YOUR NOTES

You have already been provided with a rationale and some ideas for outlining in Chapters 3 and 4. Some people find they can draft simple papers that require little or no research without an outline or list. They can later rearrange material on the computer until it is in a logical order. Most people, however, need some sort of outline or list to guide their writing when they are working with their own ideas or with material from outside sources.

Try making an outline or list for your research paper, and make it one that works best for you. Think of your outline as a guide that will help you write later. At the very least, indicate on your outline the major ideas, in the order you intend to write about them, and add the ideas and research you will use for support and development. Read your original ideas and research notes, and check to make certain that all are cross-referenced in some way to the outline. Identify the places where you need more information and research. If you have stored research material in computer files, reread each item, check to make certain you have placed quotation marks around quoted material, and make certain you have recorded the original source for every quoted, paraphrased, or summarized item. Arrange the items under headings on your outline in the order you think you are likely to use them. If you have photocopied or printed material from online, use numbers to cross-reference to your outline the highlighted passages you intend to quote. If you have gathered research material on cards, paper-clip the cards to the places on the outline where you will use them later. Work with your outline until it flows logically and makes sense. Pay attention to the parts, the order of the parts, and the relationships among the parts.

If you have the opportunity, discuss your outline or plan with your instructor, a peer editing group, or a friend. Someone else can often tell you whether the organization is clear and logical, whether you will need more support and evidence, and whether the warrants will be generally acceptable to your audience.

The following sample outline is more complete than the research plan described in Chapter 3 (on page 66). It is an outline of the student-written researched position paper that appears in Appendix 1 on pages 276–286. This outline would be complete enough to guide writing for some people. Others might want to add more detail to it before attempting the first draft. It is the sort of outline one might take to a peer editing group to discuss and receive suggestions for the actual writing of the paper.

SAMPLE OUTLINE

Working Title: "The Big Barbie Controversy"*

Strategy for Paper: Summarize positions in exploratory paper in introductory paragraphs and describe personal interest in Barbie to create my own *ethos*; establish and apply criteria for judging Barbie doll as both good as a role model for building girls' self-esteem and bad for that purpose; conclude by stating that Barbie is neither good nor bad and should not be the focus of this issue; instead, parents and community are responsible for helping children build self-esteem. Value claim at the end.

Introduction (summary of positions in exploratory paper and background history):

- My childhood interest in Barbie—loved her. My sister's disinterest
- Feminism—how changed my view: new respect for sister
- New common sense view: Barbie just a doll with marketable appeal
- History of Barbie doll: new concept in 1959; offers choices to girls; evidence of success

Is Barbie good for building girls' confidence and self-esteem?

- A powerful icon; evidence of the doll's popularity
- Criteria for showing Barbie is good: Barbie is everywhere; people all over the world play with these dolls; it is fun to play with Barbie; Barbie stimulates imagination and is a good role model because she can take on many roles.

Is Barbie bad for harming girls' confidence and self-esteem?

- Criteria for showing Barbie is bad for girls: the doll creates a poor body image; encourages eating disorders; encourages stereotypes; is a negative role model.

(continued)

_____

*This is an example of an outline that was used to guide writing. The paper developed from this outline appears in Appendix 1, pages 276–286.

SAMPLE OUTLINE *(continued)*

Refutation: Does Barbie have to be either good or bad?

- Refute those who say all bad: anorexia older than Barbie; cannot protect children from everything that might be a negative influence
- Refute those who say all good: people who played with Barbie still self-critical and have limited insight into themselves

Conclusion: It is not Barbie's responsibility to create a self-image in children.

Claim: Adults and society are responsible for children's self-images. Barbie doll is being used as a scapegoat.

Note that this outline is worked out in detail in some areas but not in others. The ideas in it so far, however, belong to the author. The peer group that critiques it at this stage would be able to help the author decide whether she has gathered enough source material to write a credible paper or whether she needs to read and take more notes. When your own research seems to be complete, and the notes you intend to include in the paper are either copied in a computer file, on cards, or highlighted on photocopies, the notes can now be cross-referenced to your outline and stacked in the order in which you will use them in the paper. You are ready to write the draft next. Most of the material in the paper will be your own insights, observations, ideas, and examples. The researched material will be incorporated into the paper to add information, interest, clarity, and credibility.

INCORPORATING RESEARCH INTO YOUR FIRST DRAFT

Use common sense in working your research materials into your draft. Your objective is to create a smooth document that can be read easily while, at the same time, demonstrating to your readers exactly which materials are yours and which are drawn from outside sources. Here are some suggestions to help you accomplish this. We draw our examples from an article by Johanne Mednick, "The Highs of Low Technology," from the *Toronto Globe and Mail*, July 23, 1993, page 16.* Mednick is a teacher who lives in Canada, and her article is about her old bicycle.

1. ***Use quoted material sparingly.*** You want to have the controlling voice in your paper. No more than 20 percent of your paper should be made up of direct quotations of other people's words. When you do quote, select material that is interesting, vivid, and best stated in the quoted words.

   Here is an example of a direct quote that you could have marked on a photocopy of the article or copied onto a note card with the author's name

---

*The examples on pages 246–248 show how and when to use research and credit its source in your writing; The Mednick article is a one-page source. Treat longer sources in exactly the same way. To find more complete MLA instructions, see pages 259–275 and the student paper on pages 276–286 or the *MLA Handbook for Writers of Research Papers*, seventh edition, Chapter 6.

and the page number recorded in MLA style to use later in your paper. In this first example, the author's name is cited with the page number at the end of the quote since she is not named in the text. This signals the reader that the full citation is available in the alphabetized list of sources at the end of the paper. The two ellipses in this quotation show that the writer omitted words before or at the end of the source's sentence and omitted at least another full sentence. This shortened quotation efficiently expresses what you want to say:

EXAMPLE: "Perhaps my bike is representative of a world gone by. . . . My bike is certainly not built for speed. . . . It's built for taking time. It makes people feel relaxed" (Mednick 16).

2. *Paraphrase or summarize when you do not know enough to use your own explanations.* Use your own words to rephrase or summarize other people's explanations and ideas so that yours is the dominant voice in your paper.

    Here is an example of paraphrased material from the same article, followed by the page number only since the author is mentioned in the text:

EXAMPLE: Mednick says that her microwave and her computer make her feel that life is getting too complicated and out of control (16).

    Here is a summary of Mednick's article, again with the author mentioned in the text so that only the page number is necessary at the end.

EXAMPLE: Mednick claims that people still long for the older, simpler machines like her old bicycle and the simpler way of life they represented (16).

3. *Begin and end your paper with your own words instead of a quotation, paraphrase, or summary of other people's ideas.* The beginning and end are emphatic places in a paper. Put *your* best ideas there, not someone else's.

4. *Whenever you can, introduce each quotation, paraphrase, or summary in your paper so that your readers will know who wrote it originally.* Make it clear where your words and ideas leave off and where someone else's begin. Introduce each quotation, paraphrase, or summary with the name of the person who wrote it. Consider also adding a description of that person's credentials to establish his or her *ethos* and authority.

EXAMPLE: According to Johanne Mednick, a teacher in Canada, an old bicycle is better than newer models (16).

5. *Integrate every quotation into your paper so that it flows with the rest of the text and makes sense to the reader.* Work in the quotations so that they make sense in context.

EXAMPLE: People have various reasons for preferring the old to the new. Mednick's reasons for preferring her old bicycle are clear in her concluding statement. In describing her bicycle, she says, "It allows me the opportunity to relax and, at best when I'm heading down the road, escape what I don't understand" (16).

6. *If your author quotes someone else and you want to use that quote in your own paper, introduce the quotation by indicating who originated it.* Make clear you are quoting someone your source quoted.

EXAMPLE: Mednick declares that other people show a great deal of interest in her old bicycle. Strangers come up to her regularly and make such comments as "Where did you get that thing?" and "I haven't seen one of those in ages" (16).

7. *Cite the source of the quotation, paraphrase, or summary in parentheses at the end of it.* Further instructions for writing in-text parenthetical citations are given in Appendix 1.

Write all quotations, paraphrases, and summaries into your first draft so that your entire paper will be in place for smooth reading. The following three paragraphs show the quoted, paraphrased, and summarized material from the Mednick article worked into the first draft so that it is absolutely clear as to what is the author's and what is Mednick's.

> Many people become nostalgic for the ways things were. Some people keep old cash registers at their businesses to remind customers of days gone by. Other people fire up wood stoves to help them remember earlier times. Johanne Mednick, a teacher in Canada, claims that many people still long for older, simpler machines and also for the way of life they represent (16).
>
> Mednick uses her old bicycle as an example. "Perhaps my bike is representative of a world gone by," she says. "My bike is certainly not built for speed. . . . It's built for taking time. It makes people feel relaxed" (16).
>
> New computers and microwave ovens, by contrast, make people feel that life is getting too complicated and out of control (Mednick 16).

Notice that in the first paragraph, Johanne Mednick's entire name is used to introduce her material, and in subsequent references she is referred to as Mednick. Notice also that in the first two paragraphs, Mednick's name is used to introduce the material that is attributed to her. Since it is clear from the context where her material begins and where it leaves off, it is only necessary to insert the page number of her article at the end of the borrowed material. In the third paragraph, Mednick's name is not included in the text, and it is less clear whose idea this is. To make it absolutely clear to the reader that this is another idea of Mednick's, her last name along with the page number is placed at the end of the borrowed idea. The full information about this source and where it was first located will be placed on bibliography pages at the end of the paper. The reader who wants to know when and where Mednick published her article can refer to those pages.

Clearly Identify Words and Ideas from Outside Sources to Avoid Plagiarism

Whenever you use quoted, paraphrased, and summarized material from other sources in your paper, you must indicate where your words leave off and someone else's begin, and you must identify the original source for all borrowed material.

Sometimes students mix their words in with the words of the author they are quoting and, as a result, the reader cannot easily sort out the student-writer's words from those of the author quoted. This is a form of plagiarism. You have seen a real example of this error in Chapter 3, page 65. Let's look at another example. The underlined words and phrases in the paragraph below have been copied exactly as the author wrote them. Notice, however, that the student does not place any of this material in quotes to show that these words belong to the author and not to the student.

> Low technology can be a high for many people. A wonderful bicycle that most people would refer to as an <u>old clunker</u> might bring its owner considerable pleasure. Its <u>two large wheels, seat, handle bars, basket, bell</u>, and pedals help its owner <u>glide past all of the riders on racers and mountain bikes who are intent on engaging the right gear for the occasion</u>. People admire her bike because it gives them a sense of <u>something manageable, not too complicated</u> (Mednick 16).

Even though the citation at the end of the paragraph indicates that some of the ideas are Mednick's, the reader does not know which words came directly from Mednick's essay and which have been supplied by the author.

Examine these two better and accurate ways to incorporate research. One is to *paraphrase the ideas in your own words*.

> Not everyone likes new bicycles. Johanne Mednick describes her old bicycle and the pleasure it brings her. She never envies people who pass her by on new bikes. She prefers the familiar comfort of her old bicycle (16).

An alternative is to *combine your words with the author's, but place the author's words in quotations marks*.

> Johanne Mednick claims in her essay "The Highs of Low Technology" that she prefers her old bicycle to new racing bikes or mountain bikes. She describes her old bicycle in admiring terms. It has, she says, "two large wheels, seat, handle bars, basket, bell and the simple mechanism that allows me to pedal my way to wherever I'm going" (16). She is often able to pass people on newer bikes because they have to slow down to shift gears (16).

Document Your Sources

Some of the main features of source acknowledgment are explained in Appendix 1, pages 259–275. Use this Appendix as a reference guide when you are working borrowed material into your paper and also when you are preparing the final list of the works you have used. These methods will inform your reader about exactly what material in your paper is yours, what belongs to other people, and where you found the material in your research.

In Appendix 1 you will first be shown examples of ways to incorporate borrowed material into the text of your paper and how to cite them in the text to indicate succinctly where they originally appeared. You will then be shown how to prepare entries for the list of sources that you have used. This list will appear at the end of your paper. Take a look at the types of sources listed in Appendix 1. Some of them may suggest resources that you have not yet thought of for your paper.

As you incorporate borrowed material from other sources, you will need to follow a system and a set of conventions that has been prescribed for this purpose. Two such systems are described in Appendix 1. MLA style, which is recommended by the Modern Language Association for papers written in the humanities, is explained first. MLA documentation style provides advice on how to acknowledge the work of other individuals in your paper itself and also how to give full information about these sources in a list of "Works Cited" at the end of your paper. Following the discussion of MLA style is a researched position paper in MLA style format (pages 276–286). It was written by a student, and you can use it as an example when you write your own paper. Study the annotations in the margins of this paper. They demonstrate how quoted and summarized material can be incorporated into papers and acknowledged according to MLA style.

The second documentation style taught in Appendix 1 is APA style, recommended by the American Psychological Association for papers written in the social sciences. APA documentation calls for a somewhat different system from MLA. Information is provided for citing sources in the text of an APA style paper and listing these sources on a "References" page at the end. The first page and the References page from a student paper written in APA style provide an illustration of this documentation format (pages 300–301).

Other documentation styles, not described in Appendix 1, include CSE style, which is recommended by the Council of Science Editors for scientific papers, including the natural sciences, chemistry, geography, and geology; and Chicago style, the style recommended by the University of Chicago Press. Chicago style (or CMS, for the *Chicago Manual of Style*) is followed throughout this book. If an instructor asks you to use either CSE or Chicago style in a paper, consult the Internet or a published manual for guidelines. No matter which system you use while writing a paper, be consistent and do not mix styles.

MAKE REVISIONS AND PREPARE THE FINAL COPY

Review Chapter 4 for additional information to help you write and revise your paper. It may take several tries, but you will eventually get a version of your paper that you are content to show to other readers. Seek the help of your peer editing group, a tutor, your instructor, or other readers once again, when you have improved your paper as much as possible on your own. When you arrive at this point, you will think your paper is pretty good. However, a new reader will always find ways to improve a paper. This is the time, then, to put aside pride and let others take a final look at what you have written. During this final revision process, you and your readers can use the Toulmin model to help you identify and revise the major elements in the paper.

1. Find your claim. Is it clear? Is it well positioned?
2. Check the quantity and quality of your support. Is there enough? Is it relevant? Is it authoritative and accurate?
3. Check your warrants. Are they likely to be acceptable to your audience?
4. Think about backing for your warrants. Would explaining the backing make your warrants stronger and more acceptable to your audience?
5. Focus on your rebuttal, if you have one. Does it effectively address the opposing arguments?
6. Consider a qualifier. Would a qualified claim make your argument stronger?

As you go through your paper these final times, make all the remaining changes, large and small. If you have not done so already, write a meaningful title that reflects the content of the paper. Rewrite parts by using more evocative words, cut out anything that does not contribute to the meaning, add text where necessary, rearrange things if you have a good reason to do so, read your paper aloud to catch additional problems, and make all final corrections. You will finally reach a point where you are satisfied. Now it is time to prepare the final copy.

Type your paper on standard 8 ½-by-11-inch paper, and double-space all of it, including the "Works Cited" (MLA) style or "References" (APA) pages. See pages 265–275 and 291–299 for further instructions. If you are following MLA style, leave 1-inch margins all around. Type your last name and the page number ½ inch from the top of the right-hand corner. Repeat this on all subsequent pages, including the "Works Cited" list. One inch from the top of the first page, by the left-hand margin, type and double-space your name, your instructor's name, the course name and number, and the date. (Your instructor may ask you to add the type of assignment.) Double-space again, and type the title, centered. Double-space once more, and begin typing your paper. Attach the "Works Cited" list at the end, continuing to number these pages sequentially.

If you are following APA style, prepare a title page (if your professor requires it) on which you type a short version of your title and the page number in the top right-hand corner and on all subsequent pages. For example, the author of the paper "Alaskan Wolf Management" uses the short title "Alaskan Wolf" on each page of his paper (pages 300–301). Next, drop down to midpage and type the title, centered. Then double-space and type your name; double-space again and type the name of your school. Begin your paper on the next page with the short title and page number in the top right-hand corner. Then double-space and type the title. Double-space again and begin your paper. Attach the list of "References" at the end, starting on a new page, numbered sequentially.

Spell-check your paper, if you are using a computer, and proofread it one last time, even if you have utilized the spell-check. Correct all of the errors that you can find. Errors in a research paper damage your *ethos* with your readers. Careless errors communicate that you do not really value your own work or your audience. When your paper is as error-free as you can make it, it is ready for submission.

REVIEW QUESTIONS

1. Name and describe the six parts of classical organization.
2. Name five examples of organizational patterns that you might use in a position paper. Describe their main features or rationale, and name the type of claim typically associated with each of them.
3. Name at least one type of proof that would be appropriate for developing each of the five types of claims.
4. What steps can you take to avoid plagiarism when you are incorporating research materials into your draft and when you are preparing the final copy?
5. What is the purpose of the "Works Cited" page (MLA) and the "References" page (APA)?

CLASS ACTIVITIES AND WRITING ASSIGNMENTS

1. **Review and Complete Invention Activities**

    Invention, a canon of classical rhetoric, is the process of creating and gathering the ideas and other materials you will use for writing argument (see page 237). As you go through the research and idea materials that you have accumulated to this point, you may discover that you need to find or develop more material in some areas. You may need to read more. You may also need to think more. Worksheet 9: Invention (page 253) provides thinking and questioning strategies that can help you produce additional material to write about. Read through the list of invention strategies on the worksheet. They represent a composite of those described in this and earlier chapters. Some of them will be "hot spots" for you. That is, they will immediately suggest profitable activity for developing your paper. Check those that you want to use at this point, and complete them. There may be only two or three. Include the Toulmin model, however. It is one of the best invention strategies for argument.

2. **Writing Assignment: The Researched Position Paper**

    a. *Write a list, outline, or partial manuscript that will serve as a plan for your paper, and bring it to class.* Refer to the example on pages 245–246 in this chapter. In peer editing groups of three or four students, explain to the group what your paper is about and how you plan to organize and develop it. Elicit suggestions from the others to help with ideas and organization and also with adding research. Review Chapter 9 and decide whether or not to use visual argument as support.

    b. *Create a class peer critique sheet.* The peer critique sheet provides a guide for critiques and revision. Make a list of all of the special requirements for a good researched position paper: a clear claim, adequate support, accurate documentation, and so on. Select five to ten items from this list that you believe are essential elements to consider during revision. Organize them on a peer critique sheet. Use these sheets in your peer editing group to critique individual student papers and make good recommendations for revision.

    c. *Write a draft of your paper, revise it, and bring it to class.* At this point it is useful to have one or more people read your paper and give you ideas for improving it. Your readers may use the peer critique sheets created in Exercise 2b and write their comments on them or on the papers. This can be accomplished in one of the following ways:

        1. Groups in class: The members of your peer group should first read all of the papers written by your group and make a few notes about each of them on the peer critique sheets or on the papers. As an alternative, the authors can read their papers aloud. Then each paper should be discussed, and members of the group should offer observations and recommendations for improvement to each author. As the discussion progresses, the peer critics may continue to add suggestions to the peer critique sheets, which should be given to the authors at the end of the session (continued on page 254).

WORKSHEET 9: INVENTION

Your claim: _____

Develop your claim by using some of the following invention strategies. If you cannot generate information and ideas, do some background reading, and then return to these.

1. Freewrite for five minutes.

2. Brainstorm additional ideas and details in brief phrases for another five minutes.

3. Make a brief outline or list that shows the parts of your paper.

4. Explain to someone in your class or group what you expect to accomplish in your paper, or talk into a tape recorder about it.

5. Write your insights in a computer file, a journal, or on sheets of paper filed in a folder.

6. Mentally visualize and write a description of a scene related to your claim.

7. Make a research plan. Write your claim plus three to five reasons. Add ideas for research and a draft plan.

8. Think about possible organizational patterns to shape your paper. What might work best—a claim with reasons, problem–solution, cause and effect, compare and contrast, chronology or narrative, or a combination of two or more patterns? How can you use classical structure?

9. Think through the rhetorical situation. Remember TRACE: text, reader, author, constraints, exigence.

10. Use the Toulmin model to develop the key parts of your paper. Consider the claim, support, warrants, backing for the warrants, rebuttal, and qualifiers.

11. Ask the claim questions: Did it happen? What is it? What caused it? Is it good or bad? What should we do about it?

12. Decide on proofs that are appropriate for your type of claim. Recall SICDADS—sign, induction, cause, deduction, analogies (literal, figurative, historical), definition, and sign—and recall VAM—value, authoritative, and motivational proofs.

13. Utilize critical thinking prompts. Start with your claim, but then make these recursive; that is, apply them at any point and more than once during the process.

Associate it.	Think about it as it is now.	Evaluate it.
Describe it.	Think about it over time.	Elaborate on it.
Compare it.	Ask if it is a part of a whole; describe the whole.	Project and predict.
Apply it.	Analyze its parts.	Ask why.
Divide it.	Synthesize it.	

14. Make a more complete outline, set of notes, or list to guide your writing.

15. Write chunks or bits of your paper as they begin to form in your mind.

2. Individuals outside of class: Trade papers with a classmate and critique them outside of class. Before the next class period, read the paper you have been assigned carefully and make as many useful suggestions as you can on the paper itself and on the peer critique sheet. When you return to class, talk through your suggestions with the author. Then listen in turn to that individual's ideas for improving your paper.

d. *Make final revisions, and prepare the final copy.* Your researched position paper should be a length specified by your instructor. It should be double-spaced and should utilize a specified number of outside sources. Use MLA or APA format throughout. The student paper on pages 276–286 demonstrates general format, in-text citations, and "Works Cited" requirements for MLA style. The sample pages from the student paper on pages 300–301 do the same for APA style. Notice that in these papers the ideas that control them are the authors' original ideas and opinions and that the quoted and paraphrased material is used to provide support.

e. *Write a one-page Toulmin analysis of your paper.* Submit it with your final paper.

f. *Write a submission letter to your instructor.* Submit a letter to your instructor with your final paper in which you describe what you like about your paper and what still dissatisfies you. Identify problems or passages on which you would like some feedback.

3. Present Your Research in a Class Symposium

Adapt your researched position paper to create a five-minute oral presentation of the research you have completed. Follow these instructions.

1. Work with your written manuscript to change it into an oral report. Underline and number the most important ideas. Since oral argument usually has fewer main ideas than written argument, limit yourself to three to five main ideas so that you can explain them in the time you have.

2. Think about your audience. How much background information about your topic will you have to present or possibly add at the beginning of your speech to help your audience understand it?

3. Remember, also, that your listeners have only one chance to understand the main ideas. Add some obvious transitions to clarify your main ideas and make them stand out. These might include, for example, explaining your main points in your introduction, numbering them as you explain them, and restating and summarizing them at the end of your speech.

4. You will not read your speech, but you will probably want some speaking notes to refer to as you speak. Accomplish this by writing a 250-word abstract of your researched position paper. State the claim, the main points made about it, some of the evidence, and your conclusion. Now go back and underline the points in the abstract that you want to talk about and number these in the margin. While you are speaking, you might need to glance at your abstract from time to time to remind yourself of the next point, and, if you find that you are stuck, you can read a sentence or two. Writing the abstract in sentences will also help you get the phrasing right so that you will speak more fluently.

5. Organize members of your class in groups around the same or related topics. The best group size is five to seven students with a moderator. The moderator will call on the students in your group to present your abstracts of your research papers.

6. Practice your speech and time it. If anything in the speech seems to be unclear or awkward, make revisions. Work with the speech until it fits the time frame of five minutes.

7. Add a visual to your presentation to make it more forceful and memorable. Copy or create single or composite pictures, graphs, or other visuals than can be used to make your claim more convincing. Or, you may want to include visuals in a PowerPoint presentation. Here are the rules for using visuals during an oral presentation: (a) make it large enough for your audience to read easily, and (b) do not put it in front of your audience until you are ready to discuss it.

8. Practice the speech several times until you can give it fluently.

9. When you give your speech, use eye contact and experiment with some gestures. Above all, concentrate on communicating with your audience.

10. Answer questions from the class. Participate in a brief class discussion of the ideas presented by your group.

HOW TO DOCUMENT SOURCES

USING
MLA STYLE
&
APA STYLE

How to Document Sources Using MLA Style

The following material will demonstrate, first, how to use in-text citations to show your readers exactly what material you have included in your paper from outside sources; and, second, how to prepare a final list of sources with publication details at the end of your paper. This list is called either Works Cited, if you are following MLA style, or References, if you are following APA style. In-text citations are structured to make clear to the reader who is to be credited with the words or ideas and where in the Works Cited or References list to find the full documentation of that source. You will have noted that this book utilizes the footnote style preferred by the University of Chicago Press and described in the *Chicago Manual of Style* (15th ed., 2003) to make the same information clear to the reader.

The first section of this appendix discusses MLA documentation. If you need information on APA style, turn to page 287. For additional detail on how to use MLA style, consult the *MLA Handbook for Writers of Research Papers* (7th ed., 2009), published by the Modern Language Association; for APA style, consult the *Publication Manual of the American Psychological Association* (6th ed., 2010), published by the American Psychological Association.

The MLA portion of this appendix is itself divided into two sections, as described above: (1) how to cite sources in the body of the text, and (2) how to cite sources in the Works Cited list. If you need information only on how to format sources for the Works Cited page, turn to page 265.

MLA: HOW TO CITE SOURCES IN THE BODY OF THE TEXT

The MLA system of documentation is very simple to learn and understand. The system asks that you show where you originally found a direct quotation or the information for a paraphrase or a summary by inserting a brief parenthetical citation at the end of the borrowed material in your written text. The typical in-text parenthetical citation contains the author's last name and the page number: (Jones 5). However, if you include the author's name in the text, then you do not need to include it in the citation. If you include a book or journal title because no author is available (an unknown or anonymous author), place the title in italics (for a book) or quotation marks (for an article).

To help you quickly find what you need, use the following list.

1. A direct quotation with the author mentioned in the text—page 260
2. A direct quotation with the author not mentioned in the text—page 260
3. A paraphrase or summary with the author mentioned in the text—page 260
4. A paraphrase or summary with the author not mentioned in the text—page 260
5. Two or more authors—pages 260–261
6. Two books by the same author—page 261
7. A corporate or group author—page 261
8. An unknown or anonymous author—page 261
9. A work reprinted in a book or journal—pages 261–262
10. Short quotations versus block quotations—page 262
11. Ellipsis points and quoted material—page 263
12. Tables—page 263
13. Graphs, artwork, photographs, and other illustrations—page 264
14. Poetry and song lyrics—page 264
15. Electronic sources—pages 264–265

1. A direct quotation with the author mentioned in the text If you introduce the author's name in the body of the text before you quote directly, then there is no need to include the name in the parenthetical citation.

> Although various critics have accused Arnold Schoenberg's musical compositions of being "atonal," Alex Ross points out that the composer was "simply offering a tonality of a less familiar kind" (176).

2. A direct quotation with the author not mentioned in the text

> Although various critics have accused Arnold Schoenberg's musical compositions of being "atonal," others argue that the composer was "simply offering a tonality of a less familiar kind" (Ross 176).

3. A paraphrase or summary with the author mentioned in the text

> According to Calvin Tomkins, the rebuilding and expansion of the New York Museum of Modern Art proves that modern art has not reached its end (72).

4. A paraphrase or summary with the author not mentioned in the text

> If the rebuilding and expansion of the New York Museum of Modern Art is any indication, claims that modern art has reached its end may soon be proven wrong (Tomkins 72).

5. Two or more authors If two or three authors have written the material you have borrowed, include all of their last names in either the introductory wording or the citation.

> Pimentel and Teixeira remind us, "Virtual reality is all about illusion" (7).

> "Virtual reality is all about illusion" (Pimentel and Teixeira 7).

For more than three authors, use only the first author's last name and add *et al.* to the citation. *(Et al.* is an abbreviation of the Latin *et alii,* meaning "and others." It is not italicized in your paper.)

> "Television is not primarily a medium of entertainment in all societies" (Comstock et al. 25).

6. Two books by the same author To indicate which book you are citing, either include the name of the book in the introductory material or add a short-ened title to the parenthetical information to differentiate between the books. For example, if you are using *The Second Self: Computers and the Human Spirit* (1984) and *Life on the Screen: Identity in the Age of the Internet* (1995), both by Sherry Turkle, document as follows:

> Sherry Turkle says the computer is like a mirror that has a strong psychological hold over her *(Second Self* 306). She explains further that "the computer tantalizes me with its holding power" *(Life* 30).

If the author is not mentioned in the text, include the author's name followed by a comma before the shortened title of the work: (Turkle, *Life* 30).

7. A corporate or group author Sometimes written materials are attributed to a corporate or group author (e.g., a corporation, company, association, or organization) rather than to an individual author. In this case, use the name of the corporation or group, preferably in the wording that precedes the quotation.

> The RAND Corporation observes that "when the No Child Left Behind Act was passed into law in January 2002, it heralded the beginning of one of the most expansive efforts to reform public education" (7).

If the corporate author is not mentioned in the text, include the corporate author's name as part of the citation before the page number.

> (RAND Corporation 7)

8. An unknown or anonymous author When no author is listed for either a book or an article, use the title or the first words of an abbreviated title in your citation.

> *Article:* ("Creativity and Television" 14)

> *Book:* (World Almanac 397)

9. A work reprinted in a book or journal If you quote an article, poem, story, or any other work that is reprinted not in its original but in another com-pilation, cite the author you are quoting in the text and the page number. The author or editor of the compilation is not cited in the parenthetical citation, but is fully cited in the Works Cited. Thus a quotation that includes words from both pages of the essay by Chris Piper on pages 25–26 of this book by Nancy V. Wood would be cited in the text as (Piper 25–6).* (See page 270, Works Cited example 18.)

10. Short quotations versus block quotations Short quotations do not exceed four lines of text. For short quotations, place quotation marks around the quoted material, insert the citation information in parentheses, and place the period outside it.

> According to Nate Stulman, many college students in his dormitory "routinely stay awake all night chatting with dormmates online. Why walk 10 feet down the hall to have a conversation when you can chat on the computer—even if it takes three times as long?" (268).

Quotations that exceed four lines of text should be blocked. To block a quotation, you should eliminate the quotation marks and indent each line 1 inch (or ten spaces) from the left margin, including the first line if you quote all or part of a single paragraph (that is, do not set a paragraph indent). If you quote two or more full paragraphs, indent the first line of each paragraph an additional ¼ inch (or three spaces), as in the example below. Place the period at the end of the text, followed by the parenthetical citation. Use double-spacing, as you do throughout your paper. It is good writing style to provide a brief introduction to a long quote and to finish the quote with a concluding thought.

> Nate Stulman describes some of the uses of computers by the students at his school that he has observed:
>
>> Several people who live in my hall routinely stay awake all night chatting with dormmates online. Why walk 10 feet down the hall to have a conversation when you can chat on the computer—even if it takes three times as long?
>>
>> You might expect that personal computers in dorm rooms would be used for nonacademic purposes, but the problem is not confined to residence halls. The other day I walked into the library's reference department, and five or six students were grouped around a computer— not conducting research, but playing Tetris. Every time I walk past the library's so-called research computers, it seems that at least half are being used to play games, chat, or surf the Internet aimlessly. (268)
>
> These experiences may be typical of students' computer use at other colleges as well.

---

*Note that inclusive page ranges in MLA style ellide the hundred- or thousand-place numeral for the closing page in the range, as long as it is clear which pages are being cited. For example, 199–203 would not be ellided.

11. Ellipsis points and quoted material   Occasionally, you will want to delete material from the original source either to make your document shorter or to make the writing that includes the quote more readable. If you do so, indicate by inserting ellipsis points to signal that you have removed words. The following example shows how to use ellipsis points to indicate you have omitted words in the middle of a sentence. (Other information on ellipsis points can be found in Chapter 3, page 62).

> "If there were a wider appreciation for motherhood in society, women might . . . hold their heads high when going to the boss and asking for a reduced hour work schedule" (Hewlett 308).

When deleting the ending of a sentence in a short quotation, indicate that deletion by using three spaced points and a fourth after the parenthetical citation. The fourth point serves as the period to the sentence.

> "A weakness of mass entertainment is its impersonality . . ." (Jones 226).

When there is no parenthetical citation (for example, within a large block quotation), then the sentence is completed by placing the period before the ellipsis.

12. Tables   Place tables as close as possible to the text they explain or illustrate. At the top left, place the word *Table* and assign an arabic numeral. On a new line, place a caption capitalized headline style. Provide source information immediately below the table. Notes, if any, follow, numbered with lowercase letters *(a, b, c,* etc.). Double-space throughout (for a small table) and align as shown. Indent a second or more lines in the caption and source lines two spaces; indent the first line of notes five spaces.

Table 1

Travel and Entertainment Cost Savings Using Electrovision

Source of Savings	Amount Saved per Year[a]
Switching from first-class to coach airfare	$2,300,000
Negotiating preferred hotel rates	940,000
Negotiating preferred rental car rates	460,000
Systematically searching for lower airfares	375,000
Reducing interdivisional travel	675,000
Reducing seminar and conference attendance	1,250,000
Total Potential Savings	$6,000,000

Source: Courtland L. Bovee and John V. Thill, *Business Communication Today,* 6th ed. (Upper Saddle River: Prentice, 2000) 539. Print.
[a]In U.S. dollars.

13. *Graphs, artwork, photographs, and other illustrations* Graphs, artwork, photographs, and other illustrations are labeled Fig., the abbreviation for *Figure,* followed by an arabic numeral; the caption (see format below) is followed on the same line by any source material. This is an example created in a word processing program.

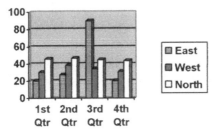

Fig. 1   Quarterly earnings according to region.

14. *Poetry and song lyrics* Quote three lines or less of poetry in your text by using quotation marks and a slash with spaces on each side [/] to separate the lines. The parenthetical citation should contain the line numbers.

> As "Gacela of the Dead Child" shows, Lorca's goal was to express the character of *duende:* "The dead wear mossy wings. / The cloudy wind and the clear wind / are two pheasants in flight through the towers," (5-7).

For more than three lines, indent the quotation 1 inch (or ten spaces) from the left margin.

> In fact, *duende* invades much of Lorca's work:

> > Death goes in
> > and death goes out
> > of the tavern
> > Black horses
> > and sinister people
> > roam the hidden trails
> > of the guitar. (1-7)

15. *Electronic sources* Cite electronic sources in the text just as you would print sources. Introduce the quotation with the author's name, or cite the author's last name (or a short title, if there is no author) with a page or paragraph number in parentheses at the end. If the source has no page or paragraph numbers or if you are citing or quoting from the whole source as a single document, place only the author's name in the parentheses. Here is an example of a quotation from an online journal that numbers paragraphs.

> "Rose represents the unnamed multitude of women who were placed in the same circumstances but whose stories were never told" (Mason, par. 8).

If you use the author's name in the body of the text introducing the quotation, then place only the paragraph number in the citation.

> According to Mason, "Rose represents the unnamed multitude of women who were placed in the same circumstances but whose stories were never told" (par. 8).

Some online sources do not provide page or paragraph numbers. There are two ways to cite such sources. If you place the author's name in the text, there is no parenthetical citation at the end.

> Carlos Oliveira phrases the question about media and reality this way: "Take, for instance, the alteration of our reality through the mass media. Do the media create reality? Or do they alter or destroy it?"

If you do not mention the author in the text, place only the author's name in the citation.

> "Take, for instance, the alteration of our reality through the mass media. Do the media create reality? Or do they alter or destroy it?" (Oliveira).

Also, some online sources are a single page, which may or may not be numbered. When your source is a single page, include any page number in the Works Cited entry but use the no-page-number model in your text. For example, look at the quotation from Rachel Sa in paragraph 16 of the MLA student research paper titled "The Big Barbie Controversy" on pages 283–284. No page number is included in the text since this is a single-page source. Now turn to page 286 and look at the Works Cited entry for Sa. Notice that the page number is included here.

MLA: HOW TO CITE SOURCES IN THE WORKS CITED PAGE

Attach to the draft a list of all the works you have quoted, paraphrased, or summarized in your paper along with full publication information for each source. This list is titled Works Cited, and it begins on a new page, which is numbered consecutively. It is alphabetized according to the last names of the authors or, if no author is listed, by the title of the works, ignoring any initial *A, An,* or *The.* Note: *All the information on the list should be double-spaced, just like the rest of your final paper.*

Look at the Works Cited page at the end of the MLA-style student paper appearing on pages 285–286. Include on any Works Cited list only those works actually cited or borrowed from in your paper. The easiest way to prepare this list for your paper is to alphabetize your bibliography cards or notes, in the manner just explained. If you have prepared an annotated bibliography, simply eliminate the annotations to create the Works Cited list. Start each citation at the left margin and indent each successive line ½ inch (or five spaces; this is called a hanging indent). Note: *Use day, month (abbreviated), year order for dates.*

The Internet has increased not only personal access to printed source material but also proliferated the number and type of published forms or mediums available as credible source material. A writer's ethical responsibility in documenting sources requires that the audience be able to locate and examine the cited sources readily. Accordingly, the Modern Language Association now requires that the medium of publication be clearly documented in all citations in MLA style. That is, all mediums or vehicles or forms of publication will be identified as a standard element of citation. Here is a list of mediums, which will usually appear at the end of an entry, followed by a period.

Print.	Web.	CD.
CD-ROM.	DVD.	DVD-ROM.
Radio.	Television.	Performance.
Audiocassette.	LP.	Film.
Videocassette.	Laser disc.	Address.
MS.	E-mail.	Microform.
Microsoft Word file.	MP3 file.	Digital file.

Examine the basic formats provided next, and then locate and use the many specific examples for documenting sources in specific mediums that follow in this section on MLA style.

Basic Format for Books, Articles, and Electronic Sources

Books and other nonperiodical sources

Author/Editor (last name, first name). *Title of Book*. Edition. City of publication: Publisher Name in Shortened Form, year of publication. Medium of publication.

Articles in journals and other periodicals

Author (last name, first name). "Title of Article." *Name of Journal* volume number.issue number, if available (year of publication): page numbers. Medium.

Author. "Title of Article." *Name of Newspaper* date of publication, edition, if relevant: page numbers. Medium.

Author. "Title of Article." *Name of Magazine* date of publication: page numbers. Medium.

Documents from the Internet that can be located by author and title search

Author. "Title."/*Title*. Print publication information. *Site*. Web. Access date.

or

Author. "Title."/*Title Database/Site*. Sponsor/Owner/Publisher, Publication date or latest update. Web. Access date.

Documents from the Internet that require a URL to be located

> Author. "Title"/*Title Database*. Print publication date. *Site*. Sponsor, publication date or latest update. Web. Access date.*

*Note: If you can find an Internet site easily by entering the author and title into a search engine, like *Google,* or a Web browser, like Firefox, omit the Web address or URL (for uniform resource locator). Add the URL when a site or document would be difficult to locate without it.

Documents from online scholarly articles located through online databases

> Author. "Title of Article." [Follow the basic model for Newspaper, Magazine, or Journal article]. *Database Name*. Medium. Access date.

Note that in book titles, article titles, names of periodicals, names of Web sites, and other titles of works or publications, MLA capitalizes all important words, headline style. Also note that article, short story, and poem titles are placed within quotation marks, whereas titles of books, newspapers, journals, magazines, Web sites, databases, software, and so forth are italicized (use underlining only if you have no access to a computer). For electronic sources, print publication information (when it exists) is listed first, followed by the electronic publication information, medium of publication, date of access, and uniform resource locator (URL) in angle brackets (included only if needed to access that specific source). A period ends the entry. Eliminate the volume number, issue number, and parentheses around the date when citing newspaper or magazine articles.

Examples of many of the types of sources most commonly cited for argument papers are provided on the next several pages. Consult the following list to quickly find the formats you need.

How to List Print Books

How to List Print Articles

How to List Electronic Sources

How to List Other Nonprint Sources

How to List Print Books

1. A book by one author

Melvern, Linda. *Conspiracy to Murder: The Rwandan Genocide.* London: Verso, 2004. Print.

2. A book by two or three authors

Chayes, Antonia H., and Martha Minow. *Imagine Coexistence: Restoring Humanity after Violent Ethnic Conflict.* San Francisco: Jossey, 2003. Print.

3. A book by more than three authors

Stewart, Charles J., et al. *Persuasion and Social Movements.* 3rd ed. Prospect Heights: Waveland, 1994. Print.

4. Two or more books by the same author

As demonstrated in the first entry of this example, an initial *The* (or *A* or *An)* is disregarded in the alphabetized titles. Replace the author's name after the first entry with three hyphens followed by a period. Shorten the words *University* and *Press* as U and P in the publisher information; note other standard abbreviations in various entries.

Shaviro, Steven. *The Cinematic Body.* Minneapolis: U of Minnesota P, 1993. Print.

---. *Connected, Or, What It Means to Live in the Networked Society.* Minneapolis: U of Minnesota P, 2003. Print.

5. A book by a corporate or group author

Harvard Business School Press. *The Results-Driven Manager: Winning Negotiations That Preserve Relationships: A Time-Saving Guide.* Boston: Harvard Business School P, 2004. Print.

6. A book with no author named

The World Almanac and Book of Facts. New York: World Almanac, 2010. Print.

7. A republished book

Locke, John. *An Essay Concerning Human Understanding.* 1690. New York: Dover, 1959. Print.

8. A translation

Virilio, Paul. *Ground Zero.* Trans. Chris Turner. London: Verso, 2002. Print.

9. A second or subsequent edition

Wood, Nancy V. *Perspectives on Argument.* 6th ed. Upper Saddle River: Prentice, 2009. Print.

10. Proceedings from a conference or symposium

Medhurst, Martin J., and H. W. Brands, eds. *Presidential Rhetoric: Critical Reflections on the Cold War Linking Rhetoric and History.* Texas A&M Conf. on Presidential Rhetoric, 5-8 Mar. 1998. College Station: Texas A&M UP, 2000. Print.

11. An introduction, preface, foreword, or afterword

Rajchman, John. Introduction. *Pure Immanence*. By Gilles Deleuze. Trans. Anne
Boyman. New York: Zone, 2001. 7-23. Print.

12. A government document

United States. FBI. Dept. of Justice. *National Instant Criminal Background Check
System*. Washington: GPO, 2004. Print.

How to List Print Articles

Include all the page numbers of the article. Use a plus sign when the pages are
not consecutive; otherwise, cite the range of inclusive pages. Elide the first digit
of the ending page above 99 (e.g., *122–25)*, but only when elliding a digit will not
cause confusion (see examples 20 and 40).

13. An article from a magazine

Tomkins, Calvin. "The Modernist." *New Yorker* 5 Nov. 2001: 72-83. Print.

14. An article from a newspaper

Rutenberg, Jim, and Micheline Maynard. "TV News That Looks Local, Even If It's
Not." *New York Times* 2 June 2003: C1+. Print.

15. An article in a periodical with no author listed

"Metamorphosis." *New Yorker* 5 Nov. 2001: 10. Print.

16. An article in a journal

Mountford, Roxanne. "The Rhetoric of Disaster and the Imperative of Writing."
Rhetoric Society Quarterly 31.1 (2001): 41-48. Print.

17. An edited collection of articles or an anthology

Handa, Carolyn, ed. *Visual Rhetoric in a Digital World*. Boston: Bedford, 2004. Print.

18. An article in an edited collection or an anthology

Stroupe, Craig. "Visualizing English: Recognizing the Hybrid Literacy of Visual
and Verbal Authorship on the Web." *Visual Rhetoric in a Digital World*. Ed.
Carolyn Handa. Boston: Bedford, 2004. 13-37. Print.

19. A cross-reference to an edited collection or an anthology To avoid duplicating information when citing more than one source from a collection or anthology,
set up a cross-reference in the Works Cited list. Cite the whole anthology or collection as you would any source. For the entire collection, the editor is the author.

Handa, Carolyn, ed. *Visual Rhetoric in a Digital World*. Boston: Bedford, 2004.
Print.

Cite each article from the anthology that you have used but instead of duplicating the anthology's full publication information, include the last name of the editor of the collection and pertinent page numbers only. Alphabetize each entry in this case by the cited article author's last name.

> Stroupe, Craig. "Visualizing English: Recognizing the Hybrid Literacy of Visual and Verbal Authorship on the Web." Handa 13-37.

20. A reprinted article in an edited volume or collection The following shows a chapter from Gunther Kress's book *Literacy in the New Media Age* reprinted in the collection by Handa.

> Kress, Gunther. "Multimodality, Multimedia, and Genre." *Literacy in the New Media Age*. London: Routledge, 2003.106–21. Rpt. in *Visual Rhetoric in a Digital World*. Ed. Carolyn Handa. Boston: Bedford, 2004. 38-54. Print.

21. A signed article in a reference work Omit page numbers for reference works that arrange entries alphabetically.

> Davidson, W. S., II. "Crime." *Encyclopedia of Psychology*. Ed. Raymond J. Corsini. 4 vols. New York: Wiley, 1984. Print.

22. An unsigned article in a reference work

> "Quindlen, Anna." *Current Biography Yearbook*. Ed. Judith Graham. New York: Wilson, 1993. Print.

23. A review

> Ottenhoff, John. "It's Complicated." Rev. of *The Moment of Complexity: Emerging Network Culture*, by Mark C. Taylor. *Christian Century* 119.21 (2002): 56-59. Print.

24. A letter to the editor

> Cooper, Martin. Letter. *Business Week* 17 May 2004: 18. Print.

25. An editorial

> "Consider Cloning Source of Organs." Editorial. *USA Today* 22 Oct. 2003: 19A. Print.

26. A published interview

> Rice, Condoleeza. Interview by Nathan Gardels. *New Perspectives Quarterly* 18.1 (2001): 35-38. Print.

27. A personal interview

> Wick, Audrey. Personal interview. 27 Dec. 2010.

28. A lecture, speech, or address

> King, Martin Luther, Jr. "I Have a Dream." March on Washington. Lincoln Memorial, Washington, DC. 28 Aug. 1963. Address.

How to List Electronic Sources

A helpful rule for electronic sources is to use Web sites that are as unchanging as possible so the reader will be able to access the information at a later date. Sites that are refereed, authoritative, or based on historical texts or that have print counterparts should prove to be stable, at least in the immediate future. Entries for Internet sources consist of six basic divisions: the author's name, title of the document, print publication information (where applicable), electronic publication information, medium, date of access, and URL (required *only* when it is necessary to lead a reader to the source directly).

29. A *document from an Internet site* List print publication information, if any, first. If none is available, list only the electronic publication information: author's name, document title or short selection (in quotes), Internet site name or title (italicized), sponsor or host (if applicable), date of electronic publication or last update (if available), medium (Web.), and date of access, ended by a period. Add a URL (in angle brackets) only if a Google search by author or title does not lead to the article, as in this example. This is an online source with no print version. The journal is archived, and this specific article can be located by using the Search box on the journal's home page, as shown here, or the URL for the document page, as in example 43. (In MLA style, break a URL *only* after a slash.)

> McPhaul, Kathleen M., and Jane A. Lipscomb. "Workplace Violence in Health Care: Recognized but Not Regulated." *Online Journal of Issues in Nursing* 9.3 (2004). American Nurses Association, 2008. Web. 17 June 2010. <http:// www.nursingworld.org/MainMenuCategories/ANAMarketplace/ ANAPeriodicals/OJIN.aspx>. Search path: McPhaul and Lipscomb.

30. A *digital file* A digital file is a document created electronically, either on a computer using a software program or on some other digital producer—a camera, sound equipment, and so on. Digital files can be uploaded to the Internet, where they can be researched on a search engine, or they can exist and be exchanged and utilized independently from it. To cite such a document, identify its form or type (a book, recorded music, a manuscript, etc.) and follow the citation model for that kind of document. The file format, for example, *PDF, XML, MP3,* or *JPEG,* is the medium of publication. When the format is not known, use *Digital file.* (The file format or medium is not italicized unless a software name is part of its name, as in *Microsoft Word.*) If the file has versions, name the version or identify the one cited as shown in the example.

> Norman. Don. "Attractive Things Work Better." *Emotional Design*, Ch. 1. File last modified 24 Feb. 2003. PDF file. 17 June 2010.

31. An *entire Internet site* Include the site name (its title) italicized, name of the editor (if available), name of any sponsoring organization, date of electronic publication, date of access.

> *CNN.com.* Cable News Network, 2010. Web. 17 June 2010.

32. A home page for a course Include the instructor's name, the course title, the label *Course home page,* dates or semester of the course, names of the department and the institution, date of access, and the URL.

> Stern, David. Heidegger. Course home page. Fall 2000. Dept. of Philosophy, U of Iowa. Web. 17 June 2010. <http://www.uiowa.edu/~c026036/>.

33. A personal home page Include the owner's name, title of the site (if available), the label *Home page,* date of the last update (if available), and an access date. Add the URL only if a name search does not lead directly to the page.

> Blakesley, David. Home page. 18 Sept. 2003. Web. 17 June 2010.

34. An online book Include the author, title of the book (italicized), print publication information (if available), title of the Web site (italicized), date of electronic publication, medium of publication, and date of access. The following is an example of an online book that is out of print.

> Mussey, R. D. *An Essay on the Influence of Tobacco Upon Life and Health.* Boston: Perkins and Marvin, 1836. *Project Gutenberg.* Project Gutenberg Online Book Catalog, 2006. Web. 17 June 2010.

35. A part of an online book

> Mussey, R. D. "Cases Illustrative of the Effects of Tobacco." *An Essay on the Influence of Tobacco Upon Life and Health.* Boston: Perkins and Marvin, 1836. *Project Gutenberg.* Project Gutenberg Online Book Catalog, 2006. Web. 17 June 2010.

36. An article in an online newspaper Include the author, title of the article, name of the newspaper, publisher, date of publication, page or paragraph numbers (if available), medium of publication, and date of access.

> Webb, Cynthia L. "The Penguin That Ate Microsoft." *Washington Post.* Washington Post, 27 May 2004. Web. 17 June 2010.

37. An article in an online magazine

> Reiss, Spencer. "The Wired 40." *Wired* July 2006. Condé Nast, 2008. Web. 17 June 2010.

38. An article in an online scholarly journal If the article is included within a database, state the name of the database (italicized) after the print publication information.

> Wishart, Jocelyn. "Academic Orientation and Parental Involvement in Education during High School." *Sociology of Education* 74.3 (2001): 210–30. *JSTOR.* Web. 17 June 2010.

39. A review

> Gray, Donna. Rev. of *Psychic Navigator*, by John Holland. *BookReview.com.* 18 Oct. 2004. Web. 17 June 2010.

40. A publication on a CD-ROM or DVD-ROM Cite as you would a book or a work in a book, and add the label *CD-ROM* or *DVD-ROM* after the publication information. The CD-ROM is the medium of publication.

> Leston, Robert. "Drops of Cruelty: Controlling the Mechanisms of Rhetorical History." *Proceedings of the Southwest/Texas Popular and American Culture Associations: Years 2000–2003.* Ed. Leslie Fife. Emporia: SW/TX PCA/ACA P, 2003. 681–91. CD-ROM.

41. A work from an online database In addition to the print information, you should include the name of the database (italicized), medium, and the date of access. Omit the URL assigned by the service to the article itself.

> Goldwasser, Joan. "Watch Your Balance." *Kiplinger's Personal Finance* 58.3 (2004): 96. *LexisNexis Academic.* Web. 17 June 2010.

42. A television or radio program If you are citing the transcript of a program instead of the program itself, at the end of the entry write *Print. Transcript.* (not italicized).

> Rehm, Diane. *The Diane Rehm Show.* With E. L. Doctorow. American University Radio, 24 May 2004. Web. 17 June 2010.

43. An advertisement Cite the product's name or company name, followed by the label *Advertisement.*

> Lanvin. Advertisement. *Haut Fashion-Africa.com.* Web. 17 June 2010.

For advertisements found in a print source, include the print publication information and eliminate the electronic publication information.

44. A cartoon or comic strip Include the creator's name and the title, followed by the label *Comic strip* and the publication and/or electronic access information.

> Adams, Scott. "Dilbert." Comic strip. *Dilbert.com.* 14 June 2010. Web. 17 June 2010.

For cartoons or comic strips found in a print source, include the print publication information and eliminate the electronic publication information. (Typically, a print archive is a more secure resource.)

How to List Other Nonprint Sources

If the sources in this section are accessed online, add the medium of publication, date of access, and the URL to the entry, if needed. See model 30 for a digital file.

45. An audio recording Include the name of the performer (or conductor or composer), the title of the recording, the manufacturer, and the date. Song titles appear in quotation marks; album titles are italicized.

> James, Bob. *Dancing on the Water.* Warner Bros., 2001. Audiocassette.

46. A film or video recording Begin with the title, list the director, distributor, and year of release. However, if you are citing a particular individual contributor, then begin with that person's name, followed by their title or functions: Capra, Frank, dir. or Chaplin, Charles, perf.

> *Rabbit-Proof Fence.* Dir. Phillip Noyce. Miramax, 2002. Film.

47. A videotape or DVD Insert the type of publication medium at the end of the entry.

> *Composition.* Prod. ABC/Prentice Hall Video Library. Prentice, 1993. Videocassette.

48. A painting, sculpture, or photograph Cite the artist's name, the title of the work, the date of creation (*N.d.* if unknown), the medium, and the name and city of either the institution that houses the work or the individual who owns it.

> Klee, Paul. *Red Balloon.* 1922. Oil painting. Guggenheim Museum, New York.

49. A map or chart Include the title of the map or chart, the label *Map* or *Chart,* and the publication information.

> *Oregon.* Map. Chicago: Rand, 2000. Print.

For an online map or chart, include the title (in quotation marks), the label *Map* or *Chart,* name of the reference source (italicized), sponsoring organization, date of publication or update, medium, date of access, and the URL, if needed.

> "New York City Transit." Map. *Mta.info.* Metropolitan Transportation Authority.
>   Web. 3 July 2010.

50. An e-mail message Here the medium of publication is *E-mail.* The title is the subject line enclosed in quotation marks.

> Harris, Omar. "Re: Artist Statement." Message to [Your Name]. 25 Apr. 2010.
>   E-mail.

I INCH

1/2 INCH

AUTHOR'S LAST NAME ⟶ Virasin 1

DOUBLE-SPACE

Prisna Virasin

Researched Position Paper

Professor Wood

English 1302

19 April 2010

PAGE NUMBER

1

The Big Barbie Controversy

As a twenty-something female who grew up in America, I am

DOUBLE-SPACE

Author establishes *ethos* in first three paragraphs

very interested in the Barbie debate. I played with Barbie dolls

almost obsessively from first to third grade. I designed clothes for

them out of handkerchiefs and tissues and dreamed about becoming

a fashion designer. I remember envying the girls who had Barbie

I INCH

Ferraris and dream houses. I looked on in horror as my little sister

I INCH

cut her Barbie's hair short and colored it hot pink with a marker.

2

I would later learn, as a first-year student in a small, liberal

Summaries of positions in exploratory paper in paragraphs 2 and 3

arts college, that by turning Barbie into a punk rocker, my sister was

actually "queering Barbie" or using the doll in a way unintended by

Mattel (the makers of Barbie). I was proud of my sister for this

creative venture because this was around the time I was introduced

to feminism. Through the lens of feminism, the horror I felt by

watching my sister destroy Barbie transformed into a reverence for

my little sister. At the age of five, she acted on her instinct to

Personal narrative

deconstruct Barbie, and I could not see her political defiance for

what it was until I was nearly twenty. In my women's studies classes,

I tried to deny any past connection to Barbie. I was ashamed to have

ever associated with this figure. I felt duped by Barbie. I thought that

I INCH

(continued)

she had tricked me into wanting to be seven feet tall with long blond hair and a body that wouldn't quit. I felt sorry for the girls who looked like walking Barbie dolls, always worried about looking perfect. It was obvious that they were still under "the Barbie spell."

3   Now, as a returning student, with a few years of working "in the real world" behind me, I'm not sure whether my feminist instinct to hate Barbie is lying dormant or whether it has been replaced by common sense. I have seen little girls playing with Barbies, and I do not have the urge to snatch the dolls out of their hands. However, I still feel a twinge of guilt because a part of my mind continues to wonder if Barbie or the image of Barbie is doing irreparable damage to the self-image of children everywhere.

4   There are many people who say that Barbie is "just a doll." These people believe that the Barbie debate is a "FemiNazi" creation to breed fear in the hearts of parents. These skeptics in the Barbie debate view Barbie as a toy, stating that she does not have power or influence over little girls or grown women. If Barbie is just a doll, then the Barbie debate is indeed without foundation. In reviewing Barbie's history, I found that she was created to make a difference in girls' lives and has succeeded in becoming a very marketable product.

5   The Barbie doll was created in 1959 by Ruth Handler, the cofounder of Mattel. Handler created the doll after seeing her daughter, whose nickname was Barbie, and her daughter's friends play with their paper dolls. According to Gaby Wood and Frances Stonor Saunders, Handler realized that little girls wanted a doll

Focus on issue

Transition to Barbie's history

Quotation: authors identified in text

(continued)

I INCH   I/2 INCH

Virasin 3

"they could aspire to be like, not aspire to look after" (38). This was a revolutionary idea because before the creation of Barbie, the toy store doll selection mainly consisted of baby dolls, which encouraged little girls to pretend to be mothers. Ruth Handler states that Barbie "has always represented the fact that a woman has choices" (39).

6   The Barbie doll has been a commercial success since the toy was first introduced on March 9, 1959. Fifty years later, on the doll's birthday, the lead story on the *History.com* Web site, entitled "Barbie Makes Her Debut," provides some highlights of the doll's success and consequent influence. By 1993, the doll and related merchandise were earning more than a billion dollars annually. By 2009, this article reports, "more than 800 million dolls in the Barbie family have been sold around the world and Barbie is now a bona fide global icon."

I INCH

Online source mentioned in text; no page number available

I INCH

7   Barbie is marketed internationally in more than 140 countries. Stephanie Deutsch, who has written a book about collecting Barbie dolls and who is a collector herself, says, "It is fascinating to see how Barbie dolls from other countries reflect the ideals of foreign societies," and she goes on to describe the "wild and sexy" dolls of Brazil, and the Barbie dolls strapped to candles for little girls in Greece to carry in religious processions (5). In 1968, Barbie dolls were first provided with the mechanism to talk. Besides English, some Barbie dolls spoke Spanish, and others spoke French, German, or Japanese. One of Barbie's friends spoke with a British accent (34).

8   I believe that Barbie's influence lies in her pervasiveness. She is everywhere, and therefore she is on the minds of many

I INCH

(continued)

Virasin 4

Transition to why Barbie's good

people. I don't think that Barbie is "just a doll." With the overarching product placement, marketing force, and popularity of the Barbie doll, she is undeniably a powerful icon of American society.

9   Avid Barbie fans span many different age groups. There are three-to six-year-olds who play with Barbie dolls, wear Barbie brand clothes, and sleep on Barbie brand beds with matching sheet sets. Barbie doll collectors have met for over twenty years to celebrate all things Barbie. Special collection Barbies are auctioned for thousands of dollars. Supporters of Barbie state that, apart from being a

Criteria for goodness

national icon, Barbie is just a fun part of growing up. They refer to the simple fun of playing with Barbie dolls. They believe that Barbie is a tool in building girls' imaginations. They also maintain that Barbie is a positive role model because she is able to do almost anything. Barbie was an astronaut before the first woman went into

Fig. 1 A President 2000 Barbie.
Source: Carlos Osorio/AP Wide World Photos. Web.

Appeals to motives and values

space. Barbie is a veterinarian, a doctor, a businesswoman, and to top it all off, a presidential candidate. Figure 1 shows the Barbie that was dressed to run for President of the United States in 2000. Included in the package are a blue campaign suit, a red ball gown, campaign material, and an Internet Web site. In her article about growing up with Barbie, Patricia O'Connell reminisces:

    What always fascinated me about Barbie
    was that she could be—and was—anything

(continued)

| 1 INCH | 1/2 INCH |

Virasin 5

I wanted her to be. By extension, I felt the same was true
for me. That's the real magic of Barbie. Deciding which
career she ought to pursue on any given day fired my
imagination far more than pushing a baby-size doll
around in a carriage ever did.

10   Handler's creation of Barbie as a challenge to the idea that the
proper role for a woman was that of a mother has become ironic in
light of feminist protests against the Barbie doll. Barbie protesters
have stated that Barbie is responsible for the development of poor
body image in girls. They believe that Barbie's proportions create
impossible images of beauty toward which girls will strive. If Barbie
were human, it has been "estimated that . . . her measurements
would be 36-18-38," and this has "led many to the claim that Barbie
provided little girls with an unrealistic and harmful example and
fostered negative body image" ("Barbie Makes Her Debut"). The
Barbie protesters also believe that the poor body image resulting
from playing with Barbie could lead to eating disorders such as
anorexia and bulimia.

11   In addition to protests of Barbie's physical appearance, there is
also the issue of Barbie's intellectual image. Barbie detractors have
criticized the Barbie lifestyle, which seems to center around clothes,
cars, dream homes, and other material possessions. According to
Jacqueline Reid-Walsh and Claudia Mitchell, the feminist leader
Betty Friedan believed that "Barbie was a product of consumerism
who spent all her time shopping, a model for women who are

Quote longer than
four lines; indent
10 spaces; no
page number
available

Transition to why
Barbie's bad

1 INCH

Criteria for
badness

1 INCH

1 INCH

Two authors
quoting another
author

(continued)

Virasin 6

defined by their relationships with men rather than their accomplishments as people" (184). Protests followed the release of the talking Barbie, which was enabled with such expressions as "Math is hard" and "Let's go shopping." Parents feared that the first sentence would reinforce the stereotype that girls were less skilled at math than boys. The second sentence seemed to reinforce the importance of clothes, physical appearance, and material goods.

12   In February 2010, Mattel, the creator of Barbie dolls, came out with a new Barbie: Computer Engineer Barbie. This doll "wears a neon-colored T-shirt with a binary code pattern and carries a smartphone and a Bluetooth headset. Her hot pink glasses will come in handy during late nights coding on her hot pink laptop" (Miller). Miller adds that Mattel asked people to vote for this most recent Barbie's career, and the idea of a Computer Engineer career doll won the vote. Few women choose computer engineering as a career, and it is hoped that this new Barbie doll may have a positive influence on attracting young women to this field. Since members of the Society of Women Engineers and the National Academy of Engineering were consulted in the creation of this doll, this doll's creators predict a more positive intellectual image for this Barbie doll than for the dolls of the early 1990s who complained that math was too hard.

13   Still, some people continue to question whether or not Barbie is a suitable American icon. They challenge Barbie's ability to represent the all-American woman positively. In 2004, Mattel announced the release of a new California Barbie doll that would more accurately

Appeals to values

(continued)

| 1 INCH | | 1/2 INCH |

reflect the times ("It's Splittsville"). This Barbie has broken up with Ken,

who is now "just a friend," and has taken up with Blaine, an Australian

surfer. California Barbie uses modern "instant messaging to stay

connected to her game. Her ears can be pierced. Her car has a working

CD player" (Verdon 18A). Still, a television advertisement following

the release of the Cali Girl Barbie shows she has not changed that

much from the old Barbie. In this ad, Barbie says she is "born to shop,"

and she can "never have too much stuff" or "too many friends."

Summary of an article

14   According to Seth M. Siegel, the government of Iran has

banned Barbie, and police officers are confiscating Barbie dolls from

toy stores all over that country. The Iranian government believes that

Barbie is "un-Islamic" because of the way she represents Western

1 INCH

immorality. She dresses provocatively and has a close relationship with a man who is not her husband. For many Iranians, Barbie has become a symbol of American women in a very negative sense (22–24). As an alternative, little Muslim girls are encouraged to play with the Razanne doll that better reflects Muslim culture and values. Figure 2 provides a picture of a Muslim girl, who lives in the United States, and her Razanne doll.

Fig. 2 Jenna Debryn shows off her Razanne doll, a modest Muslim alternative to Barbie.
Source: Reed Saxon/AP Wide World Photos. Web.

15   Transition to refutation

Does the Barbie debate boil down to whether Barbie is good or bad? I believe that if she has the power to convey all of the positivity

1 INCH

(continued)

I INCH

1/2 INCH

that Barbie fans believe she embodies, then the same power can be used to contaminate the world with all of the negativity that the Barbie protesters warn us against. She is a pervasive image in American society, but that does not necessarily mean that we have to label her as either good or bad. As a feminist, I am willing to concede that women are neither all good nor all bad. As a female image, Barbie plays the dual role quite well. We can make Barbie into whatever we want. She can be an astronaut or a punk rocker or a punk-rock astronaut. I believe that Barbie supporters have made her into a goddess, while Barbie protesters have turned her into a demon. In both cases, I believe she has become a scapegoat.

I INCH

I INCH

16   In addressing the issue that Barbie causes poor body image that could lead to eating disorders, the obvious statement that I can make is that eating disorders were around long before Barbie was created. Also, because of Barbie's immense popularity, if the doll truly caused eating disorders, eating disorders would have reached epidemic proportions. In actuality, only about five percent of women suffer from eating disorders. Barbie supporters also ask why male action dolls are not protested against when they have similar unattainable proportions.

Refutation of those who say Barbie's all bad

17   By banning Barbie, we will not be solving the problem of poor body image. Also, Barbie's image is so pervasive that it would be almost impossible to shelter children from her. In a satirical editorial by Rachel Sa, she muses on the absurdity of sheltering children from all things Barbie: "Maybe the safest thing is to just keep your little

No need to cite a page number for a one-page source

I INCH

(continued)

I INCH ↕   I/2 INCH ↕

Virasin 9

girls in their bedrooms. Yes! Just keep them shut away until all of
that icky stuff disappears or until they grow up—surely by then they
will have figured out how to deal with it all on their own."

18   If one were to believe the argument made by Barbie supporters
that Barbie creates positive self-image in girls, and combine this

Refutation of those who say Barbie's all good

belief with the fact that Barbie is very pervasive in the United States,
it should follow that American females who have played with Barbie
would have nearly eradicated any thoughts of negative self-image.
Theoretically then, most American women would have conquered
self-critical thoughts about their physical or intellectual state as a
result of their contact with Barbie. However, women know that these

I INCH ←→   ←→ I INCH

self-critical thoughts are a part of many women's daily lives,
and even the most ardent Barbie fanatic has "bad hair days" or
"fat days."

19   It is not the responsibility of the Barbie doll to create positive or

The real issue

negative self-images in children. The ability to influence children
falls mainly on the shoulders of all adults in the communities in
which these children live. This includes the global community in
which we now find ourselves living. The issue of self-image should
be addressed by all cultures early on and continuously in children's
lives. Only by positively reinforcing unconditional acceptance of
children's physical appearance are we going to be able to curb the
problem of negative body image. We, as an entire culture, need to
look at our ideologies on beauty and what we are teaching children
about themselves.

I INCH

(continued)

Virasin 10

20   The Barbie controversy is so called because the Barbie sometimes becomes the focus of how we view ourselves as women. I realize now that I cannot blame thoughts of being fat, short, or out of style on a doll or girls that look like dolls. The Barbie debate between "Barbie good" and "Barbie bad" has actually masked the true issue. Instead, we need to address how we value beauty, how we value ourselves, and how we act upon these beliefs in the larger context of our community. As a first step, we need to take the doll off of the pedestal and stop blaming Barbie.

Value claim [margin note]

Virasin 11

Works Cited

"Barbie Makes Her Debut." *History.com*, 9 Mar. 2009. Web. 17 Feb. 2010.

California Barbie. Advertisement. The WB Network, 18 Mar. 2004. Television.

Deutsch, Stephanie. *Barbie: The First Thirty Years*. 2nd ed. Paducah: Collector, 2003. Print.

"It's Splitsville for Barbie and Ken." *CNN.com*. 12 Feb. 2004. Web. 17 Apr. 2010. <http://forums.yellowworld.org/showthread.php?t=13541>.

Miller, Claire Cain. "Barbie's Next Career? Computer Engineer." *bits.blogs.nytimes.com*, 12 Feb. 2010. Web. 17 Feb. 2010.

O'Connell, Patricia. "To Ruth Handler: A 21 Barbie Salute." *BusinessWeekOnline* 1 May 2002. *Academic Search Complete*. Web. 11 Apr. 2010.

[margin note:] The Works Cited follows the text, but always on a new page, numbered consecutively. Center the title, double-space, and use a hanging indent, as shown.

[margin note:] In MLA style, divide a URL only after a slash; include URL only when necessary to locate source.

[margin note:] 5 SPACES

(continued)

1 INCH

1/2 INCH

Virasin 12

Reid-Walsh, Jacqueline, and Claudia Mitchell. "Just a Doll? Liberating

Accounts of Barbie-Play." *Review of Education/Pedagogy/

Cultural Studies* 22.2 (Aug. 2000): 175–90. *Academic Search

Complete.* Web. 3 Apr. 2010.

Sa, Rachel. "Blame It on Barbie: How Was I Supposed to Know She

Was Warping Our Minds?" *Toronto Sun* 4 May 2002: 15.

LexisNexis. Web. 3 Apr. 2010.

Seigel, Seth M. "Sell the West as a Brand." *Brandweek* 10 June 2002:

22–24. *Academic Search Complete.* Web. 3 Apr. 2010.

Verdon, Joan. "Barbie Says, Bye-Bye Doll." *Fort Worth Star-Telegram*

13 Feb. 2004: 1A+. Print.

Wood, Gaby, and Frances Stonor Saunders. "Dream Doll." *New

Statesman* 15 Apr. 2002: 38–40. *Academic Search Complete.* Web.

3 Apr. 2010.

1 INCH

1 INCH

1 INCH

How to Document Sources Using APA Style

T his section is provided as a concise resource for documenting sources in APA style. If you need similar information on MLA style, go to page 259. For additional detail on how to use APA style, consult the *Publication Manual of the American Psychological Association* (6th ed., 2010) published by the American Psychological Association.

The APA portion of this appendix is itself divided into two sections: (1) how to cite sources in the body of the text, and (2) how to cite sources in the References list. If you need information on how to format sources for the References page, go to pages 291–299.

APA: HOW TO CITE SOURCES IN THE BODY OF THE TEXT

As in MLA style, the APA system of documentation asks that you show where you originally found a direct quotation or the information for a paraphrase or a summary by inserting a brief parenthetical citation at the end of the borrowed material in your written text. The APA system requires that you provide the author's last name, the date of publication, and the page numbers, which are introduced by *p.* or *pp.*: (Jones, 2003, p. 5). If, however, you mention the name of the author in the text, you do not need to repeat the author's name in the parenthetical material.

To help you quickly find what you need, use the following list.

1. A direct quotation with the author mentioned in the text—page 288
2. A direct quotation with the author not mentioned in the text—page 288
3. A paraphrase or summary with the author mentioned in the text—page 288
4. A paraphrase or summary with the author not mentioned in the text—page 288
5. Two or more authors—page 288
6. Two books by the same author—pages 288–289
7. A corporate or group author—page 289
8. An unknown author—page 289
9. A work reprinted in a book or journal—page 289

1. A direct quotation with the author mentioned in the text If you introduce the author's name in the body of the text before you quote directly, then there is no need to include the name in the parentheses. Note that the year of publication follows the author's name, while the page number follows the quotation.

> Although various critics have accused Arnold Schoenberg's musical compositions of being "atonal," Alex Ross (2001) points out that the composer was "simply offering a tonality of a less familiar kind" (p. 176).

2. A direct quotation with the author not mentioned in the text Note that in this case, the author's last name, year of publication, and page number appear together in parentheses after the quotation.

> Although various critics have accused Arnold Schoenberg's musical compositions of being "atonal," others argue that the composer was "simply offering a tonality of a less familiar kind" (Ross, 2001, p. 176).

3. A paraphrase or summary with the author mentioned in the text

> According to Calvin Tomkins (2001), the rebuilding and expansion of the New York Museum of Modern Art proves that modern art has not reached its end (p. 72).

4. A paraphrase or summary with the author not mentioned in the text

> If the rebuilding and expansion of the New York Museum of Modern Art is any indication, claims that modern art has reached its end may soon be proven wrong (Tomkins, 2001, p. 72).

5. Two or more authors If two authors have written the material you have borrowed, list both of their last names in either the introductory wording or the citation for all references. In APA style, use *and* in your text, but use the & sign inside parentheses and in tables or other context features.

> Pimentel and Teixeira (1993) remind us, "Virtual reality is all about illusion" (p. 7).

> "Virtual reality is all about illusion" (Pimentel & Teixeira, 1993, p. 7).

If a work has three, four, five, or six authors, list all of the authors' last names for the first reference, then use only the first author's last name and the abbreviated term *et al.* (but not italicized) for subsequent references.

> "Television is not primarily a medium of entertainment in all societies" (Comstock et al., 1978, p. 25).

For more than six authors, use only the first author's last name followed by et al. (an abbreviation for *et alii*, "and others") in all citations.

6. Two books by the same author To indicate which book you are citing, use the publication dates to distinguish between the books. For example, if you are using *The Second Self: Computers and the Human Spirit* (1984) and *Life on the Screen: Identity in the Age of the Internet* (1995), both by Sherry Turkle, document as follows:

> The computer can have a strong psychological hold over some individuals (Turkle, 1984, p. 306). In fact, the computer can tantalize "with its holding power—in my case, the promise that if I do it right, *it* will do it right, and right away" (Turkle, 1995, p. 30).

7. A corporate or group author Sometimes written materials are attributed to a corporate or group author (e.g., a corporation, company, association, or organization) rather than to an individual author. In this case, use the name of the corporation or group, preferably in the wording that precedes the quotation.

> The RAND Corporation (2004) observes that "when the No Child Left Behind Act was passed into law in January 2002, it heralded the beginning of one of the most expansive efforts to reform public education" (p. 7).

Otherwise, mention the corporate author in the citation after the quotation.

> (RAND Corporation, 2004, p. 7)

8. An unknown author When no author is listed for either a book or an article, use the title or the first words of an abbreviated title in your citation.

> *Article:* ("Creativity and Television," 1973, p. 14)

> *Book:* (*World Almanac*, 2003, p. 397)

9. A work reprinted in a book or journal If you quote an article, poem, story, or any other work that is reprinted from its original, cite the author of the work you are quoting, not the author or editor who reprinted it, but use the date of the reprint. Thus a quotation from the Chris Piper essay on pages 25–26 of this book would be cited as (Piper, 2011, pp. 25–26). Note that in APA style, no numbers are ellided in page ranges.

10. Short quotations versus block quotations Quotations should not be formatted as block quotations unless they exceed forty words. For short quotations, place quotation marks around the quoted material, insert the citation information, and place the period outside of the parentheses.

> Author Benjamin Cheever (1999) says he uses his computer to "write and read letters, and if it did not involve the elimination of envelopes and a certain parallel loosening of style, the process would be similar to the one that once involved lambskins and sharpened feathers" (p. 7).

Quotations that exceed forty words are blocked. To block a quotation, you eliminate the quotation marks and indent each line 1/2 inch (or five spaces) from the left margin. Blocked quotations are double-spaced like all of your text.

If you quote two or more paragraphs, indent the first line of the second and each subsequent paragraph an additional 1/2 inch (or five spaces). Place the period at the end of the text, followed by the parenthetical citation. It is good writing style to provide a brief introduction to a long quote and to finish the quote with a concluding thought.

Author Benjamin Cheever (1999) contrasts his use of the computer with that of individuals who spend a lot of time on the Internet.

> The news bulges with stories about dispensing therapy on the Net, doing business on the Net, trolling for unsuspecting sexual prey on the Net. Not on this computer. Most of what I do on the electronic superhighway is write and read letters, and if it did not involve the elimination of envelopes and a certain parallel loosening of style, the process would be similar to the one that once involved lambskins and sharpened feathers. (p. 7)

Cheever has essentially substituted his computer and its word processing program for his old typewriter.

11. Ellipsis points and quoted material Occasionally, you will want to delete material from the original source either to make your document shorter or more readable. Always indicate that you have removed words by inserting ellipsis points. The following example shows how to use ellipsis points to indicate you have omitted words in the middle of a sentence.

> "If there were a wider appreciation for motherhood in society, women might . . . hold their heads high when going to the boss and asking for a reduced hour work schedule" (Hewlett, 2002, p. 308).

Do not insert ellipsis points at the beginning or ending of a quotation except in the unusual instance that you want to emphasize that it begins or ends in mid-sentence, as in the following example.

> "A weakness of mass entertainment is its impersonality . . ." (Jones, 2002, p. 226).

To indicate an omission between two sentences of a quotation, however, you must use a period followed by three spaced ellipsis points.

12. Tables Tables should be placed as closely as possible to the text they explain or illustrate. Label with the word *Table* (not italicized), assign it an arabic

Table 1

Travel and Entertainment Cost Savings Using Electrovision

Source of savings	Amount saved
Switching from first-class to coach airfare	$2,300,000
Negotiating preferred hotel rates	940,000
Negotiating preferred rental car rates	460,000
Systematically searching for lower airfares	375,000
Reducing interdivisional travel	675,000
Reducing seminar and conference attendance	1,250,000
Total Potential Savings	$6,000,000

Note: From *Business Communication Today* (p. 539), by C. L. Bovee and J. V. Thill, 2000, Upper Saddle River: Prentice Hall.

numeral, and give it a brief explanatory title, which appears above the table on a new line and is italicized. Provide the citation information immediately below the table, labeled with the word *Note* in italics followed by a period. Double-space throughout and align to the left margin. (Note that APA style requires that you use italics, not underlining, when you have access to a computer.)

13. *Graphs, artwork, photographs, and other illustrations* Graphs, artworks, photographs, and other illustrations should be placed close to the text they illustrate. Below each visual, place the label *Figure*, assign a number in sequence, followed by a period, all italicized. A caption (if there is one), formatted sentence style as shown, and then the source information follows on the same line. See page 300 for an example of a visual image used as an illustration in a student paper. The example below was created in a word processing program.

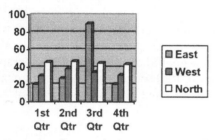

Figure 1.   Quarterly earnings according to region.

14. *Electronic sources* If a page number is available in an electronic source, cite as you would a print source. Some electronic journals number paragraphs rather than providing page numbers. If this is the case, then include the author's name, the year, and the page or paragraph number (if available) in parentheses, just as you would for a print source. If paragraph numbers are available, use the abbreviation *para.* (not italicized) to show you are citing a paragraph number. For more information, see the next section or consult more complete APA publications.

> "Rose represents the unnamed multitude of women who were placed in the same circumstances but whose stories were never told" (Mason, 2003, para. 8).

If no page or paragraph number is provided, cite a heading in the work and direct the reader to the paragraph in that section by number:

> (Regelin, 2002, Management plan section, para. 4)

If no author is listed, cite a short title, headline style, and place it in quotes.

> ("Wolf in Alaska," 2003)

APA: HOW TO CITE SOURCES IN THE REFERENCES PAGE

Attach to your draft a list of all the works you have quoted, paraphrased, or summarized in your paper along with full publication information for each of them. This list begins on a new page, is titled References, and is alphabetized according to the last names of the authors or, if no author is listed, by the title of the work, ignoring any initial *A, An,* or *The* when alphabetizing. For exceptions to this rule, consult the latest edition of the APA style manual. All the information on the list should be double-spaced, just like the rest of your final paper.

Some of the formats below advise you to include a DOI number as one way to identify where an article may be located. DOI stands for "digital object identifier." It is a special number that always begins with the number 10 and is assigned by the publisher to an article when it is accepted for publication. Not all articles have DOIs, but when they do, you can usually locate them near the copyright notice on the first page of the article, often in the upper right-hand corner. Include the DOI, when it is available, for both print and online articles as shown in the examples below. Follow this form: doi: followed by the number, *with no period at the end*. When no DOI is available, use the URL, and follow this form: Retrieved from http://www.xxxxxxxx *with no period at the end*.

Look at the example of a References list that appears on page 301. Include on your list only the works you have actually cited in your paper. The easiest way to prepare this list is to alphabetize your bibliography cards or notes, as explained in the previous paragraph. If you have prepared an annotated bibliography, simply eliminate the annotations to create the References list. Start each citation at the left margin and indent each successive line 1/2 inch (or five spaces).

Basic Format for Books, Articles, and Electronic Sources

Books

Author, A. A. (year published). *Title of book.* City, State: Publisher name in full.

Articles in periodicals

Author, A., & Author, B. (Date of publication). Title of article. *Name of the Periodical, volume number* (issue number), page numbers in full. doi: (if one is assigned.)

Online documents

Author, A. (Date of publication). *Title of document.* doi: or Retrieved from source URL (no retrieval date is needed, no period after doi or URL)

Online periodicals with print or without print version

Author, A. (Date of publication). Title of article. *Title of Periodical, volume number* (issue number), page numbers. doi: or Retrieved from source URL (no URL is included when there is a print version)

A document from an online periodical located through an online database

Author, A. (Date of publication). Title of article. *Title of Periodical, volume number* (issue number, if applicable), page numbers. Retrieved from name of database.

Note that in book and article titles, APA capitalizes only the first word of the title, the first word of a subtitle, and all proper nouns, sentence style. Also note that

APA does not require quotation marks for article titles. Titles of periodicals are written headline style with important words capitalized. Titles of books, newspapers, and journals or magazines are italicized. The volume numbers of periodicals are also italicized, but the issue numbers are not. For electronic sources, publication information is listed first, and, if it is a source likely to change, use the URL of the home page for the publication.

Here are examples of the types of sources most commonly cited for argument papers. To help you quickly find what you need, consult the following list.

How to List Books

How to List Articles

How to List Electronic Sources

How to List Other Nonprint Sources

How to List Books

1. A book by one author

Melvern, L. (2004). *Conspiracy to murder: The Rwandan genocide*. London, UK: Verso.

2. A book by two to six authors

Chayes, A. H., & Minow, M. (2003). *Imagine coexistence: Restoring humanity after violent ethnic conflict*. San Francisco, CA: Jossey-Bass.

Comstock, G., Chaffee, S., Katzman, N., McCombs, M., & Roberts, D. (1978). *Television and human behavior*. New York, NY: Columbia University Press.

3. A book by more than six authors When a book has more than six authors, list the first six names, just as in the example above that lists five, followed by et al.

4. Two or more books by the same author Alphabetize the titles by publication date, with the earliest date first.

Shaviro, S. (1993). *The cinematic body*. Minneapolis, MN: University of Minnesota Press.

Shaviro, S. (2003). *Connected, or, what it means to live in the networked society*. Minneapolis, MN: University of Minnesota Press.

5. A book by a corporate or group author When the author and the publisher are the same, as they are in the following example, use the word *Author* (not italicized) as the name of the publisher.

Harvard Business School Press. (2004). *The results-driven manager: Winning negotiations that preserve relationships*. Boston, MA: Author.

6. A book with no author named

The world almanac and book of facts. (2007). New York, NY: World Almanac Books.

7. A republished book

Locke, J. (1959). *An essay concerning human understanding.* New York, NY: Dover. (Original work published 1690)

8. A translation

Virilio, P. (2002). *Ground zero* (C. Turner, Trans.). London, UK: Verso.

9. A second or subsequent edition

Bovee, C. L., & Thill, J. V. (2000). *Business communication today* (6th ed.). Upper Saddle River, NJ: Prentice Hall.

10. Proceedings from a conference or symposium   Treat the title of the conference or symposium as a proper noun.

Gray, W. D. (Ed.). (2004). *Proceedings of the Twenty-Fifth Annual Conference of the Cognitive Science Society.* Mahwah, NJ: Erlbaum.

11. An introduction, preface, foreword, or afterword

Rajchman, J. (2001). Introduction. In G. Deleuze, *Pure immanence* (A. Boyman, Trans.) (pp. 7–23). New York, NY: Zone.

12. A government document

Federal Bureau of Investigation. U.S. Department of Justice. (2004). *National instant criminal background check system.* Washington, DC: U.S. Government Printing Office.

How to List Articles

List all the pages on which the article is printed, whether they are successive or interrupted by other pages. Insert *p.* or *pp.* only for newspaper articles and articles or chapters in books. Omit *p.* or *pp.* for journal and magazine articles.

13. An article from a magazine

Tomkins, C. (2001, November 5). The modernist. *The New Yorker,* 72–83.

If a volume number is available, insert it in italics after the comma following the magazine title: *Natural History,* 96, 12–15.

14. An article from a newspaper

Rutenberg, J., & Maynard, M. (2003, June 2). TV news that looks local, even if it's not. *The New York Times,* p. C1.

15. An article in a periodical with no author listed

Metamorphosis. (2001, November 5). *The New Yorker,* 10.

16. An article in a journal with continuous pagination in each volume

Hanlon, J. (2004). It is possible to give money to the poor. *Development and Change, 35,* 375–384.

17. An article in a journal paginated by issue

Kruse, C. R. (2001). The movement and the media: Framing the debate over animal experimentation. *Political Communication, 18*(1), 67–88.

18. An edited collection of articles or an anthology

Johnson, V. D., & Lyne, B. (Eds.). (2002). *Walkin' the talk: An anthology of African American literature.* Upper Saddle River, NJ: Prentice-Hall.

19. An article or chapter in an edited collection or an anthology

Willis, C. (2002). Heaven defend me from political or highly educated women! Packaging the new woman for mass consumption. In A. Richardson & C. Willis (Eds.), *The new woman in fact and in fiction: Fin-de-siècle feminisms* (pp. 53–65). New York, NY: Palgrave Macmillan.

20. A reprinted article in an edited volume or collection

Kress, G. (2004). Multimodality, multimedia, and genre. In C. Handa (Ed.), *Visual rhetoric in a digital world* (pp. 106–121). Boston, MA: Bedford/St. Martin's. (Original work published 2003)

21. A signed article in a reference work

Davidson, W. S., II. (1984). Crime. In R. J. Corsini (Ed.), *Encyclopedia of psychology* (Vol. 1, pp. 310–312). New York, NY: Wiley.

22. An unsigned article in a reference work

Quindlen, Anna. (1993). In J. Graham (Ed.), *Current biography yearbook* (pp. 477–481). New York, NY: Wilson.

23. A review

Ottenhoff, J. (2002). It's complicated [Review of the book *The moment of complexity,* by M. C. Taylor]. *Christian Century, 119* (21), 56–59.

24. A letter to the editor

Cooper, M. (2004, May 17). [Letter to the editor]. *Business Week,* 18.

25. An editorial

Consider cloning source of organs [Editorial]. (2003, October 22). *USA Today,* p. A19.

26. A published interview

Gardels, N. (2001, January). [Interview with C. Rice]. *New Perspectives Quarterly, 18*(1), 35–38.

27. A personal interview
You would not cite this in the References list. Cite it instead in the text.

Audrey Wick (personal communication, December 27, 2007) holds a different perspective.

28. A lecture, speech, or address

King, M. L., Jr. (1963, August 28). I have a dream. Speech delivered at the Lincoln Memorial, Washington, DC.

How to List Electronic Sources

A helpful rule to keep in mind in your research and when citing electronic sources is to use Web sites that are as reliable and unchanging as possible so a reader can access the information at a later date. Web sites that are refereed, authoritative, based on historical texts, have print counterparts, or provide archival versions of articles and other material should prove to be stable.

The basic elements of an electronic APA References list entry are author, publication date in parentheses, title of the article, title of the periodical or electronic text, volume and issue number, and pages (if any), DOI or the URL with no brackets and no period at the end. Provide URLs that link as directly as possible to the work or to the document page. If doing so is not possible, provide the URL for the home page. Like some content, URLs are changeable. Increasingly, publishers are assigning a Digital Object Identifier (DOI) to journal articles and other documents. The DOI is linked to the content no matter its portability from location to location on the Internet. When you have a DOI for your source, it replaces the URL. To cite a source with a DOI, first list the publication information as in example 17. Then, if there is a DOI, enter *doi:* (not italicized) followed by the number. No final period is used.

29. An online journal article with DOI

Hunter, C. D. & Joseph, N. (2010, January 5). Racial group identification and its relations to individualism/interdependence and race-related stress in African Americans. *Journal of Black Psychology.* doi: 10.1177/0095798409355794

30. An online magazine article without DOI

Dixit, J. (2010, January 1). Heartbreak and home runs: The power of first experiences. *Psychology Today.* Retrieved from http://www.psychologytoday.com/articles/200912/heartbreak-and-home-runs-the-power-first-experiences

31. An entire Internet site For a multipage document Internet site, provide the URL for the home page that contains the document. It can also be cited within the text, with the URL, in parentheses, rather than in the References page.

CNN.com. (2010). Retrieved from http://www.cnn.com

32. A document from a professional Web site Use n.d. (no date) when a publication date is not available, and provide a URL that links directly to the chapter or section. URLs can be divided at the end of a line *after* a slash or *before* a period or symbol.

Herman, P. (n.d.). Events. *Milton-L Home Page.* Retrieved from http://www.richmond.edu/~creamer/milton/events.html

33. *A home page for a course* Include the name of the instructor, date of publication or latest update, course title, and retrieval information.

> Stern, D. (2000). Heidegger. Retrieved from http://www.uiowa.edu/~c026036/

34. *A personal home page* Include the name of the owner, date of publication or latest update, title of the site (if available), and retrieval information.

> Blakesley, D. (2003, September 18). Home page. Retrieved from http://
> web.ics.purdue.edu/~blakesle/

35. *An online book*

> Mussey, R. D. (1836). *An essay on the influence of tobacco upon life and health.*
> Retrieved from http://www.gutenberg.org/dirs/1/9/6/6/19667/19667.txt

36. *A part of an online book* Provide the URL that links directly to the book chapter or section. If the URL leads to a page that directs the reader to locate the text within it, use the language *Available from* (not italicized) instead.

> Mussey, R. D. (1836). Cases illustrative of the effects of tobacco. *An essay on the*
> *influence of tobacco upon life and health.* Retrieved from http://
> www.gutenberg.org/dirs/1/9/6/6/19667/19667.txt

37. *An article in an online newspaper* Include the author, date of publication, title of the article, and name of the periodical, and URL.

> Webb, C. L. (2004, May 27). The penguin that ate Microsoft. *The Washington Post.*
> Retrieved from http://www.washingtonpost.com/wp-dyn/articles/
> A59941-004May27.html

38. *An article from an online database* If the article is included within an online database, state the name of the database rather than providing the URL.

> Wishart, J. (2001). Academic orientation and parental involvement in education
> during high school. *Sociology of Education, 74,* 210-230. Available from
> *JSTOR* database.

39. *A review*

> Gray, D. (2004). [Review of the book *Psychic Navigator,* by J. Holland].
> *BookReview.com.* Available from http://www.bookreview.com

40. *A publication on a CD-ROM or DVD-ROM*

> Leston, R. (2002). Drops of cruelty: Controlling the mechanisms of rhetorical
> history. *Proceedings of the Southwest/Texas Popular and American Culture*
> *Associations: Years 2000-2003.* Ed. Leslie Fife. [CD-ROM]. (681–691). Emporia,
> KS: SW/TX PCA/ACA Press, 2003.

41. *Electronic mail (e-mail)* You would not cite this in the References list. Cite it instead in the text, as in this example.

> Byron Hawks (personal communication, October 4, 2010) suggests a different
> approach.

42. A television or radio program Include the URL if an archive version or transcript exists online so a reader may access the program in the future.

> Rehm, D. (Executive producer & host). (2004, May 24). *The Diane Rehm Show with E. L. Doctorow* [Radio broadcast]. Washington, DC: American University Radio.

How to List Other Nonprint Sources

43. An audio recording

> James, B. (Artist). (2001). *Dancing on the water* [CD]. New York, NY: Warner Brothers.

44. A motion picture Include the name of the director or producer or both, the title, the label *Motion picture* (not italicized) in square brackets, the country of origin of the motion picture, and the name of the studio.

> Noyce, P. (Director). (2002). *Rabbit-proof fence* [Motion picture]. United States: Miramax Films.

45. A videotape or DVD Place the type of medium in square brackets.

> ABC/Prentice Hall Video Library (Producer). (1993). *Composition* [Videotape]. Englewood Cliffs, NJ: Prentice Hall.

46. Graphs, artworks, photographs, advertisements, and other illustrations Illustrations such as artworks, photographs, maps, comic strips, and advertisements are not included in the References list. They are documented within the text. See *Graphs, artworks, photographs, and other illustrations* on page 291.

SHORTENED TITLE → Alaskan Wolf 1

PAGE NUMBER

1 INCH

1/2 INCH

DOUBLE-SPACE

Darrell D. Greer*

Researched Position Paper

Professor Smith

English 1302

22 April 2010

Alaskan Wolf Management

Introduction and background of problem

Whether or not to control the wolf population by aerial shooting when wolves become plentiful enough to threaten other animal populations has been a contested issue in Alaska for more than fifty years (see Figure 1). The Alaska Department of Fish and Game has the responsibility for conserving wildlife in Alaska. When they determine caribou and moose are endangered by a growing wolf population, they periodically recommend that the wolf population be reduced, usually by hunters who shoot the wolves from airplanes and helicopters or who land their planes and shoot the wolves when they are exhausted from running. The position of the Department of Fish and Game is that the wolf population must be reduced at times in Alaska when

DOUBLE-SPACE

1 INCH

1 INCH

Figure 1. Whether or not to thin out the wolf population by aerial shooting when these animals are believed to threaten other wildlife is a persistent issue in Alaska. From www.shutterstock.com

1 INCH

*APA guidelines call for a separate title page, which includes a running head for publication, the full title, and the author's name and institutional affiliation (see the *Publication Manual of the American Psychological Association,* 6th ed., 2010). Your professor, however, may ask you to present your identifying information as shown here.

Alaskan Wolf

References

Alaska wolves. (2008) Retrieved from http://www.defenders.org

Cockerham, S. (2008, January 30). Palin wants to shoot down wolf lawsuits. *Anchorage Daily News*. Retrieved from http://www.adn.com/news/alaska/wildlife/wolves/story/298522.html

History of wolf control in Alaska (2008). Retrieved from http://www.defenders.org

Keszler, E. (1993, May). Wolves and big game: Searching for balance in Alaska. *American Hunter,* 38–39, 65–67.

Protect America's wildlife ads. (2009) Retrieved from http://www.defenders.org

Regelin, W. L. (2002, March). *Wolf management in Alaska with an historic perspective.* Retrieved from http://www.wc.adfg.state.ak.us/index.cfm?adfg=wolf.wolf_mgt

Williams, T. (1993, May–June). Alaska's war on the wolves. *Audubon,* 44–47, 49–50.

Wolf "control" in Alaska [Editorial]. (2004, March 14). *The New York Times*, p. A12.

The wolf in Alaska (2008). Retrieved from: http://www.wildlife.alaska.gov

1 INCH

1/2 INCH

1 INCH

1 INCH

1 INCH

In APA format, break long URLs before a period or after a slash. Never add a hyphen.

APA APA APA APA APA APA APA APA APA APA APA APA APA APA APA APA APA APA APA APA

SUMMARY CHARTS

TRACE: THE RHETORICAL SITUATION

THE TOULMIN MODEL

TYPES OF CLAIMS

TYPES OF PROOF AND TESTS
OF VALIDITY

TRACE

THE RHETORICAL SITUATION

FOR YOU AS THE READER

Text. What kind of text is it? What are its special qualities and features? What is it about?

Reader. Are you one of the readers the writer anticipated? Do you share common ground with the author and other audience members? Are you open to change?

Author. Who is the author? How is the author influenced by background, experience, education, affiliations, values? What is the author's motivation to write?

Constraints.* What beliefs, attitudes, habits, affiliations, or traditions will influence the way you and the author view the argument?

Exigence. What caused the argument, and do you perceive it as a defect or problem?

FOR THE TARGETED READER AT THE TIME THE TEXT WAS WRITTEN

Text. What kind of text is it? Is it unique to its time?

Reader. Who were the targeted readers? What qualities did they have? Were they convinced? How are they different from other or modern readers?

Author. Who is the author? What influenced the author? Why was the author motivated to write?

Constraints.* What beliefs, attitudes, habits, affiliations, or traditions influenced the author's and the readers' views in this argument?

Exigence. What happened to cause the argument? Why was it a problem? Has it recurred?

FOR YOU AS THE WRITER

Text. What is the assignment? What should your completed paper look like?

Reader. Who are your readers? Where do they stand on the issue? How can you establish common ground? Can they change?

Author. What is your argumentation strategy? What is your purpose and perspective? How will you make your paper convincing?

Constraints.* How are your training, background, affiliations, and values either in harmony or in conflict with your audience? Will they drive you apart or help build common ground?

Exigence. What happened? What is motivating you to write on this issue? Why is it compelling to you?

*Do not confuse constraints with warrants. Constraints are a broader concept. See pages 28–29 and 103.

THE TOULMIN MODEL

WHEN YOU ARE THE READER

1. ***What is the claim?*** What is this author trying to prove? Look for the claim at the beginning or at the end, or infer it.

2. ***What is the support?*** What information does the author use to convince you of the claim? Look for reasons, explanations, facts, opinions, personal narratives, and examples.

3. ***What are the warrants?*** What assumptions, general principles, values, beliefs, and appeals to human motives are implicit in the argument? How do they link the claim and the support? Do you share the author's values? Does the support develop the claim? Are the warrants stated, or must they be inferred?

4. ***Is backing supplied for the warrants?*** See whether additional support or appeals to widely accepted values and belief systems are provided to make the warrants more acceptable to the reader.

5. ***Is there a rebuttal?*** Are other perspectives on the issue stated in the argument? Are they refuted? Are counterarguments given?

6. ***Has the claim been qualified?*** Look for qualifying words such as *sometimes, most, probably,* and *possibly.* Decide what is probably the best position to take on the issue, for now.

WHEN YOU ARE THE WRITER

1. ***What is my claim?*** Decide on the type of claim and the subclaims. Decide where to put the claim in your paper.

2. ***What support will I use?*** Invent reasons, opinions, and examples. Research and quote authorities and facts. Consider using personal narratives.

3. ***What are my warrants?*** Write out the warrants. Do they strengthen the argument by linking the support to the claim? Do you believe them yourself? Will the audience share them or reject them?

4. ***What backing for the warrants should I provide?*** Add polls, studies, reports, expert opinions, or facts to make your warrants convincing. Refer to generally accepted values and widely held belief systems to strengthen the warrants.

5. ***How should I handle rebuttal?*** Include other perspectives and point out what is wrong with them. Make counterarguments.

6. ***Will I need to qualify my claim?*** Decide whether you can strengthen your claim by adding qualifying words such as *usually, often,* or *probably.*

TYPES OF CLAIMS

CLAIMS OF FACT

What happened? Is it true? Does it exist? Is it a fact?

Examples:

Increasing population threatens the environment.
Television content promotes violence.
Women are not as effective as men in combat.

READERS

WRITERS

- Look for claims that state facts.
- Look for facts, statistics, real examples, and quotations from reliable authorities.
- Anticipate induction, analogies, and signs.
- Look for chronological or topical organization or a claim with reasons.

- State the claim as a fact, even though it is controversial.
- Use factual evidence and expert opinion.
- Use induction, historical and literal analogies, and signs.
- Consider arranging your material as a claim with reasons.

CLAIMS OF DEFINITION

What is it? What is it like? How should it be classified? How should it be interpreted?
How does its usual meaning change in a particular context?

Examples:

We need to define what constitutes a family before we discuss family values.
A definition will demonstrate that the riots were an instance of civil disobedience.
Waterboarding can be defined as a form of torture.

READERS

WRITERS

- Look for a claim that contains or is followed by a definition.
- Look for reliable authorities and sources for definitions.
- Look for comparisons and examples.
- Look for compare-and-contrast, topical, or deductive organization.

- State your claim and define the key terms.
- Quote authorities or go to dictionaries, encyclopedias, or other reliable sources for definitions.
- If you are comparing to help define, use compare-and-contrast organization.
- Use vivid description and narrative.
- Use deductive organization.

CLAIMS OF CAUSE

What caused it? Where did it come from? Why did it happen? What are the effects?
What probably will be the results on both a short-term and a long-term basis?

Examples:

Clear-cutting is the main cause of the destruction of ancient forests.
Censorship can result in limits on freedom of speech.
The American people's current mood has been caused by the state of the economy.

READERS

WRITERS

- Look for a claim that states or implies cause or effect.

- Make a claim that states or implies cause or effect.

(continued)

TYPES OF CLAIMS *(continued)*

READERS

- Look for facts and statistics, comparisons such as historical analogies, signs, induction, deduction, and causal arguments.
- Look for cause-and-effect or effect-and-cause organization.

WRITERS

- Use facts and statistics.
- Use historical analogies, signs, induction, and deduction.
- Consider using cause-and-effect or effect-and-cause organization.

CLAIMS OF VALUE

Is it good or bad? How good? How bad? Of what worth is it? Is it moral or immoral? Who thinks so?
What do those people value? What values or criteria should I use to determine its goodness or badness?
Are my values different from other people's or the author's?

Examples:

Computers are a valuable addition to modern education.
School prayer has a moral function in the public schools.
Animal rights are as important as human rights.

READERS

- Look for claims that make a value statement.
- Look for value proofs, motivational proofs, literal and figurative analogies, quotations from authorities, signs, and definitions.
- Expect emotional language.
- Look for applied criteria, topical, and narrative patterns of organization.

WRITERS

- State your claim as a judgment or value statement.
- Analyze your audience's needs and values and appeal to them.
- Use literal and figurative analogies, quotations from authorities, signs, and definitions.
- Use emotional language appropriately.
- Consider the applied criteria, claim with reasons, or narrative organizational patterns.

CLAIMS OF POLICY

What should we do? How should we act? What should future policy be? How can we solve this problem?
What course of action should we pursue?

Examples:

The criminal should be sent to prison rather than to a psychiatric hospital.
Sex education should be part of the public school curriculum.
Battered women who take revenge should not be placed in jail.

READERS

- Look for claims that state that something should be done.
- Look for statistical data, motivational appeals, literal analogies, and argument from authority.
- Anticipate the problem–solution pattern of organization.

WRITERS

- State the claim as something that should be done.
- Use statistical data, motivational appeals, analogies, and authorities as proof.
- Use emotional language appropriately.
- Consider the problem–solution pattern of organization.

LOGICAL PROOFS

Do not confuse proofs with support. A proof represents a complete line of argument, which includes a claim, its support(s), and the warrant(s). A proof demonstrates a particular way of thinking about and developing the main claim of the argument. The logical proofs have been arranged according to the mnemonic SICDADS: Sign, Induction, Cause, Deduction, Analogies, Definition, Statistics.

WHEN YOU ARE THE READER	**WHEN YOU ARE THE WRITER**
	Think of symptoms or signs that you can use to show or demonstrate that something is so.

SIGN

WHEN YOU ARE THE READER	
Look for clues, symptoms, and occurrences that are explained as signs or symptoms that something is so.	Pointing out the symptoms or signs that something is so.
	Example:
	Claim: The child has chicken pox.
	Support: The child has spots.
	Warrant: Those spots are a sign of chicken pox.
	Tests of Validity: Ask whether this is really a sign of what the author claims. Always ask whether there is another explanation.

INDUCTION

Look for a conclusion or claim based on examples or cases.	Drawing a conclusion (claim) from several representative cases or examples.
	Example:
	Claim: Everyone liked that movie.
	Support: I know three people who liked it.
	Warrant: Three examples are enough.
	Tests of Validity: Ask whether there are enough examples, or whether this is a "hasty" conclusion or provable claim. Try to think of an exception that would change the conclusion or claim. See whether you can make the "inductive leap" from the examples to the conclusion or claim and accept it as probably true.

	Give some examples and draw a conclusion/claim based on them; *or* make the claim and back it up with a series of examples.

(continued)

TYPES OF PROOF AND TESTS OF VALIDITY *(continued)*

When You Are the Reader	LOGICAL PROOFS	When You Are the Writer
	CAUSE	
Look for examples, trends, people, or events that are cited as causes for the claim. Look for the effect(s) of the claim.	Placing the claim in a cause-and-effect relationship to show that it is either the cause of an effect or an effect of a cause. *Example:* *Warrant:* Depression in a group of people has increased. *Support:* This group of people has also increased its use of the Internet. *Claim/conclusion:* The Internet may be causing depression. **Tests of Validity:** Ask whether one or more causes alone are sufficient to create certain effects or whether these effects could result from other causes. Try to think of exceptions to the cause-and-effect outcome.	Make a claim, and ask what caused it. Think of examples, trends, people, or events as possible causes. Analyze effects.
	DEDUCTION	
Locate or infer the general principle (warrant). Apply it to the example or case. Draw a conclusion or claim.	Applying a general principle (warrant) to an example or a case and drawing a conclusion. *Example:* *Warrant:* Most uneven footprints are left by people who limp. *Support:* These footprints are uneven. *Claim:* The person who left these footprints walks with a limp. **Test of Validity:** Ask whether the general principle (warrant) and the support are probably true because then the claim is also probably true.	Make a general statement. Apply it to an example or a case. Draw a conclusion. Decide whether to make the general statement (warrant) explicit or implicit.

(continued)

LOGICAL PROOFS

WHEN YOU ARE THE READER		WHEN YOU ARE THE WRITER

ANALOGIES: LITERAL, HISTORICAL, AND FIGURATIVE

Interpreting what we do not understand by comparing it with something we do. Literal and historical analogies compare similar items, and figurative analogies compare items from radically different categories.

When You Are the Reader

Literal and historical analogy:
Look for items, events, people, periods of time that are being compared.

Figurative analogy:
Look for extended metaphors or items being compared that are from totally different categories.

When You Are the Writer

Literal and historical analogy: Think of items in the same category that can be compared. Show that what happened in one case will also happen in the other. Or, demonstrate that history repeats itself.

Figurative analogy:
Think of comparisons with items from other categories. Try to compare items that have similar qualities, characteristics, or outcomes.

Example of historical analogy:
Claim: Many people will die of AIDS.
Support: Many people died of the Black Death.
Warrant: AIDS and the Black Death are similar.

Example of literal analogy:
Claim: The state should spend more money on education.
Support: Another state spent more money with good results.
Warrant: The two states are similar, and the results of one will be the results of the other.

Example of figurative analogy:
Claim: Reading a difficult book should take time.
Support: Digesting a large meal takes time.
Warrant: Reading and eating are sufficiently alike that they can be compared.

Tests of Validity: For literal analogies, ask whether the cases are so similar that the results of one will be the results of the other. For historical analogies, ask whether history will repeat itself. For figurative analogies, ask whether the qualities of the items being compared are real enough to provide logical support or are they so dissimilar that they do not prove anything.

(continued)

TYPES OF PROOF AND TESTS OF VALIDITY *(continued)*

WHEN YOU ARE THE READER	LOGICAL PROOFS	WHEN YOU ARE THE WRITER
	DEFINITION	
Look for definitions of key words or concepts. Definitions can be short (a word or sentence) or long (several paragraphs or an entire essay). Notice whether the reader is asked to accept the claim "by definition" because it has been placed in an established category.	Describing the fundamental properties and qualities of a term or placing an item in a category and proving it "by definition." *Example:* *Warrant:* Family values characterize the good citizen. *Support:* Radical feminists lack family values. *Claim:* Radical feminists are not good citizens. **Tests of Validity:** Ask whether the definition is accurate and reliable or are there exceptions or other definitions that would make it less reliable? Ask whether the item belongs in the category in which it has been placed.	Define the key terms and concepts in your claim. Define all other terms that you and your reader must agree on for the argument to work. Place some ideas or items in established categories and argue that they are so or true "by definition."
	STATISTICS	
Look for numbers, data, and tables of figures along with adequate interpretations of them.	Using figures or data to prove a claim. *Example:* *Claim:* We were right to end draft registration. *Support:* It cost $27.5 million per year. *Warrant:* That was too much; it proves we did the right thing. **Test of Validity:** Ask where the statistics came from, to what dates they apply, and whether they are fair and accurate. Ask whether they have been exaggerated or skewed. Ask whether they prove what they are supposed to prove.	Find data, statistics, and tables of figures to use as evidence to back your claim. Make clear where you find the statistics, and add your interpretations and those of experts.

(continued)

TYPES OF PROOF AND TESTS OF VALIDITY *(continued)*

WHEN YOU ARE THE READER	PROOF TO ESTABLISH *ETHOS*	WHEN YOU ARE THE WRITER
	AUTHORITY	
Look for the references to the author's credentials, background, and training. Look for credential statements about quoted authorities.	Quoting or citing established authorities or experts or by establishing one's own authority and credibility. *Example:* *Claim:* California will have an earthquake. *Support:* Professors, scientists, and government officials say so. *Warrant:* These experts are reliable. **Tests of Validity:** Ask whether the experts, including both outside authorities and the author, are really experts. Remember that argument from authority is only as good as the authorities themselves.	Refer to your own experience and background to establish expertise. Quote the best, most reliable, and relevant authorities. Establish common ground and respect by using appropriate language and tone.
	EMOTIONAL PROOFS	
	MOTIVES	
Look for references to items or qualities you might need, want, or fear and advice on how to get them or avoid them. Look for emotional language, description, and tone.	Appealing to what all audiences are supposed to need, such as food, drink, warmth, shelter, sex, security, belonging, self-esteem, creativity, and self-expression. Urging audiences to take steps to meet their needs. Considering also what they fear. *Example:* *Claim:* You should support this candidate. *Support:* The candidate can help you achieve job security and have safe neighborhoods. *Warrant:* You want job security and safe neighborhoods.	Think about audience members' needs or fears, and show how your ideas will help them meet these needs or avoid what they fear. Use emotional language and tone where appropriate.

(continued)

311

TYPES OF PROOF AND TESTS OF VALIDITY *(continued)*

WHEN YOU ARE THE READER	EMOTIONAL PROOFS	WHEN YOU ARE THE WRITER

MOTIVES *(continued)*

WHEN YOU ARE THE READER

EMOTIONAL PROOFS

Tests of Validity: Ask whether you really need what the author assumes you need. Ask whether doing what is recommended will satisfy the need as described.

WHEN YOU ARE THE WRITER

VALUES

Look for examples or narratives that display values or that threaten values. Infer values (warrants) that are not explicitly stated.

Look for emotional language and tone.

Appealing to what all audiences are supposed to value, such as reliability, honesty, loyalty, industry, patriotism, courage, conviction, faithfulness, dependability, creativity, integrity, freedom, equality, devotion to duty, and acceptance by others.

Alternatively, appealing to threats to these values.

Example:

Claim: The curriculum should be multicultural.

Support: A multicultural curriculum will contribute to equality and acceptance.

Warrant: You value equality and acceptance.

Tests of Validity: Ask whether you share that author's values. Ask about the effect that differences in values or threats to values will have on the argument.

Appeal to your audience's values through warrants, explicit value statements, and narratives that illustrate values. Or, use these means to show what threatens their values.

Use emotional language and tone where appropriate.

Credits

Index